This page - Pete Robins sets off on Byways, E3 6b. Stanage. Photo: Graham Parkes. Page 142
Cover: Chris Craggs on Kirkus's Corner, E1 5b. Stanage. Photo: Graham Parkes. Page 142

Peak Gritstone *EAST*

A rock climbing guidebook to selected routes on the eastern gritstone edges of the Peak District

Text, topos, photo-topos and maps
Chris Craggs and Alan James.

All photos Chris Craggs unless otherwise credited.

Original ROCKFAX design
Ben Walker, Mick Ryan and Alan James.

Printed by Clearpoint Colourprint, Nottingham.
Distributed by Cordee (Tel: (+int) 44 (0) 116 254 3579)

Published by ROCKFAX Ltd. December 2001
© ROCKFAX Ltd. and Chris Craggs 2001

This book incorporates information previously collated
by volunteers on behalf of, and published by, the British
Mountaineering Council. It is published with the agree-
ment of the BMC. The BMC reserves its copyright and
other intellectual property rights.

ROCKFAX
rockfax.com

Sheffield, UK and Bishop, CA, USA
Email UK: alan@rockfax.co.uk
Email USA: mick@rockfax.com
RRP £18.95 ($28, 32 Euros)

ROCKFAX

COAST BLANCA, MALLORCA, EL CHORRO (2001) - rockfax.com/spain
Third edition of the most popular ROCKFAX guidebook to three brilliant climbing areas in Spain. Sport and some trad climbing. Now with 360 pages and nearly 3000 routes.
"This easily lives up to the very high standards that we have accustomed to from the ROCKFAX range over the past eleven years" - Ben Heason, Planet Fear web site

YORKSHIRE GRITSTONE BOULDERING (2000) -
rockfax.com/yorkshire_bouldering
All the bouldering on the brilliant gritstone outcrops of Yorkshire, England. 320 pages, nearly 3500 problems over 17+ locations.
"..one day all guidebooks will look like this" - Simon Panton, Climber, February 2001

DORSET (2000) - rockfax.com/dorset
Sport climbing, trad climbing, deep water soloing and bouldering on the south coast of England. 1500 routes on 272 pages including 32 pages of colour.
"Mighty fine; a job well done" - Mike Robertson, OTE, May 2000

COSTA DAURADA (1998) - rockfax.com/costa_daurada
Winter sun destination near Barcelona in northern Spain. Single pitch sport climbing on perfect limestone. 172 pages, 1000+ routes and all major areas.
"It is the most comprehensive and up-to-date guide available for this area, superseding the Spanish guide." - - John Adams, Climber, March 1999

PEAK BOULDERING (1998 and 2000) - rockfax.com/peak_bouldering
Gritstone bouldering in the Peak District, near Sheffield, England. The only guidebook available. 2nd Edition - 224 pages, 38 locations and 1600+ separate problems.
"Having had a chance to use the guide for myself, plus liaising with others, it has become apparent that it is pretty damn good." - Neil Bentley, High, August 1998

NORTH WALES LIMESTONE and NORTH WALES BOULDERING (1997)
rockfax.com/north_wales_limestone
Sport and traditional climbing found on the spectacular Ormes of Llandudno. Also includes a bouldering guide to North Wales. 224 pages, 800+ routes, 34 separate crags.

ISLANDS IN THE SKY - VEGAS LIMESTONE (2001) - rockfax.com/vegas
A guidebook to the rock climbing on Las Vegas and Great basin limestone in the USA. 224 pages, 652 routes.

RIFLE - BITE THE BULLET (1997)
Sport climbing on the limestone of Rifle Mountain Park in Colorado. 72 pages, 200+ routes.

PEMBROKE (1995)
Traditional climbing on the Pembrokeshire Coast of South Wales. All the important routes are included. 112 pages, 450+ routes.

BISHOP BOULDERING SURVIVAL KIT (1999)
All the information you need for bouldering around Bishop in California.

NEW BOOKS

PEAK LIMESTONE (2002) - rockfax.com/peak_limestone
All the best trad and sport routes on Peak limestone in one book.

YORKSHIRE and SOUTH LAKES LIMESTONE (2002)
rockfax.com/yorkshire_limestone
All the best trad and sport routes on Yorkshire and South Lakes limestone in one book.

CONTENTS

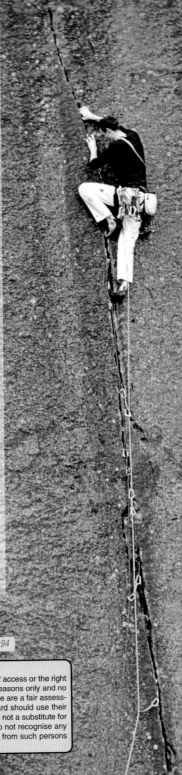

Classic finger jamming, *Embankment 3*, E1 5b, Millstone. Photo: Ian Parnell. *Page 194*

INTRODUCTION

The harsh gritstone cliffs that form the rim of the Derwent Valley in north Derbyshire are a superb climbers playground. The magnificent quality of the rock, dramatic settings and an august history combine to provide a climbing experience that is unique in the World. Although the climbs are rarely more than 20m high the routes are action-packed and classic climbs are jammed shoulder to shoulder on these thin ribbons of gritstone.

In 1988 I was on an extended trip to Yosemite and gathered around the fire one evening there were a group of luminaries from the British scene, including John Allen, fresh from ascents of *The Nose* on El Capitan and the *South Face of Mount Watkins*. The talk turned to the possibility of compiling a list of the ten best routes in the world and John said, "Well they are bound to be on grit then". The assembled team only took a moment to concur. Gritstone is the finest climbing medium on the planet; 35 years spent climbing all over the world have not managed to shake this conviction one iota!

THE BOOK

I have harboured the idea of a selected climbs guide to what are probably the most popular cliffs in the world for a long time. I originally envisaged textural descriptions backed up by black and white photographs (taken from coloured prints) with coloured lines to mark the different grade bands. I took the idea to Alan James and it turned out he had already been thinking along the same lines, he just needed someone with the required time available and an intimate (even obsessive) knowledge of grit – bingo! Together we modified and adapted the concept until it evolved to the format you see here. Between us we photographed all of the Eastern Edges using a high-resolution digital camera (Olympus 3040), where needed these images have been manipulated to remove people (you could never tell) add a suitable sky or modified so as to improve salient morphological features.

The overriding concept from the very beginning was to produce a book that would be inspiring, elegant and above all prove infallible to use, I wonder how close we got? Any feedback is welcome, please visit **www.rockfax.com** and tell it how it is!

Dominic Lee high on *Five Finger Exercise*, E2 5c, Cratcliffe. Page 262

THE HISTORY

It all began with James W. Puttrell back in about 1885 who scratched the rocks of Wharncliffe and gradually left his mark on most of the more important outcrops, and even had a tickle at some limestone. By the First World War the sport had developed into a recognisable format with ropes used for safety (at least for the second man), guidebooks being written to the main cliffs, and a rudimentary grading system developed. Since then things have become ever more refined; protection techniques have developed to the point where falling off has become (almost) the norm and still grades of difficulty continue to rise. The names of those who have developed the superb collection of climbs we now have on Gritstone reads like a Who's Who of British Climbing, Colin Kirkus, Peter Harding, Don Whillans, Joe Brown, Ed Drummond, John Allen, Pete Livesey, Ron Fawcett, Jerry Moffatt, Johnny Dawes, John Dunne, Seb Grieve, Robin Barker and John Arran and each year new names are added to the list.
It is beyond the scope of this book to cover the history in any great depth but we have included brief first ascent details.

BOULDERING

Plenty of bouldering areas are described within this book and located on the maps with the adjacent symbol. The idea behind including this information is to cater for those who like to indulge in a bit of bouldering from time to time, but don't require the more in-depth approach provided by a bouldering guide. The ROCKFAX guidebook to Peak Bouldering covers all the areas in great detail and many more across the Peak District. Check **www.rockfax.com** for more information. Bouldering grades are covered on page 14.

WEB SITE

The section of the ROCKFAX web site at the specific address **www.rockfax.com/peak_gritstone/** contains extra information relating to this book. As things develop we will be posting pdf updates and free pdf downloads of other crags (Portable Document Format - *a universal format which can be viewed and printed out on all modern computers using the free application Adobe Acrobat Reader*).

PEAK GRITSTONE ROUTE DATABASE

www.rockfax.com/peak_gritstone/grit_database/
This database contains a listing of every route in the book with the possibility for you to lodge comments and vote on grades and star ratings. This information is essential to help us ensure complete and up-to-date coverage for all the climbs. We can then produce updates and make sure we get it right in subsequent editions. To make this system work we need the help of everyone who climbs on Peak Gritstone. We can not reflect opinions if we have not got them so if you think you have found a big sandbag of a route, or discovered a hidden gem that we have only given a single star to, let us know about it. We also want to know your general comments on all other aspects of this book. Basically if you have anything to say about Peak Gritstone East, don't just say it to your mates down at the pub, say it to ROCKFAX.
Use the forms at **www.rockfax.com/feedback/**

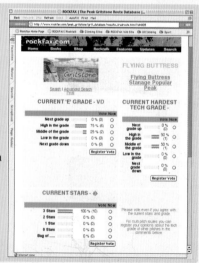

Gritstone is somewhere very special – respect and enjoy – we will see you out there.

Chris Craggs and Alan James, November 2001

ACCESS CONSIDERATIONS

Rock climbing becomes ever more popular; with the growth of indoor climbing walls and ever larger numbers of people wanting access to the cliffs, the pressures have never been greater. Any of the climbers who were incidental in developing these great cliffs would doubtless be absolutely flabbergasted to see the number of climbers on Stanage on a sunny summer's day. The rock is a finite resource and we all have a responsibility to ensure access is maintained, and that the effects of erosion due to over-use are minimised.

ACCESS

Much of the area covered in this guidebook does not have a historical right of access. The heather moors that crown many of the cliffs have been used for grouse shooting for well over a century and the moor's characteristic environment has developed through systematic burning of small areas in a controlled fashion. We are fortunate indeed that the work done on our behalf over the years has left the current positive situation. As anywhere in the country, a continued freedom of access requires a responsible approach, the freedoms already won could be so easily lost, and this is all our responsibility. Crags with individual access arrangments are listed in relevant sections of their introductions. If you do encounter access problems contact the BMC at The British Mountaineering Council, 177-179 Burton Road, West Didsbury, Manchester, M20 2BB.

GENERAL BEHAVIOUR

Simple reasonable requests such as make no fires, leave no litter, close gates after you, park sensibly and avoid disturbing farm animals should be obvious to all.

Pay and Display car parks are appearing all over the Peak, as is the habit of making popular roadside parking areas inaccessible using wooden posts or mounds of earth. Please use the designated parking area whenever possible and be aware of the increased incidence of car crime. The tell-tale sign of broken glass in the car park means it is a good idea to leave nothing of value in the car. If you park away from the recognised areas the car needs to be right off the road or you risk getting ticketed.

All the moors in Derbyshire are grazed by sheep and as such make an unsuitable destination for domestic dogs. If you really must take your best friend on a climbing trip it should be tied up and kept quiet and the place should be cleaned up before you leave!

CLOSURES

Infrequently access restrictions (signs will be posted) do occur mainly due either to nesting birds, or through potential fire hazards, although in both these cases a balance has to be struck. Closing huge swathes of moor because Ring Ouzels may just be interested in nesting appears a bit heavy-handed as does shutting Stanage and Froggatt because there is a potential fire risk on the peat moors of Kinder.

CHALK

The use of magnesium carbonate (gymnast's chalk) has become almost universal and for many climbers new to the sport a chalk-bag is second only in essential purchases to a pair of rock boots. Despite this, chalk is an unsightly addition to these dark gritstone cliffs and being alkaline is alien to the acid moorlands. The pale streaks below well-used holds show where the dark lichen that gives the rock its characteristic dark colour is being killed off. Before topping out (in the usual windy conditions) it is worth nipping your bag shut to avoid being blinded as the bag upends, releasing most of its contents. Closing your bag before starting down the descent gullies, will lessen the chances of loosing 50p worth of chalk!

Chalk on Tody's Wall. Photo: Alan James

Graham Parkes climbing *Valediction*, HVS 5a, Stanage End. *Page 92.*

ACCESS CONSIDERATIONS

TOP ROPING/GROUPS

The development of indoor walls has introduced a new generation to climbing and often they enjoy it for the physical/technical aspect, not needing to seek the adrenaline high generated when leading climbs. This has led to the monopolisation of popular and/or classic routes at busy times; a selfish and unreasonable approach so please be aware of the needs of others. The wear and tear that climbs are suffering is another growing problem, a visit to Yarncliffe Quarry will reveal the damage that can be done through over-use. If you must visit the cliffs in a large group, please consider other climbers. What might feel like good-humoured banter and horseplay can seem like yobbish behaviour to others on the cliff who are there for a bit of peace and quiet. Keep your kit in one area and try to avoid monopolising popular routes for extended periods of time.

A busy day at Birchen.

'EFFICS'

The way individuals choose to climb a piece of rock is up to them, although the way they report the ascent is a more public affair. Preplacing gear, hanging on a runner whilst clipping it, taking tension from the rope, and other nefarious activities, are all signs of an ever-downward ethical spiral. This stems at least in part from the sport climbing idea that only the end result matters – balderdash! There is only ONE pure form of ascent but if you want to tick the route having sat on half a dozen runners then so be it; be warned though, Judgment Day may not be far away! Gritstone has always been home to a particularly pure ethic and the best form of ascent is a ground-up lead, placing the gear as you go, in a single push. On the harder and more serious routes, the individual moves are often practised extensively and then the route led or soloed in what has become known as a 'headpoint'. This is exactly what Joe Brown did on *Brown's Eliminate* 50 years ago, though in those days the more transparent title of 'practiced on a top rope first' (less sexy but a truer reflection of what went on) was used. Nobody really cares how you do the route as long as the rock doesn't suffer, but will you be able to live with yourself after?

There is no reason for attempting to improve holds on any of the 1900 free routes in this guide and if you think otherwise then you are wrong. Wire brushing on the harder routes needs to be done with great care as even iron-hard gritstone can be damaged by over-zealous cleaning. Most modern damage to the crags in this book has occurred when climbers have attempted to retrieve stuck gear. Equipment that gets stuck is invariably gear that is badly placed, so think before you place it. If it does get well and truly jammed it may be better leaving it for someone who can get it out without wrecking the rock!

Cloud inversion at Curbar.

"A veritable indoor grit crag!" - OTE 82

"This wall has a greater variety of shapes, sizes and types of lead and top-rope walls than any other" - OTE 100

ROCKCITY

Outdoor Retailer - Online Shop - Climbing Centre

info@rockcity.co.uk
www.rockcity.co.uk

Hawthorn Avenue
Hull 01482 223030

Sun - Fri 10am - 10pm
Saturday 10am - 8pm

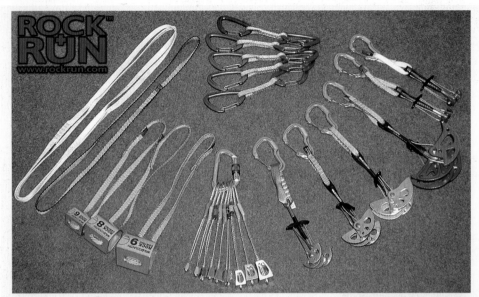

Virtually every piece of gear you place on the routes in this book will have to be carried up the crag by you so starting with the correct equipment is essential.

RUNNERS - The wide breaks and cracks make gritstone an ideal place for Friends and other camming devices. Many old routes which were bold and unprotected leads in their day are now relatively safe with the modern protection devices available. Wires and hexes will be found useful for the narrower cracks. The photo above illustrates a typical general gritstone rack. It consists of a single set of wires, a few hexes and a full range of Friends. One or two slings will also be found useful on some routes and often on the cliff-top belays. For harder routes micro-wires and more advanced camming devices may be found essential.

Kenton Cool fiddling gear into a break. Photo: Ian Parnell

ROPES - Most grit routes are short enough to be climbed on a single 10mm or 11mm rope. The only exceptions to this are routes which wander around in which case you may need 2 x 9mm ropes.

OTHER GEAR - Beyond these essentials you may find tape for bandaging your hands before, or after, they are wrecked by some savage crack. A tooth brush is useful for cleaning the smaller holds on the harder routes and a bouldering mat can be very welcome on those unprotected starts.

The only other thing you need is this book!

UKClimbing.com

The best place for climbing on the web

- **Searchable Crag and Wall Databases**
- **Regular News and Features**
- **The Most Popular Climbing Discussion Forums**

This is gritstone, the home of British climbing, so as you would expect we are using the British trad grade. The table below is an attempt to compare the grades with several other systems across the world. It is a slightly different table from the ones in previous books, and the one on the ROCKFAX web site, because of the unique nature of gritstone routes.

BOLD ROUTES - Many gritstone routes have limited protection and you can find yourself in some very serious situations, especially on the harder climbs. This should be clear from the text but please make sure you use your own skill and judgment as to whether you will be able to safely complete a chosen climb. A bold E2 may only feel like a Sport grade 6a on a top-rope but it is a very different proposition as a lead or solo.

BRITISH TRAD GRADE

1) **Adjectival grade (Diff, VDiff, Severe, Hard Severe (HS), Very Severe (VS), Hard Very Severe (HVS), E1, E2,.... to E9).**
An overall picture of the route including how well protected it is, how sustained and a general indication of the level of difficulty of the whole route.

2) **Technical grade (4a, 4b, 4c,..... to 7a).**
The difficulty of the hardest single move, or short section.

COLOUR CODING

The routes are all given a colour-coded dot corresponding to a grade band.
GREEN ROUTES - **Everything at grade Severe and under.** Mostly these should be good for beginners and those wanting and easy life.
ORANGE ROUTES - **Hard Severe to HVS inclusive.** General ticking routes for those with more experience.
RED ROUTES - **E1 to E3 inclusive.** Routes for the experienced and keen climber. A grade band which includes many of the Peak's great classics.
BLACK SPOTS - **E4 and above.**

BOULDERING

The boulder problems in this book are given a UK tech grade and a V-grade.

ROUTE GRADES

BRITISH TRAD GRADE (See note on bold gritstone routes)	Sport Grade	UIAA	USA
Mod (Moderate)	1	I	5.1
	2	II	5.2
Diff (Difficult)	2+	III	5.3
VDiff (Very Difficult)	3-	III+	5.4
		IV-	
HVD (Hard Very Difficult)	3	IV	5.5
Sev (Severe)	3+	IV+	5.6
		V-	
HS (Hard Severe) 4a/4b BOLD SAFE	4	V	5.7
VS (Very Severe) 4b/5a BOLD SAFE	4+	V+	5.8
HVS (Hard Very Severe) 4b/5b BOLD SAFE	5	VI-	5.9
E1 5a/5c BOLD SAFE	5+	VI	5.10a
E2 5a/6a BOLD SAFE	6a	VI+	5.10b
E3 5b/6a BOLD SAFE	6a+	VII-	5.10c
E4 5c/6b BOLD SAFE	6b	VII	5.10d
E5 6a/6c BOLD SAFE	6b+	VII+	5.11a
E6 6b/6c BOLD SAFE	6c		5.11b
E7 6c/7a BOLD SAFE	6c+	VIII-	5.11c
E8 6c/7a BOLD SAFE	7a	VIII	5.11d
E9 7a/7a BOLD SAFE	7a+	VIII+	5.12a
E10 7b/7b BOLD SAFE	7b	IX-	5.12b
	7b+		5.12c
	7c	IX	5.12d
	7c+	IX+	5.13a
	8a	X-	5.13b
	8a+	X	5.13c
	8b		5.13d
	8b+	X+	5.14a
	8c	XI-	5.14b
	8c+	XI	5.14c
	9a		5.14d
	9a+	XI+	5.15a

Bouldering Grade	V0-	V0	V0+	V1	V2	V3	V4	V5	V6	V7	V8	V9	V10	V11	V12	V13	V14
UK Tech Grade	4c or easier /	5a / 5b	5c	6a	6b		6c		7a	7b							
Font Grade		4	4+	5	5+	6a	6b	6c	6c+	7a	7a+	7b	7b+	7c	7c+	8a	8a+	8b	8b+

Route Symbols

 A good route

 A very good route

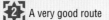 A brilliant route

 Technical climbing involving complex or trick moves

 Powerful moves requiring big arms

 Sustained climbing, either long and pumpy or with lots of hard moves

 Fingery climbing - sharp holds!

 Fluttery climbing with big fall potential

 A long reach is helpful/essential

 Rounded holds typical of gritstone

Photo-topos

Crag Symbols

 Approach - Approach walk time and angle

 Sunshine - Approximate time when the sun is on the crag

 Green and damp in the winter with lichen and moss

 Sheltered from the wind

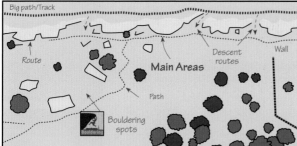 **Bouldering spots** - Marked on the maps and described in the text

Grade Colour Codes

The colour-coded route numbers correspond to the following grade bands:

❶ - Grade Severe and under
❷ - Grade Hard Severe to HVS
❸ - Grade E1 to E3
❹ - Grade E4 and above

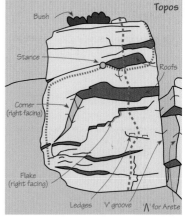

Topos

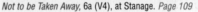

Not to be Taken Away, 6a (V4), at Stanage. *Page 109*

This book is a selective guidebook which means that it only covers the major buttresses, on the major gritstone crags, on the eastern side of the Peak District. The coverage averages about 50% of the climbs which, considering the number of routes included, gives you some impression of the wealth of climbing to be found on Peak Gritstone. A more complete list of routes on these crags, and many other smaller crags, is provided by the BMC. For any frequent visitor to the area, their books will be found to be indispensable.

STANAGE (1989)
Soon to be updated by a new volume dedicated to Stanage itself and a separate volume for the Sheffield Area crags (Wharncliffe, Dovestone Tor, Rivelin and Bamford from this book).

FROGGATT (1991)
Covers all the crags from the Burbage Valley to Froggatt and Curbar, including Millstone.

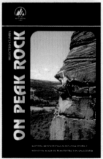

CHATSWORTH (1996)
Covers Gardoms, Birchen, Chatsworth and Cratcliffe from this book, but also several good venues further south including Black Rocks.

ON PEAK ROCK (1995)
An attractive selected climb book covering the whole of the Peak District. All the crags in this book, plus the western grit crags and the limestone.

THE BMC ACCESS FUND
A contribution is made from the proceeds of this guidebook to the BMC Access Fund which supports access and conservation work in the Peak District.

Le type d'escalade le plus populaire au Royaume-Uni c'est celui qui se fait sur les falaises de grès du Peak District, dans la région de Derbyshire. Peu nombreux sont les grimpeurs britanniques qui n'ont pas passé des moments dans les endroits ci-décrits, et pour beaucoup d'entre eux c'est là où ils ont grimpé pour la première fois. Il y a tellement de voies majeures de tous les niveaux: de la voie la plus facile pour les débutants en allant jusqu'à l'une des voies traditionnelles (sans spits) les plus difficiles du monde actuellement, qui se trouve à Burbage South. Récemment on a commencé à parler internationalement de cet endroit comme un site de bloc, mais c'est depuis la fin des années 1800 que l'on y grimpe, et pour bien des grimpeurs britanniques c'est plus connu pour l'escalade encordée. Beaucoup de voies dures modernes dites classiques ont figuré dans l'excellent vidéo Hard Grit, de la maison Slackjaw.

La plupart des voies sont courtes, d'une longeur, et requièrent une protection naturelle: il n'y a un seul spit dans ce livre. Le rocher – le grès – [There is a difficulty here because the word for sandstone and gritstone is the same in French.] offre des formations avec des lignes magnifiques et une adhérence fabuleuse. Même après beaucoup d'années d'escalade, bien des voies ne sont pas patinées, tellement le grain est rugueux.

Le Peak District lui-même est très beau et comprend des landes sauvages très attirantes. La plupart des falaises se trouvent dans un beau cadre avec des vues magnifiques vers l'ouest.

LE GUIDE

Ce guide contient tous les renseignements nécessaires pour trouver les meilleures voies sur les falaises décrites. Il y a des plans de situation, des photo-topos et des descriptions pour pouvoir localiser les voies. On utilise aussi beaucoup de symboles avec les voies pour donner une idée du type d'escalade : vous les trouverez tous en face avec des explications.

L'ÉQUIPMENT

Toute la protection sur les voies est naturelle, et vous en aurez besoin d'une bonne sélection. Ce qui est le plus utile c'est les friends car ils s'adaptent bien aux fissures qui se trouvent fréquemment sur les falaises. Vous aurez besoin également d'un jeu de coinceurs et de quelques sangles. Pour de bonnes promotions sur le matériel, consulter **www.rockrun.com**

COTATIONS

Toutes les voies dans ce livre ont une cotation "traditionnelle" qui comprend deux éléments:
1) La note qualificative (Diff, ..., Very Severe (VS ou "très difficile"), ... E1, E2, ... jusqu'à E9). Ceci vous donnera une vue d'ensemble de la voie, y compris son niveau de protection, d'intensité, ainsi qu'une indication du niveau de difficulté de l'ensemble de la voie.
2) La note technique (4a, 4b, 4c, 5a, ... jusqu'à 7a). Ceci fait référence au niveau de difficulté du mouvement individuel ou de la portion la plus ardue de la voie.
Il y a une table de conversion à la page 14.

INFORMATION SUPPLÉMENTAIRE

Pour en savoir plus sur le grès du Peak District, consulter ce website spécialisé:
www.rockfax.com/peak_gritstone/

ROCKFAX

ROCKFAX consiste d'Alan James au Royaume-Uni et de Mick Ryan aux États-Unis. Ça fait depuis 1990 que nous faisons des guides d'escalade sur des endroits situées dans le monde entier. Vous trouverez des renseignements sur toutes nos publications sur notre website **www.rockfax.com**

Email (Royaume-Uni): alan@rockfax.co.uk Email (États-Unis): mick@rockfax.com

Symboles des voies

 Bonne voie

 Très bonne voie

 Voie majeure

 Escalade technique nécessitant des mouvements complexes ou astucieux

Requiert des bras solides pour des mouvements de force

Escalade de continuité, longue et avec bouteilles garanties ou bien avec beaucoup de mouvements durs

 Escalade à doigts – prises coupantes!

Escalade angoissante avec possibilité de grandes chutes

Les grands seront avantagés.

Prises arrondies ou inclinées

Photo-topos

Symboles des parois

 Approche - Temps de marche d'approche et pente.

 Soleil - Heures approximatives auxquelles la paroi est exposée au soleil.

 Couvert de lichen et mousse en hiver.

Protégé du vent

 Secteurs de bloc – signalés sur les plans et décrits dans le texte

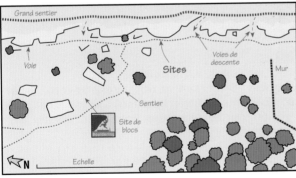

Couleurs Différentes

Les numéros des voies en couleurs différentes correspondent aux bandes de cotations suivantes:

1 - Niveau 3+ ou au-dessous

2 - Niveau 4 à 5+.

3 - Niveau 6a à 6c.

4 - Niveau 6c+ et au-dessus

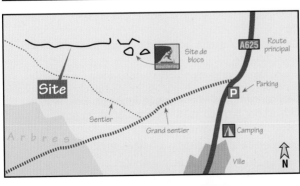

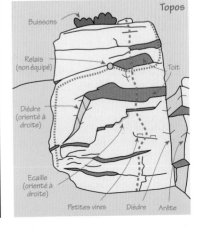

Topos

EINFÜHRUNG

Das beliebteste Klettergebiet Großbritanniens ist der Peak District in Derbyshire mit seinen Gritstone-Felsen (eine Art grober Sandstein). Fast jeder britische Kletterer ist viel in der in diesem Buch beschriebenen Gegend geklettert und für viele ist dies der Ort, wo sie klettern gelernt haben. Es gibt unzählige sehr schöne Routen in allen Schwierigkeitsgraden: von leichten Routen für Anfänger bis hin zu einer der zur Zeit härtesten traditionellen / ungebohrten Kletterei der Welt in Burbage South. Seit kurzem ist die Gegend auch international als Bouldergebiet bekannt, aber im Peak District wird schon seit dem Ende des 19. Jh. geklettert und das Gebiet ist - für britische Kletterer - sehr viel berühmter für seine mit Seil zu kletternden Routen. Viele der modernen schweren klassischen Routen sind in dem faszinierenden Slackjaw Video "Hard Grit" beschrieben.

Die Routen sind hauptsächliche kurze, selbst zu sichernde Einseillängentouren. Im ganzen Buch ist kein einziger Haken beschrieben. Der Fels, Gritstone, ist eine Art grober Sandstein, der fantastische Felsformationen mit großartigen natürlichen Linien und hervorragender Reibung bietet. Viele Routen sind, obwohl sie schon seit Jahren viel geklettert werden, wegen der groben Felsstruktur dennoch nicht speckig.

Der Peak District selbst ist eine sehr schöne Gegend mit reizvollen Mooren und die meisten Felsen sind schön gelegen und bieten eine eindrucksvolle Aussicht nach Westen.

DER KLETTERFÜHRER

Dieses Buch beinhaltet alle Informationen, die nötig sind, um die besten Routen an den Felsen zu finden. Dies umfaßt Zustiegsskizzen, Phototopos und Beschreibungen, die die Routenfindung erleichtern. Außerdem werden viele Symbole benutzt, um zu verdeutlichen, von welcher Art Kletterei eine Route ist. Diese Symbole sind auf der nächsten Seite erklärt.

AUSRÜSTUNG

Alle Sicherungen in diesem Gebiet sind selbst zu legen und eine gute Auswahl an Material ist nötig, um hier zu klettern. Am nützlichsten für Gritstone sind Friends, die hervorragend in die sehr häufig auftretenden Risse passen. Ein Satz Keile und einige lange Schlingen sind ebenfalls nötig.

SCHWIERIGKEITSBEWERTUNG

Alle Routen sind traditionell britisch bewertet, d.h. zweiteilig:

1) Eine adjektivische Bewertung wie "Diff" (schwierig), "Very Severe" (sehr ernst), [...], "E1, E2, ..., bis E9" (Extreme Schwierigkeiten). Diese stellt eine Gesamtbewertung der Schwierigkeiten der bezeichneten Route dar, wie sie abgesichert, wie anhaltend schwer sie ist.

2) Die klettertechnische Bewertung 4a, 4b, 4c, 5a, ... bis 7a. Sie bezieht sich auf die Schwierigkeit des härtesten Einzelzuges (der härtesten Einzelstelle) der Tour. Eine Umrechnungstabelle befindet sich auf Seite 14.

ZUSÄTZLICHE INFORMATION

Zusätzliche Informationen zum Peak District Gritstone befinden sich auf der ROCKFAX Webseite **www.rockfax.com/peak_gritstone/**

ROCKFAX

ROCKFAX sind Alan James in Großbritannien und Mick Ryan in Amerika. Seit 1990 schreiben wir Kletterführer für Gebiete in der ganzen Welt. Informationen zu unseren Publikationen befinden sich auf unserer Webseite www.rockfax.com.

E-mail (UK): alan@rockfax.co.uk E-mail (USA): mick@rockfax.com

Symbole

 Lohnende Kletterei

 Sehr lohnende Kletterei

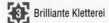 Brilliante Kletterei

 Technisch anspruchsvolle Tour mit trickreichen Zügen.

 Heikle Kletterei mit hohem Sturzpotential, aber nicht allzu gefährlich.

 Durchgehend anstrengende Tour; entweder anhaltend schwer oder mit einer Reihe harter Züge.

 Kleingriffige, rauhe Kletterei - nichts für zarte Hände.

 Anstrengende Züge. Erfordert kräftige Oberarme.

 Lange Arme sind hilfreich.

 Abgerundete und abwärtsgeneigte Griffe

Photo-topos

Abstieg

13

12

11

14

Alternativen für dieselbe Route

15 16 nächstes Gebiet

Felsymbole

 Zugang - Zeit und Steilheit des Zugangsweges.
10 min

 Sonnenschein - Zeit, zu der der Felsen in der Sonne liegt.
Afternoon

 Grün, im Winter mit Flechten und Moos bedeckt
Green

 windgeschützt
Sheltered

 Bouldergebiete - auf den Karten eingezeichnet und im Text beschrieben
Bouldering

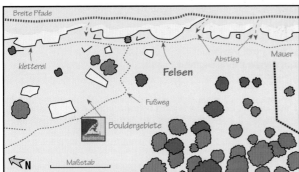

Breite Pfade

kletterei

Abstieg

Mauer

Felsen

Fußweg

Bouldergebiete

Bouldering

Maßstab

N

Farbig markierte Routennummern

Die farbigen Routennummern entsprechen den folgenden Schwierigkeitsbereichen:

① - Grad IV+ und darunter

② - Grad V bis VI

③ - Grad VI+ bis VII+

④ - Grad VIII und darüber

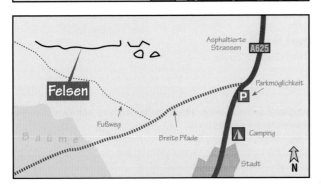

Asphaltierte Strassen A625

Felsen

Parkmöglichkeit
P

Fußweg

Baume

Breite Pfade

Camping

Stadt

N

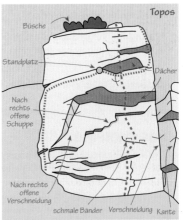

Topos

Büsche

Standplatz

Dächer

Nach rechts offene Schuppe

Nach rechts offene Verschneidung

schmale Bänder   Verschneidung   Kante

INFORMATION

MOUNTAIN RESCUE

In the event of an accident requiring the assistance of Mountain Rescue:

Dial 999 and ask for 'POLICE - MOUNTAIN RESCUE'

All mountain rescue incidents in the Peak District area fall under the responsibility of Derbyshire Constabulary. If in any doubt request Derbyshire Police Operations Room.

MOBILE PHONES

All the crags described in this book have excellent mobile phone coverage across the major networks.

BRITISH MOUNTAINEERING COUNCIL

British Mountaineering Council, 177-179 Burton Road, West Manchester, Manchester, M20 2BB.
Tel: 0161 445 4747 Fax: 0161 445 4500 **www.thebmc.co.uk**
The BMC is the official body representing climbers in Britain. If you have problems regarding access to any of the areas in this book, then get in touch with the BMC Access Officer at the address above.

TOURIST INFORMATION OFFICES

If you are short of ideas of what to do on a wet day, need some accommodation, want some tickets for the theatre or are just interested in local history; take a look at the **Tourist Information Offices**. They contain much more useful information than is possible to include on these pages.
Sheffield - The Peace Gardens. Tel: 0114 273 4672
Buxton - The Crescent. Tel: 01298 25106
Bakewell - Old Market Hall, Bridge Street. Tel: 01629 813227
Leek - Market Place, Leek. Tel: 01538 381000
Chesterfield - Peacock Information Centre, Lower Pavement. Tel: 01246 207777
More information and other travel tips are at - **www.travelengland.org.uk**

CAMPING

There are many more campsites in the Peak District but the two listed below are the most popular with climbers. More sites can be found on the following 2 web sites - **www.ukclimbing.com/listings/campsites.html**
www.campingcar.co.uk

Stanage - North Lees Camp Site
Birley Lane, Hathersage (see map on page 88). Tel: 01433 650838
The most popular climbers' campsite.

Baslow - Eric Byne Memorial Campsite
Below Birchen Edge, off the A619 (see map on page 256).
Rudimentary site but in a good location.

- Tents only
- Showers

NOT CAMPING

The free *Peakland Post* newspaper, produced 2 or three times a year, includes an extensive accommodation list. It is available from the Tourist Information Offices.
Youth Hostels - There are YHAs in Bakewell, Hathersage, Buxton, Elton (near Cratcliffe), Youlgreave (near Rheinstor) and Eyam (near Stoney). Check - **www.yha.org.uk**

Lucy Creamer on *Goosey Goosey Gander*, E5 6a, Marble Wall at Stanage. Photo: Ian Parnell. *Page 94*
Katherine Schirmacher on *Time for Tea*, E3 5c, on the Embankment at Millstone. Photo: Ian Parnell. *Page 194*

INFORMATION

GETTING AROUND

The areas in this book extend down the eastern edge of the Peak District and the easiest way to get to most of them is by car. The approach descriptions are written assuming you have access to a car. However if you are trying to get to the crags by public transport, firstly good luck, and secondly, here is a list of useful contacts which may help.

Buses - Derbyshire County Council provide an up to date listing of the bus services throughout the Peak District. This can be obtained from a Tourist Information Office or by post from Derbyshire County Council, Public Transport Unit, Chatsworth hall, Chesterfield Road, Matlock, DE4 3FW. You can also telephone Derby (01332) 292200 or South Yorkshire Traveline (01709) 515151, for more details.

South Yorkshire Transport - www.sypte.co.uk

Public Transport in Derbyshire - www.derbysbus.net

East Midlands Travel - www.scbeastmidstravel.co.uk

Trains - There is a regular service from Sheffield and Manchester to Grindleford. A long but pleasant walk leads up the Padley Gorge to Burbage South, Millstone and Lawrencefield. You can also reach Froggatt from here but there are few other crags you can reach using trains.

CLIMBING SHOPS

More shops listed at - www.ukclimbing.com/listings/shops.html

Rock+Run - 98 Devonshire Street, Sheffield, S1 4GY. Tel: 0114 275 6429

Outside - Main Road, Hathersage. Tel: 01433 651936

CCC - Hill Street, Sheffield, S2 4SZ. Tel: 0114 2729733

Outside - 45 Mowbray Street, Sheffield, S3 8EW. Tel: 0114 279 7427

Jo Royles - 6 Market Place, Buxton, SK17 6EB. Tel: 01298 25824

Hitch 'n' Hike - Hope Valley. Tel: 01433 651013

Nevisport - 26 Park Road, Chesterfield, S40 1XZ. Tel: 01246 201437

CAFES

Grindleford Station Cafe - Just off the B6001 through Grindleford (see map on page 114). Popular with climbers and walkers. Large portions of food and great entertainment in reading the polite (?) little notices.

Longland's Cafe - Above Outside in the centre of Hathersage (see main map on page 31). Excellent cafe with good food and its own gear shop.

PUBS

More pubs listed at - www.pub-explorer.com
There are loads of pubs in the area. The ones listed below are near bouldering areas.

The Fox House - near Burbage South.

The Grouse - above the parking area for Froggatt.

Robin Hood Inn - parking area for Birchen and Chatsworth.

The Moon - on the main road in Stoney Middleton.

The Druid - in Birchover near Cratcliffe.

Three Stags Heads - near Wardlow Mires on the A623. A great pub.

The Broadfield - on Abbeydale Road in Nether Edge in Sheffield. The right-hand room here has long been a meeting place of Sheffield climbers.

Curbar Edge.

CLIMBING WALLS

Although it is a well known fact that it never rains in the Peak District, there are occasional times of year when you may not be able to actually climb on the wonderful gritstone. The list below should help you find somewhere to climb. We haven't got enough room for approach directions so you will have to ring them up to find out how to get there. More information on the UKClimbing web site at - **www.ukclimbing.com/walls/**

- Lead routes
- Bouldering
- Showers
- Cafe
- Shop

SHEFFIELD

The Foundry - **see travel advert on page 25**
45 Mowbray Street, Sheffield. Tel: 0114 279 6331 or 0114 275 4802
Dedicated climbing centre. Built and added to by various people since 1991. Up to 16m lead wall and curved resin bouldering wall by Bendcrete. Special cellar-style training room with own membership arrangements. Bouldering competitions in the winter. Open all week 10am to 10pm (8pm at weekends). Different in summer. Winter bouldering league. Cafe, showers, weights room and function room. **www.foundryclimbing.com**
ROCKFAX Rating - ★★★★ - The original climbing centre. Lots of lead routes, a good bouldering wall and an intense cellar with plenty of powerful locals to boulder with.

The Edge - **see advert opposite**
John Street, Sheffield. Tel: 0114 275 8899
Dedicated climbing centre. Built in 1994 with new developments for each new season. Up to 15m lead and top rope climbs with two articulating walls. Extensive featured curved resin bouldering area. Popular winter bouldering league. Huge new Woodie now open with 10m roof, stepped and 10/30/45 degree boards. Open all week 10am-10.30pm (8pm weekends and bank holidays). Cafe and technical gear shop open till 9pm weekdays and 6pm weekends. **www.sheffield-climbing.co.uk**
ROCKFAX Rating - ★★★★ - Excellent centre with good range of routes which are changed regularly and a quality bouldering room.

HULL

Rock City - **see advert on page 11**
Hawthorn Avenue, Humberside, HU3 5JX. Tel: 01482 223030
Dedicated climbing centre. Built and added to by various people since 1994. Open all week 10 am to 10 pm (Saturday to 8pm only). Lead & top rope walls of all angles, curved resin bouldering plus cave and cellar, unique traditionally protected wall. Over 50% more top-rope walls were added in 2001. Fully safety matted and heated throughout. **www.rockcity.co.uk**
ROCKFAX Rating - ★★★★ - Excellent centre with new extended bouldering.

HUDDERSFIELD

Huddersfield Sports Centre
Southgate, Huddersfield. Tel: 01484 223630
Dedicated room in sports centre. Built and added to by DR since 1992. Panelled leading wall and curved-resin bouldering wall. Open Mon - Fri 7:15 am to 10:30pm, weekends 9am to 9pm.
ROCKFAX Rating - ★★★ - Good extensive centre with interesting bouldering feature.

CLIMBING WALLS

LIVERPOOL

Awesome Walls Climbing Centre 🜲📷🍴🛒 - see advert opposite
St. Albans Church, Athol Street, Liverpool. Tel: 0151 2982422
Large dedicated Climbing Centre. Major 16.5m lead wall plus 12m free-standing pillar. 4 separate bouldering areas with marked problems. Course, gear hire. Cafe and shop. Open Monday to Friday 12am till 10pm, weekends and bank holidays 10am till 6pm.
ROCKFAX Rating - ★★★★ - Excellent centre with new extended bouldering.

GLOSSOP

Glossop Leisure Centre 📷🚿
High Street East, Glossop. Tel: 01457 863223
Moulded concrete bouldering wall built by Bendcrete in 1990. Given a face lift in 1997 with new discs and 50 colour-coded problems. Open Mon - Fri 9am to 10:30pm, Sat 10am to 8pm, Sun 10am to 9pm.
ROCKFAX Rating - ★★★ - Cramped little wall with surprisingly good bouldering.

NOTTINGHAM

Nottingham Climbing Centre 🜲📷🚿🛒
The Sports Ground, Haydn Road, Nottingham. Tel: 0115 924 5388
Dedicated climbing centre. Built by DR in 1994. Cellar-style training area recently added. Up to 10m lead wall and large area of walls, and arch, for bouldering. Bouldering competitions in the winter. Open Mon - Fri 10am to 10pm, weekends 10am to 7pm. Cafe.
ROCKFAX Rating - ★★★★ - Large centre. Lead walls lack height but is probably the best bouldering wall in the country.

LEEDS

The Leeds Wall 🜲📷🚿🛒🍴 - see advert on page 17
100a Gelderd Road, Leeds LS12 6BY Tel: 0113 234 1554
Large dedicated Climbing Centre. Gear shop with extensive range of boots, harnesses, ropes and hard wear. Variety of climbing walls for all ages and abilities. Taster sessions, beginner and improver courses available. Lizard Club for kids at weekends and during school holidays. Cafe and vending on site. Open Monday to Friday 10am till 10pm, weekends and bank holidays 10am till 8pm. **www.theleedswall.co.uk**
ROCKFAX Rating - ★★★★ - Cheap and small.

STOCKPORT

Rope Race 🜲📷🚿🍴🛒
Goyt Mill, Upper Hibbert Lane, Marple. Tel: 0161 426 0226
Dedicated climbing centre. Built and added to by various people since 1993. Curved resin bouldering wall and separate cellar-style area. One 18m lead featured wall and plenty of other panel lead walls. Open Mon - Fri 10am to 10pm, weekends 10am to 7pm.
ROCKFAX Rating - ★★★ - Complex arrangement of walls. Good small bouldering section. Lead routes suit lower grade climbers.

🜲	- Lead routes
📷	- Bouldering
🚿	- Showers
🍴	- Cafe
🛒	- Shop

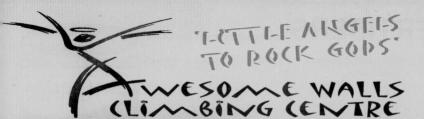
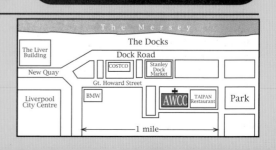

ADVERTISERS

ROCKFAX is very grateful companies, shops and climbing walls, who have supported this guidebook.

AWESOME WALLS (page 29) - Climbing wall
AWCC, St. Alban's Church, Athol Street, Liverpool, L5 9XT. Tel: 0191 2303793

BENDCRETE (Page 119) - Climbing walls, holds, mats
Bendcrete, Aqueduct Mill, Tame Street, Stalybridge, Cheshire, SK15 1ST.
Tel: 0161 3383046 Fax: 0161 3387956 www.bendcrete.com

ROCK + RUN (Page 12) - Shops and online shop
The Lakes - 3-4 Cheapside, Ambleside, LA22 0AB. Tel: 01539 433660
Sheffield - 98 Devonshire Street, Sheffield, S1 4GY. Tel: 0114 275 6429
Mail Order - Tel: 015394 32855 www.rockrun.com

SCARPA (Back cover) - Climbing footware
The Mountain Boot Company Ltd., 8 Nelson Street, Newcastle, NE1 5AW.
Tel: 0191 232 3565 Fax: 0191 222 1764 www.scarpa.co.uk

SNOW & ROCK (Inside front cover) - Shops
M25 Superstore - 99 Fordwater Road, Chertsey, KT16 8HH. Tel:01932 566 886
Bristol Superstore - Shield Retail Centre, Bristol, BS32. Tel: 0117 914 3000
Kensington - 188 Kensington High Street, London, W8 7RG. Tel:0207 937 0872
Hemel Ski Centre - St. Albans Hill, London, HP3 9NH. Tel:01442 253 305
Holborn - 150 Holborn, Corner Gray's Inn Road, EC1N 2LC. Tel: 0207 831 6900
Sheffield Ski Village - Vale Road, Sheffield, S3 9SL. Tel: 0114 275 1700
Birmingham - 14 Priory Queensway, Birmingham, B4 6BS. Tel: 0121 236 8280
www.snowandrock.com

THE EDGE CLIMBING CENTRE (Page 27) - Climbing wall
The Edge Climbing Centre, John Street, Sheffield, S2 4QU.
Tel: 0114 275 8899 Fax: 0114 273 8899 www.sheffieldclimbing.co.uk

UKCLIMBING.COM (Page 13) - Climbing web site
www.ukclimbing.com

OUTSIDE (Inside back cover) - Shops
Peak - Main Road, Hathersage. Tel: 01433 651936
Wales - The Old Baptist Chapel, High Street, Llanberis. Tel: 01286 871534
Sheffield (Clearance shop)- 45 Mowbray Street, Sheffield, S3 8EW.
Tel:0114 279 7427 Fax:0114 275 4802 www.outside.co.uk

ROCK CITY (Page 11) - Climbing Wall
Hawthorn Avenue, Humberside, HU3 5JX. Tel: 01482 223030
www.rockcity.co.uk

THE FOUNDRY INSURANCE (Page 25) - Insurance
The Foundry, 45 Mowbray Street, Sheffield. Tel: 0114 275 5806
www.foundrytravel.com

THE LEEDS WALL (Page 17) - Climbing wall
100a Gelderd Road, Leeds LS12 6BY. Tel: 0113 234 1554
www.theleedswall.co.uk

SPORTIVA (Page 225) - Climbing boots
Contact Big Stone. Tel: 01433 639433
www.lasportiva.co.uk

BEYOND THE EDGE (Page 17) - Climbing instruction
51 Plymouth Road, Sheffield, S7 2DE. Tel: 0114 249 7059

MOUNTAIN EQUIPMENT (Page 173) - Outdoor clothing and equipment
Contact local stockist or telephone 01457 854424
www.mountain-equipment.co.uk

ADVENTUREWORKS / JAGGED GLOBE (Page 25) - Climbing trips, courses
The Foundry Studios, 45 Mowbray Street, Sheffield S3 8EN. Tel: 0114 2763344
www.jagged-globe.co.uk

ACKNOWLEDGEMENTS

I first climbed on the Eastern Edges back in 1967 when I travelled down in the back of a van, through torrential rain to camp below Stanage. That weekend introduction to the wonderful world of gritstone climbing, with visits to Stanage, Burbage and Millstone, fired my imagination. My two companions on that trip were Colin Binks and Peter Ackroyd, both of whom I still manage to climb with on occasions. In 1970 I moved to Sheffield to train as a teacher and climbed in the Peak every weekend for three years, come rain or shine, with Steve Warwick, Nigel Baker and Dave Spencer. In the late 70s I climbed with the gritstone gurus of the late Ed Wood, Mark Stokes, Martin Veale, Pete O'Donovan and also began climbing with Graham Parkes. Graham has now been a regular partner for over 20 years, from Stanage to Cloggy, the Verdon and Yosemite, and back to Burbage. More recently I have climbed with Jim Rubery and that gritstone legend Dave Gregory whose tales from over 50 years on the grit never fail to entertain. On a recent day on Stanage, Colin, Daves Spencer and Gregory, Graham, Martin and Pete were all out there, enjoying the routes as ever, not a bad turnout all those years on!

A special thanks must got to my parents who never understood the attraction of climbing but realised that it meant so much to me that they never tried to stand in the way.

Thanks to Alan James who had the vision to see what we might be able to achieve with the superb combination of our combined fifty odd years of experience and his creative vision - I think we might just have set the guidebook world on fire!

Finally to Sherri Davy, my constant 'other-half' for the past 15 years, I hope the finished product is worth all the time I have spent on it, locked in the back room or tramping the Edges for one more checking session - thanks for all the support, now what's next?

Chris Craggs - November 2001

The job of documenting the information on the routes on Peak Grit was started way back in the 1920s by the likes of Fergus Graham and Rice Kemper Evans. The work was later carried forward by Peter Harding, Eric Byne, Nat Allen, Paul Nunn and others. In the 1970s the newly formed BMC Guidebook Committee took over the proceedings with people like Dave Gregory, Graham Hoey, Keith Sharples, Geoff Radcliffe, Malc Baxter and Geoff Milburn taking leading roles. We would like to thank all the individuals who have carried out this onerous task over the years. We would also like to acknowledge the role of the BMC in coordinating the work of the Guidebook Committee since 1971 and publishing the last three series of guidebooks.

Thanks to Susan Harvey of Harvey Maps (www.harveymaps.co.uk) whose superb 1:25,000 sheet *The Dark Peak* has been a great resource when working on this volume.

We have received hundreds of comments and votes via the Gritstone Route Database as well as masses of other feedback. I would like to thank all those who have taken an interest in the Internet side of this guidebook and hope that you will continue to let us know what you think in the future.

Thanks also to the following:

John Read, Neil Foster and Ben Heason for their extensive feedback and comments; to Mike James (Dad - getting his first new route credit in one of my books on page 188) and Dave Gregory for proof reading; to Jana Sticht and Juan Varela-Nex for their translations; to Ian Parnell, Dave Wilkinson, Jon Barton and Simon Richardson for their excellent photographic contributions; to Nick Smith for his superb work on the Gritstone Route Database; to Andy Hyslop for business advice and commitment to the idea; to Pete O'Donovan for loaning his scanner; to John Cox for an entertaining day out and an insight into better grading; to Mick Ryan for flying the ROCKFAX flag in the States and to my mother Liz James for her general help and support.

I would personally like to thank all the people whom I have climbed with on the gritstone edges over the years especially Nigel Boothroyd, Tudor Griffiths, Matt Snape, Paul Dearden, Lewis Grundy, Dave Ranby, Sophie Milner and Rory Park.

A big 'hats off' to Chris Craggs for the magnificent effort he has put in. Starting from the day we decided to 'go for it' to the day of the last key stroke, he has been a continual hive of activity; always reliable and a font of knowledge on Peak Grit; there is no-one better to have authored this book. Thanks also to Sherri for her patience and supply of butties.

Finally thanks to my family. The latest arrival Lydia gets her first mention in a book but the older ones are now dictating their own credits. Hannah has asked me to write, "Hannah and Sam are both very good at climbing." Special thanks to Henriette for her support, putting up with all my late nights and her contribution to the great guidebook debate.

Alan James - November 2001

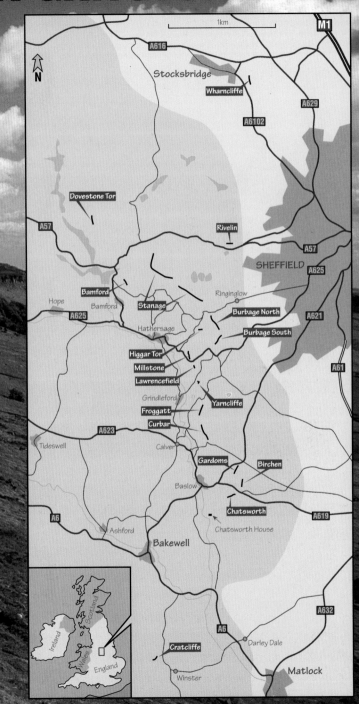

1km

M1

Wharncliffe

Dovestone Tor

Rivelin

Bamford

Stanage

Burbage North

Higgar Tor

Burbage South

Millstone

Lawrencefield

Yarncliffe

Froggatt

Curbar

Gardoms

Birchen

Chatsworth

Cratcliffe

A616

Stocksbridge

Wharncliffe

A6102

A629

Dovestone Tor

A57

Rivelin

SHEFFIELD

A57

A625

Bamford

Hope

Bamford

A625

Stanage

Ringinglow

Burbage North

Hathersage

Burbage South

A621

Higgar Tor

Millstone

Lawrencefield

A61

Grindleford

Yarncliffe

Froggatt

Curbar

A623

Calver

Tideswell

Gardoms

Birchen

Baslow

Chatsworth

A619

Chatsworth House

A6

Ashford

Bakewell

Ireland

Scotland

Wales

England

A6

Darley Dale

Cratcliffe

Winster

Matlock

A632

CRAG	No. of ROUTES	Mod	Diff	VDiff	HVD	Sev	HS	VS	HVS	E1	E2	E3	E4	E5	E6	E7
WHARNCLIFFE	88	1	8	10	3	10	5	8	6	12	8	4	4	5	3	1
DOVESTONES	88	2	5	8		13	5	18	19	12	2	2	1	1		
RIVELIN	76	1	2	4	1	6	3	9	12	10	4	6	7	9	2	
BAMFORD	112	10	8	4		12	5	22	17	7	9	5	5	1	4	3
STANAGE	591	6	22	37	15	49	47	111	88	59	39	30	31	22	26	9
BURBAGE NORTH	130	8	6	17	6	21	3	28	18	11	1	2	2	2	3	2
HIGGAR TOR	30		1	4		2	4	3	2	3	2		4	3	2	
BURBAGE SOUTH	81	2		1	2	5	2	15	18	6	6	1	5	9	3	6
MILLSTONE	107		1	3		3	4	18	21	10	12	9	4	13	5	4
LAWRENCEFIELD	40			3	1	1		9	2	4	4	2	12	2		
YARNCLIFFE	24				2	1	1	11	4	2	2				1	
FROGGATT	115	1	4	6		6	7	16	12	6	12	7	5	10	11	12
CURBAR	127	1	1	3		7	6	15	15	12	11	10	11	13	11	10
GARDOMS	73		2	4	1	5	7	18	6	7	7	7	1		4	2
BIRCHEN	143	8	10	27	3	29	12	27	8	10	4	2	3			
CHATSWORTH	42			5		2	7	3	5	6	5	6	2	1		
CRATCLIFFE	32			3		1	1	1	1	6	9	3	3	3	1	

Approach walk	Sunshine or shade	Access	Green	Sheltered	SUMMARY	Page	
15 min to 30 min	Mostly afternoon				A short outcrop in a rather urbane setting. Routes tend to be steep, fingery and hard for the grade. The landings are bad. **Best feature**: the Hell Gate Area	44	Wharncliffe
40 min	Afternoon			Bouldering	A wild and remote crag reached by one of the longest walk-ins in the Peak. Can be rather green and gritty after rain. **Best feature**: the fantastic setting.	54	Dovestones
10 min to 15 min	Lots of sun			Sheltered	A city crag; actually within the Sheffield boundary. South facing and low. A good bet for cold days but gets green and midgy. **Best feature**: the Rivelin Needle.	64	Rivelin
15 min to 25 min	Afternoon	Restrictions			Some of the roughest gritstone overlooking the dramatic setting of the Ladybower Reservoir. Restricted access. **Best feature**: the rock on the Lower Tier.	74	Bamford
10 min to 25 min	Afternoon and evening			Bouldering	As good as grit gets; there is something here for everyone and enough routes for years and years of visits. **Best feature**: glorious sunsets after great grit evenings.	86	Stanage
2 min to 20 min	From mid morning			Bouldering	Roadside bouldering and plenty of short routes. Easy access, and quality rock, the perfect combination. **Best feature**: accessible for when you need a quick fix.	152	Burbage North
5 min	From mid morning			Bouldering	Steep abrasive routes in a great setting, often a bit windy so ideal on hot or midgy days. Some of the steepest grit around. **Best feature**: the huge horn of a belay on top of The Rasp.	168	Higgar Tor
10 min to 20 min	Summer evenings only	Green		Bouldering	A series of short (and not so short) shady buttresses and a couple of quarries. Has many of grit's very hardest offerings. **Best feature**: a good retreat on hot days.	172	Burbage South
10 min to 15 min	Afternoon and evening			Bouldering	The grandest of the quarries, superb walls and soaring cracks. Once the empire of aid, now has the best cracks in the country. **Best feature**: finger jamming par excellence.	184	Millstone
5 min	Afternoon			Sheltered	Millstone's little sister, an idyllic quarry with a fine set of steep routes around a smelly pond. Quite good for beginners. **Best feature**: a great retreat in cold weather.	200	Lawrencefield
Roadside	From mid morning			Sheltered	A battered hole in the ground. The easy climbs in the first bay have been loved to death although there are better routes here. **Best feature**: 5 minutes from Grindleford Cafe.	206	Yarncliffe
10 min to 20 min	Afternoon			Bouldering	Some great cracks and the best set of slabby routes in the Peak, although many of them are very bold. **Best feature**: Valkyrie, a two-pitch route to a proper summit.	210	Froggatt
5 min to 15 min	Afternoon			Bouldering	The Cloggy of grit, fearsome cracks and desperate face climbs make this a place to visit when you are 'on a roll'. **Best feature**: the final jug on L'Horla.	228	Curbar
10 min to 25 min	Afternoon and some shade	Green	Sheltered	Bouldering	A rather overgrown edge of jutting buttresses above a tree covered hillside. Can be green and midgy when humid. **Best feature**: Moyer's Buttress, simply magnificent.	244	Gardoms
10 min to 15 min	Afternoon			Bouldering	The baby of the Eastern Edges, short routes, a friendly setting and stacks of lower grade offerings. Can be very busy. **Best feature**: a great place for starting out.	256	Birchen
10 min to 12 min	Summer evenings only	Green	Sheltered		A sister to Gardoms, neglected and a little overgrown, although great when the conditions are right. Avoid after rain. **Best feature**: the fist jams on the lip of Sentinel Crack.	272	Chatsworth
10 min	Until mid afternoon	Green	Sheltered	Bouldering	The most rural of the cliffs in this guide; not very extensive but a real bijou experience with some surprisingly big routes. **Best feature**: the walls of Owl Gully – grit to die for.	278	Cratcliffe

FIFTY OF THE BEST

☐ Black Hawk Traverse Right	Stanage	Diff
☐ Flying Buttress	Stanage	VDiff
☐ Heaven Crack	Stanage	VDiff
☐ Pulpit Groove	Lawrencefield	VDiff
☐ Hollybush Crack	Stanage	VDiff
☐ N.M.C Crack	Gardoms	HVD
☐ Heather Wall	Froggatt	S 3c
☐ Green Gut	Froggatt	S 4a
☐ Bishop's Route	Stanage	S 4a
☐ Balcony Buttress	Stanage	S 4a
☐ Black Hawk Hell Crack	Stanage	S 4a
☐ Twisting Crack	Stanage	S 4a
☐ Christmas Crack	Stanage	HS 4a
☐ Robin Hood's RH Buttress Direct	Stanage	HS 4a
☐ Inverted V	Stanage	VS 4c
☐ High Neb Buttress	Stanage	VS 4c
☐ The File	Higgar Tor	VS 4c
☐ Mississippi Buttress Direct	Stanage	VS 4c
☐ Great North Road	Millstone	HVS 5a
☐ Valkyrie	Froggatt	HVS 5a
☐ Croton Oil	Rivelin	HVS 5a
☐ Goliath's Groove	Stanage	HVS 5a
☐ Right Unconquerable	Stanage	HVS 5a
☐ Suicide Wall	Cratcliffe	HVS 5a
☐ The Peapod	Curbar	HVS 5b
☐ Left Unconquerable	Stanage	E1 5b
☐ Moyer's Buttress	Gardoms	E1 5b
☐ Brown's Eliminate	Froggatt	E2 5b
☐ Tower Face Direct	Stanage	E2 5b
☐ Regent Street	Millstone	E2 5c
☐ The Rasp	Higgar Tor	E2 5c
☐ Elder Crack	Curbar	E2 5b
☐ Quietus	Stanage	E2 5c
☐ Billy Whiz	Lawrencefield	E2 5c
☐ Great Slab	Froggatt	E3 5b
☐ The Archangel	Stanage	E3 5b
☐ Requiem	Cratcliffe	E3 6a
☐ Sentinel Crack	Chatsworth	E3 5c
☐ Calvary	Stanage	E4 6a
☐ Moon Walk	Curbar	E4 6a
☐ Old Friends	Stanage	E4 5c
☐ Nectar	Stanage	E4 6b
☐ Strapadictomy	Froggatt	E5 6b
☐ Goosey Goosey Gander	Stanage	E5 6a
☐ Profit of Doom	Curbar	E5 6b
☐ Green Death	Millstone	E5 5c
☐ London Wall	Millstone	E5 6a
☐ Linden	Curbar	E6 6b
☐ Beau Geste	Froggatt	E7 6c
☐ End Of The Affair	Curbar	E8 6c

Wharncliffe
Dovestone Tor
Rivelin
Bamford
Stanage
Burbage North
Higgar Tor
Burbage South
Millstone
Lawrencefield
Yarncliffe
Froggatt
Curbar
Gardoms
Birchen
Chatsworth
Cratcliffe

GRADED LIST

The following list contains 500 of the best routes on Peak Gritstone arranged in order of difficulty. This should provide you with hours of entertainment as you see how high up the list you can tick. Just to make it more complex there are three tick boxes for three styles of ascent.

1st Class (GOLD AWARD)
A clean lead, bottom up. No pre-placed gear, no weighting the gear. Sport equivalent of a flash.

2nd Class (SILVER AWARD)
Led with a fall but returned to the ground. Led after pre-practice on a top-rope (headpoint). Followed the route (seconding or top roping) first try without weighting the gear or rope.

3rd ....(AWARD! you've got to be joking)
"Covered the ground". Sat on a runner, top-roped with falls, winched, human pyramid, stood in slings, used a ladder. Sport equivalent of working the route!

Graham Parkes and Dave Spencer on
Nectar, E4 6b, Marble Wall, Stanage. Page 94

1 2 3	E10	Page
★★★ ❑❑❑	Equilibrium	175
★★★ ❑❑❑	Doctor Doolittle	237

1 2 3	E9	Page
★★ ❑❑❑	The Zone	243
★★★ ❑❑❑	Parthian Shot	175
★★★ ❑❑❑	Knockin' on Heaven's Door	238

1 2 3	E8	Page
★★ ❑❑❑	Soul Doubt	216
★★★ ❑❑❑	Marbellous	94
★★★ ❑❑❑	Captain Invincible	183
★★★ ❑❑❑	Unfamiliar	115
★★ ❑❑❑	Smoked Salmon	77
★ ❑❑❑	Stampede	174
★★ ❑❑❑	Renegade Master	211
★★★ ❑❑❑	The End of the Affair	231

1 2 3	E7	Page
★★★ ❑❑❑	Slab and Crack (Curbar)	237
★★★ ❑❑❑	Little Women	150
★★ ❑❑❑	Scritto's Republic	194
★★ ❑❑❑	Screaming Dream	211
★★★ ❑❑❑	Groove Is In The Heart	150
★ ❑❑❑	Strappotente	212
★★ ❑❑❑	Sad Amongst Friends	151
★★★ ❑❑❑	Beau Geste	216
★★★ ❑❑❑	Master's Edge	193
★★★ ❑❑❑	Balance It Is	175
★★★ ❑❑❑	Braille Trail	175
★★ ❑❑❑	Black Car Burning	150
★★ ❑❑❑	Cemetery Waits	123
★★★ ❑❑❑	Top Loader	185
★★★ ❑❑❑	White Lines	234
★★★ ❑❑❑	Shine On	123
★★★ ❑❑❑	Flight of Ideas	112
★★★ ❑❑❑	Janus	238
★★★ ❑❑❑	Cool Moon	230
★★ ❑❑❑	Jasmin	81
★★ ❑❑❑	Benign Lives	212
★★ ❑❑❑	The Salmon	77

1 2 3	E6	Page
★ ❑❑❑	Cock Robin	212
★★ ❑❑❑	Warmlove	151
★★★ ❑❑❑	Adam Smith's Invisible Hand	198
★★★ ❑❑❑	Careless Torque	109
★ ❑❑❑	Dragon's Hoard	50
★★★ ❑❑❑	Spanish Fly	246
★★★ ❑❑❑	Messiah	180
★★★ ❑❑❑	Ulysses' Bow	109
★★ ❑❑❑	Slackers	233
★★ ❑❑❑	Wall Of Sound	137
★★ ❑❑❑	The 9 O'clock Watershed	144
★★★ ❑❑❑	Heath Robinson	91
★★★ ❑❑❑	Boys Will Be Boys	118
★★ ❑❑❑	My Herald of Free Enterprise	114
★★★ ❑❑❑	Mickey Finn	246
★★★ ❑❑❑	Salmon Direct	76
★★★ ❑❑❑	Mother's Pride	185
★★★ ❑❑❑	Perplexity	185
★★ ❑❑❑	Carpe Diem	134
★★ ❑❑❑	Block and Tackle	170
★ ❑❑❑	Skinless Wonder	150
★★ ❑❑❑	Epiphany Left-Hand	216
★★★ ❑❑❑	Desolation Angel	51
★★ ❑❑❑	The Cool Curl	104
★ ❑❑❑	Master of Disguise	144
★★ ❑❑❑	Mean Streak	217
★★★ ❑❑❑	Linden	243
★★★ ❑❑❑	Narcissus	220
★★★ ❑❑❑	Crème de la Crème	209
★★★ ❑❑❑	The Crypt Trip	102
★★ ❑❑❑	One Step Beyond	236
★★ ❑❑❑	Grace and Danger	112
★★★ ❑❑❑	Defying Destiny	120
★★ ❑❑❑	Skidoo	113
★★ ❑❑❑	Genocide	280
★★★ ❑❑❑	Indian Summer	112
★★ ❑❑❑	Make It Snappy	253
★ ❑❑❑	Science Friction	214

Adrian Berry on *Goliath*, E4 5c, Burbage South.
Photo: Ian Parnell. *Page 180*

Jim Rubery on *The Rasp*, E2 5b, Higgar Tor. *Page 170*

Dave Gregory on *The Peapod*, HVS 5b, Curbar. *Page 243*

Bilberry Crack, VS 5a, Bamford. Page 76

Colin Binks on *Hargreave's Original*, Black Slab, VS 4c, Stanage. *Page 138*

Stanage sunset. Photo: Dave Wilkinson.

WHARNCLIFFE

Wharncliffe
Dovestone Tor
Rivelin
Bamford
Stanage
Burbage North
Higgar Tor
Burbage South
Millstone
Lawrencefield
Yarncliffe
Froggatt
Curbar
Gardoms
Birchen
Chatsworth
Cratcliffe

Wharncliffe has long had a bit of a rogue reputation as a grim place to climb owing to its slightly urban location overlooking the upper Don Valley and the steel rolling mills of Stocksbridge. As you can see from the photo-topos, this is just rumour mongering by the locals who want to keep the place to themselves; well their cover has been blown! The main section of cliff has routes across the full grade spectrum and, although many only rise to 12m in height, they are usually action-packed and quite intense. The climbing tends to be steep and fingery, with many small sharp holds rather than the roundedness of true gritstone. The grades here have long been regarded as being on the tough side and we have made some effort to redress this. One rumour that is true is that the landings are awful; make a point of getting an early runner in, small Friends are especially useful in this respect!

Wharncliffe was very significant at the birth of British outcrop climbing with J.W.Puttrell first scratching the rock here with his nailed boots back in 1885. By 1900, and due in large part to the nearby railway line, Wharncliffe was the most popular cliff in the country. An article published in 1910 described 110 separate routes here. The heady days have never returned and a century on Wharncliffe is a place to escape the crowds that have become so much of climbing elsewhere in the Peak; strange to think that the place is probably less popular now than it was 100 years ago, surely the only venue in Britain where this can be said.

APPROACH (SK297977)

The cliff flanks the eastern edge of the Don Valley 10km north of Sheffield city centre. It is most easily approached from Stocksbridge. Locate Station Road which is a small road off the main road connecting the A616 with the traffic light junction at the south of the town. 400m down Station Road is a steep left turn which is almost impossible to access travelling in this direction so turn around. A short distance up here is parking on the left. It is also possible to park on Station Road although it should be pointed out that both locations are prime venues for car crime. From either parking follow the track uphill under two sludgy tunnels below the railway-line and across a cycle track. Continue to a pool and turn right. The path rises soon emerging from the trees above the first buttress on the cliff.

CONDITIONS

The cliff is high enough to catch much of the bad weather that afflicts the Peak though being north and east of the main mass of hills there is a rain shadow effect here and Wharncliffe can be in the sun when Stanage is swathed in clinging mist and dampened by drizzle. The cliff dries rapidly and is relatively midge-free when compared to the main crags. On winter afternoons, with the sun out and an easterly wind, the dark rock absorbs the sun's radiation and warms up nicely.

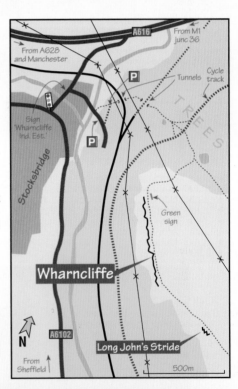

OTHER GUIDEBOOKS - A more complete list of routes at Wharncliffe is published in the 1989 BMC *Stanage* guidebook. A new book including Wharncliffe is due to be published by the BMC and it will be called the *Sheffield Area* guidebook.

5m gap

Tensile Test Area 50m →

Descent

Wharncliffe
Dovestone Tor
Rivelin
Bamford
Stanage
Burbage North
Higgar Tor
Burbage South
Millstone
Lawrencefield
Yarncliffe
Froggatt
Curbar
Gardoms
Birchen
Chatsworth
Cratcliffe

PROW ROCK AREA

The first section of Wharncliffe is the pointed pinnacle of Prow Rock. This worthy mini-summit usually requires a flying leap to escape. To the right of the pinnacle is a well-cracked buttress once capped with a pylon.

❶ Steeltown E5 6b
8m. The leaning north face of Prow Rock. Reach the central break then use layaways and an undercut to gain the sloping top. Swing left to better holds to finish.
FA. Howie Darwin 1989

❷ The Moire E5 6b
8m. The outer arete of the Prow is taxing and poorly protected. The landing is typical Wharncliffe. Enough said!
FA. Don Barr 1978

❸ Querp E3 6b
10m. Gain the base of the scoop in the centre of the west face from the right and make fingery pulls to enter it.
FA. Howie Darwin 1989

❹ Outside Route .... S 4a
8m. From the south tip of the tower trend left via a niche.
FA. J.W.Puttrell c.1900

❺ The Nose .... VS 4c
6m. The juggy south arete of the tower.
FA. Fred Jones 1933

❻ Inside Route .... Diff
8m. The shady face is the easiest way up and down the tower.
FA. J.W.Puttrell 1885

❼ Exonian's Return .... HVS 5c
8m. A fingery left to right traverse of the wall behind the Prow.
FA. Reg Addey early 1960s

❽ Pylon Crack .... VDiff
8m. The steep and protectable left-hand crack in the north face.
FA. J.W.Puttrell and friends c.1900

❾ Quern Crack .... S 4a
8m. ...and the steeper fissure just to the right.
FA. J.W.Puttrell and friends c.1900

❿ Hamlet's Climb .... HVD
10m. The steep crack in the left-hand side of the buttress leads to a notch. Escape leftwards. A **Direct Finish** is **VS 4c**.
FA. J.W.Puttrell and friends c.1900

⓫ Requiem of Hamlet's Ghost . HVS 5a
10m. The face between the two cracks gives steep climbing over a series of overlaps.
FA. Terry Hirst 1976

⓬ The Crack of Doom ..... HS 4b
10m. The steep off-width was a good effort for its day.
FA. J.W.Puttrell and friends c.1900

⓭ Despair E2 5c
10m. Climb the steep pillar on the right-hand side of the buttress, passing a roof early on.
FA. Nick White 1982

Wharncliffe · Dovestone Tor · Rivelin · Bamford · Stanage · Burbage North · Higgar Tor · Burbage South · Millstone · Lawrencefield · Yarncliffe · Froggatt · Curbar · Gardoms · Birchen · Chatsworth · Cratcliffe

Descent ←---

Afternoon | 15 min

Change in viewing angle

⑤ ⑥ ⑦

Mantelshelf Pillar 10m ▶

TENSILE TEST AREA

A smooth face of good quality rock with some enjoyable if short climbs and some fingery bouldering. A couple of the routes hereabouts are of great antiquity

① Suspense . . . . [ ] **HVS 5b**
6m. The left-edge of the wall.
FA. Pete Crew late 1950s

② Mellicious . . . . [ ] **E1 5c**
6m. The wall between the arete and the shallow groove.
FA. John Camateras 2000

③ Tensile Test . . . . [ ] **E1 5c**
6m. The technical slab and beckoning shallow groove above is the best offering here.
FA. Terry Hirst 1977

④ Elastic Limit . . . . [ ] **E1 5c**
6m. Climb the middle of the steep slab to the crease followed by *Abair*, then step left to finish.
FA. Michael Anderson 1977

⑤ Forget-me-not . . . . [ ] **S 4b**
6m. Mantel onto a finger ledge just left of the gully then climb the wall above.

⑥ Abair . . . . [ ] **E1 5b**
14m. Finger traverse the prominent thin break from right to left to a finish on the arete.
FA. Don Barr 1978

⑦ Handover Arete . . . . [ ] **HVS 4c**
8m. Climb the arete to the block overhang and pull over this at its left-hand edge where it is narrowest.
FA. Frank Fitzgerald 1955

⑧ Mantelshelf Pillar . . . . [ ] **HVS 5a**
6m. The left-hand arete of the prominent square pillar.
FA. John Fearon late 1950s

⑨ The Mantelshelf . . . . [ ] **HS 4b**
6m. The right arete of the pillar via a hard mantelshelf move.
FA. J.W.Puttrell c1900

⑩ Back and Foot . . . . [ ] **Diff**
6m. A good place to practise the suggested technique.
FA. J.W.Puttrell c1900

MANTELSHELF PILLAR

⑩

⑨

⑧

Photo Finish 30m ▶

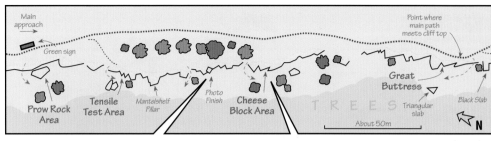

Wharncliffe

Dovestone Tor

Rivelin

Bamford

Stanage

Burbage North

Higgar Tor

Burbage South

Millstone

Lawrencefield

Yarncliffe

Froggatt

Curbar

Gardoms

Birchen

Chatsworth

Cratcliffe

PHOTO FINISH

A fine slab with a huge rocking block perched on top.

⑪ Slab and Corner . . . . 🔲 **VS 4b**
8m. From the centre of the slab trend left to climb the shallow groove in the arete.
FA. Fred Jones 1933

⑫ Photo Finish . . . . 🔲 **E1 5b**
10m. From part way up *Slab and Corner* step right and climb the slab and the rocking block above.
FA. Terry Hirst 1979

⑬ Dead Heat . . . . . . 🔲 **E4 5c**
10m. The slab just right of centre is technical, tenuous and unprotected.
FA. Nick White 1985

⑭ Renrock . . . . 🔲 **HVS 5a**
8m. The right-hand edge of the slab is pleasant, though protection is lacking.
FA. Rod Wilson late 1950s

CHEESE BLOCK AREA

A blocky buttress split by a series of cracks and grooves which is a great area for beginners.

⑮ Black Wall . . . . 🔲 **S 4a**
6m. The north-facing wall is climbed centrally by a couple of tricky mantelshelves.

⑯ Cheese Cut . . . . 🔲 **Diff**
6m. The angular groove gives pleasant bridging at a very amenable grade.
FA. J.W.Puttrell c1900

⑰ Cheese Cut Crack . . . . 🔲 **VDiff**
6m. The crack in the right-hand wall of the groove starts steeply and leads rapidly to easy ground.
FA. J.W.Puttrell c1900

⑱ Cheese Block . . . . 🔲 **VDiff**
8m. To the right of the arete is a crack leading to a perched flake. Follow this steeply to easier ground.

⑲ Cheese Cut Flake . . . . 🔲 **VDiff**
8m. Climb the wide crack past an awkward overhang then continue up the pleasant twisting crack above.
FA. J.W.Puttrell c1900

Descent

Descent

On the side wall

Black Slab 20m

Wharncliffe

Dovestone Tor

Rivelin

Bamford

Stanage

Burbage North

Higgar Tor

Burbage South

Millstone

Lawrencefield

Yarncliffe

Froggatt

Curbar

Gardoms

Birchen

Chatsworth

Cratcliffe

GREAT BUTTRESS

Not surprisingly this is one of the tallest buttresses on the cliff with a good set of worthwhile routes on the main piece of rock and some much milder offerings on its slumped neighbour just to the left.

DIRECT APPROACH - From the green sign above Prow Rock continue on the cliff-top path for about 250m to a point where the path approaches the edge for the first time. You should be able to see the triangular slab below the Great Buttress.

① Alpha . . . . **Diff**
10m. Follow flakes up the left-hand side of the slabby buttress to blocky ledges and a finish on the left-hand arete.
FA. J.W.Puttrell et al c1900

② Beta Crack . . . . **VDiff**
10m. The long continuous flake that runs up the right-hand side of the slab gives a fine pitch moving left at the top. Alternatively finish over a small overhang (**S 4a**).
FA. J.W.Puttrell et al c1900

③ Trapezium **E1 5b**
10m. Climb the wide crack to a notch and then the steep wall above passing the right-hand edge of the overlap. Steep and hard on the fingers.
FA.Don Barr 1978

④ The Great Chimney . . . . . **Diff**
8m. The obvious cleft gives a good old fashioned climb with blocky ground leading to some steep bridging.
FA. J.W.Puttrell et al c1900

⑤ Great Chimney Crack . . . . **S 4a**
10m. In the right-hand wall of the chimney is a steep left-trending crack. Follow this on good (and occasionally creaky) holds until it is possible to stride into the chimney to finish.
FA. J.W.Puttrell et al c1900

⑥ Thrown Away **E2 5c**
12m. The right-hand wall of the chimney is climbed centrally, starting up a thin crack and trending left towards the top. Escapable but with some good stretchy moves.
FA. Gary Gibson 1981

⑦ Great Buttress Arete **E1 5b**
12m. A fine climb up the long arete. A tape can be placed over a flake early on for protection. Above this the route gives good sustained climbing. For a long time this was a Wharncliffe rarity; an over-graded route.
FA. Pete Crew early 1960's

⑧ Great Buttress . . . . **VS 4c**
12m. Start up the arete but traverse right just below the useful sapling into the centre of the face. Climb to a deep horizontal slot then step left to a steep finish.
FA. Fred Jones 1933

⑨ Romulus . . . . **VDiff**
8m. The straight crack passing a small overhang early on and finishing on a spacious rocky ledge.
FA. J.W.Puttrell et al c1900

⑩ Remus . . . . **S 4a**
8m. A thin crack which leads to a tiny shallow groove and the same rocky ledge as *Romulus*.
FA. J.W.Puttrell et al c1900

⑪ Fly Wall . . . . **HS 4a**
8m. The centre of the short wall gives a pleasant but poorly protected piece of climbing.
FA. Frank Fitzgerald 1955

⑫ Leaf Arete **E1 5b**
8m. Climb the arete of the Leaf, initially up its edge and then at half height up its left-hand side via a good slot.
FA. John Camateras 2001

⑬ Leaf Buttress . . . . **VS 4c**
8m. The front face of the Leaf trending left throughout via a flake and tiny groove.
FA. Pete Crew late 1950s

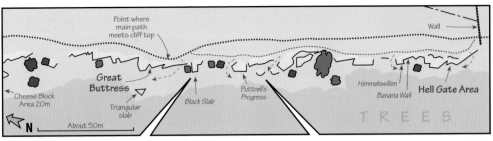

Point where main path meets cliff top

Wall

Cheese Block Area 20m

Great Buttress

Triangular slab

Black Slab

Puttrell's Progress

Himmelswillen

Banana Wall

Hell Gate Area

N

About 50m

TREES

Wharncliffe
Dovestone Tor
Rivelin
Bamford
Stanage
Burbage North
Higgar Tor
Burbage South
Millstone
Lawrencefield
Yarncliffe
Froggatt
Curbar
Gardoms
Birchen
Chatsworth
Cratcliffe

BLACK SLAB

30m gap

Afternoon · 18 min

14 · 15 · 16

17 · 18 · 19

Change in viewing angle

The Monolith

22 · 23

21

20

Himmelswillen 70m

BLACK SLAB

A delightful and very popular piece of rock with three variations.

⑭ Black Slab Left . . . . 🔲 **Diff**
10m. The left-hand line on the slab trending slightly right then back left to finish.
FA. J.W.Puttrell 1885

⑮ Black Slab Centre . . . . . . 🔲 **VDiff**
10m. The central line crossing an overlap in the centre of the slab and finishing up a tiny groove.

⑯ Black Slab Right . . . . 🔲 **VDiff**
10m. The right-hand line starts from a block, passes a flake, and finishes with a steeper section.

PUTTRELL'S PROGRESS AREA

⑰ Black Finger . . . . 🔲 **E3 5c**
10m. Climb the tower that supports the rest of the main buttress to its top then follow a series of spidery cracks left-wards below an overlap to a finish up the left-hand arete.
FA. John Allen 1973

⑱ Anzio Breakout/Pilgrimage 🔲 **E5 6b**
10m. Take *Black Finger* to the roof, reach right for small holds and make a fierce pull to reach the break on *Puttrell's Progress*. Pull through the centre of the roof and finish up the wall above.
FA. Jon Darwin 1987/ Don Barr 1978

PUTTRELL'S PROGRESS AREA

A buttress that has been slowly collapsing over the years. Get the classic Puttrell's Progress done before the whole thing goes west!

⑲ Puttrell's Progress . . . . 🔲 **S 4a**
12m. Climb the right arete of the big cave and squirm into the vertical slot with difficulty. Make an intimidating traverse left and finish up the steep juggy crack.
FA. J.W.Puttrell et al c1900

⑳ Helping Hand . . . . . . 🔲 **E1 5c**
10m. Climb the centre of the right-hand pillar to a break and the hard wall above trending left.
FA. John Allen 1973

㉑ As You Like It . . . . 🔲 **VDiff**
8m. The left crack in the right wall of the gully is escapable.
FA. J.W.Puttrell et al c1900

㉒ Black Crack . . . . 🔲 **HVD**
8m. The right-hand crack in the right wall of the gully.
FA. J.W.Puttrell et al c1900

㉓ Black Cap . . . . 🔲 **E2 6a**
8m. The short sharp arete of the gully.
FA. Roger Doherty 1985

HIMMELSWILLEN and BANANA WALL

An impressive buttress and wall with a good set of routes across the grades. *Tower Face* and *Himmelswillen* are superb routes in the lower grades and the hard climbs based around *Banana Wall* are a sterling set of fingery test-pieces.

DIRECT APPROACH - From the green sign continue on the cliff-top path for about 500m until you reach a wall. Descend to the right to reach Hell Gate Area and *Himmelswillen* just beyond.

❶ Sidewinder . . . . S 4a
8m. The centre of the steep north-facing wall is climbed on small holds starting from a block and finishing with a long reach.

❷ Himmelswillen . . . . VS 4c
14m. The classic of the crag. Climb the left arete to ledges then step right and layback into the finger crack that splits the centre of the tower. Finish on the left arete.
FA. Tom Stobart (solo) 1933

❸ Serrated Edge E1 5b
14m. The right-and arete can be followed throughout. It is rather close to *Himmelswillen* in its central section but features good steep climbing.
FA. Gary Gibson 1981

❹ Teufelsweg . . . . Diff
14m. The rift that splits the face.
FA. Hans Teufel (of Munich Climb fame)1936

❺ Wango Tango E6 6c
12m. The left-hand side of the smooth face on the smallest of holds imaginable.
FA. Roger Doherty 1987

❻ Dragon's Hoard E6 6b
12m. From the right-hand side of a block tiny cracks lead up the centre of the face to a desperate, grasping final sequence. Originally the route was *Cardinal's Treasure* E4 6b and it swung right to finish as for *Banana Wall*.
FA. (DH) Simon Jones 1993. FA. (CT) John Allen 1984

❼ Banana Wall E4 6a
12m. A rare beast indeed, a soft touch Wharncliffe route! Climb the small wall right of centre using undercuts (good Friend) and poor holds to reach easier ground by a long stretch. Finish rapidly.
FA. Don Barr 1977

❽ Tower Face . . . . HS 4b
12m. The face on the left-hand edge of the square buttress is split by a thin crack. Approach the crack via a short awkward slab (poor protection) then climb it using the arete on the right when required. *Photo page 53.*
FA. Eric Byne 1933

HELL GATE AREA

The finest set of hard climbs on the cliff based around three jutting aretes. Half a dozen routes weigh in at E4 and above, with *Journey into Freedom* currently the hardest offering on the cliff. All are steep, fingery and very poorly protected. Those in search of something a lot less serious should enjoy the three *Hell Gate* routes.

⑨ Down to Earth **E4 5c**
12m. The valley face of the buttress is fingery, sustained and unprotected where it really matters, and the landing is pretty poor too! Side runners drop the grade a notch or two.
FA. Roger Doherty 1985

⑩ On the Air **E5 6a**
12m. The right-hand arete of the face is climbed on its right side until it is possible to teeter around onto the front face to finish. Bold and precarious.
FA. Terry Hirst 1978

⑪ Journey into Freedom .. **E7 6b**
12m. Bridge out of the wide central cleft in the left wall and climb leftwards using undercuts to slap for the arete. After a couple of moves up this swing right and climb the wall to join and finish as for *On the Air*.
FA. Simon Jones 1993

⑫ Seconds Out **E5 6b**
12m. Mantel onto the jutting block, then move up before finger-traversing the thin crack all the way to the arete and a finish as for the last pair of climbs.
FA. Don Barr 1978

⑬ Hell Gate Gully .... **Mod**
12m. The blocky central gully provides a little light relief in this crucible of daring deeds. Climb a slab then bridge past blocks to reach easier ground above. All very historical.
FA. J.W.Puttrell et al c1900

⑭ News at Zen **E3 5c**
10m. The right-hand wall of the gully is climbed centrally passing a useful black pocket. A rather sensible side runner lowers the grade to E1.
FA. Simon Jones 1993

⑮ Desolation Angel **E6 6b**
12m. The main central arete gives a superb and technical route,. It is climbed on its left-hand side throughout by laying-away and using holds on the left. A rather distant side runner is more normal at E5, though the upper section still remains bold.
FA. Terry Hirst (with side runner) 1978 Simon Jones (solo) 1992

⑯ Hell Gate .... **VDiff**
14m. The deep groove has a tricky bulge early on and another to leave the half-height niche. Not a bad effort for a hundred plus years ago.
FA. J.W.Puttrell et al c1900

⑰ Gavel Neese **E2 5b**
14m. The blunt arete has a very height-dependent start (at least 6a for shorties) and no runners (large Friends on the left) until after the crux. The upper arete is much easier and has good holds and protection as well as great positions.
FA. Reg Addey (solo) early 1960s.

⑱ Lucifer **E2 5c**
12m. Climb *Hell Gate Crack* to the first overhang then step left and climb a crack to the roof. Pull over this and climb the open groove with difficulty.
FA. Terry Hirst 1984

⑲ Hell Gate Crack .... **HS 4b**
12m. The steep and awkward flake-crack in centre of the face leads to the large overhang. Step right for an easier finish.

Wharncliffe
Dovestone Tor
Rivelin
Bamford
Stanage
Burbage North
Higgar Tor
Burbage South
Millstone
Lawrencefield
Yarncliffe
Froggatt
Curbar
Gardoms
Birchen
Chatsworth
Cratcliffe

Descent

The 'inside' arete of the tower

10m gap

The left arete

① October Climb . . . . [ ] **S 4a**
14m. Climb a crack passing a tall jammed block to ledges then finish up the left-hand side of the face above.
FA. John Fearon 1955

② October Arete Original . . . . [icons] **VS 4c**
12m. Start up *October Climb* to the jammed block then make tricky and exposed moves out to the arete. Finish more easily.
FA. John Fearon 1955

③ October Arete . . . . [icons] **E2 5c**
12m. The left-hand arete of the left-hand tower has a hard, reachy and poorly protected start until it joins the VS.
FA. Pete Crew early 1960s

④ Autumn Wall . . . . [icons] **E4 6a**
12m. The left-hand side of the face of the tower is climbed, passing an overlap early on and with thin moves on poor holds at half height.
FA. Terry Hirst (solo) 1978

⑤ Equinox . . . . [icons] **E3 6a**
12m. The right-hand arete of the wall with increasing difficulty.
FA. Terry Hirst (left-hand finish) 1978. FA. (Direct) John Hesketh 1988

⑥ Grammarian's Progress . . . [icons] **VS 4b**
14m. Starting at the wind tunnel and climb the arete on the left-hand side of the detached tower, before pulling round onto the front face. A poorly protected mantelshelf reaches better holds, then traverse right to a wide crack to finish.
FA. R.A.Brown 1944

⑦ Long John's Ordinary . . . . . . [ ] **S 4a**
6m. The easiest way up the tower. Climb the inside arete of the tower moving left to gain the top. Now try and escape!
FA. J.W.Puttrell late 1800s

LONG JOHN'S STRIDE
An isolated set of quiet buttresses with a good selection of climbs. It can be green here in winter.
APPROACH - From above Hell Gate Area continue on the cliff top path for 10 mins.

⑧ Gwyn . . . . [icons] **E1 6a**
12m. The centre of the north-facing wall of the central tower has a taxing moves and no gear.
FA. Reg Addey (solo) early 1960s

⑨ Grammarian's Face . . . . . . [icons] **E2 5b**
12m. The right-hand arete of the central tower face is easier than it looks but no better protected.
FA. Gary Gibson 1982

⑩ Long John's Eliminate . [icons] **E2 5b**
16m. Climb the arete as for the previous climb but traverse the face on the right to a groove in the opposite arete. Climb this then traverse back left to a crack. Bold.
FA. Pete Crew early 1960s

⑪ Impish . . . . [icons] **E1 6b**
6m. The short left arete of the chimney. Spotter or mat advised.
FA. Simon Jones 1994

⑫ Long Chimney . . . . [icons] **Diff**
10m. The prominent narrowing cleft.
FA. J.W.Puttrell et al c1900

⑬ Richard's Revenge . . . . [icons] **VS 5a**
10m. The smart crack is tough to start, passing an old peg scar, and features excellent jamming above.
FA. Dick Brown late 1940s

⑭ Lincoln Crack . . . . [icons] **HVD**
8m. The pleasant crack on the right is sometimes green.
FA. Dick Brown late 1940s

DOVESTONE TOR

Dovestone Tor is well worth a visit if you want to escape the crowds of Froggatt and Stanage and to experience climbing in the Peak as it was fifty years ago. The cliff is basically a long west-facing wall riddled with many circular holes. The rock can be dirty, especially after rain, but the outlook is as fine as any cliff in the Peak and sunny afternoons spent here can be enthralling with superb views out into the wilderness of Bleaklow.

Developments in the mid-1990s dramatically increased the number of routes and brought to light inaccuracies in the existing information. In the earlier days of the exploration of the edge, teams of climbers claimed routes without leaving precise details of who did what. In particular a team of Ted Howard, Barry Pedlar, and Tanky Stokes climbed routes attributed here to 'Ted Howard et al.' although exactly who led what is not recorded. Many of the new climbs, described here for the first time, will have been climbed in the past, especially the easier lines. Any information on these would be gratefully received. Some of the climbs described here might not be of the quality you might expect in a selected routes guide, but as they have never been listed elsewhere, it was felt appropriate to include a wide selection here.

BOULDERING - There is some bouldering on the rocks below the main edge. Also two of the formations passed on the Cut Throat Bridge approach to the crag have some fine, esoteric bouldering.

ACCESS

Much of the moor to either side of Dovestone Tor is controlled to promote the grouse population. Access is freely given but on shooting days (notices posted) you need to stay on the normal paths.

APPROACHES (SK197898)

Dovestone Tor is situated high above the Ladybower Reservoir. There are 2 main approaches:

1) Cut-throat Bridge (50 mins walk). Park in the lay-by on the A57 above the bridge. From the bridge pick up one of two possible paths up to the crest of the moor where a right turn leads past some good bouldering, to the Tor.

2) Foulstone Delf near the Strines Inn (40 mins walk). Follow a good track that runs to the crest of the ridge, then turn left (south) onto the flagged path which leads to the cliff.

WARNING - Both car parks, especially Foulstone Delf, are visited regularly by thieves. Leave nothing in your car.

CONDITIONS

The cliff is set at an altitude of 600m and facing due west it will catch any bad weather going. It can be green and is at its best on summer afternoons when the grassy base to the crag can be utilised to the full.

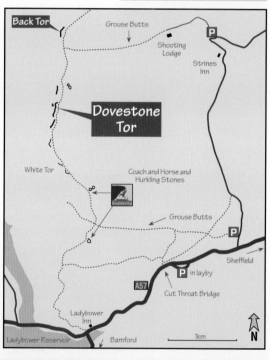

OTHER GUIDEBOOKS - Other routes on Dovestone Tor and the surrounding crags are covered in the 1989 BMC *Stanage* guidebook. A new book including Dovestone Tor and the other Derwent edges is due to be published by the BMC and it will be called the *Sheffield Area* guidebook. The bouldering is in the 1998 Peak Bouldering ROCKFAX.

Martin Veale on *Lancaster Flyby*, E1 5b, Gargoyle Buttress Area, Dovestone Tor. *Page 61*

Descent

Descent

5m gap

TITANIC AREA
The left-hand side of the cliff has some pleasant routes on good rock. Fast drying and clean.

Wharncliffe
Dovestone Tor
Rivelin
Bamford
Stanage
Burbage North
Higgar Tor
Burbage South
Millstone
Lawrencefield
Yarncliffe
Froggatt
Curbar
Gardoms
Birchen
Chatsworth
Cratcliffe

From Strines

Boulderin

From Cut Throat Bridge

Start of slabs

Titanic Area   The Great Buttress   Gargoyle Buttress Area   Route 1   Upper Buttress

← N   About 100m

Afternoon   40 min

① Squawk .... HVS 5b
8m. The leaning arete to the right of the overhangs to a long reach for the break. A tricky (and avoidable) mantel remains.
FA. Chris Craggs 1996

② Sick as a Parrot .... HVS 5a
8m. Start by a big pocket at ground level and climb straight up the wall before trending slightly right to a precarious exit.
FA. Chris Craggs 1996

③ Sick Bay .... HS 4b
12m. Start just left of a groove and shuffle left on good jams to a rounded exit on the far left, above the overhangs.
FA. Ted Howard et al. 1957

④ Handy Wall Hole .... S 4a
10m. Climb the easy groove to a ledge and then the wall above and right passing the eponymous pocket.
FA. Dave Gregory 1996

⑤ Thunderbirds .... S 4a
8m. Start in the centre of the wall and climb onto a ledge, through a bulge and diagonally left across the final wall.
FA. Jim Rubery 1996

⑥ Woodentops .... S 4a
8m. Climb the thinner left-hand crack to ledges then move left to another crack to finish.
FA. Jim Rubery 1996

⑦ Stingray .... VDiff
8m. The hand-jamming crack just left of the arete leads steeply to ledges. Finish around to the right.
FA. Ted Howard et al. 1957

⑧ Windblasted .... Diff
8m. The pleasant wall 4m left of the chimney climbed direct.

⑨ Windblown .... VDiff
8m. Directly up the steep juggy wall 3m left of the chimney.
FA. Ted Howard et al. 1957

⑩ Jonah .... Diff
8m. The chimney is about as pleasant as it looks and the apparent chockstone isn't one.
FA. Ted Howard et al. 1957

⑪ Tight 'uns .... VS 5a
10m. Climb the slab just right of the chimney (avoid using the arete) to a ledge. A short awkward wall (loose blocks lurk here) leads to the easier cracked wall above.
FA. Chris Craggs 1995

⑫ Titanium .... VS 5a
10m. The centre of the thin slab from a gravel patch, and then the bulging wall above just left of the blunt central rib.
FA. Chris Craggs 1994

⑬ Titanic .... VS 4c
10m. Climb past an elongated pocket in the right side of the slab and up steep rock directly above by a short slanting crack.
FA. Chris Craggs 1996

⑭ Titania .... VS 4c
10m. Climb the left arete of the slab and the leaning wall on spaced (and well-hidden) buckets. Graded VDiff for years!
FA. Ted Howard Et al. 1957

⑮ Itis .... HS 4b
10m. Climb the steepening right side of the arete to an awkward exit onto a shelf using a huge hidden jug.
FA. Ted Howard et al. 1957

Between the overhangs,
Dave Spencer on
Great Buttress, E1 5b,
Dovestone Tor. *Page 59*

Wharncliffe
Dovestone Tor
Rivelin
Bamford
Stanage
Burbage North
Higgar Tor
Burbage South
Millstone
Lawrencefield
Yarncliffe
Froggatt
Curbar
Gardoms
Birchen
Chatsworth
Cratcliffe

1 Poll Taxed . . . . [ ] S 4a
10m. Climb just left of the central rib of the bay, through the mid-height bulge to side-step the upper one.
FA. Chris Craggs 1996

2 Pole-axed . . . . [icon][ ] S 4a
10m. Climb the wall just right of the centre of the bay on a collection of large pockets, then pull through the bulge at a flake. Trend left up the slab to finish.
FA. Chris Craggs 1996

3 Jacobite's Route . . . . [icon][ ] VDiff
12m. Possibly the best route of its grade on the cliff. Climb the slab just left of the projecting buttress then a groove to its top. Step out right onto the crest of the buttress then climb to the bulges that cap the wall. Trend left below these to finish up a flake crack.
FA. Albert Shutt 1949

4 Slow Cooker . . . . [icon][ ] S 4a
12m. Climb the shallow central groove of the projecting buttress to join *Jacobite's Route*. Follow this until it is possible to make a tricky (height-dependent) move up the steep scoop just left of the capping overhang.
FA. Chris Craggs 1996

5 Slocum . . . . [icon][ ] S 4a
12m. Trend out right above a flat roof to reach a prominent flake. Follow this then more broken rock towards the bulges that cap the wall. A short loop left then right is needed to get onto the good ledge below these. Finish out right easily.
FA. Ted Howard et al. 1957

6 First Come . . . . [ ] HVS 5a
12m. A series of variations on *Slocum*, slightly artificial but with some interesting moves. Pull over the centre of the low roof then keep right to avoid the parent route. Gain the large ledge just below the top by a tough mantelshelf move and then finish out left with difficulty.
FA. Chris Craggs 1996

7 Gruyere . . . . [ ] VS 4c
12m. Start at the left toe of the gully and climb the 'cheesy' wall to a series of bulges. Step left under these then pull back right onto the nose. Finish easily.
FA. Dave Gregory 1996

8 Dovestone Gully . . . . [ ] Mod
20m. The deep chimney is 'interesting' and often well-limed. Climb the debris then cross the right wall to gain the front face of the buttress. Up this then cross a giant jammed boulder to an exit on the left. I am surprised JWP didn't stick his nose up here, but then again!
FA. Ted Howard et al. 1957

9 Dovestone Edge . . . . [ ] S 4a
20m. Climb the bulges immediately right of the gully (odd rock) and then the face just right of the arete to a final short slab that is taken centrally.
FA. Chris Craggs 1996

BOULDERING - The block below the edge (the actual Dovestone) has some good high problems with fine 'hueco-style' rock formations.

Descent (awkward)

THE GREAT BUTTRESS
This is the appropriately named dominant feature of the crag. The long routes here mostly provide absorbing climbing with the route *Great Buttress* being a fine example of a reasonably-graded route weaving through territory usually reserved for much harder grades. The whole buttress sometimes retains its greenness.
APPROACH - The quickest approach is from the left (looking in) side of the crag, under the Titanic Area.

10 Dovestone Wall . . . . [icon][ ] Diff
20m. A worthwhile low-grade climb although the start is steep. Begin 2m right of the gully and climb hole-ridden rock to the base of the slab. Climb this slightly to the right until below the overhangs, then back to the left to finish in the bay above the lower section of *Dovestone Gully*.
FA. Albert Shutt 1949

11 A Little Green Eyed God . . . [icon][ ] VS 4c
20m. Start 3m right of the gully and climb onto a large jammed block. Head straight up the steep wall to a wide break and pull awkwardly onto the slab between twinned green 'eyes'. Up the slab then take the final steepening leftwards to finish on the arete in a fine position.
FA. Chris Craggs 1996

12 Barney Rubble . . . . [icon][ ] VS 4c
20m. Start 5m right of the gully and just right of a large block on the floor. Climb into a large sandy cave (the left-hand of a pair) then on up juggy rock above this. Pull through the prominent notch in the flat roof that crosses this part of the cliff to an easy finish.
FA. Paul Harrison 1984

13 Thread Flintstone . . . . [icon][icon][ ] HVS 5b
20m. Cross the roof directly below the rib that divides the twin caves and climb straight up the bulging wall (thread on the left) to the capping roof. Pull over this with difficulty 1.5 metres right of *Barney Rubble's* notch.
FA. Mike Appleton 1996

Photo page 57.

⑭ Brown Windsor . . . . . 🎯🏞️⬜ **VS 4b**
28m. A good but devious climb. Start at a soft orange thread under the centre of the wall and trend up and right to a pale square block. Step left and pull over the bulge (strenuous - crux) to a rest under the big roof then make a long traverse left until past the end of this and pull onto the slab for an easy finish trending right.
FA. Ted Howard et al. 1957

⑮ Mock Turtle . . . . 🏞️⬜ **E1 5b**
20m. An eliminate with some good moves. From an embedded spike pull over the roof then climb straight up the bulging rib between *Brown Windsor* and *Great Buttress Eliminate*. Continue up a scoop then hand traverse 3m to the right and pull strenuously over the right edge of the large capping roof.
FA. Mike Appleton 1996

⑯ Great Buttress Eliminate 🎯🏞️⬜ **HVS 5a**
22m. Start under the blunt arete below a patch of orange rock, and pull strenuously over the initial overhang.. Continue in a direct line through bulges and up a steep crack until it possible to traverse right to join *Great Buttress*.
FA. Stuart Gascoyne 1981

⑰ Great Buttress . . . . . 🎯🏞️⬜ **E1 5b**
20m. The classic of the cliff; the place is worth visiting just for this route which is pleasantly low in the grade. Start on the right in a green corner below a huge roof and trend left to pass the arete. Climb straight up the steep wall then trend strenuously right through the bulges keeping just above the lip of the overhang to where a tricky pull gains the final delicate slab.
Photo page 57.
FA. Ted Howard et al. 1957

⑱ Sforzando . . . . . . 🎯🖼️🦅⬜ **E4 6a**
16m. The large roof that hangs over the bay is tackled via its left edge where there are a couple of useful flakes. Possibly unrepeated.
FA. Alan Monks 1985

The next pair of routes are expeditions when compared to most grit outings.

⑲ Central Climb . . . . 🎯⬜ **VS 5a**
1) 4c, 12m. Start at the corner under the big roof and climb up and right to bypass the overhang and gain the groove on its right with difficulty. Climb to a belay on the large ledge.
2) 5a, 12m. From the belay ledge move left and climb awkwardly into an undercut crack. Finish up this.
FA. Albert Shutt, Robert Gratton 1949

⑳ Fennario . . . . 🎯⬜ **VS 4c**
1) 4b, 12m. Climb the left-slanting crack left of stepped overhangs to a grassy vertical crack and then the terrace stance.
1) 4c, 12m. Climb straight up the wall to a sloping ledge gained awkwardly and finish up the steep crack and bulge directly above. A more direct start is also possible.
FA. Ted Howard et al. 1957

㉑ Nippon, Nippoff . . . . ⬜ **E3 6a**
8m. Follow the break that runs out left from a short way up the second pitch of *Fennario*. This leads to an exposed arete and an easy finish. Short but with exciting positions
FA. Andy Bailey 1983

Descent

Descent
down chimney
(awkward)

GARGOYLE BUTTRESS AREA

Gargoyle Buttress features a slab on its left, a crenellated tower in the centre and a walled-in bivvy cave at its foot. It has a collection of routes of which *Stony Faced* and *Gargoyle Buttress* are the choicest cuts. The taller buttress to the right is home to a classic VS and some other worthwhile routes in the middle grades. *Route 1* is a real gem and would be a polished horror on a more popular cliff. The relatively recently discovered *Lancaster Flyby* is the pick of the rest of the routes here. The prominent overhang remains unclimbed despite its having been 'looked at'.

APPROACH - This area is set above and right of the Great Buttress. It can be easily reached from below or above, see map on page 56.

① Gargoyle Traverse . . . . **HS 4b**
20m. Begin up the slab on the left and climb to its top right-hand corner. Traverse right around the buttress, with tricky and exposed moves midway, to finish up a block-filled chimney.
FA. Albert Shutt 1949

② Caveman . . . . **S 4b**
12m. Start in the roofed recess on the left side of the buttress. Climb to the roof and escape out left. Follow the easy crack then climb the tower above starting at its right corner.
FA. Chris Craggs 1996

③ Dead on a Rival **E5 6b**
14m. Climb the arete to the left of the bivvy cave to the break then traverse right into the middle of the wall. Climb directly up this to a ledge and finish easily through the bulges.
FA. Nick White 1985

④ Woodhouse's Wandering Way . . **E3 5c**
18m. Make bouldery moves up the wall 1.5m right of the arete using some rather creaky flakes then traverse the break left to the arete. Climb the slab and the bulging wall above. A very unbalanced route.
FA. John Stevenson 1980s

To the right of the bivvy cave is an grotty corner blocked by a large roof and immediately left of this a leaning wall.

⑤ Stony Faced **E2 5c**
14m. Take the left arete of the leaning wall to a slab then the bulging wall left of a crack to a baffling final move.
FA. Mike Appleton 1996

⑥ Gargoyle Buttress . . . . . . **VS 4c**
14m. Climb the corner to a landing on a sloping shelf on the left (damn pigeons). Continue on 'stonking' jams up the bulging crack to a finish through the crenellations.
FA. Geoffrey Sutton 1957

⑦ Barker's Got a Sweat On . . . . . **HVS 5a**
10m. A route up the wall and right-slanting flakes to a finish up the bulging rib.
FA. Martin Veale 1996

⑧ Conservative Tendencies . . . . . **VS 4c**
10m. Climb the lower wall past a large pocket and the awkward right-trending groove above.
FA. Chris Craggs 1996

To the right is the deep well-named chimney of Wind Tunnel.

⑨ Canker . . . . **VDiff**
10m. Climb the wall 3m left of the chimney slightly rightwards. Step left onto a ledge then trend right to finish in a bay.
FA. Ted Howard et al. 1957

⑩ Back Blast . . . . **HVS 5b**
10m. Start just left of the foot of the gully of *Wind Tunnel* and climb the steep wall trending slightly rightwards, linking horizontal breaks via long reaches. Finish up a short slab avoiding easy escape out to the left.
FA. Chris Craggs 1996

⑪ Wind Tunnel . . . . **Mod**
14m. The dark chimney often lives up to its name and is much used as a way down by the competent.
FA. J.W.Puttrell 1890s

Descent
down chimney
(awkward)

Descent

Upper Tier 100m

⑫ Hurricane . . . . **VDiff**
14m. Start up the square arete on the right of the chimney then step left and climb the centre of the steep wall on good holds. A pleasant pitch considering its grim and windy setting.
FA. Ted Howard et al. 1957

⑬ Typhoon . . . . **HVS 5b**
14m. An eliminate. Climb centrally up the smooth wall between the two aretes (hard for the short) then cross bulges to an overhang. Mantelshelf over this on the right then finish left and back right through the final bulges.
FA. Mike Appleton 1996

⑭ Route 1 . . . . **VS 4c**
16m. An underrated (and long under-graded) classic. Start up the outer arete of the buttress and mantelshelf awkwardly onto a ledge. Step left and make a second mantelshelf over a bulge onto a sloping shelf then step right and climb a short undercut crack (crux). Finish out to the right.
FA. Albert Shutt 1949

⑮ The Shylock Finish . . . . . **VS 5a**
6m. From the ledge above the crux on *Route 1* follow the lowest horizontal break awkwardly out to the left. Finish easily in an exposed position, always remembering to pay with a pound of flesh.
FA. Stuart Gascoyne 1981

⑯ Blue Velvet **E1 6a**
12m. Start just right of the arete and make hard moves to the beckoning thin crack, then pull through the bulges to a ledge to the right of the crux crack of *Route 1*. Move right under a bulge and mantelshelf awkwardly onto a ledge just below the cliff top. The short can gain the route from *Route 1* via a short traverse using an elongated pocket, reducing the grade to **HVS 5a**.
FA. Chris Craggs 1996

Next is a broad flat (and unclimbed) roof at 6m with a deeply recessed groove running up to its right-hand edge.

⑰ Claw Climb . . . . **HVS 5a**
14m. Start under the roof and trend left to pass it strenuously using a large (and possibly loose?) block just above the lip. Once established step back right and finish more easily up the slabby face.
FA. Ted Howard et al. 1957

⑱ Talon . . . . **VS 4b**
14m. Climb the deeply-recessed v-groove until forced to step right onto the bounding rib at the level of the roof. Pull straight up into a thin crack just above and use this to reach easier ground.
FA. Ted Howard et al. 1957

⑲ Lancaster Flyby **E1 5b**
14m. Begin just right of the arete and climb the wall to a deep horizontal break (good gear). A difficult pull on small holds reaches another break. Continue trending rightwards up the interesting wall with one trickier move where things steepen to reach easy ground. *Photo page 55.*
FA. Chris Craggs 1996

⑳ Route 2 . . . . **VS 4b**
14m. Climb onto the large grass ledge on the right then follow the diagonal break out left strenuously until past the arete. Finish up easier rock.
FA. Albert Shutt 1949

Whamcliffe

Dovestone Tor

Rivelin

Bamford

Stanage

Burbage North

Higgar Tor

Burbage South

Millstone

Lawrencefield

Yarncliffe

Froggatt

Curbar

Gardoms

Birchen

Chatsworth

Cratcliffe

UPPER BUTTRESS

Above and right of the main edge is a smaller cliff of excellent quality rock. This has a maximum height of 8m and presents a series of fine buttresses that are generally cleaner than the main cliff.

APPROACH - From above via a small, indistinct path leading down from the section of stone-slabbed path.

❶ Barefoot . . . . **Diff**
6m. The left arete of the wall leads past a handy pocket. Finish over the block.
FA. Chris Craggs 1996. Definitely done before.

❷ Slab Happy . . . . **S 4b**
6m. The centre of the slab is delicate.
FA. Dave Gregory 1996. Probably done before.

❸ Step It Up . . . . **S 4c**
6m. The slab just left of the central groove has a tricky start and leads to a deep crack.
FA. Dave Gregory 1996

❹ Groovy Moves . . . . **S 4b**
6m. A shallow right-facing groove leads to a bulge. Pull over this on jams and continue direct.
FA. Dave Gregory 1996

To the right are twin cracks above an overhang.

❺ Jam On It . . . . **HVS 5a**
6m. The left-hand crack is entered from the left and is easier than it looks. You may end up with one foot in the next climb briefly if you are tall enough to reach it.
FA. Chris Craggs 1996

❻ Squirm . . . . **HVS 5a**
6m. The right-hand crack is also entered from the left and is everything that it appears and that the name suggests.
FA. Chris Craggs 1996

❼ Hang 'em High . . . . **HS 5b**
4m. The short hanging corner is entered with difficulty from a convenient block (overhead protection) and eases instantly.
FA. Dave Gregory 1996

❽ Chicken Head **E2 5c**
6m. Gain the prow from the right or left by a swinging hand traverse and make a couple of dramatic moves to easy ground.
FA. Paul Mitchell 1991

❾ Pleasant . . . . **Diff**
6m. From blocks in the gully follow the pleasant slabby arete on the right.
FA. Dave Gregory 1996

❿ Spring Night . . . . **HVS 5b**
8m. Trend left to climb the left edge of the wall on good horizontal breaks to a reachy finish.
FA. Chris Craggs 1982

⓫ Autumn Day . . . **E1 5b**
8m. The centre of the wall is climbed via a hard pull on small holds and a final long reach for a rounded edge.
FA. Graham Hoey 1981

⓬ Stretch Marks **E1 6a**
8m. Gain the initial ledge from the right then climb the wall trending right passing a floral hole to a huge final reach.
FA. Chris Craggs 1996

⓭ Razor Cut . . . . **VS 4b**
8m. Sadly the thin straight crack on the right side of the wall is escapable, especially in its lower section. Beware of the big rocking block near the top.
FA. Chris Craggs 1996

To the right is a blocky descent gully.

⓮ Rocky . . . . **VDiff**
6m. The front of the pillar.
FA. Dave Gregory 1996

⓯ Blocky . . . . **VDiff**
6m. The crack on the right side of the leaning pillar of rock has an awkward entry.
FA. Dave Gregory 1996

⓰ Hanging Tree . . . . **HVS 5b**
8m. Pull into the tiny hanging groove on the left-hand side of the overhang from holds on the right. Continue easily.
FA. Chris Craggs 1996

Wharncliffe

Dovestone Tor

Rivelin

Bamford

Stanage

Burbage North

Higgar Tor

Burbage South

Millstone

Lawrencefield

Yarncliffe

Froggatt

Curbar

Gardoms

Birchen

Chatsworth

Cratcliffe

⑰ Easy Ground . . . . ▨▧ [   ] **HVS 5b**
8m. The left-hand side of the roof is crossed using a perfect finger hold in its centre though it requires a bit of an 'udge' to pass the lip.
FA.Graham Hoey 1981

⑱ Excel . . . . ▨2▧ [   ] **HVS 5b**
8m. Cross the centre of the roof to an awkward move around the lip. Excel(lent) and strangely Tippler-esque.
FA. Con Carey 1976

⑲ Swinwood . . . . [   ] **E1 5b**
8m. Climb the left arete of the square recess until it is possible to traverse out onto the front face. Finish up the centre of this.
FA. Dick Swindon 1981. Originally graded Hard Severe.

⑳ Smokin' . . . . ▨ [   ] **E1 5b**
10m. Climb awkwardly on to the ledge then from the porthole traverse the improving break out left to the arete. Climb the short precarious slab just round the corner.
FA. Dave Spencer 1996

㉑ Landing Craft . . . . [   ] **HVS 5b**
6m. Climb awkwardly onto the ledge then pass the porthole and a perfect nut slot to a tough exit.
FA. Martin Veale 1996

㉒ Amen Corner . . . . [   ] **HS 4b**
6m. The left corner of the recess is reached via an awkward wide crack and climbed steeply.
FA. Chris Craggs 1996

㉓ Old Man's Corner . . . . [   ] **VDiff**
6m. The often rather lurid right-hand corner of the recess is climbed in two stages.
FA. Dave Gregory 1996

㉔ Village Green . . . . [   ] **VS 5a**
6m. Climb straight up the steep slab finishing just left of a short crack. Can be as the name suggests.
FA. Chris Craggs 1996

㉕ Iambo . . . . ▨ [   ] **S 4a**
6m. Follow the thin crack rightwards on continually surprising holds.
FA. Oliver Woolcock 1960s

㉖ Bertie . . . . ▨▧ [   ] **E1 5c**
8m. Climb the leaning wall just right of the arete on good but spaced holds to a more delicate finish where the angle starts to drop back.
FA. Martin Veale 1996

㉗ Blunt . . . . ▨▧ [   ] **HVS 5b**
8m. The centre of the bulging wall via a blunt nose and tricky mantelshelf.
FA.Chris Craggs 1982

㉘ Philby . . . . [   ] **HVS 5a**
8m. The right side of the wall, passing an elongated jammed block at two-thirds height.
FA. Paul Harrison 1984

A deep chimney offers an awkward descent route over blocks. Next is an steeply overhanging arete.

㉙ Granny Smith . . . . ▨ [   ] **E1 5b**
8m. The sharp and very overhanging arete is fortunately 'well endowed' and is best climbed quickly.
FA. Graham Hoey 1981

㉚ Cox's Pippin . . . . ▨▮ [   ] **HVS 5a**
8m. The obvious roof crack to the right proves to be reachy and a bit of a corker.
FA. Oliver Woolcock 1960s

㉛ Ganges . . . . [   ] **VDiff**
8m. The block-filled chimney is tricky towards the top.
FA. Oliver Woolcock 1960s

㉜ Crackless Bottom . . . . [   ] **E1 5b**
8m. Climb the centre of the right-hand buttress of the cliff. Pull into a hanging crack and exit awkwardly.
FA. Chris Craggs 1996

㉝ Soft Top . . . . ▧ [   ] **E1 5a**
6m. Start at the right arete of the cliff and climb the flat wall on the right easily (small Friends) to a harrowing exit.
FA. Martin Veale 1996

RIVELIN

Wharncliffe
Dovestone Tor
Rivelin
Bamford
Stanage
Burbage North
Higgar Tor
Burbage South
Millstone
Lawrencefield
Yarncliffe
Froggatt
Curbar
Gardoms
Birchen
Chatsworth
Cratcliffe

The low-level, south-facing outcrop of Rivelin Edge is often ignored because of a rogue reputation for midges and greenery. Whilst this can be true on a hot summer's day, in autumn and winter the cliff comes into its own, getting all the sun that is going, drying rapidly and being sheltered enough to be climbable when the other edges are a frozen, wind-blasted wasteland. The simple approach and the fact that it is inside the Sheffield city boundary makes it a popular quick-hit-crag when time is short. There is the possibility to finish work and nip out for an ascent of the Needle before the sun sets; alternatively grab the opportunity of a beautiful winter's day to have a go at one of the big aretes or blank walls whilst the friction is good. The central area of the cliff, around the Rivelin Needle, has the highest quality concentration but hidden away in the trees are some real gems across the grade range. Overall the place is well worth a few trips and after each visit it is likely that you will have spotted another excellent route to aim for next time.

APPROACH (SK279872)

The crag looks south over the Rivelin valley, above the A57, on the western side of Sheffield. The best parking spot is in the large free car park on the far side of the dam at Rivelin Reservoir (avoid parking on the side of the A57 by the turning for the dam). Walk back to the main road and locate a path opposite that runs towards the cliff and then veers right through a damp area into the trees, gradually rising. At a marker post take the left fork which rises more steeply. Continue fairly directly up the hill, ignoring any paths leading off right, and you will emerge suddenly just to the left of the Rivelin Needle. This approach is much harder to follow in the summer when the vegetation drowns many of the paths in the trees.

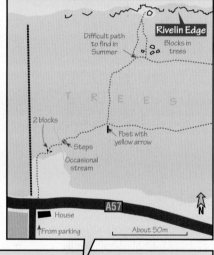

CONDITIONS

Originally the slope below the cliff was open heath but over time woodland has grown up and now the silver birch and other species grow almost up the to cliff face. This tree cover gives shelter on windy days but makes the place green in the depths of winter, although the Rivelin Needle itself stands proud of the trees and is seldom green. As mentioned above, it is a south-facing sun-trap.

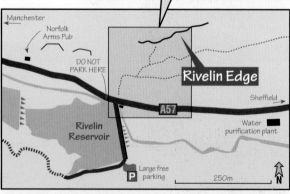

OTHER GUIDEBOOKS - A more complete list of routes at Rivelin is published in the 1989 BMC *Stanage* guidebook. A new book including Rivelin is due to be published by the BMC and it will be called the *Sheffield Area* guidebook.

Wharncliffe
Dovestone Tor
Rivelin
Bamford
Stanage
Burbage North
Higgar Tor
Burbage South
Millstone
Lawrencefield
Yarncliffe
Froggatt
Curbar
Gardoms
Birchen
Chatsworth
Cratcliffe

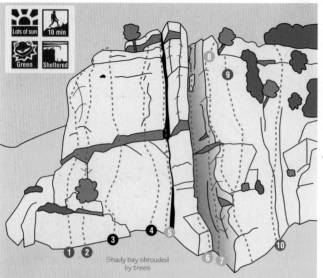

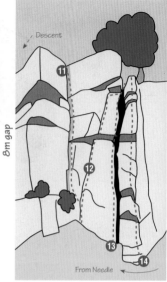

KREMLIN KRACK AREA

The left-hand end of the main section of the cliff is a tree-shrouded bay bounded on the right by some low-angled slabs. The routes in the bay tend to be well-sheltered, even staying dry in the rain, and are generally hard and fingery. The twin chimneys to the right are safe graunches whereas the slab to the right again has more open and airy affairs.

APPROACH - From the point where the path arrives at the crag, scramble up some blocks and walk left for 50m.

❶ Ausfahrt **E2 5c**
12m. The left arete of the wall with an overhang early on and a bold finish up the rounded rib.
FA. Chris Craggs 1983

❷ Exit **E3 5c**
12m. Climb a thin crack through the bulge and the delicate wall above trending rightwards. Protected by tiny wires.
FA. Roger Greatrick 1983

❸ Jaded **E4 6b**
12m. Climb the centre of the wall to the bulge and make a hard pull on tiny holds to pass this. Above is easier.
FA. Graham Hoey 1989. The route Der Komissar (Roger Greatrick 1983) has now been superseded by more direct offerings.

❹ Moontan **E5 6c**
10m. The right-hand side of the wall is desperate to the break and only a little easier above.
FA. John Allen 1987

❺ Kremlin Krack . . . . **HVS 5a**
10m. An intimidating leaning chimney is hard to enter, although fortunately protection is adequate without the need to resort to giant cams.

❻ Scarlett's Chimney . . . . . . **HS 4a**
10m. The chimney on the other side of the hanging rib is an altogether easier affair than its left-hand neighbour.
FA. Harry Scarlett late 1920s

❼ Left Under . . . . **HVS 5a**
12m. A groove to the left of *Left Edge* leads awkwardly to a standing position below the flake of *Left Edge*. Layback up and right to join and finish as for that route.
FA. Bruce Goodwin 1992

❽ Left Edge . . . . **VS 4c**
10m. The arete of the slab is pleasantly delicate with an 'on edge' feeling and is not especially well protected.
FA. Pete Crew early 1960

❾ Left Edge Slab **E1 5a**
10m. Tackle the slab direct, it is delicate and poorly protected.

❿ Rivelin Slab . . . . **Mod**
10m. The heathery slab is quite a popular route for beginners although it is almost too easy to be a challenge.

Beyond a gritty descent route is a smart blocky buttress.

⓫ Angle Crack . . . . **Diff**
8m. The pleasant main groove passing a block.

⓬ Solitaire . . . . **VDiff**
8m. Take the crack just right of the corner and follow it trending right to a move right again just below the top.

⓭ Isolation . . . . **S 4a**
10m. A deeper crack on the right set in a shallow corner is straightforward enough.

⓮ Rodney's Dilemma . . . . . . **S 4a**
12m. The arete gives a pleasant piece of climbing with good runners in the horizontal breaks.

About 50m

Blizzard Ridge Area

N

Face Climb

Kremlin Krack Area

Main approach

Rivelin Needle

The Brush Off Area

Plague Auto da Fe

Wilkinson's Wall

Roof Route

Altar Crack Area

T R E E S

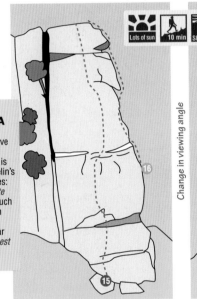

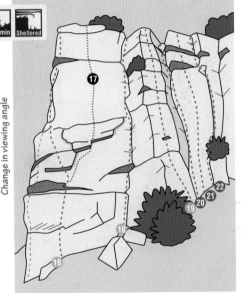

Lots of sun | 10 min | Sheltered

Change in viewing angle

BLIZZARD RIDGE AREA

A fine piece of rock situated directly above the point where you arrive at the crag. It is home to one of Rivelin's 'must-do' HVS routes: *Blizzard Ridge*. *White Out* is a nice soft-touch E2 for those after an easy life, *David's Chimney* is a popular VDiff and *The Tempest* is a fine blank slab climb.

⑮ White Out **E2 5c**
12m. The centre of the left-hand wall avoiding the tendency to drift towards the arete. Mild at the grade, so don't get too excited if you find it easy.
FA. Bob Bradley 1983

⑯ Blizzard Ridge . . . . . . **HVS 5a**
14m. The juggy lower wall and fine bold arete above are superb and very photogenic. The central section is pleasantly airy which puts the route at the upper end of the grade. The bold upper moves can be protected by a rather odd sideways nut. It can also be started direct (strenuous) up the lower arete for a full **E1 5b** tick. *Photo page 65.*
FA. Allan Austin 1958. Direct start Peter Stone 1998.

⑰ The Tempest **E5 6b**
14m. The narrow wall to the right has a big rattling flake, a hand-placed peg runner and hard moves on sloping holds. Markedly easier for the tall and slightly escapable where it really matters.
FA. Graham Hoey 1983

⑱ Jonathan's Chimney . . . . . **VS 4c**
12m. The left-hand rift is of a classical kind and is rather poorly protected where it counts.
FA. Harry Scarlett late 1920s

⑲ Jonad Rib . . . . **HVS 4c**
12m. The delicate rib between the chimneys proves to be quite mild for HVS but then again it is not all that well protected. Care required unless you are 'solid' at the grade.
FA. Glyn Owen 1955

⑳ David's Chimney . . . . . . **VDiff**
10m. *David's* rift is even more classical than *Jonathan's* and also more worthwhile despite being of a much lower grade. Check the climbing manual for the full variety of techniques needed.
FA. Harry Scarlett late 1920s

㉑ OFSTED Wall **E1 5c**
10m. Climb the narrow wall between *Layback Crack* and *David's Chimney*, without deviation and keep the inspectors happy!
FA. Percy Bishton 1997

㉒ Layback Crack . . . . **Diff**
8m. The short clean-cut crack left of the groove that bounds the end of the wall can be laybacked though other techniques work as well.
FA. Eric Byne 1933

Wharncliffe
Dovestone Tor
Rivelin
Bamford
Stanage
Burbage North
Higgar Tor
Burbage South
Millstone
Lawrencefield
Yarncliffe
Froggatt
Curbar
Gardoms
Birchen
Chatsworth
Cratcliffe

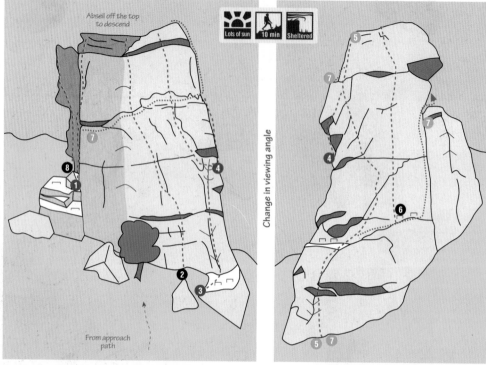

Abseil off the top to descend

Lots of sun | 10 min | Sheltered

Change in viewing angle

From approach path

THE RIVELIN NEEDLE

Standing in front of the cliff is the obelisk of the Rivelin Needle, one of grit's more inaccessible summits. All the routes on the pinnacle are worth doing. Several climbs arrive at the small ledge of The Notch from where a rickety flake leads to the summit. This flake needs handling with great care.

DESCENT - From its steeply-shelving top a short abseil (from a chipped notch or old chains) is the easiest method of escape.

❶ The Eye . . . . ▨▨▮ ☐ **E2 6a**
8m. The right-hand arete on the short side of the Needle. If you can't reach the holds, try a leg-lock in the break.
FA. Bill Briggs 1976

❷ Declaration . . . . . . ▨▨▨ ☐ **E5 6c**
12m. The blunt rib in the middle of the northwest arete is highly technical and relies upon some suspiciously broken holds.
FA. Dave Pegg 1986

❸ Angst . . . . ▨▨♡ ☐ **E3 5c**
12m. Climb the groove to the flat roof then step left to a grasping, shelving exit. Fortunately large Friends in the final break reduce the angst factor a little.
FA. Ian Riddington 1984

❹ The Original Route . . . . ▨▨ ☐ **E2 5c**
12m. Climb the groove to the roof then exit right with considerable difficulty to join *Croton Oil* and a finish up the rickety flake.
FA. Joe Brown 1954

2nd 10/03
❺ Croton Oil . . . . ▨ ☐ **HVS 5a**
20m. A classic with fine climbing and positions and good protection throughout. From the centre of the south face climb a wide crack then the wall trending left (good wires) to reach The Notch. Finish up the rickety flake with care. *Photo opposite.*
FA. Pete Crew 1963

❻ Only Human . . . . ▨▨ ☐ **E5 6c**
14m. The right-hand side of the south face leads to a desperate sequence where a peg used to be, up the final steep wall.
FA. John Allen 1988

❼ The Spiral Route . . . . ▨✦ ☐ **VS 4c**
24m. The easiest way to the summit although it is not that easy! Start as for *Croton Oil* then move right to a crack, which leads to the ledges behind the tower, and the feeling that you are still on the ground. From the opposite end of the ledges hand-traverse the horizontal break out right (pumpy) to gain The Notch and the rickety-flake finish.
FA. Don Wooller 1950

❽ Jumpy Wooller . . . . ▨▨♡ ☐ **E6 6c**
8m. The left-hand arete of the back wall is climbed by sustained, slappy moves using a layaway high on the right. A small Hex in a sandy pocket offers some (dubious) protection.
FA. Niall Grimes 1998

Jim Rubery and Brian Rossiter on *Croton Oil*, HVS 5a, Rivelin Needle. *Opposite*

Whamcliffe · Dovestone Tor · Rivelin · Bamford · Stanage · Burbage North · Higgar Tor · Burbage South · Millstone · Lawrencefield · Yarncliffe · Froggatt · Curbar · Gardoms · Birchen · Chatsworth · Cratcliffe

About 50m

N

Face Climb

Kremlin Krack Area · Main approach · Blizzard Ridge Area · Rivelin Needle · The Brush Off Area · Plague · Auto da Fe · Wilkinson's Wall · Roof Route · Altar Crack Area

T R E E S

FACE CLIMB and THE BRUSH OFF AREA

The clean, quarried wall behind the Rivelin Needle has some pleasant if short routes on good rock. Across the bay to the right the slabby face of Brush Off Buttress has some much bolder offerings, including the magnificent *Brush Off* and the pleasant *Fringe Benefit*. Those who like their sport short and sharp should find *Easy Picking* to their liking.

Lots of sun · 10 min · Green · Sheltered

❶ Face Climb 1 . . . . HVD
6m. Follow 'flatties' up the left-hand side of the face with little in the way of protection.
FA. Frank Burgess 1933

❷ Face Climb 1.5 VS 4c
6m. Trend right across the unprotected face then finish direct.
FA. Geoff Milburn 1962

❸ I'm Back E4 6a
6m. The technical and fingery wall just to the right, bold.
FA. Nick Stokes 1985

❹ Jelly Baby . . . . HVS 5b
6m. The narrow leaning corner is quite technical and escapable.
FA. Chris Addy 1977

❺ Face Climb Number 2 . . . . HS 4b
6m. The narrow face has a tricky finish. Side runners may be needed at this grade otherwise it is more like solid VS.
FA. Frank Burgess 1933

❻ Crack One . . . . S 4a
6m. The awkward corner crack.
FA. Dick Brown 1950

❼ Shelf Wall . . . . VS 4c
6m. Mantel-a-way up the short-lived wall 8m to the right.
FA. Dick Brown 1950

❽ Easy Picking E2 6b
8m. The thin crack left of the corner has a desperate start and even more desperate moves to reach the wider upper section.
FA. Steve Bancroft 1976

❾ Oliver's Twist . . . . VS 4b
8m. The right-hand crack of a pair just right of the main corner.
FA. Oliver Woolcock 1963

❿ The Terminator . . . E5 6c
8m. The centre of the steep wall to the right. A side runner protects the lower section but not the finish.
FA. John Allen 1985

⓫ The Brush Off E4 5c
10m. The slabby left arete is precarious and effectively unprotected. A stunning effort for its day, it still requires a cool head.
FA. Pete Crew 1963

⓬ Party Animal E2 5c
10m. The centre of the slab is mildly bold to the midway break (small Friends) and mildly technical above.
FA. John Allen 1985

⓭ Fringe Benefit E1 5b
10m. The right-hand side of the slab is pleasantly delicate and poorly protected. Finish at a perched block. Low in the grade.
FA. Graham Parkes (in a school lunch break) 1980

Up and right is a short wall.

L 10/03

⓮ Fumf . . . . VS 5a
4m. The arete has a funny starting sequence but soon eases.

⓯ Wobbly Wall . . . . HVS 5b
4m. Small holds allow the blank wall to the right to be climbed.
FA. Ed Drummond 1969

⓰ Europe After Rain E4 6b
4m. The right-hand side of the wall to a hairy exit. Short but quite intense.
FA. John Allen 1984

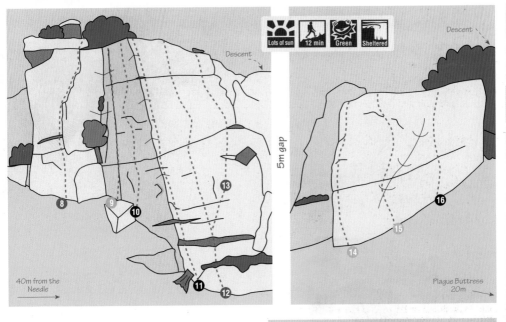

PLAGUE

A buttress with a couple of highly technical outings both protected by one of the last bolts on natural grit. It is about time someone did their stuff to make honest women of *Plague* and *Big Al*.

17 Caravaggio E3 6a
8m. The side-wall of the buttress on sloping holds leads to a hard finale.
FA. Mark Stokes 1979

18 Outsider E2 5c
10m. Climb the left wall to the break then traverse round the arete on jams to where a couple of steep pulls are needed heading back left to the top.
FA. Bill Briggs 1976

19 Ring of Roses ...... HVS 5a
14m. Start as for *Outsider* but traverse the whole buttress on good jams.
FA. Chris Craggs 1981

20 Big Al E5 6c
10m. Start up *Plague* but then climb the left-hand side of the face with great difficulty. Unfortunately the bolt on *Plague* has to be pre-clipped.
FA. Neil Stokes 1986

21 Plague E4 6b
10m. The centre of the overlapping wall past an ancient ethically indefensible and unwelded bolt. The move to pass the overlap containing the bolt is desperate.
FA. Johnny Woodward 1981

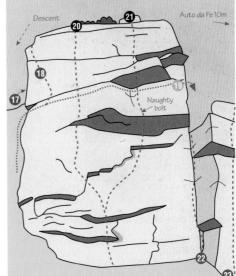

22 The Crevice .... VDiff
8m. The steep corner crack just to the right.

23 Lichen Slab .... S 4a
8m. The slab and overlap around to the right are cleaner and pleasanter than the name might suggest.

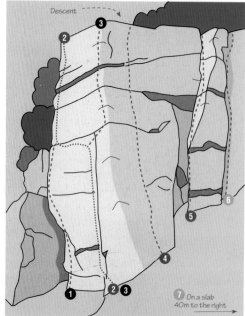

Wharncliffe
Dovestone Tor
Rivelin
Bamford
Stanage
Burbage North
Higgar Tor
Burbage South
Millstone
Lawrencefield
Yarncliffe
Froggatt
Curbar
Gardoms
Birchen
Chatsworth
Cratcliffe

AUTO DA FE and ROOF ROUTE

The edge continues past a series of isolated and impressive buttresses. These offer some great challenges and are rarely busy although the enclosed nature means they can be green and damp.

❶ Sparks **E5 7a**
10m. Scratch up the fierce left arete to join *Palm Charmer*.
FA. Adrian Berry 1993

❷ Palm Charmer **E3 5c**
10m. The thin crack in the front of the buttress is awkward (crux) then step left and palm smartly up the arete to finish.
FA. Paul Harrison 1985

❸ Auto da Fe **E4 6a**
12m. Rivelin's other great E4 arete is technically harder than *The Brush Off* but this one has adequate gear. Climb the short crack to the break and arrange a few wires and Friends. If not pumped solid, make a committing pull onto the arete and sprint for the top. Beautiful!
FA. Andy Parkin 1976

❹ Reprieve **E3 5c**
10m. An unprotected face with hard moves just below the top.
FA. Dave Mirthin 1976

❺ Left Holly Pillar Crack . . . . . . **S 4a**
6m. A right-slanting crack in the wall to the right.

❻ Right Holly Pillar Crack . . . . . . **HS 4b**
6m. The steep and strenuous series of flakes just left of the vegetated corner.

40m right is a clean wall which is not shown on the topos.

❼ Wilkinson's Wall . . . . **VS 4b**
8m. Climb the wall leftwards on holds that were once razor edges to reach the arete and then finish direct.
FA. Peter Wilkinson 1951

15m to the right is a large slab protruding from the hillside.

❽ Summertime **E3 5c**
8m. Climb the undercut left arete of the large slab, approaching it from the right. It feels bold but soon eases.
FA. Dave Morgan 1976

❾ Small Time **E2 6b**
8m. The thin centre of the slab, with a side-runner to the right.
FA. John Allen 1985

❿ Regular Route . . . . **HVS 5a**
10m. The centre of the slab to the left of the big overhang of *Roof Route* was a surprisingly late discovery.
FA. John Allen 1988

To the right is a vertical buttress with a prominent roof and an overlapping wall to the right.

⓫ Groove Route . . . . . . **HVS 5b**
10m. Climb the pleasant shallow groove left of the jutting roof, it is more difficult than it appears.
FA. Bill Briggs 1976

⓬ Roof Route . . . . **HVS 5b**
10m. The brutal roof crack is as good, and as hard, as it looks. Rumours that the crack is lined with skin are not completely without foundation.
FA. Joe Brown late 1950s

ALTAR CRACK AREA

Rivelin finishes off with a fine buttress, *Altar Crack* and *Nonsuch* are good crack climbs whereas *New Mediterranean* and *Moolah* are a couple of excellent and hard face routes.

13 Root Route . . . . S 4a
10m. A pleasant route up the groove to the right of the roof.

14 Dynasty E4 6a
8m. The cramped wall just to the right. Fiddly wires under the roof protect the hardest moves.
FA. Keith Sharples 1984

15 April Fool E2 5b
8m. The wall and overhang to the left of the arete are bold but not too technical.
FA. Andy Parkin 1976

16 Steph . . . . HVS 5a
6m. The reachy but juggy wall just right of the arete.
FA. Bill Briggs 1976

ALTAR CRACK AREA

17 New Mediterranean . . . E5 6c
10m. The left-hand line on the smooth wall is desperate and reachy. Runners are normally placed in the next route first.
FA. John Allen 1985

18 Moolah E5 6b
10m. The right-hand line on the wall is also desperate, try a right-facing 'egyptian' to avoid the huge reach.
FA. John Allen 1988

19 Altar Crack . . . . VS 4c
10m. The clean-cut corner crack is the scene of many an epic. Establish yourself in the crack, bung in some gear, and layback like your life depends on it. Higher up it becomes clear that it does so try not to pump out before the break. Sketch right and belly-flop over the top.
FA. Dick Brown late 1940s

20 Nonsuch E1 5b
10m. The thin crack has perfect protection and superb finger jams but still manages to be hard work.
FA. Alan Clarke early 1960s

21 Gettin' Kinda Squirrelly E6 6b
8m. The left arete of *Vestry Chimney*, climbed on its left-hand side, finishing via the flake on the left wall.
FA. Mark Hundleby 1990s

22 Vestry Chimney . . . . VDiff
8m. The awkward chimney.

23 Too Much E2 6a
8m. The thin crack in the slab has the discomforting combination of low runners and a high crux.
FA. Andy Parkin 1976

BAMFORD

Wharncliffe
Dovestone Tor
Rivelin
Bamford
Stanage
Burbage North
Higgar Tor
Burbage South
Millstone
Lawrencefield
Yarncliffe
Froggatt
Curbar
Gardoms
Birchen
Chatsworth
Cratcliffe

Bamford Edge is a series of buttresses set in spectacular situation overlooking the upper reaches of the Derwent Valley and the Ladybower Reservoir. The restrictive access situation has meant that the edge has become something of a backwater over the years. You won't find the eroded dirt patches under the starts of the routes here, in fact for many of today's climbers the edge provides a pleasant reflection on how the things used to look on the Peak's grit edges. However it is important to remember that this lack of attention is not an indication of the quality of climbing found on the edge and most visitors will be very pleasantly surprised by the superb routes.

ACCESS - This has sometimes been problematical over the years and the current situation, though far from ideal, at least works. Small groups can visit the edge from 1st October to 31st March providing they contact the keeper, Mr Chris Bush on (0114) 2630892 first. Please make the effort.

CONDITIONS
The rock is some of the roughest gritstone around, although the lack of traffic makes the cliff occasionally rather lichenous. It is well-exposed to the weather but can be delightful on summer evenings as the sun goes down over Ladybower.

APPROACH (SK208848)
A minor road (New Road) runs below the cliff from a point 1km north of the village of Bamford and just south of the Yorkshire Bridge pub. Above the last trees and on the up-hill side of the road there is a small lay-by (room for 3-4 well-parked cars) by a gate and below an old collapsed stone building. Cross the fence carefully, head straight up the bank to the moor edge then turn left to locate your chosen buttress, fifteen to twenty minutes from the road. It is also possible to park at the top of the hill and follow the crest of the moor to the cliff, a longer approach though with less ascent.

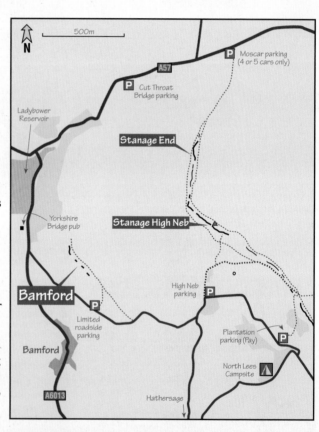

OTHER GUIDEBOOKS - A more complete list of routes at Bamford is published in the 1989 BMC *Stanage* guidebook. A new book including Bamford is due to be published by the BMC and it will be called the *Sheffield Area* guidebook.

The finest location on eastern grit? Jim Rubery on *Quien Sabe?*, VS 4c, Bamford. *Page 76*

Wharncliffe
Dovestone Tor
Rivelin
Bamford
Stanage
Burbage North
Higgar Tor
Burbage South
Millstone
Lawrencefield
Yarncliffe
Froggatt
Curbar
Gardoms
Birchen
Chatsworth
Cratcliffe

GREAT TOR - LOWER TIER

The best rock on the cliff, in a great setting and with a small collection of excellent climbs from the mild to the desperate. The well-protected *Bilberry Crack*, the superb jamming on *Brown's Crack* and the well-positioned *Quien Sabe?* are the classic in the 'orange zone'. *The Salmon Slab* has a great collection of intense 'black zone' routes.

APPROACH - See map on next page. Scramble down from below the overhang of the Upper Tier.

① Hasta La Vista . . . . **S 4a**
8m. Climb the wide crack on the left then make an awkward and ungainly stomach traverse out right to escape the overhangs.
FA. Geoffrey Sutton 1957

② Back Flip . . . . **VS 4c**
10m. Climb the left arete of the wall, passing an overlap, to the capstone. Make an odd off-balance move to get out left then finish direct.
FA. Gwyn Arnold 1991

③ The Naked Eye **E3 5c**
10m. The centre of the wall is strenuous and poorly protected. Some of the flakes feel creaky.
FA. Gary Gibson 1982

④ Benberry Wall **E3 5c**
10m. The right-hand side of the wall using flakes and then the evermore-harrowing arete, eventually on its right-hand side.
FA. John Allen 1976

⑤ Bilberry Crack . . . . **VS 5a**
10m. The thin crack in the corner is technical and protectable.
Photo page 42.
FA. Dick Brown 1952

⑥ Recess Crack . . . . **VDiff**
10m. The juggy right-hand corner of the recess is a pleasant lower grade climb with good holds and plenty of protection.
FA. Dick Brown 1952

⑦ Recess Groove . . . . **VS 4c**
10m. The V-groove and short wall just left of the arete.
FA. Dave Gregory 2000

⑧ Nemmes Pas Harry **E1 5b**
12m. The steep bulging wall on creaking jugs and nicely-delicate scoop above and right.
FA. Gary Gibson 1981

⑨ Quien Sabe? . . . . **VS 4c**
14m. Start up *Brown's Crack* but follow ramps left then tackle the crucial crack that splits the bulge. Well protected but quite taxing. Should the route be 5a, who knows? Starting up *Nemmes Pas Harry* makes an excellent **HVS 5a**. *Photo page 75.*
FA. Brian Evans 1958

⑩ Brown's Crack . . . . **HS 4b**
12m. Classic. The striking straight crack is awkward to enter and superb above. Protection is perfect throughout.
FA. Dick Brown 1951

⑪ Jetrunner **E4 6a**
12m. Climb the wall via the tiny pocket to the top break. Then step left and sprint up the arete on its right-hand side.
FA. Andy Bailey 1983

⑫ Salmon Left-Hand **E6 6b**
12m. As for *Jetrunner* to the top break. Make a high step into twin pockets, right foot into high right pocket, smear left and reach the top. Can be combined with *Salmon Direct* by making a tricky left-foot cross-through into high pocket to gain the *Direct*.
FA. Nick Dixon 1995

⑬ Salmon Direct **E6 6c**
12m. As for *Jetrunner* to the top break. then make some hard moves to gain a high pocket from the right (left foot in pocket). Smear high rightwards and reach for the sky.
FA. Jon Read 1998. In mistake for The Salmon.

⑭ The Salmon E7 6c
12m. As for *Salmon Direct* to stand in the high pocket. Traverse right to the small group of poor pockets, and finish as for *Smoked Salmon*. Slightly artificial as it's easier to make the final move of *Direct* than to head rightwards.
FA. Johnny Dawes 1984. Reclimbed by Dawes 1995, after it lost a crucial pebble (used to rock up onto to gain the far right-hand pockets).

⑮ Smoked Salmon ... E8 7b
12m. How you gain the top break is nothing considering what lies above though direct is best. From the break make three wild moves up to a poor edge and then a slightly better pocket to the right. Finish direct on pockets. Hard for the short!
FA. Johnny Dawes 1995

⑯ Curving Crack .... VS 4c
10m. Loop along the curving crack then swing right around the arete and finish up *Sandy Crack* which may be the crux!
FA. Allan Austin 1958

⑰ Poached Salmon .. E5 6b
12m. The arete right of *Curving Crack* direct via a series of slaps to the break. Get some gear in and reach up and left for a short flake (hard for the short) to finish.
FA. Jon Read 1999

⑱ Sandy Crack .... S 4b
8m. The wide crack in the corner has a tricky exit passing a large threadable chockstone.
FA. Eric Byne 1930

⑲ Quebec City .... VS 4c
30m. From *Sandy Crack* follow the inviting horizontal break, through some hard territory, all the way to *Quien Sabe?*
FA. Chris Craggs 1981

GREAT TOR - SALMON SLAB
Johnny Dawes originally climbed this magnificent wall in 1984 as *The Salmon*, E6 6c. The loss of a crucial pebble left the wall 'unclimbable' until Johnny called in again in 1995 to find two even harder ways up it! It is now laced with six recognisable outings. For those looking for milder sport *Curving Crack* and *Sandy Crack* are both worthwhile.

To the right is a short wall with two distinct lines.

⑳ Greydon Boddington ... HVS 5b
6m. The left-hand line in the wall passing a shelf and finishing up a short crack.
FA. Martin Veale 1977

㉑ Fizz E1 5b
6m. The right-hand line with two pairs of strange pockets that provide both holds and runners.
FA. Martin Veale 1980

50m right across the steep hillside, through clinging vegetation and past broken rock, is an attractive shallow scoop behind a rowan tree.

㉒ The Egg E4 6a
10m. The elegant scoop is entered from the left and exited rapidly to the right.
FA. Johnny Dawes 1984

㉓ High and Dry E6 6b
10m. The scoop direct to a harrowing exit. No sideways chicanery is allowed on this one.
FA. John Dunne 1986

GREAT TOR - UPPER TIER

Although not of the quality of the Lower Tier, the Upper Tier of Great Tor has a few worthwhile offerings with *Undercut Crack* being the best (if you like that kind of thing). There is also an interesting collection of easy chimney climbs from the start of the 20th century, the work of J.W.Puttrell and his associates, so get those tweeds on. *Gargoyle Flake* is one of the better VS climbs on the cliff with good moves in a spectacular setting. The routes on Tinner Buttress are worth doing if you are used to using rounded holds to make progress.

APPROACH - To go straight to the Great Tor, follow the main path over the top of the other buttresses and then drop down once you arrive at the Upper Tier. To reach the Lower Tier drop down below *Undercut Crack* or skirt the left edge of the cliff.

❶ Easy Chimney . . . . Mod
8m. A deep historical rift on the far left leads into a through cave to reach the cliff top.
FA. J.W.Puttrell 1900

❷ Palpitation . . . . S 4b
8m. The undercut left arete is awkward to reach holds over the bulge but then has easier climbing on sloping holds.
FA. Eric Byne 1930

On the front of the buttress to the right are two steep lines both of which are poorly protected and have hard exits.

❸ Thin on Top E2 5b
8m. The left-hand line passing a hole to a harrowing exit on poor, sloping holds.
FA. Colin Binks 1981

❹ Green and Nasty E2 5c
8m. The right-hand line starting up a flake also has a tough exit that will keep you on your toes.
FA. Chris Craggs 1981

❺ Deep Chimney . . . . Mod
8m. Another profound historical cleft for lovers of the dark and dingy. Approached over ledges and squirmed to safety.
FA. J.W.Puttrell 1900

❻ Kelly . . . . S 4a
10m. The left arete of the next buttress via a shelf, an awkward wide crack and a rightwards exit.
FA. Harry Kelly 1918

❼ Astronaut's Wall . . . . . HVS 5a
12m. The centre of the undercut buttress is strenuous and then delicate, though the situations are hardly space-walking.
FA. Pete Hatton 1963

❽ Possibility . . . . S 4a
12m. Tackle the side wall to the right of the buttress and make an exit round to the left.
FA. Bob Downes 1957

❾ Primitive Chimney . . . . Mod
10m. Climb the deep chimney that separates the two buttresses in classic fashion passing a jammed boulder.
FA. J.W.Puttrell 1901

Wharncliffe
Dovestone Tor
Rivelin
Bamford
Stanage
Burbage North
Higgar Tor
Burbage South
Millstone
Lawrencefield
Yarncliffe
Froggatt
Curbar
Gardoms
Birchen
Chatsworth
Cratcliffe

Descent

Descent

20m gap

Afternoon | 23 min

13

14

15

16

17

18

10 Undercut Crack E2 5b
8m. The short but brutal roof crack is a real gritstoner's glory where subtlety is definitely not required; tape up only if you really must.
FA. Allan Austin 1958

11 A35/M35 .... E? 6?
8m. The vague break in the roof right of the overhanging crack awaits a reascent....
FA. Joe Brown (with one sling for aid) 1958. FFA. John Allen 1975. Reclimbed by Steve Allen in 1984 after most of the crucial flake disappeared. The rest of the flake has now gone.

12 Avoiding the Traitors E7 6c
8m. The superb inverted dish and hanging flutings in the roof to the right of *M35* just had to be done, though it waited a while for someone with the required talent.
FA. Johnny Dawes 1995

To the right past a deep vegetated corner is a jutting buttress with prominent large hanging flake.

13 Old Wall .... HVS 5b
12m. Climb on to the tip of the perched flake at the base of the wall then climb through a notch and up the face on poor holds.

14 Gargoyle Flake .... VS 4c
14m. A delicate slabby arete on the right leads to a superb layback and an exposed finish swinging by the gargoyles (painful!).
FA. Pete Hatton 1963

15 Bum Deal .... HVS 5b
10m. The bottom-shaped crack and its continuation lead to romping up the easier wall above.
FA. Chris Craggs 1981

To the right is a descent gully and beyond this a heavily striated buttress which has a trio of routes that involve steep climbing on sloping and lichenous holds.

16 Tinner .... HVS 5b
10m. The left-hand side of the steep wall trending right on holds that are less than generous, though at least the protection is reasonable.
FA. Allan Austin 1958

17 Right-hand Twin .... HVS 5a
10m. The centre of the wall via a right-trending ramp is strangely similar to its left-hand twin.
FA. Allan Austin 1958

17 Solstice Arete .... VS 4c
10m. Climb the wide crack below the right-hand side of the buttress then the narrow and rather lichenous arete and rounded bulges above.
FA. Peter Stone 1997

Wharncliffe
Dovestone Tor
Rivelin
Bamford
Stanage
Burbage North
Higgar Tor
Burbage South
Millstone
Lawrencefield
Yarncliffe
Froggatt
Curbar
Gardoms
Birchen
Chatsworth
Cratcliffe

WRINKLED WALL AREA

A small collection of interesting buttresses with the projecting fin of *Wrinkled Wall* being the most significant piece of rock.

There is also some good bouldering on the collection of blocks aretes and boulders to the left of the fin.

APPROACH - See map on next page. The crag-top path provides the best approach. Drop down when you can see the distinct prow of the 'wrinkled wall'.

① **Que? Slab Direct** . . . . **VDiff**
8m. The centre of the slab on the far left is pleasant.
FA. Jim McCall 1998

② **K Buttress Slab** . . . . **Diff**
8m. The leaning slab on the left trending right throughout.
FA. Dick Brown early 1950s

③ **K Buttress Crack** . . . . **VDiff**
8m. The deep, slanting cleft is the perfect antidote to the climbing wall.
FA. Dick Brown early 1950s

④ **Wrong Hand Route** **E1 5c**
10m. The leaning crack has a useful pocket and turns out to be especially well named.
FA. John Gosling 1971

⑤ **Skarlati** **E2 5b**
10m. Scramble on to the ledge on the arete from the right then climb the committing rounded bulges trending left.
FA. Martin Boysen 1969

⑥ **Fern Chimney** . . . . **Mod**
8m. The fern-filled chimney is a botanist's delight, although most climbers might not get too much pleasure from it.

⑦ **Bracken Crack** . . . . **VDiff**
8m. The crack, moving right at the bulge.
FA. Pete Hatton 1963

⑧ **Down to Earth** **E4 6a**
8m. The short leaning arete of the biggest boulder is tricky though the landing is fairly soft.
FA. Al Rouse 1985

⑨ **Deb** . . . . **VS 4c**
4m. The square-cut arete of the boulder is a two-move wonder.
FA. Peter Stone 1997

The next three routes are at a higher level, starting from a terrace and most easily reached from the right. All follow short steep cracks.

⑩ **Special K** . . . . **HVS 5a**
8m. The short-lived left-hand crack in the side-wall passing the 'blank' section on a good jug.
FA. Arthur Robinson 1971

⑪ **Dead Mouse Crack** . . . . **HS 5a**
8m. The steep, left-slanting central crack in the front face feels pushy and exposed.
FA. Allan Austin 1958

⑫ **Hanging Crack** . . . . **S 4a**
6m. The right-hand crack is approached steeply from the right.
FA. Allan Austin 1958

The next routes are located on the attractive fin of rock jutting from the hillside.

⑬ **Bamboozer** **E2 6a**
12m. The wide crack on the left-hand edge of the buttress is climbed until it is possible to swing right to access the hard upper left-hand section of the face.
FA. Andy Popp 1993

⑭ **Jasmin** **E6 6b**
12m. The fearsome centre of the north-facing wall starting at the obvious notch. The climbing is desperate, on poor holds, and has no runners.
FA. Ron Fawcett 1990s

Wharncliffe
Dovestone Tor
Rivelin
Bamford
Stanage
Burbage North
Higgar Tor
Burbage South
Millstone
Lawrencefield
Yarncliffe
Froggatt
Curbar
Gardoms
Birchen
Chatsworth
Cratcliffe

Descent

⑮ Access Account . . . . 🖾 ☐ **E1 5c**
12m. Hard moves past the overhang on the right-hand side of the face gain the break, then step right to climb the arete on its left-hand side throughout.
FA. Al Rouse 1985

The rest of the routes are on the sunny south face of the fin and are not overly well protected.

⑯ Wrinkled Wall . . . . 🖾2 ☐ **VS 4c**
14m. From a short crack/slot climb diagonally left along a horizontal break to reach the easier but well-positioned arete. A very photogenic pitch
FA. Allan Austin 1958

⑰ Old and Wrinkled . . . . 🖾 🖾 ☐ **HVS 5a**
12m. Start as for the last route but climb the face just to the left of centre and keeping to the right of the arete. Delicate.

⑱ The Crease . . . . 🖾2 🖾 ☐ **E1 5a**
12m. Pleasantly precarious climbing up the right-hand side of the wall starting up the short crack/slot and then continuing in the same line.
FA. Mark Davies 1979

⑲ Sinuous Crack . . . . 🖾1 ☐ **Diff**
10m. The strangely-named straight crack that bounds the right-hand side of the face passing a useful chockstone just below the top.

← - - - - Descent

Afternoon · 18 min

1
2
3
4
5
6
7
8
9
12

Wrinkled Wall 70m

NEB BUTTRESS

The finest part of the cliff with an excellent collection of climbs on a fine series of jutting buttress and undercut walls. On any other crag in the Peak queues would be the norm, but here you may well have the place to yourself.
APPROACH - There is a lower path from Gun Buttress, otherwise use the crag-top path and drop down the left-hand side (looking in).

Great Tor Upper Tier From parking

Lower Tier Salmon Slab Tinner Wrinkle Wall Area Neb Buttress Porthole Buttress Gun Buttress

The Egg

About 50m N

Wharncliffe
Dovestone Tor
Rivelin
Bamford
Stanage
Burbage North
Higgar Tor
Burbage South
Millstone
Lawrencefield
Yarncliffe
Froggatt
Curbar
Gardoms
Birchen
Chatsworth
Cratcliffe

① Cleopatra .... VS 4c
8m. The hanging crack left of the arete is approached up a steep groove and gives strenuous climbing

② Samson's Delight .... HS 4c
8m. The cracked arete is also steep as well as short.
FA. Pete Hatton 1963

③ Dirty Stop Out E2 5b
8m. The thin crack and bulging wall, trending right to finish.
FA. Chris Lawson 1981

④ Delilah .... S 4b
8m. The awkward crack is soon over.

⑤ Short Curve .... VDiff
8m. As might be expected, this follows the short curving crack in the wall to the right.

⑥ The Business Boy E2 6b
6m. Bounce up the short wall to the left of the deep corner
FA. Martin Veale 1987

⑦ N.B. Corner .... Mod
8m. The deep angle is only just noteworthy.

⑧ Big Ben .... VS 4b
8m. The steep left-hand crack shouldn't cause too much of a dingdong as it is juggy and well protected.

⑨ Parliament .... HVS 5b
12m. The thinner right-hand crack in the north-facing wall feels best if you keep to the its right-hand side.
FA. Chris Craggs 1981

⑩ Auricle E2 5c
16m. The face just right of the arete has hard moves above the break using an 'ear'. Escape out right at the top below the roofs.
FA. John Gosling 1971

Afternoon | **18 min**

Descent

Wharncliffe
Dovestone Tor
Rivelin
Bamford
Stanage
Burbage North
Higgar Tor
Burbage South
Millstone
Lawrencefield
Yarncliffe
Froggatt
Curbar
Gardoms
Birchen
Chatsworth
Cratcliffe

11 Jumping Jack Longland — E3 5c
14m. The direct finish to *Auricle* is worthwhile and pumpy.
FA. Steve Bancroft 1979

12 Neb Buttress — HVS 5a
20m. Climb the crack to its top then traverse left to round the arete where a crack and short wall lead to an escape out right. A direct start up the lower arete is also possible with no change in grade, and less problems with the ropes, though it doesn't feel quite as good.
FA. Allan Austin 1958

13 Bamford Rib — HVS 5a
16m. The rounded rib to the right of the crack and the bumpy wall above give good sustained climbing.
FA. John Allen 1973

14 The Happy Wanderer — HVS 5a
14m. The arete is steep and sustained at an amenable grade and with good protection. Nicely elegant.
FA. Geoff Morgan 1967

15 Reach — VS 4c
14m. A direct line 2m right of the arete with the expected couple of long stretches.
FA. Chris Craggs 1981

16 Bamford Wall — S 4a
14m. Climb the slanting flake to its crest then move right to a crack. Up this to good ledges then move back out left for a more exposed finale if required.
FA. Hugh Banner 1960

17 Bamford Buttress — S 4a
12m. From an ochre coloured hole, climb to top of the flake then trend right to finish up the final section of *Twin Flakes*.
FA. Brian Evans 1958

18 Busy Day at Bamford — HVS 5a
12m. The blunt arete on the right is followed through a series of bulges to easier angled ground.
FA. Chris Craggs 1991

19 Twin Cracks — VS 4b
10m. From the cave climb the steep cracks by jamming and bridging, left then right.
FA. Hugh Banner 1960

20 Deep Cleft — Mod
14m. The deep dark chimney is always a windy experience.
FA. I put my money on JWP c1900

21 Oracle — VS 4b
14m. Climb the chimney until the fine exposed arete on the right can be gained by a bold swing. Finish in a superb position.
FA. Paul Nunn 1971

22 Sterling Moss — E4 6b
16m. The wall and flat roof right of the hanging arete have perplexing moves to pass the bulge.
FA. Johnny Dawes 1984

23 Ontos — E3 6b
16m. The centre of the impressive wall, approached by an easy rib, has a hideous 'stopper' move at the bulge. Apparently long thumbs help with the crucial moves.
FA. John Allen 1975

24 Trouble with Lichen — HVS 5a
25m. A nicely-positioned right-to-left girdle of the buttress, finishing up the left arete.
FA. John Allen 1973

25 Slanting Slab — Mod
14m. The easy slab on the right-hand side of the face is mild but still worthwhile at the grade.

Neb Buttress 60m

Porthole Buttress below

PORTHOLE BUTTRESS

Descent

GUN BUTTRESS
The buttress nearest the road has a good collection of easier routes on great, rough rock. With the added attraction of with a delightful grassy base, the place is worth half a day and don't forget to bring the picnic.
APPROACH - This is the first bit of rock you come to on the usual approach. You can't really miss the characteristic 'gun' on the top of the main buttress.

⑥ **Shadow Wall** . . . . ▨▮ ▭ **VS 4c**
12m. The left-hand side of the buttress has one long reach. Exit to the right under the gun and mantelshelf to finish.
FA. Chris Craggs 1981

⑦ **Life During Wartime** . . . ▨▧ ▭ **E3 5c**
10m. The bulging left arete of the buttress is short-lived but strenuous despite this.
FA. Keith Ashton 1985

⑧ **Randy's Wall** . . . . . ▨▮▧ ▭ **VS 5a**
14m. Start under the arete but trend up and right to pass an overhang and gain the centre of the wall strenuously. Finish more delicately.
FA. John Robson early 1960s

⑨ **Magnum Force** . . . . . . ▨▧ ▭ **VS 5b**
14m. Climb through the centre of the bulges to the ledge of *Randy's Wall* then traverse left to climb close to the arete.
FA. Chris Craggs 1981

⑩ **Gunpowder Crack** . . . . ▨▧ ▭ **VS 5b**
12m. The enticing hand-jamming crack is a pig to enter and much more pleasant above.
FA. Hugh Banner 1961

⑪ **Master Blaster** . . . . ▨▧▧ ▭ **E1 5c**
10m. The right-hand side-wall on a poor set holds, to a final long reach for a shallow crack Tiny wires protect.
FA. Chris Craggs 1981

① **Slab and Crack** . . . . ▭ **Diff**
8m. The named features left of the slanting chimney.

② **Möglichkeit** . . . . ▭ **HS 4b**
8m. The chimney itself is a bit of a grovel especially at the top.
FA. Allan Austin 1958

③ **Plimsoll Line** . . . . ▧ ▭ **HVS 5b**
10m. Gain the porthole from the cave and finish up the wall above on a poor selection of holds.
FA. Colin Binks 1981

④ **Porthole** . . . . ▮▧ ▭ **HVS 5b**
10m. Climb to the hole then head left to the arete to finish.

⑤ **Leaning Slab** . . . . ▭ **VDiff**
10m. The slab on the right and the steeper wall above.

12 Loader's Bay . . . . ☐ **Diff**
8m. The deep and ferny groove gives easy bridging.

13 Ammo . . . . ☐ **S 4a**
8m. The short arete and wall above.

14 Long John . . . . ☐ **VS 5b**
8m. The jutting snout is gained by a leap and a tussle. The short may have to use lateral thinking.

15 Three Real Men Dancing ☐ **E2 6a**
8m. The undercut wall on the right is short and sharp, and difficult to get established on.
FA. Martin Veale 1982

16 Green Chimney . . . . ☐ **Diff**
8m. As the name suggests chimney is often verdant.

17 Artillery Corner . . . . ☐ **Diff**
8m. .. and just right again is a similar feature.

18 Gangway . . . . ☐ **Diff**
8m. The ramp on the right wall. It can also be reached direct, at S 4c, by a swift pull.
FA. (Direct start) Chris Craggs 1981

19 Green Parrot . . . . ☐ **VS 5b**
8m. Gaining the beak is a touch squawkward.
FA. Martin Veale 1981

20 Bosun's Slab . . . . ☐ **Mod**
8m. The mild slab on the right-hand side of the prow.

21 Concave Slab . . . . ☐ **Mod**
8m. The scooped slab is also pretty straightforward.

22 Convex or Perplexed . . . . ☐ **VS 5b**
8m. Pull awkwardly over the nose and continue easily.
FA. Chris Craggs 1991

23 Adjacent Slab . . . . ☐ **Diff**
8m. The narrow slab is easy enough.

24 Hypotenuse . . . . ☐ **Mod**
8m. The open corner by mild bridging and jamming.

25 Opposite . . . . ☐ **S 4a**
8m. Start just right of the corner and climb straight up the wall on good holds.
FA. Chris Craggs 1991

26 Vertigo . . . . ☐ **HS 4c**
10m. The undercut left-hand arete of the buttress has a steep start on jams and is pleasant above.
FA. Pete Hatton 1963

27 Armed and Dangerous . . ☐ **E4 6a**
10m. The roof is crossed leftwards at its maximum width.
FA. Mark Stokes 1987

28 Dynamite Groove . . . . ☐ **HVS 5b**
10m. From a conveniently placed block pull into the hanging groove then continue direct.
FA. Martin Veale 1981

29 Sunny Side . . . . ☐ **S 4a**
6m. The centre of the final short wall on the far right.
FA. Chris Craggs 1981

30 Slopey Side . . . . ☐ **E1 5c**
6m. The right-hand side of the final face starting at a hole.
FA. Colin Binks 1991.

85

Whamcliffe
Dovestone Tor
Rivelin
Bamford
Stanage
Burbage North
Higgar Tor
Burbage South
Millstone
Lawrencefield
Yarncliffe
Froggatt
Curbar
Gardoms
Birchen
Chatsworth
Cratcliffe

STANAGE

The greatest of all the gritstone edges, with over 4km of exposed rock, in a setting of magnificent grandeur. Stanage must be the most popular climbing destination in the country and presumably that means in the world. I first climbed on Stanage back in August 1968 and thirty-odd years later it remains my favourite climbing destination, although I must admit it gets harder and harder to find new things to do! The cliff has routes of every grade from the easiest of bumbles to climbs at the limit of human ability. Stanage also has climbing of every style and there is enough here to keep most climbers ticking over for at least half a lifetime. The rock is of impeccable quality and climbing is possible throughout the year, always bearing in mind the vagaries of our climate. Some sections of the cliff have been quarried in the distant past for the production of millstones, most notably the Marble Wall and Wobbler areas. The climbing here is characterised by clean-cut grooves and aretes, whereas the rest of the cliff has the more usual rounded breaks and sloping tops that gritstone climbers grow to love.

Most people's first encounter with Stanage is at the well-named Popular End where there are enough classics for many months of superb climbing. Next a visit to the magical arena of the Plantation Area is a must, usually followed by a trip up the long bracken-covered slopes to sample the delights of the High Neb region. Once you have climbed on each of these three main areas a few times your true Stanage apprenticeship can begin by calling in at a few of the more out-of-the-way locations. Try checking out End Slab Surgeon's Saunter, Marble Wall, The Blurter, Count's Buttress, Tower Face, The Unconquerables and Millsom's Minion; you will then begin to get a feel for the place.

The popularity of the cliff can make climbing here a bit of a public affair especially in the arena-like atmosphere of The Popular End. A 10 minute walk to the left will almost invariably leave the crowds behind and give you some chance to perform without the feeling that you are the star attraction in a circus. Whatever your aspirations are, welcome to Stanage - this one place you will enjoy.

BOULDERING - Stanage has masses of bouldering possibilities both on the edge and on boulders below. Most of the main areas on Stanage are briefly described on the relevant pages.

CONDITIONS

As mentioned above the cliff is climbable at anytime of the year if the weather is being kind. Days when the bracken below the cliff glows like burnished gold in the low winter sun can be just as memorable as those long drawn-out evenings of high summer. Short crisp winter days can be magical, with superb friction and a quiet cliff, and the first spring evening after the clocks go forward is always a very special time.

Most of Stanage comes into condition very rapidly after poor weather, although the northern end of the cliff can be green in winter or after periods of rain. Midges can make life unpleasant (or even unbearable) on calm days between June and August.

Set at an altitude of 450 metres and facing west-southwest, conditions on the Edge are often best described as bracing. The almost ever-present west wind is equally good at drying the cliff and blasting away the cobwebs. On the rare occasions when an easterly is blowing (and this is especially the case in winter) conditions on the Edge can be warm and calm at the foot of the cliff, wild and freezing up on the belay.

Facing west, the cliff receives the afternoon sun until it sets and the sunsets here can be particularly magnificent.

OTHER GUIDEBOOKS - There are over 1200 routes at Stanage. A complete list of these routes is published by the BMC in their 2001 Stanage guidebook. The bouldering is in the 1998 Peak Bouldering ROCKFAX.

It doesn't have to be hard to be good. *Black Hawk Traverse Left*, VDiff, Stanage. *Page 145*

APPROACHES (SK226866 to SK254834)

Car thieves visit all the car-parking areas described below. It is sensible to leave nothing in the car and remove the parcel shelf so that the lack of any valuables is evident to these dim individuals who prey on innocent climbers.

There are four main access points that are commonly used to reach the cliff; approach generally times take between 10 and 25 minutes.

1) Moscar Top (SK 232878). By the A57 Snake Pass Road, best for Stanage End. (Note: recent work here has reduced the already-limited parking and raised the size of the kerb). Cross the gate and follow the obvious wide track gently up hill to the start of the cliff, just out of view over the horizon.

2) Dennis Knoll (SK 227843). The cattle-grid directly below High Neb, best for the section of cliff between Crow Chin and High Neb. Follow the Long Causeway to stiles on the left, which give access to the slope below the cliff.

3) The Plantation (SK 238838). Pay and Display parking. Best for areas between Count's Buttress and the Unconquerables. Follow the path to the trees then choose your destination, left on the path for Goliath's, right past the bouldering to reach the Unconquerables.

4) Hook's Car or The Popular End (SK 244829). The reinforced verge is best for the Popular End. The less-frequented areas of Apparent North Buttress and the Cowper Stone can be approached from either Burbage Bridge or from the verge on the road dropping down to Hook's Car Parking. Access to the central part of the cliff is also possible from parking by the Redmires Reservoirs on the outskirts of Sheffield although it is a long walk.

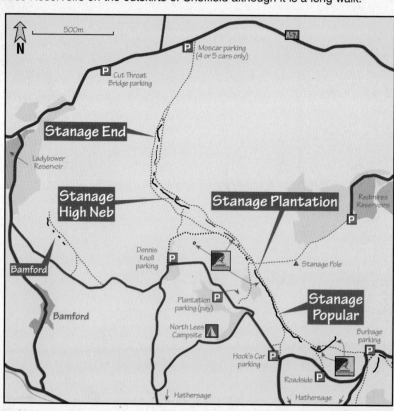

Wharncliffe
Dovestone Tor
Rivelin
Bamford
Stanage
Burbage North
Higgar Tor
Burbage South
Millstone
Lawrencefield
Yarncliffe
Froggatt
Curbar
Gardoms
Birchen
Chatsworth
Cratcliffe

Robin Barker crimping for England on the first ascent of *Black Car Burning*, E7 6c, Apparent North, Stanage. *Page 150*

Surgeon's Saunter Area 20m

END SLAB AREA

An excellent and secluded slab with some poorly protected routes. Behind is another slab with some worthwhile lower grade routes which are well-protected, and a vicious crack that is a carnivore. The area is best visited late on summer evenings when it gets the sun.

APPROACH - The slabs are reached in 20 minutes from Moscar (limited parking) and in 30 minutes from the High Neb parking. See map on page 97.

❶ Another Turn . . . . 🖾 🖾 ⬜ **VS 4a**
12m. The first route on the cliff is delicate and unprotected in its lower section. The steeper upper part has runners and holds.

❷ Steamin' . . . . 🔲 ⬜ **E1 5b**
14m. Start just right of the arete and climb delicately, passing the right-hand edge of a thin overlap. From the ledge, climb a short crack, a wall and the final roof centrally.
FA. Chris Craggs 1983

❸ The Pinion . . . . 🖾 ⬜ **HVD**
16m. Begin as for *Steaming* and but trend rightwards to the corbel-ledge. Move right then go up to the break, then right and up to finish. A varied selection of Friends helps protect this one.
FA. Harry Kelly 1921

❹ The Ariel . . . . 🖾 ⬜ **HVD**
16m. Start just left of the small cutaway and trend diagonally leftwards to join *The Pinion* on the corbel-ledge. Climb to the break and then traverse left to round the corner and finish as for *Another Turn*.
FA. Fred Pigott et al. early 1920s

❺ The Green Streak . . . . . . 🖾 ⬜ **VS 4c**
12m. Go directly up the slab just left of the overhang with some delicate moves on pockets. Small cams protect.
FA. Fred Pigott et al. early 1920s

❻ Incursion . . . . 🖾 🖾 ⬜ **E1 5b**
14m. Go direct up the slab just left of the cutaway until a delicate traverse out right gains the centre of the slab. The next couple of moves are the crux and low Friends protect the start of the difficulties. The route has also been done one-legged and with no hands.
FA. Paul Nunn 1962. FAOLAWNH. Johnny Dawes 1990s

❼ Incursion Direct . . . . . 🖾 🔲 ⬜ **E1 6a**
12m. Climb the centre of the overhang of the cutaway to pull over rightwards to pockets. Finish up the slab as for the original. A hard move but jump-off-able, if you miss the puddle.
FA. Andy Parkin 1976

❽ High Flyer . . . . 🖾 🖾 ⬜ **E4 6a**
12m. From a boulder under the overhanging right-hand arete make a swinging leap leftwards to gain a hand hold and a foot ledge down and left. Pull around and follow the right-hand edge of the slab to a scary, semi-mantelshelf move to easy ground.
FA. Lee Bowyer 1979

❾ Chip Shop Brawl . . 🖾 🖾 🖾 ⬜ **E5 6c**
12m. From the tip of the block under the right edge of the overhang, leap on to the hanging arete and power up it.
FA. John Allen 1987

❿ Caliban's Cave . . . . 🖾 ⬜ **HS 4b**
12m. The dark and narrowing recess gives awkward back-and-footing to a ledge on the left. Tricky moves are needed to pass the overhang. Can be green and slippery.
FA. Harry Kelly 1921

⓫ Prospero's Climb . . . . . . 🖾 ⬜ **VDiff**
12m. Climb the middle of the slab to the first ledge then move left to reach and climb the prominent layback flake.
FA. Harry Kelly 1921

⓬ The Crab Crawl . . . . 🖾 ⬜ **S 4a**
12m. Start below the left-hand edge of a small overlap at 3m. Climb past the overlap then continue up the slab in a direct line.
FA. Fred Pigott et al. early 1920s

Wharncliffe · Dovestone Tor · Rivelin · Bamford · Stanage · Burbage North · Higgar Tor · Burbage South · Millstone · Lawrencefield · Yarncliffe · Froggatt · Curbar · Gardoms · Birchen · Chatsworth · Cratcliffe

SURGEON'S SAUNTER AREA
This tall tower split by a chimney on its left-hand side and thinner cracks to the right has a trio of excellent routes across the grade spectrum.

Descent

Wobbler Area 40m

Whamcliffe · Dovestone Tor · Rivelin · Bamford · Stanage · Burbage North · Higgar Tor · Burbage South · Millstone · Lawrencefield · Yarncliffe · Froggatt · Curbar · Gardoms · Birchen · Chatsworth · Cratcliffe

---

⑬ Crab Crawl Arete . . . . VS 4c
12m. Start at the right-hand corner of the slab and follow the right-hand arete throughout by pleasantly delicate climbing.
FA. Andy Parkin 1976

⑭ The Vice E1 5b
10m. The leaning, leering crack is climbed by technical jamming to a gruesome shelving exit. Gritstone brutality at its best. Hideous, unless you are proficient jammer with big hands, in which case you will find it something of a HVS path.
FA. Clive Rowland 1962. (Pete Crew according to some).

⑮ Nursery Crack . . . . HVS 5b
6m. The wide crack in the tower in the bay is impossible to grade and just about as hard to climb. Graded Diff for years.

SURGEON'S SAUNTER AREA

⑯ Cripple's Crack . . . . S 4a
10m. The wide right-slanting crack that splits the centre of the north-facing wall of the next tower is an awkward customer.
FA. Fred Pigott et al. early 1920s

⑰ Which Doctor E5 6a
16m. Climb a flake, then the face above, until a horizontal break can be followed out right to the arete (small Friends). Finish up this with a flourish.
FA. Martin Veale 1991

⑱ Doctor's Chimney . . . . . . S 4a
18m. Climb the crack up the left side of the pillar to reach the impressive chimney system. Tricky moves are then needed to enter the main fissure before following it with pleasure.
FA. Fred Pigott 1919

⑲ Surgeon's Saunter . . . . . . VS 4c
20m. The original way of accessing the twin cracks. Start up the crack to the right of *Doctor's Chimney* then hand-traverse the lowest break to reach the cracks a short distance below the jammed block. Finish steeply up the left-hand crack.
FA. F.Pigott, Morley Wood 1929. Named after Dr. Rice Kemper Adams.

⑳ Surgeon's Saunter Direct . . . HVS 5b
18m. The twin cracks that split the tower give a great route with a hard, but highly-protectable start and excellent jamming above. The dubious jammed tooth at half-height has resisted many years of efforts to wrench it from its socket. Finish up the right-hand crack for the full effect.
FA. Peter Biven 1953

㉑ Heath Robinson . . . E6 6b
16m. Direct up the bulging right arete of the tower. The sloping exit requires some skill to avoid slithering off backwards; try undercutting the break to reach the slopers, then go!
FA. Johnny Dawes 1984

㉒ Manhattan Chimney . . . . . . S 4a
6m. A short chimney capped by a flat block. Classic back-and-footing leads to the well-protected crux at the capstone.
Fred Pigott 1919

**㉓ New York, New York /
Sir Chilled E4 6b**
7m. A short arete (E1 6a) leads to a trickier upper section. This gives a little exercise in dynamic climbing.
FA. John Allen 1986/Richard Heap 1999

㉔ Manhattan Crack . . . . VS 4b
6m. The excellent, but short-lived, layback crack with a steep and strenuous upper section.

Afternoon | 25 min | Green

Descent

15 16 17
On wall to right

Surgeon's Saunter 40m

Marble Wall 500m

Sidebar (vertical tabs): Wharncliffe · Dovestone Tor · Rivelin · Bamford · **Stanage** · Burbage North · Higgar Tor · Burbage South · Millstone · Lawrencefield · Yarncliffe · Froggatt · Curbar · Gardoms · Birchen · Chatsworth · Cratcliffe

THE WOBBLER AREA

Short, steep walls and quality cracks alternate. The area was quarried in antiquity which explains the angular nature of the rock and the piles of rubble in front. The right-hand side offers some extended problems for the boulderer/soloist.

❶ The Iain Farrar Experience **E5 7a**
10m. The blunt arete direct without recourse to side runners.
FA. Don Honneyman late 1990s

❷ Good Clean Fun **E4 6b**
10m. From a couple of moves up *The Wobbler* stride left onto the face and climb it by fierce moves.
FA. John Allen 1984

❸ The Wobbler **E1 5c**
10m. Climb the fierce left-hand crack by finger jamming. Then layback the cluster of cracks rightwards with a bit of a wobbler.
FA. Pete Crew 1962

④ Avril .... **HS 4b**
8m. The pleasant right-hand jamming crack on 'solid lockers'.

❺ Mars .... **HVD 4a**
8m. The diagonal flake left of the groove has a tricky start.

⑥ February Crack .... **HS 4b**
6m. Short and steep climbing up the angular corner.

❼ Exaltation **E6 6c**
8m. Fierce climbing which is a good target for a hot day since the wall is north-facing. The original line, *Saltation*, finished by scuttling off to join *Old Salt*. A hand-placed peg in a slot can protect the first crux, lowering the grade a notch - E5 6c. Small Friends and wires protect the stretch at the top.
FA. Paul Smith 1989. FA. (Saltation) Johnny Dawes 1984
FA. (Without peg) Pete Robins 2000

❽ Old Salt .... **HVS 5a**
10m. Climb the front arete of the buttress using a thin curving crack to gain a small ledge (5b for shorties). Move leftwards to follow flakes out on to the face to a finish in a splendid position.
FA. Paul Nunn 1963

❾ Valediction .... **HVS 5a**
8m. Just around the arete is a steep smooth-sided crack. Climb this through overhangs to a rocky ledge. The crack contains some hidden holds and is friendly on the jams. *Photo page 9.*
FA. Geoff Sutton 1959

❿ Monad **E2 6a**
6m. The wall left of the chimney has a desperate start on a tiny, polished foothold. Bridging back to the opposite wall is one possible (cheating?) solution however above this there is still a hard move to complete.
FA. Steve Bancroft 1979

⓫ Boomerang Chimney .... **S 4b**
6m. The banana-shaped rift is usually a greasy battle.

⓬ Twin Cracks .... **VDiff**
6m. The mild parallel cracks just right of the chimney are climbed in (not 'on a') tandem.

⓭ Quiver .... **HVS 5c**
5m. Climb the short crack which ends in the middle of the wall. Undercut for the break and quiver up the final move on rounded holds.
FA. Graham Hoey 1981

⓮ Arrow Crack .... **VS 5a**
5m. The crack right of *Quiver* doesn't run out half way up the wall and, as such, proves to be a bit less demanding.

The next three routes are in the short quarried wall to the right, just off the photograph above.

⓯ Microbe .... **HVS 5c**
6m. Climb the thin crack on the left of the wall, passing a narrow overlap early on.
FA. Steve Bancroft 1975

⓰ Germ **E2 6a**
6m. The thinner crack on the right has a taxing finale.
FA. Chris Sowden 1980

⓱ Problem Corner .... **VS 5b**
6m. Bridge the blank groove which bounds the wall. Short, sweet and far too petite.

← Wobbler Area 500m

Descent ←

1 **Marble Tower Flake** . . . . **S 4c**
12m. Reach the good ledge on the arete by a jump from the left (a move of 4c) then traverse left and exit from the ledge via the tall flake at its left extremity.
FA. Eric Byne 1950

2 **Marble Arete** . . . . **HS 4c**
10m. Start as for the previous route and follow the arete above. Mildly bold but with good moves in a nice position.
FA. Paul Nunn 1960s. Reclimbed and named by Chris Craggs 1970s

3 **Sceptic** . . . . **HVS 5b**
12m. Start right of the arete of the wall. From a block move out right and climb the unprotected wall on flat holds to ledges and a spectacular finale over the juggy roof.
FA. Al Parker 1970s. Reclimbed and named by Chris Craggs 1970s

4 **The Lamia** **E2 5c**
A superb girdle, the best of several on the cliff.
1) 5b, 12m. Start as for *Sceptic* but swing right along the break to *Nectar*. Continue to a hanging-stance on *Orang-outang*.
2) 5c, 16m. Ape along the same line to an awkward move upwards by a diagonal overlap to a deep break under the roof. Continue right to finish up the hard roof-crack.
FA. Steve Bancroft, John Allen 1975

5 **Terrazza Crack** . . . . . . **HVS 5a**
12m. The superb straight crack is a classic jamming product of the Rock and Ice. Well-protected but surprisingly hard work.
FA. Joe Brown 1952

6 **Harvest** **E4 6b**
4m. The short and savage roof crack above and right of *Terrazza Crack*. The jam at the lip is a good one but above that it all gets very flared. Those with flexibility will be able to use the foot holds under the roof to great effect.
FA. John Allen 1975

7 **Nectar** **E4 6b**
A blank corner and desperate roof crack give a well-protected classic of the 70s which is slightly spoilt by the fact that you can walk off from the top of the first pitch. *Photo page 38.*
1) E3 6b, 12m. A delicate start followed by tough bridging moves leads up the corner to a belay below the roof. Often climbed on its own.
2) E4 6b, 4m. Stretch into the roof-crack, shuffle towards the lip with your feet on the side wall then levitate the final short section. Even harder than *Harvest*.
FA. John Allen, Steve Bancroft 1976

8 **Orang-outang** **E2 5c**
12m. Yet another classic. Start to the left of the arete and climb a small corner to a narrow stepped-overhang. Layback onto the front face to a poor rest then follow the thin crack. On the crux the left arete will probably be of use.
FA. John Allen 1973

9 **Marbellous** **E8 7a**
12m. ...and another classic. The centre of the smooth wall to the right was perhaps the true 'last great problem' of Stanage. Start up a ramp left of *Goosey Goosey Gander* to reach the break then place small Friends in the horizontal slot out to the left. (Attempt to reverse to the ground from here then your runners can stay in place when you fail on the next bit). The upper section succumbs to a desperate move on thin undercut flakes.
FA. Robin Barker 1997

10 **Goosey**
Goosey Gander **E5 6a**
12m. ...and just one more classic. This short action-packed pitch follows the thin crack splitting the bulges. Protection is good but hard to place hence E5 for effort. Access the crack by a series of left-facing layback moves and sprint through the bulges (hint: a wrapped undercut with your right hand is found useful by some, but not all, on the crux). Things ease above, as long as you have some puff left. *Photo page 93 and 23.*
FA. Gabe Regan 1976

Whamcliffe · Dovestone Tor · Rivelin · Bamford · Stanage · Burbage North · Higgar Tor · Burbage South · Millstone · Lawrencefield · Yarncliffe · Froggatt · Curbar · Gardoms · Birchen · Chatsworth · Cratcliffe

MARBLE WALL

Another place where the quarry-men showed what great craftsmen they were, leaving us a *marbellous* set of classic routes to go at. Green in the winter but superb for the rest of the year and only a 20 minute stroll from the parking below High Neb.

The main part of the wall has such hard but well-protected classics as *Nectar*, *Goosey Goosey Gander* and the modern desperate of *Marbellous*. For something milder the superb *Terraza Crack* should delight the those in search of classic jamming and the pleasant routes on the *Sister's* wall are easier again.

The most surprising thing about Marble Wall is, despite the fact there are so many good routes here, the place is rarely busy.

APPROACH - It is virtually midway between the Moscar parking and the High Neb parking. The latter is probably better since it is more extensive. See map on next page.

---

⑪ Don's Delight . . . . HVS 5b
8m. A short slab on the right side of the bay is climbed trending rightwards to a precarious and unprotected moves to gain a shallow groove and easier climbing.
FA. Don Whillans 1962

The next routes are on the tower in front and right of the main Marble Wall.

⑫ Hideous Hidare 6b (V5)
6m. Climb the rib of the block on slopers then step right and mantelshelf back left with considerable difficulty. One to tease.
FA. Paul Mitchell 1993

⑬ Left Hand Tower . . . . VS 4c
16m. Climb the awkward crack on the left of the wall to the tip of the block on the left. Traverse the wide break rightwards to a finish just round the arete on the side-wall of the gully.

⑭ Turtle Power . . . . (E6 6c)
14m. The centre of the fine concave wall is a hard lead. Small RPs offer limited protection for the crucial moves to reach the beckoning break. Above this things become safer but another hard move is required before things ease. The route may not have been repeated since the loss of crucial pebbles.
FA. Neal Travers 1990

⑮ Slap 'n' Spittle E4 6a
14m. The right arete of the concave wall is tackled on its left-hand side with the crux passing the bulge early on. The gear arrives after the hard lower section. Finish on the right.
FA. Andy Lewondowski 1983

⑯ Pacemaker . . . . HVS 5b
16m. Bridge up the gradually widening chimney to the right until it becomes essential to leap on to the right wall expediently, just above the crucial long reach of *Vena Cave-in*.
FA. Colin Binks 1983

⑰ Vena Cave-in E3 5c
16m. An entertaining trip up the right-hand wall of the cleft with good protection from large Friends although the closeness of the opposite wall detracts. From the end of the initial crack of *Right-hand Tower* trend gradually left up well-separated rounded breaks to some particularly stretchy moves.
FA. Gary Gibson 1981

⑱ Right-hand Tower . . . . HVS 5a
16m. Like a fine wine; well rounded. Climb a thin crack left of the arete and continue straight up to the final break. Move round the corner on to the south face to find a precarious final couple of moves. Well protected by large Friends.

⑲ Wild and Woolly E1 5b
16m. From a collapsing wall move left to good holds in the break. Climb straight up well, initially on pockets. Keep just right of the arete to reach the final ledge of *Right-hand Tower*. Finish up the left-hand side of the nose using a small flake.
FA. Chris Craggs 1995

⑳ Tempskya E3 5c
14m. Start from the remains of the wall and climb directly up the bulging face on spaced and rounded holds to a short crack. Finish as for *Right-hand Tower*.
FA. Clive Jones 1978

㉑ First Sister . . . . VS 4c
12m. Start under the left-hand continuous crack and climb the thin lower section to good jams in the deeper upper section of the crack. Up this to the top.

㉒ Second Sister . . . . VS 4c
10m. The continous thin crack is pleasant.
FA. Alan McHardy 1961

㉓ Richard's Sister . . . . HS 4b
10m. The widening right-hand crack on the wall.
FA. Alan McHardy 1961

Wharncliffe
Dovestone Tor
Rivelin
Bamford
Stanage
Burbage North
Higgar Tor
Burbage South
Millstone
Lawrencefield
Yarncliffe
Froggatt
Curbar
Gardoms
Birchen
Chatsworth
Cratcliffe

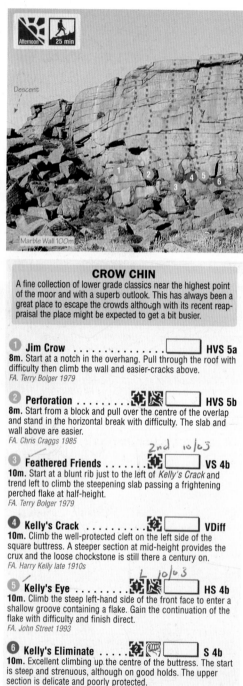

Descent

Descent

14

10

1 2 3 4 5 6 7 8 9 11 12 13

← *Marble Wall 100m*

Exodus 300m →

CROW CHIN

A fine collection of lower grade classics near the highest point of the moor and with a superb outlook. This has always been a great place to escape the crowds although with its recent reappraisal the place might be expected to get a bit busier.

1 Jim Crow . . . . **HVS 5a**
8m. Start at a notch in the overhang. Pull through the roof with difficulty then climb the wall and easier-cracks above.
FA. Terry Bolger 1979

2 Perforation . . . . **HVS 5b**
8m. Start from a block and pull over the centre of the overlap and stand in the horizontal break with difficulty. The slab and wall above are easier.
FA. Chris Craggs 1985

2nd 10/03

3 Feathered Friends . . . . **VS 4b**
10m. Start at a blunt rib just to the left of *Kelly's Crack* and trend left to climb the steepening slab passing a frightening perched flake at half-height.
FA. Terry Bolger 1979

4 Kelly's Crack . . . . **VDiff**
10m. Climb the well-protected cleft on the left side of the square buttress. A steeper section at mid-height provides the crux and the loose chockstone is still there a century on.
FA. Harry Kelly late 1910s

L 10/03

5 Kelly's Eye . . . . **HS 4b**
10m. Climb the steep left-hand side of the front face to enter a shallow groove containing a flake. Gain the continuation of the flake with difficulty and finish direct.
FA. John Street 1993

6 Kelly's Eliminate . . . . . **S 4b**
10m. Excellent climbing up the centre of the buttress. The start is steep and strenuous, although on good holds. The upper section is delicate and poorly protected.
FA. Harry Kelly late 1910s

7 October Crack . . . . **Diff**
10m. Ascend the wide crack that splits the centre of the face. Another worthwhile lower-grade route.

8 May Crack . . . . **VS 4c**
10m. Climb above the left edge of a triangular recess then take the thin crack that splits the diagonal overlap above.
FA. Chris Craggs 1985

9 October Slab . . . . **HS 4b**
10m. Start up the right-hand arete of the triangular niche then follow the thin seam above (small wires) finishing through a stepped overlap. Well worth doing.

10 Bent Crack . . . . **HVD**
10m. On the right, the face is bounded by a left-facing corner. Climb the initial steep corner-crack to ledges then the easier corner to below the capping roof. Traverse out left to finish.

10/03

11 New Year's Eve . . . . **S 4a**
10m. Climb the fingery, square arete to the right of *Bent Crack*, a short angular groove just to the right, and the final crack.
FA. John Street 1993

12 The Marmoset . . . . . . **HS 4c**
8m. Climb through the centre of the roof of the cave using the jammed blocks gently. Easy climbing follows. The route has historically oscillated between Diff and "impossible", lets hope we have finally got it right.

13 Autumn Gold . . . . **HS 4a**
10m. Take the face to the right of *The Marmoset* cave and then the steep crack above.
FA. D.Leversidge 1983

14 Bright Eyed . . . . **VS 4b**
8m. The pleasant slab at the right-hand side of the buttress is climbed centrally.
FA. Chris Craggs 1985

Whamcliffe · Dovestone Tor · Rivelin · Bamford · Stanage · Burbage North · Higgar Tor · Burbage South · Millstone · Lawrencefield · Yarncliffe · Froggatt · Curbar · Gardoms · Birchen · Chatsworth · Cratcliffe

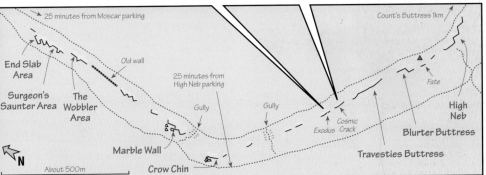

Wharncliffe · Dovestone Tor · Rivelin · Bamford · Stanage · Burbage North · Higgar Tor · Burbage South · Millstone · Lawrencefield · Yarncliffe · Froggatt · Curbar · Gardoms · Birchen · Chatsworth · Cratcliffe

EXODUS and COSMIC CRACK

Two isolated buttresses which are well worth a look if you are after *orange spot* routes. The challenges are provided by some fine crack climbs on the *Exodus* wall and stacked overhangs of *Cosmic Crack*.

15 Exodus .... HVS 5a
10m. The left-hand cracks starting from a sentry box give steep jamming to a mildly harrowing exit.
FA. Alan McHardy 1959

16 Deuteronomy ...... HVS 5b
10m. From the lowest point of the wall climb the jamming crack then step left and take a brace of cracks steeply.
FA. John Allen 1974

17 Leviticus .... HVS 5b
10m. The best defined crack just to the right of the centre of the wall gives more steep and well-protected jamming.

18 Missing Numbers .... HVS 5a
8m. The right-most crack in the wall is shorter but no less steep than its near neighbours.
FA. Graham Hoey 1981

19 Treatment .... VS 5a
8m. The left edge of the square-fronted tower across the gully is approached up easy rock and has one long reach.
FA. Gary Gibson 1979

20 Sudoxe .... HVS 5a
8m. The centre of the square-fronted tower is climbed pleasantly on 'blisters'. Avoid sneaking off right for the full effect.

30m to the right is a steep overhung buttress.

21 Beanpod .... S 4a
10m. Climb the pod-shaped crack. Exit left or finish up the arete.
FA. Al Parker 1959

22 X-ray .... HS 4b
10m. A thin crack splitting the centre of the wall.
FA. Al Parker 1961

23 Electron .... VS 4c
10m. Bridge the groove and crack just left of the central roofs.
FA. Alan Clarke 1964

24 Quantum Crack .... VS 5a
10m. Climb the central buttress passing an overhang early on to a tricky leftwards exit below the final roof.
FFA. Alan Clarke 1964

25 Cosmic Crack ...... VS 4c
10m. The crack on the right gives good laybacking and is the best of the routes hereabouts.
FA. Al Parker 1959

Wharncliffe
Dovestone Tor
Rivelin
Bamford
Stanage
Burbage North
Higgar Tor
Burbage South
Millstone
Lawrencefield
Yarncliffe
Froggatt
Curbar
Gardoms
Birchen
Chatsworth
Cratcliffe

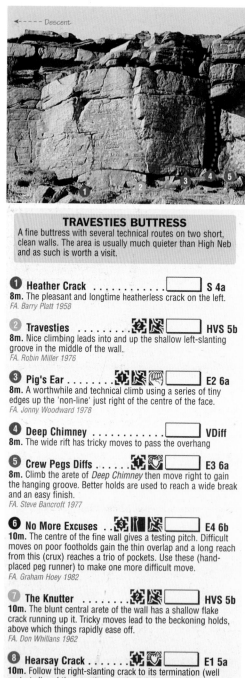

TRAVESTIES BUTTRESS
A fine buttress with several technical routes on two short, clean walls. The area is usually much quieter than High Neb and as such is worth a visit.

1 Heather Crack . . . . ☐ **S 4a**
8m. The pleasant and longtime heatherless crack on the left.
FA. Barry Platt 1958

2 Travesties . . . . 🔣🔣 ☐ **HVS 5b**
8m. Nice climbing leads into and up the shallow left-slanting groove in the middle of the wall.
FA. Robin Miller 1976

3 Pig's Ear . . . . 🔣🔣🔣 ☐ **E2 6a**
8m. A worthwhile and technical climb using a series of tiny edges up the 'non-line' just right of the centre of the face.
FA. Jonny Woodward 1978

4 Deep Chimney . . . . ☐ **VDiff**
8m. The wide rift has tricky moves to pass the overhang

5 Crew Pegs Diffs . . . . . 🔣🔣 ☐ **E3 6a**
8m. Climb the arete of *Deep Chimney* then move right to gain the hanging groove. Better holds are used to reach a wide break and an easy finish.
FA. Steve Bancroft 1977

6 No More Excuses . . 🔣🔣🔣 ☐ **E4 6b**
10m. The centre of the fine wall gives a testing pitch. Difficult moves on poor footholds gain the thin overlap and a long reach from this (crux) reaches a trio of pockets. Use these (hand-placed peg runner) to make one more difficult move.
FA. Graham Hoey 1982

7 The Knutter . . . . . . 🔣🔣 ☐ **HVS 5b**
10m. The blunt central arete of the wall has a shallow flake crack running up it. Tricky moves lead to the beckoning holds, above which things rapidly ease off.
FA. Don Whillans 1962

8 Hearsay Crack . . . . . . 🔣🔣 ☐ **E1 5a**
10m. Follow the right-slanting crack to its termination (well protected) and then continue up the bulging wall above (poorly protected) on sloping holds.

BLURTER BUTTRESS

9 Overcoat . . . . ☐ **HVS 5b**
12m. The left-hand pillar and parallel cracks in the overhang.
FA. Chris Calow 1981

10 Lucy's Slab . . . . 🔣 ☐ **HVS 5b**
12m. The right-hand pillar and tricky scoop in the roof.
FA. Al Parker 1978

11 Meddle . . . . 🔣 ☐ **E2 5c**
18m. Climb the arete of the buttress on its right-hand side until level with the bottom of *The Blurter* groove then swing left around the arete and sprint to a large ledge. Finish direct.
FA. Paul Millward 1976

12 The Blurter . . . . 🔣🔣 ☐ **HVS 5b**
22m. An devious climb, care with rope work required. Climb the chimney to a sketchy traverse left below the overhang. Enter the groove awkwardly and climb it to a step right. Pull over a bulge then trend left past the arete to the juggy north-facing wall.
FA. Al Parker 1959

13 Overhanging Chimney . . . . 🔣 ☐ **HVD**
16m. The central chimney is a bit of a thrash. Easy climbing leads to the constricted central portion. This is most easily climbed facing left (or is it right?) then things ease off.
FA. Harry Kelly 1915

14 Wolf Solent . . . . 🔣🔣 ☐ **E4 5c**
16m. A taxing beast. Start on the right and teeter leftwards up the slab until just right of the chimney. Pull through the overlap, rightwards (first good runners) then back left, with difficulty and a poor pocket. Continue delicately up the slab to a large ledge and easy finish. A **Direct Start** is a bold and bouldery **6a**.
FA. Martin Berzins 1978

15 Typhoon . . . . 🔣🔣 ☐ **VS 4b**
12m. Climb the square groove just left of the arete to half-height then step left around the arete and follow a curving crack to a sloping ledge. Breeze up rounded rock above.
FA. Al Parker 1959

16 Aries . . . . 🔣 ☐ **HS 4b**
8m. Start as for *Typhoon* and continue up the groove to an airy and bulging exit. Good gear.
FA. Al Parker 1957

Afternoon | 15 min

Wharncliffe
Dovestone Tor
Rivelin
Bamford
Stanage
Burbage North
Higgar Tor
Burbage South
Millstone
Lawrencefield
Yarncliffe
Froggatt
Curbar
Gardoms
Birchen
Chatsworth
Cratcliffe

Descent

13
15
16
12
10
9
11
13
14

Traversties Buttress 60m

---

⑰ Ono . . . . **S 4a**
8m. The pleasant left-hand line on the slab.
FA. Brian Cropper 1976

⑱ Uno Cracks . . . . **Diff**
8m. The main crack splitting the left-hand side of the slab.

⑲ Fate **E1 5c**
8m. The centre of the pocketed slab is especially taxing for the short; beware the final reachy moves.
FA. Gary Gibson 1978

⑳ Rinty . . . . **VS 5a**
8m. The thin cracks just right are pleasantly technical.
FA. Clive Rowland 1961

㉑ Duo Crack Climb . . . . **VDiff**
8m. The parallel cracks on the right.
FA. Harry Kelly 1921

BLURTER BUTTRESS and FATE

The classic Blurter is the main attraction of this area but there are a couple of other gems to be found. A couple of easy slabs on the far right are also popular with those looking for a mild introduction to gritstone.

㉒ Frosty . . . . **Diff**
8m. The cracks and open groove on the left-hand side of the right-hand slab.

㉓ Icy Crack . . . . **VS 4c**
8m. The shallow cracks in the centre of the slab are good.
FA. Bill McKee 1978

㉔ Youth . . . . **VDiff**
8m. The deepening cracks in the right-hand of the slab.

High Neb 30m →

The Blurter 30m
←

17 18 19 20 21
22 23 24

- Descent
- Blurter Buttress 100m

Whamcliffe
Dovestone Tor
Rivelin
Bamford
Stanage
Burbage North
Higgar Tor
Burbage South
Millstone
Lawrencefield
Yarncliffe
Froggatt
Curbar
Gardoms
Birchen
Chatsworth
Cratcliffe

HIGH NEB

High Neb offers some superb climbing in a majestic location and, except for sunny summer weekends, it is rarely as busy as the Popular End. There are classics of all grades to go at with some notable test-pieces including such greats as *High Neb Buttress*, *Quietus* and *Old Friends*.

① Gunter . . . . **VS 4c**
12m. The kinked crack on the far left is tricky towards the top.
FA. T.Norcliffe 1966

② Straight Crack . . . . **HS 4b**
12m. Follow the straight crack as it gradually widens. Difficulties escalate to a wide and awkward exit.

③ Eric's Eliminate . . . . **S 4a**
14m. Take the short crack in the flat face and the continuation above. Only spoilt by its proximity to *Twisting Crack*.

④ Twisting Crack . . . . **S 4a**
14m. A neglected classic, steep and quite intimidating, but on good holds. Climb the deep groove to the left edge of the big overhang (thread). Step out left on to the exposed arete and make a hard pull to gain the excellent juggy cracks above.
FA. Harry Kelly 1915

⑤ Kelly's Overhang **E1 5c**
16m. An amazing ascent for its day, up-graded by popular demand. From *Twisting Crack* make awkward moves to a poor rest on the block beneath the overhang. Bridge out right along the lip (hint: stay low) and make a hard move up and right to reach holds on the wall. Finish easily.
FA. Morley Wood 1926

⑥ Inaccessible Slab . . . . **S 4c**
6m. Climb the short slab with one tricky move to attain a standing position in the horizontal break. The green groove just to the left is the easiest way off.
FA. Henry Bishop et al. 1912

⑦ Inaccessible Crack Direct . . . **VS 4c**
14m. Climb the left arete of the recess and the crack above to the foot of the prominent groove. This gives a steep and exciting finish with tricky moves to pass the jutting nose.

⑧ The Beautician **E4 5c**
14m. From *Inaccessible Crack* make a precarious step out left above the overhang on the left and climb the slab to the break. The tricky wall and the right-trending scoop above give committing and delicate moves. Low in the grade but bold.
FA. Steve Bancroft 1984

⑨ Inaccessible Crack . . . . . . **VS 4c**
16m. The original way is devious but also good. Follow the crack that sprouts from the right-hand edge of the recess to its end, then traverse left to join and finish as for the *Direct* variation. Again the final crack is the crux.
FA. Harry Kelly 1915

⑩ Impossible Slab . . . **E3 5c**
14m. A steep slab with a bold finale. Start up the short crack 1m left of the arete and at its end make a couple of tough moves (6a?) to easier ground. Continue to ledges, lace the horizontal break then teeter up the final slab into ever more harassing territory. Side-runners lower the grade and the buzz.

⑪ Eckhard's Chimney . . . . . . **VDiff**
14m. Enter and squirm the overhanging chimney passing the narrowing close to the outside edge. Once above the protruding blocks things get easier.
FA. Ms Eckhard, early 1910s

⑫ Quietus **E2 5c**
14m. A brilliant and exciting roof climb which is high in the grade. Start under the roof and climb a groove direct to ledges below the huge overhang. Place runners that can not be kicked out then cross the roof using good flakes to a position on the lip. The crux follows and getting established on the head-wall is most easily effected by using the left-most cracks.
Photo page 103.
FA. Joe Brown 1954

Whamcliffe

Dovestone Tor

Rivelin

Bamford

Stanage

Burbage North

Higgar Tor

Burbage South

Millstone

Lawrencefield

Yamcliffe

Froggatt

Curbar

Gardoms

Birchen

Chatsworth

Cratcliffe

⑬ Norse Corner Climb ... **HS 4c**
16m. An old technical test-piece. Pull on to the slab using a big pocket then follow it rightwards under the overlap to where delicate moves gain a flat ledge. Finish up the polished corner.
FA. Henry Bishop et al. early 1910s

⑭ Quietus Right-hand **E4 6a**
14m. Starting from the large ledge on *NCC*, stick a large Friend in yer' teeth and make a difficult move to reach a wild hand-traverse leading left to the hanging arete. Pause briefly to place the gear and have some photos taken then pull up to the top. All over in about 30 seconds if you do it right.
FA. Ian Maisey 1981

⑮ Kelly's Variation .... **S 4a**
14m. A worthwhile variation start to *Norse Corner Climb*. Begin at a shallow scoop and climb up to the first horizontal break. Move left to a shallow groove and climb this to a good flat ledge. Continue up the slippery corner behind.
FA. Harry Kelly late 1910s

⑯ King Kong **E3 6a**
12m. Climb up to the shallow scoop that runs up to the overhang, bridge past this then reach straight over for a good hold on the upper wall. Progress from here is by means of a awful mantelshelf. The tall will just topple over backwards.
FA. Al Parker 1978

⑰ The Logic Book ... **E3 5c**
12m. The blunt arete is fingery and bold, especially for the short who will find it more like 6a.
FA. Gary Gibson 1981

⑱ Boyd's Crack .... **VDiff**
12m. The crack right of the corner. It eases with height but becomes awkward to protect. Big boots might also help.
FA. W.A.Boyd early 1910s

⑲ Limbo .... **S 4a**
14m. Start right of the easy break then step left to climb the poorly protected slab above the break.
FA. Chris Craggs 1978

⑳ Tango Crack .... **VDiff**
14m. The straight crack has an awkward initial section. Waltz up the easier crack above.
FA. F.C.Aldous early 1910s

㉑ Tango Buttress ..... **HS 5a**
14m. A smooth slab with sketchy initial moves. Continue up the centre to another delicate section, which leads to the curving finishing flake. Not too well protected in its upper reaches.
FA. Fred Pigott et al. early 1920s

㉒ Where did my Tan Go? . **HVS 5a**
14m. Climb just left of the arete to a break, move right and layback the arete passing a flake at 7m. The crucial moves are not too well protected and short climbers may query the grade.
FA. Chris Craggs 1989

㉓ High Neb Buttress ..... **VS 4c**
20m. A classic route of great antiquity and a bold climb until tamed by modern gear. Climb the projecting rib under the centre of the buttress to a narrow ledge (hard for the short). Continue to a ledge (good small Friend runners) then move right and climb the centre of the slab by the crucial mantelshelf. Continue more easily on the arete in a grand position.
Photo page 32.
FA. Ivar Berg 1914

㉔ High Neb Buttress Variations **VS 5a**
20m. A good route which uses a series of popular variations on the original. Climb a thin crack near the right edge of the buttress (crux) to the first break. Continue in the same line until below the crux of the original, then traverse left to good runners (small Friends). Make mantelshelf moves to reach better holds and continue up the left-hand side of the upper face.

Count's Buttress 1km →

Descent

① High Neb Edge .... HVS 5c
20m. Start up the fingery shallow groove 1m right of the arete (crux) to reach the horizontal break on the left (Friends). Continue up the flake and stay on the right-hand side of the arete until finally obliged to 'rock around' on to the front face. Finish much more easily.

❷ The Crypt Trip E6 6b
20m. The sheer wall left of *Old Friends* is tackled by this fingery and bold trip. Start under the right end of a thin overlap and climb up and left through a notch by a massive reach, or using undercuts and thin flakes, to the first proper break. More difficult (and safer) moves lead past a pocket to the main horizontal break and an easier finish up the final wall.
FA. Ron Fawcett 1983

❸ Old Friends E4 5c
18m. One of Stanage's classic E4s from the 1970s, and still a bold outing. From the bottom right-hand corner of the face gain a tiny groove which leads to a poor rest (and dodgy RPs) below and right of the hanging flake. Swing left and pull up with difficulty (a Friend in the base of the flake is hard to place) then make the crucial layback/stretch to reach the deep horizontal break. Move right and use the good pocket to gain the easier final wall.
FA. John Allen 1973

④ The Dalesman .... HVS 5a
22m. The striking horizontal break gives a good pumpy pitch with a whole stack of solid jams and great gear.
FA. Roger Greatrick 1983

❺ Mantelshelf Climb .... VDiff
14m. The slabby face 1m right of the corner is climbed by a series of mantelshelf moves. Finish up the shallow right-facing corner above.
FA. Fred Pigott et al. early 1920s

❻ It's a Cracker .... S 4b
12m. The centre of the slabby face to the right has an awkward but well-protected move to get into the thin crack. Finish up steeper rock on good holds.
FA. Jim Rubery 1997

❼ Sneezy .... HS 5a
12m. The right-hand arete of the slab has a tricky little move to pass the overhanging nose.
FA. Chris Craggs 1996

❽ Typical Grit .... HS 4a
10m. Climb the delicate narrow slab on the right-hand side of the bay to easier rock. Poorly protected; it must have been a gripper in nailed boots
FA. Fred Pigott et al. early 1920s

❾ Cave Buttress .... S 4b
16m. Start just to the left of the cave recess and climb the buttress, passing the perched flakes with care, to ledges below the overhang. Move right around the corner and finish up the juggy face directly above a crack.
FA. Fred Pigott et al. early 1920s

❿ High and Wild E3 5c
14m. Follow *Cave Buttress* to below the overhangs then launch across these, initially by a long reach and then by a ladder of jugs. A well-named climb that is hard for the short.
FA. Chris Craggs 1985

⓫ Jeepers Creepers E1 5b
14m. Follow the previous route to the overhang then attack the jamming crack that splits the right-hand edge of the roof. Climbers proficient in upside-down jamming might consider the route only HVS.
FA. Joe Brown 1958

⓬ Cave Buttress Right-hand ..... S 4b
12m. Start around to the right of the large fallen blocks and climb the crack and final steep wall on generally good holds.

Wharncliffe

Dovestone Tor

Rivelin

Bamford

Stanage

Burbage North

Higgar Tor

Burbage South

Millstone

Lawrencefield

Yarncliffe

Froggatt

Curbar

Gardoms

Birchen

Chatsworth

Cratcliffe

Descent

High Neb 1km

Afternoon   15 min

COUNT'S BUTTRESS

Below the gap in the edge, where the *Long Causeway* links the Hope Valley with western Sheffield, is the undercut face of Count's Buttress. This neglected area is home to a fine set of climbs that seem to be best suited to tall climbers with big balls. Those without one or the other advantage will be in for a hard time and those without both had better head elsewhere.

APPROACH - From the Plantation parking, follow the normal approach path under Wall End Slab. From the top of the flagstone section cut left across the hillside for about 200m.

❶ Nightmare Slab ... 🔲 E1 5b
8m. Climb the left-hand edge of the slab and make a bold high step to a good horizontal break and gear. Pass the bulge above by a long reach then stride out right to finish.
FA. Al Parker 1959

❷ Daydreamer ... 🔲 E2 6b
8m. Start in the middle of the slab at some polished holds and a short vertical flake. Make technical moves (sticky rubber sure helps) to gain the ledge, and then finish easily.
FA. Bob Brayshaw 1960

❸ Sleepwalker ... 🔲 E2 6a
8m. Start 2m left of the corner and climb the slab passing a couple of tiny overlaps early on.
FA. Chris Calow 1977

❹ Out For the Count ... 🔲 E4 6a
14m. The left arete of the lower buttress has a bold move at half height. A side runner reduces the danger but also knocks off an E-point.
FA. Chris Calow 1977

❺ The Cool Curl ... 🔲 E6 6b
14m. Ascend the lower buttress just left of its right edge to a ledge then step up and left to a precarious pull and crucial high step to get established on the central slab. Above this things ease dramatically. Scary stuff!
FA. Johnny Dawes 1984

❻ Count's Chimney ... 🔲 Diff
14m. The dark rift that splits the face is vintage. Climb the easy lower section then back and foot past the chockstone.
FA. J.W.Puttrell late 1800s

❼ Counterfeit ... 🔲 E2 5b
14m. The right-hand arete of the deep chimney is climbed on its right-hand side. Side runners would lower the grade to HVS.
FA. Graham Parkes 1997

❽ Count's Wall ... 🔲 E1 5b
16m. Climb the left-hand arete of the central cave to ledges then the thin crack (small wires) to a bolder exit. Finish easily.
FA. Dave Mithen 1976

❾ Counterblast ... 🔲 E2 5b
16m. Climb the right-hand arete of the cave then move left until above its left edge. Climb the slab using a pocket and a small crease: bold. Continue with one more stretch to easier ground.
FA. Gary Gibson 1981

❿ Abacus ... 🔲 E3 5c
16m. Follow the previous route to the first ledge then climb straight up the bold wall, directly above the right-hand edge of the cave. From the horizontal break things get easier and safer.
FA. Dave Mithen 1976

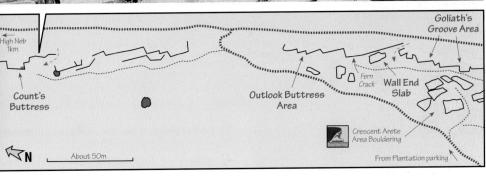

⑪ Count's Buttress **E1 5b**

16m. The original and best! A great route with a devious but logical line. Start to the right of the edge of the cave and climb the blunt arete on side pulls (unprotected) to a small ledge below the steep slab. Make an awkward traverse out right to the arete then reach the horizontal break above with difficulty before traversing back left to the short finishing crack. The finishing crack can be reached more directly from the start at **E3 6a**.
FA. Joe Brown 1955

⑫ Count Me Out **E2 5c**

14m. From the ledge on the traverse of *Count's Buttress* pull up just to the right, using three small pockets, to reach the centre of the horizontal break. Finish up the steep wall passing another useful pocket.
FA. John Allen 1985

⑬ The Count **E2 5c**

14m. A good route with a bold start. From blocks under the right-hand edge of the buttress use a loose flake to reach the break above the lip where Friends protect the move to the ledge on the arete. Climb up to jams under the bulge then follow the upper arete in a fine position.
FA. Dave Morgan 1976

⑭ Count's Crack . . . . **VS 4c**

12m. Approach the crack in the side wall from the right by a short traverse out of the corner via the horizontal break. Once entered it gives classic jamming.
FA. Eric Byne early 1930s

⑮ B Crack . . . . **S 4b**

10m. The deep right-angled corner that bounds the main bulk of Count's Buttress has an awkward bulge to start. Above it gets easier.
FA. Henry Bishop et al. c.1915

⑯ Dracula . . . . **HVS 5c**

10m. The arete at a higher level is approached over a tricky bulge. Then climb it on its left-hand side by well-protected laybacking. Markedly easier for the tall.
FA. John Gosling 1967

⑰ Shirley's Shining Temple . . **E5 7a**

8m. A desperate technical outing up the left edge of the blank slab sees few repeats. Start at a small overlap and climb up and left before tackling the final section direct. About as thin as they come.
FA. John Allen 1984. Direct start added by Graham Hoey.

⑱ Shock Horror Slab **E2 6b**

10m. Another technical test-piece. Start below and right of a slight rib and scrape up the lower bulges to an easier finish.
FA. Steve Bancroft 1980

⑲ Flaked Crack . . . . **S 4a**

10m. The left-slanting crack is harder than it looks especially if the grassy ledge to the left is avoided.

⑳ The Trickledown Fairy **E5 6b**

8m. The easy rib and sketchy upper slab give a precarious and bold piece of climbing.
FA. John Allen 1988

Wharncliffe

Dovestone Tor

Rivelin

Bamford

Stanage

Burbage North

Higgar Tor

Burbage South

Millstone

Lawrencefield

Yarncliffe

Froggatt

Curbar

Gardoms

Birchen

Chatsworth

Cratcliffe

Afternoon — 12 min

Descent

Descent

Count's Buttress 250m

OUTLOOK BUTTRESS AREA

Above the upper section of flagged path that runs from the Plantation car park to Stanage Pole is a series of short walls with an interesting collection of routes that is always quiet. The most renowned climb here is the Dawes desperate of *Weather Report*.

❶ Outlook Buttress . . . . **HVS 5b**
10m. Climb the left edge of the buttress then follow the rounded break rightwards to a steep finish on sloping holds.

❷ Look Before you Leap **E1 6b**
8m. The centre of the wall via an wild flying leap - boing!
FA. Chris Craggs 1981

❸ Outlook Layback . . . . **S 4a**
8m. The steep corner crack at the back of the ledge.

❹ Weather Report . . . **E6 6c**
10m. Climb the centre of the face trending left with a crux slap over the bulge for slopers. Finish direct.
FA. Johnny Dawes 1984

❺ Outlook Crack . . . . **HS 4b**
8m. The thin crack in the left-hand side wall of the gully has a couple of pleasant moves.

❻ Outlook Chimney . . . . **VS 5a**
8m. The fissure behind the leaning flake is hard to enter and to exit from. Ughhh! The grade is open to question.

❼ I Didn't Get Where I am Today . **E2 5c**
8m. Gain the front face of the flake, over the pocketed overhang, and climb it right then left.
FA. Johnny Dawes 1984

❽ Lookout Flake . . . . **HS 4b**
8m. A quick layback move gains the flake which eases rapidly

❾ Shard . . . . **HVS 5b**
6m. Climb straight up the delicate slab to a mantelshelf finish.
FA. Chris Craggs 1997

❿ Splinter . . . . **HVS 5c**
6m. Trend right to climb the blunt rib in the centre of the slab.
FA. Greg Griffith 1985

⓫ Tales of Yankee Power . . **E1 5c**
10m. The left side of the front of the block on small finger-holds to its crest and the wall behind.

⓬ Flaky Wall . . . . **HVS 5b**
10m. The flaky right side of the block leads to a swing left to reach its top. Finish easily.

⓭ Bastille **E1 5b**
10m. The right arete of the face on its left-hand side.
FA. Jim Rubery 1992

⓮ Shaky Gully . . . . **S 4a**
10m. The awkward wide corner crack and continuation behind.
FA. Dave Gregory 1992

⓯ Amphitheatre Face . . . . . . **VS 5a**
8m. Reach the wall right of the groove with a triple jump start, or by traversing in from the left.

⓰ Ladder Cracks . . . . **Diff**
8m. The parallel cracks just left of the corner.

⓱ Ladder Corner . . . . **Mod**
8m. The amiable corner that bounds the wall on its right.

Descent

Goliath's Groove Area 30m

Afternoon · 12 min

Wharncliffe · Dovestone Tor · Rivelin · Bamford · Stanage · Burbage North · Higgar Tor · Burbage South · Millstone · Lawrencefield · Yarncliffe · Froggatt · Curbar · Gardoms · Birchen · Chatsworth · Cratcliffe

FERN CRACK and WALL END SLAB
This large slumped sheet of rock features a good set of climbs from VS to E4. To the left is a tall tower with the prominent fissure of *Fern Crack*, and the tantalising crease of *Fern Groove*. Both are worth a little of your time if you are in the area.

18 Argus **E2 5b**
8m. Low in the grade. Climb the upper arete left of *Fern Crack* starting from a ledge on the left. Swing onto the arete and layback the arete smartly, keeping on its left-hand side. Pulling around to the right is easier and a bit pointless.
FA. Tim Carruthers 1977

19 Silk **E5 6c**
10m. An unprotected outing up the 'slabby' face to the left of *Fern Crack*. Start just left of the crack and swarm the bulge to where tough friction moves lead leftwards to parallel breaks. A variety of poor pockets enabled a swift finish to be made.
FA. Johnny Dawes 1984

20 Fern Crack ..... **VS 4c**
16m. The long crack is the major feature of the buttress and it proves to be an awkward customer. A layback start (5a?) leads to an awkward wide section off the ledge and another section to enter the upper crack. Escape out left at the top. High in the grade.

21 Help the Aged .... **6c (V7)**
6m. The direct start to *Fern Groove* is a popular boulder problem. Very condition dependent.
FA. Johnny Dawes 1985

22 Fern Groove **E2 5c**
16m. Climb the right-hand edge of the slab then reach the hanging groove by a traverse from the right. Enter it by a puzzling layback sequence then sprint to safety. Hard for E2!
FA. Pat Fearneough 1961-63

23 Smash Your Glasses **E5 6b**
14m. Follow *Fern Groove* to the first grassy ledge then tackle the right arete of the buttress keeping on its left-hand side throughout. The crux is protected though the upper arete is not.
FA. John Allen 1988

24 Wall End Slab .... **VS 5a**
22m. A devious classic. The initial slab can be ascended in several places at 5a/b. From the ledge climb through the bulge just to the right of the left arete to another ledge then step down (low runners) and traverse across the slab to reach its right arete. Follow the right side of this to the top. Poorly protected although at least the upper section is 'only' 4b.
FA. Fred Pigott et al. early 1920s

25 Wall End Slab
Super Duper Direct ... **E3 5c**
14m. Climb the centre of the lower slab and the bulge above on pockets. The final rib is the main challenge of the route due to the remote nature of the runners. Scary and reachy.
FA. Chris Craggs 1991

26 Wall End Slab Direct .. **E3 5c**
14m. A great effort for its day. Climb the lower slab right of centre to a break and runners. Step right and balance up the slab using an undercut flake to make a right-facing mantelshelf (5b) a worrying distance above the gear. Continue to the next break and escape out right to the easy upper arete (E2) or better, teeter warily up the scoop in the steepening wall to a reachy finish an even more worrying distance above your gear.
Photo page 111.
FA. Frank Elliott 1930. FA. (Direct finish) Chris Craggs 1983

BOULDERING - Despite the height of the edge there are some good problems on this section for those who have done everything on the Crescent Arete area. The main areas of interest are the section around *Help the Aged* and a small boulder over the flagstoned-path below *Lookout Flake*.

Descent

Afternoon · 10 min

Descent

Wall End Slab 30m

Satin Area 30m

GOLIATH'S GROOVE AREA

This attractive series of aretes and walls includes some of the very best offerings on the whole cliff and indeed in all of the Peak. As might be expected the area is always popular.

❶ Slanting Chimney . . . . **S 4a**
10m. The obviously named chimney in the side wall of the buttress is climbed awkwardly.

❷ The Coign . . . . **HS 4b**
L 5/03
16m. The left-hand arete of this section of rock. Climb the short crack and arete, then step up on to the main arete which is followed with a couple of steeper moves at half height.
FA. Geoffry Sutton 1958

❸ Outlook Slab . . . . **VS 5a**
16m. Climb the horizontally-cracked slab up its centre. The well-protected crux move is at the steepening.
FA. Martin Veale 1978

❹ Wall End Crack Direct . . . . **HS 4b**
16m. The widening upper crack is approached up a short jamming crack. The upper part is not too well protected.
FA. Henry Bishop et al. c1914

❺ Death, Night and Blood . . **E1 5b**
18m. Start as for the last route but step right onto the exposed and delicate arete. The final precarious section proves especially harrowing for the short. Not well protected.
FA. Gary Gibson 1978

❻ Wall End Flake Crack . . . . . **VS 4c**
20m. Climb the corner-crack of *Wall End Crack Direct* then take the sloping ramp to the foot of twin flakes. Climb the left-hand of these by well-protected (big gear) laybacking and jamming.
FA. Fred Pigott et al. early 1920s

❼ Wall End Holly Tree Crack . . . **HS 4b**
18m. Reach the flake via the thin crack in the left wall of *Helfenstein's Struggle* and follow it by jamming and bridging. The other crack is hard to ignore.

❽ Helfenstein's Struggle . . . . **HVD 4a**
16m. The wide black rift is strangely alluring. Climb a short polished corner then follow easier ground to below the large boulder blocking the rift. Either squeeze through the hole that gripped Helfenstein, or make an exposed 'outside' exit at **HS 4a**.
FA. Helfenstein - well almost. c1910

❾ The Archangel **E3 5b**
22m. A totally committing layback up the left-hand side of the immaculate arete. Side runners should be avoided at this grade. From the starting blocks, take a deep breath, and sprint for the midway break. Things are easier above.
FA. Ed Drummond 1972

❿ Don **E4 5c**
22m. The right-hand side of the arete is also good and harder and unprotected.
FA. Ed Drummond 1985. Appeared shortly after I suggested to Ed that to climb the 'other' side of the arete would be fun!

⓫ Goliath's Groove . . . . **HVS 5a**
22m. The stunning twisting groove may be the best route on the crag. The initial corner proves to be the crux for many and the midway ledge provides an optional stance with chockstone belay. The upper bulging section of the groove can be laybacked or bridged. Protection is perfect throughout.
FA. Peter Harding 1947

⓬ Doncaster's Route . . . . **HVS 5a**
24m. Ascend *Goliath's Groove* to the midway ledge then continue up the short slab on the right to another ledge. Finish up the thin crack in the wall (4b after the *Goliath's* section).
FA. Michael Doncaster 1930s

Descent

Afternoon 10 min

Satin Area

Wharncliffe

Dovestone Tor

Rivelin

Bamford

Stanage

Burbage North

Higgar Tor

Burbage South

Millstone

Lawrencefield

Yarncliffe

Froggatt

Curbar

Gardoms

Birchen

Chatsworth

Cratcliffe

⑬ Ulysses' Bow . . . . . 🔲🔲🔲 **E6 6b**
20m. The square-cut arete to the right requires stacks of commitment and technique. Each move is a notch harder than the one before but none is as hard as the ground. Sometimes done above a pile of mats but this is cheating. *Photo page 1.*
FA. Jerry Moffatt 1983

⑭ Hollybush Gully Left . . . . . 🔲🔲 **HS 4b**
20m. The square-cut corner is climbed via the awkward left-hand crack to reach the top of the flakes. Continue up the groove passing the exposed chockstone to the easier upper gully and an exit
FA. Henry Bishop et al. c.1914

⑮ White Wand . . . . 🔲🔲🔲 **E5 6a**
22m. Another bald and bold arete. Getting established on the sharp section of the arete is the crux; a thumb lock on a pebble might prove useful. Above this a traumatic-feeling layback leads to the halfway break. Finish more easily.
FA. John Allen 1975

⑯ Hollybush Gully Right . . . . 🔲🔲 **VDiff**
20m. A vintage outing from JWP. Climb a blocky rib rightwards and make a mild hand traverse back left to the gully. The upper section is easier. The **Direct Start** is strenuous S 4b.
FA. J.W.Puttrell late 1800s

⑰ Fairy Steps . . . . 🔲🔲 **VS 4a**
16m. An excellent route crossing a wide smooth wall. From a grassy ledge climb the steep slab just left of the corner to the start of a narrow ledge system. A delicate traverse leads out left until better holds can be followed directly to the top.
FA. Alan Clarke early 1960s

BOULDERING - *The blocks below the edge have some of the best boulder problems in the Peak District. The following selection includes the best of the boulder problems and some that are really routes, albeit with no gear.*

⑱ Crescent Arete . . . . . 🔲🔲 **5b (V2)**
The superb elegant arete right above the path succumbs to precarious laybacking then a sprint once it begins to ease.
FA. Gabe Reagan 1976

⑲ Deadline . . . . . . 🔲🔲🔲 **E5 6c**
Traverse the left-hand wall of the boulder to a pocket then make a very hard move to reach the final hold on the arete. Scary **V8**.
FA. Richie Patterson 1999

⑳ Beneath the Breadline . . . . . . 🔲🔲🔲 **E5 6c**
The arete of the block is followed from ground level. **V7** ish.
FA. Pat King 1999

㉑ Breadline . . . . 🔲🔲 **E4 6b**
Hop across the gap and climb the the blunt technical arete above a nasty landing. **V4/5**.
FA. John Allen 1984

㉒ Big Air . . . . 🔲🔲 **E6 6b**
Bizarre but superb moves. Leap the crevasse for the beckoning square hold and mantel a way to glory. Not a boulder problem!
FA. Martin Veale 1987

㉓ Careless Torque . . . 🔲🔲🔲 **E6 7a**
The big jutting arete has an impossible start coming in from the right. Above that is seldom travelled. Given **V12**.
FA. Ron Fawcett 1987

㉔ Not to be Taken Away . . 🔲🔲 **6a (V4)**
Boulder out the moves to access the ramp then hand traverse up this to one more tricky move at a gap in the ramp which gains the finishing jugs. Probably **V5** for the short. *Photo page 16.*
FA. John Allen 1976

㉕ Brad Pit . . . . . 🔲🔲🔲🔲 **7a (V11)**
Probably the most famous boulder problem in the Peak is located in the dark pit behind the large block. There are various cunning methods available depending on your body dimensions. Best consult a local first.
FA. Jason Myers 1995

Goliath's Groove Area 30m

Tower Face 50m

SATIN AREA and FINA

A couple of short buttresses squeezed between the ever-popular *Goliath's Groove* and *Tower Face* areas. Although of less stature, they are well worth a visit.

❶ Spur Slab . . . . **VDiff**
12m. Mantelshelf onto the tip of the slab then trend right to climb the flaky arete to the top of the block.

❷ Satin . . . . **6b (V5)**
8m. The overlap and slab are climbed infrequently as most climbers discover "there ain't no grips".
FA. Johnny Dawes 1984

❸ Living at the Speed **E1 5b**
10m. Climb the central chimney then traverse the break left-wards into the middle of the slab. Make a tricky mantelshelf move and continue delicately.
FA. Gary Gibson 1979

❹ Mark's Slab . . . . **VS 5a**
8m. Climb the chimney then hand-traverse the lowest break and climb the centre of the slab on the right.
FA. Mark Whitfield 1978

❺ Pullover . . . . **5b (V2)**
8m. A flake under the lip of the overhang allows a tough pull up and left to a layaway, use this to attain a standing position. Finish direct much more easily.
FA. Allan Austin 1958

❻ Roll Neck . . . . **VS 5a**
8m. From a block at the bottom right edge of the slab pull awkwardly leftwards, then follow the right-hand side of the slab.
FA. Dave Gregory 1992

❼ Fina . . . . **HVS 5b**
16m. Climb the crack in the left-hand arete of the buttress and hand-traverse right along the lowest break. Climb the blunt arete and tricky rib above.
FA. Al Parker 1958

❽ Four Star **E5 6b**
14m. The right arete is climbed on its left-hand side by fiercely technical laybacking above a poor landing. Join *Fina* and escape left or finish direct.
FA. Simon Horrox 1982

❾ Centaur **E1 5c**
8m. A right swine. From the cave battle into the hanging crack and heave on the frightening creaky flake until things ease. An exhausting and bloody battle for most.
FA. Don Whillans 1958

❿ Additive Chimney . . . . **HS 4b**
6m. The wide chimney above the previous route is hard to enter, hard to make progress on and not well protected. Graded VDiff for years.

BOULDERING - The direct starts to *Spur Slab*, and the two problems described above, are of most interest to boulderers. Also check out the lone boulder in the field below.

Lawrencefield · Yarncliffe · Froggatt · Curbar · Gardens · Birchen · Chatsworth · Cratcliffe

Whamcliffe
Dovestone Tor
Rivelin
Bamford
Stanage
Burbage North
Higgar Tor
Burbage South
Millstone
Lawrencefield
Yarncliffe
Froggatt
Curbar
Gardoms
Birchen
Chatsworth
Craticliffe

Up and left of the main *Tower Face* is a slabby arete most easily reached by scrambling around to the left.

❶ Cinturato **E1 5c**
14m. From the tip of the slab make an awkward move to start and then get smokin'. Delicate and unprotected.
FA. John Gosling 1967

❷ Grace and Danger . **E6 6c**
14m. The scooped wall right of *Cinturato* requires stacks of commitment not to mention technical ability. Fortunately there are more holds than appearances suggest.
.FA. John Allen 1986

❸ Esso Extra **E1 5b**
12m. From square-cut recess in the left-hand wall of the gully, swing left and pull up to a grim alcove with difficulty. From here jam up the short, strenuous and gritty crack that rises from its apex. All very Whillansian.
FA. Joe Brown 1957

❹ Tower Gully .... **VS 4b**
14m. The long corner system in the right-hand wall of the gully gives an impressive pitch. Bridge the initial groove to ledges then take the steep upper section to an escape beneath the massive chockstone.

❺ Tower Crack .... **HVS 5a**
24m. A smart hand-jamming crack. The central section is tough, although bridging helps, and the pull on to the ledge can be a poser. Climb the corner on the right and then traverse awkwardly around the arete to the ledge above *Tower Face*. *Miserable Miracle* provides a suitably contrasting finish.
FA. Joe Brown early 1950s

❻ Tower Chimney **E1 5b**
20m. The chimney to the right is always compelling and often avoided. The bell-shaped upper section is the crux. Good gear is available in the depths of the recess.
FA. Eric Byne 1933

The high rectangular wall of Tower Face is one of the tallest on the cliff. All the routes here are well worth doing.

❼ Flight of Ideas **E7 7a**
22m. An inspiring route up the soaring arete. Highly technical and with good runners below the crucial upper section. Start below a curving sandy overlap and climb through this to the break then move left to the arete. The blank upper section is climbed on its right-hand side.
FA. Simon Jones 1994

❽ Indian Summer ... **E6 6c**
22m. Another great route. Follow *Flight of Ideas* to the first horizontal break. Then use poor holds to reach the next break. Continue trending left up the crucial near-vertical upper wall above on tiny holds.
FA. John Allen 1986

❾ Tower Face Direct **E2 5b**
22m. An excellent route which is a touch bold. Climb directly up centre of the face, using the creaking flake, to a rest on the left. A strange side-ways nut protects the harrowing series of moves up and right to gain the upper flake which is much easier.
FA. Peter Biven 1956

❿ Tower Face .... **HVS 5a**
26m. Climb the Direct to some good nut slots. Either foot-traverse rightwards (safer) or go higher (easier but bolder) to a crusty flake just before the arete; either way is the crux. Climb the flake to the break then traverse left to gain the superb finishing flake.

TOWER FACE

The tallest wall on the cliff with routes to match. *Tower Face Direct* and *Flight of Ideas* are bench-mark routes for quality and all the other routes described here are worth doing. The shorter walls above and to the right also have some unsung gems if you want to be alone.

Hathersage Trip Area 50m ➡

⑪ Tower Face Indirect 🔷▢ **VS 4c**
24m. A pleasant route with a good finale. Climb the easy chimney on the right-hand side of the face until it is possible to step out to the left and then make a short traverse (crux) to reach the base of the central flake-line. Romp up this in superb positions.
FA. John Allen 1976

Right of Tower Face is a short attractive buttress split by two horizontal cracks.

⑫ Stretcher Case 🔷▢ **E2 5c**
10m. Climb the crack in the left-hand wall of the face to its top then swing right passing the arete and make a mighty stretch for the top.
FA. Chris Jackson 1981

⑬ Scuppered 🔷▢ **E4 6a**
10m. From the left-hand end of the ledge below the face, swing along the break and climb the technical arete on its right-hand side by difficult laybacking.
FA. John Allen 1988

⑭ Invisible Maniac 🔷▢ **E3 6b**
8m. A direct line up the middle of the wall arriving below the hard moves of *Nuke the Midges*. Features a cheek-grinding mantelshelf as the crux.
FA. Richie Patterson 1996

⑮ Nuke the Midges 🔷▢ **E1 5b**
10m. Start on the right up ledges then head left for 5m (a pumpy dangle for the short) to a good hold. A hard mantel on this (crux) may reach the top. The route is substantially harder for the short.
FA. Al Manson 1977

Above Tower Face is a short wall with a collection of climbs that will enable you to avoid the crowds.

⑯ Miserable Miracle 🔷▢ **E1 5b**
6m. A good extension to any of the *Tower Face* routes. The tiny left-hand arete of face feels a mite bold and very exposed. The potential fall is at least twice the size of the route.
FA. John Allen 1976

⑰ Scapa Flow 🔷▢ **E6 6c**
10m. Start at the left-hand end of the overhang and climb right-wards on pebbles towards the centre of the wall where a gripping and technical finale awaits.
FA. Andy Barker

⑱ The Mangler **E1 5c**
10m. The wide crack is fearsome, and is traditionally climbed by squirming. Those with a modern approach and huge cams might want to try laybacking.
FA. Don Whillans 1959

⑲ Crescent .... **VS 5a**
10m. The curving crack gives pleasant and well protected moves leading to easier bulges above
FA. Don Whillans 1959

Past some big oak trees is an attractive slab with three routes. Left of this is a smaller, retiring slab with one hard outing.

⑳ Swooper 🔷▢ **E5 6b**
6m. Climb the centre of the small slab trending leftwards near the top. Despite its diminutive size the route is a gripper. Beware the sandy exit. Precarious and unprotected.
FA. Johnny Dawes 1984

㉑ The Strangler ...... 🔷▢ **E4 5c**
12m. Climb the left-hand arete of the front face throughout. The lower section is straightforward and the crux is near the top. This is reasonably well protected but goes on for a couple of moves more than you might want it to.
FA. Gabriel Regan 1977

㉒ Skidoo .... 🔷▢ **E6 6b**
12m. The slab 2m right of the arete is climbed directly and provides a scary challenge requiring neat footwork and a degree of coolness.
FA. John Allen 1985

㉓ Skidoo .... 🔷▢ **E6 6c**
12m. Climb the right-hand line on the slab from right to left starting at an overlap and passing three small pockets.
FA. Niall Grimes 1997. Climbed in mistake for the original Skidoo and there is no mistake in the name.

Afternoon | 10 min

Wharncliffe
Dovestone Tor
Rivelin
Bamford
Stanage
Burbage North
Higgar Tor
Burbage South
Millstone
Lawrencefield
Yarncliffe
Froggatt
Curbar
Gardoms
Birchen
Chatsworth
Cratcliffe

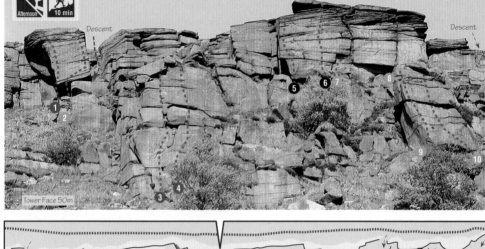

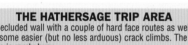

THE HATHERSAGE TRIP AREA

A secluded wall with a couple of hard face routes as well as some easier (but no less arduous) crack climbs. The area is rarely busy.

① Small Dreams **E2 6a**
10m. The undercut left arete of the buttress is taxing to access and delicate above.
FA. Chris Calow 1978

② Scorpion Slab . . . . **HS 4a**
10m. The right-hand edge of the tilted block is approached by the lower section of the descent route. Its upper part is precarious and unprotected.

③ Hercules Crack . . . . . **S 4a**
14m. Climb the flake and continue up the wider crack above. The whole affair is about as strenuous as you might expect from its name.

④ Shelf Life **E3 5c**
14m. Start just right of *Hercules Crack* and climb a tricky wall on small holds to a bulge split by a thin crack. Head rightwards on sloping holds to a ledge then step back left to climb the upper wall.
FA. Chris Craggs 1991

⑤ My Herald of Free Enterprise **E6 6c**
10m. A technical and serious route up the left arete of the wall. Gain it from the right and don't flounder! A dubious Friend 1 may provide a much-needed life-line.
FA. Dave Thomas 1989

⑥ The Hathersage Trip . . . **E4 6a**
10m. Climb the sustained centre of the wall to the left of the crack. Protection is adequate though hard-won.
FA. Bob Berzins (solo) 1982

⑦ Overhanging Crack . . . . **VS 5a**
10m. The wide crack splitting the wall is approached from the left up a thinner fissure. Awkward and strenuous.

⑧ Corner Crack . . . . **VS 4c**
10m. The leaning groove is tricky to enter and then eases.

Below the main face is a slumped slab.

⑨ Seesaw . . . . **VS 4c**
14m. Climb the left arete of the slab starting from a block on the left. The 'seesawing' flake that sits in the break snapped some years ago.

⑩ Margery Daw . . . . **VS 4c**
10m. Climb the scooped centre of the slab and the overlap from a start on the right.

Wharncliffe · Dovestone Tor · Rivelin · Bamford · Stanage · Burbage North · Higgar Tor · Burbage South · Millstone · Lawrencefield · Yarncliffe · Froggatt · Curbar · Gardoms · Birchen · Chatsworth · Cratcliffe

Descent

Paradise Wall 30m

PEGASUS WALL AREA

Probably the most important feature here is the tall block with the desperate *Unfamiliar* up its front face. This was known as Budgie Rock in days of old because of its profile when seen from the north. Of the other routes here *Overhanging Wall* is popular and mild at the grade.

⑪ Crime .... 🔲 **E4 6a**
6m. The north-east arete of the pinnacle is tackled via its shady left-hand side.
FA. Martin Veale 1986

⑫ Punishment .... 🔲 **E5 6b**
8m. The right-hand side is scarier and harder than its twin.
FA. John Allen 1986

⑬ Unfamiliar ..... 🔲 **E8 6c**
10m. A sensational route up the imposing frontal arete of the tower. Can be started direct by a jump or by leaning in from the left from a pile of stones. Gear consists of a Friend 0.5 or small wires in the diagonal crack at two-thirds height.
FA. Robin Barker 1992

⑭ Walking the Whippet .. 🔲 **E3 5b**
8m. The delicate right-hand arete of the valley face is scary and unprotected where it matters.
FA. John Allen 1984

Back up on the main edge things get a little easier.

⑮ Taurus Crack .... 🔲 **VS 4c**
10m. The flake-crack that bounds the left-hand edge of the smooth wall is over far too soon.

⑯ Star Trek .... 🔲 **E6 6b**
10m. The left-hand side of the smooth wall starting from a block. Trend right to the centre of the face, then head up and right to reach a good handhold (small Friend) below the overlap. Finish on slopers.
FA. Graham Parkes 1989

⑰ Klingon .... 🔲 **E6 7a**
10m. A route for the next generation featuring spaced holds and gear. Undercuts in the centre of the smooth wall enable a lunar leap to poor pockets, some gear and an easier finish.
FA. Mike Lea 2000

⑱ Valhalla .... 🔲 **VS 5a**
10m. To the right is a prominent straight crack in a shallow left-facing groove. Gain it from the left via an awkward crack and heathery ledge then jam the short but sweet crack.
FA. Wilf White 1948

⑲ Pegasus Wall .... 🔲 **VS 4c**
12m. To the right thin cracks run slightly leftwards up the wall. Reach these awkwardly then follow them as they kink back right to an awkward finish.

⑳ Pegasus Rib .... 🔲 **E1 5a**
12m. The right-hand arete of the buttress. Climb the flake crack to the arete and finish up this on its left-hand side. Sparsely protected, as the grade suggests.
FA. John Allen early 1970s

㉑ Flake Gully .... 🔲 **Diff**
12m. The gully between the two buttresses can be climbed left or right of the eponymous piece of rock. The left-hand side is easier whereas the right-hand side is more like VDiff.

㉒ Overhanging Wall ...... 🔲 **HVS 5a**
14m. Start below the left side of the overhang which caps the buttress and climb an awkward thin crack to a poor rest at a flake below the roof. Traverse right below the overhang and swing round the arete to finish up the south facing side-wall.
FA. Joe Brown early 1950s

㉓ Crossover .... 🔲 **E2 5c**
14m. Gain and climb the slabby right-hand rib to the roof. Traverse left to reach the flake (last runners here) then swing around the corner and finish up the mildly hairy wall on sloping holds without sneaking off to the left.

Pegasus Wall Area 30m

PARADISE WALL

A cynic might consider this a slightly misleading name but never-the-less it is a worthy and popular venue. Best at the VS/HVS range, with good protection from the cracks and breaks. Add the closeness of *Millsom's Minion* and you have a prime venue.

1 Parasite . . . . **HVS 5a**
12m. Climb the tiny square groove in the arete then step out right and climb the the narrow wall crossing a small overhang.
FA. Chris Craggs 1981

2 Paradise Arete . . . . . . **VS 4c**
14m. Climb the flake crack, that starts from a ledge 2m right of the arete, to its end. Shuffle awkwardly left to a small ledge then climb the arete with a tricky start.

3 Paradise Wall . . . . **VS 4c**
14m. A small piece of paradise. Climb the parallel cracks until they become one, then take the continuation to the top. Well protected and well worth the effort.

4 Milton's Meander . . . . . . **VS 4c**
18m. Devious but still well worthwhile. Climb *Paradise Wall* to just below where the right-hand crack ends, then traverse right all the way to the exposed arete and finish up this.
FA. Alan Clarke 1962

5 Comet **E3 5c**
14m. A rather contrived start (and easily placed side runner) runs up the pocketed wall and leads rapidly to better and easier climbing on the upper wall.
FA. Jonathan Wyatt 1985

6 Comus **E4 6a**
14m. The right-hand line of pockets in the face is bold to start involving fierce fingery climbing. The upper section is a little easier and much safer.
FA. Martin Berzins 1979

7 Paradise Crack . . . . **S 4a**
14m. The holly-shrouded crack in the right-hand edge of the face is approached from the right (ouch) and leads to a wide and tricky finish. Threaded chockstones protect.

8 Sand Gully . . . . **Diff**
10m. The groove to the right of the holly. Start to the left of a flake and climb the groove to a bilberry ledge. Continue using any combination of the diverging cracks.

9 Silica **E2 5c**
12m. To the right is a thin flake in an undercut slab. Gain the slab by using the flake (wires) and then continue precariously up the flake also utilising the right arete. Hard and scary.
FA. John Fleming 1977

10 Sand Crack . . . . **S 4a**
14m. Just to the right is a crack in a corner. Climb this by bridging past a holly bush to finish up a pleasant groove. Despite the name the route is not normally especially sandy.

11 Curved Crack . . . . **HS 4c**
18m. The curving fissure that bounds the left side of the buttress is 'interesting'. The start is awkward but the wide leaning section provides the crux and is best tackled lying on your back! Reckoned by some to be harder than *Billiard Buttress*.

Afternoon
10 min
13
14
Descent
18 19 20
9
16
17
10
11
13
15
12
14
Wall Buttress 80m

MILLSOM'S MINION AREA

A fine companion to Paradise wall. Good for HVS to E3 routes offering hard starts on steep pocketed rock with some bold slabs above. The classic *Millsom's Minion* is the pick of the routes, its one-time reputation for boldness no longer stands.

12 Pot Black **E2 5b**
20m. Start up the leaning pocketed wall just right of the arete to reach a good ledge. Then teeter up the steep slab directly above, using elusive pocket foot-holds, to make an irreversible high step to enter and finish up a shallow groove. Mild at the grade but manages to feel bold
FA. Giles Barker 1976

13 Billiard Buttress ..... **HVS 5a**
20m. A bold line up the left-hand side of the buttress. Start up the leaning wall 3m right of the arete and climb rightwards to a flange. Mantelshelf to reach the deep horizontal break that divides the face. Move left and climb the delicate arete by a hidden flake and then the pleasant slab above.
FA. Al Parker 1959

14 Millsom's Minion **E1 5b**
22m. A great classic that will be ripe for down-grading if the gear gets any better. Start as for *Billiard Buttress* to the break then move right along this for 3m. Step up and right to reach the arete (small Friends out right) then balance up again to reach a large shallow pocket and use this to gain a scoop and easier rock.
FA. Len Millsom 1962

15 Millsom's Minion Direct **E3 5c**
20m. Start under the left-hand edge of the overlap that runs along the right-hand side of the face. Using pockets pull rightwards over this and make bold moves to the horizontal break. Continue straight up the wall into the base of the scoop to reach the point where *Millsom's Minion* comes in from the right. Finish easily.
FA. Steve Bancroft 1988

16 Back in the Y.M.C.A ... **E5 6c**
16m. Start around the arete. Pull over the overlap and climb the desperate pocketed wall to join *Millsom's Minion,* just below its crux, and a relatively easily finish.
FA. Neal Travers 1991

17 Cue .... **HVS 5b**
22m. Awkward but strangely appealing. Thrash up the slanting chimney-groove to reach a trough. Then hand-traverse left below the overhang until a steep pull gains the thin finishing crack.
FA. Bob Brayshaw 1959

18 Pool Cracks .... **Diff**
8m. 12m right of Cue are two cracks. The right-hand one is easier.

19 Between the Two .... **HVS 5b**
8m. Just to the right of *Pool Cracks* above a grassy landing.

20 Pool Wall .... **VS 4c**
8m. The rib on the right with a pocketed start.

WALL BUTTRESS
Namenlos and *Wall Buttress* are popular.
The other climbs here see less traffic.

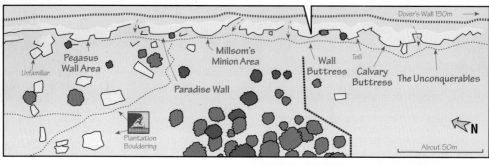

❶ O.D.G's Chimney . . . . [   ] **VDiff**
8m. The rift on the left was missed by the old timers. Enter it awkwardly to reach the top of a flake. Finish up the easy corner behind the chimney.
FA. Dave Gregory 1998

❷ Boys Will Be Boys . . . . [   ] **E6 6c**
10m. The steep blank wall offers a serious outing, following the non-line just left of centre. Unprotected and intense.
FA. John Allen 1986

❸ Capstone Chimney . . . . . . [   ] **S 4c**
10m. The deep dark chimney is steady as far as the boulder that blocks it. The thin will be able to squirm out using the through route, the rest of us face a taxing exit right.

❹ Moribund . . . . [   ] **E3 5c**
10m. Climb past the left-hand edge of the overlap to a break and swing right and make reachy moves past pockets to a second break. One more hard pull gains a flake on the left and easier ground. The route is E4 6a for the short.
FA. Steve Bancroft 1980

❺ Wall Buttress . . . . [   ] **VS 5a**
12m. Either sprint up the right-slanting layback flake then swing right to enter the wide upper crack, or take the jamming crack in the centre of the face to the same place. Continue to an awkward finish or step left for a rather easier exit.
FA. Frank Elliot 1930

❻ Direct Loss . . . . [   ] **E4 6a**
12m. Climb the right-hand crack to its top then the thinner crack-line above, before stepping right to scale the blunt arete (hand-placed blade-peg). Finish over the precarious-looking mushroom block.
FA. John Allen 1986

❼ Improbability Drive . [   ] **E3 6b**
12m. Start in the centre of the wall and climb a short crack and thin flakes to a good break. Use a small pebble to pull up the wall to a break. Finish more easily up right.
FA. John Hart 1978

❽ Namenlos . . . . [   ] **E1 5a**
14m. Delicate and bold. Climb the crack to a ledge then move left and balance up the delicate ramp line (small wires). Finish up the chimney behind the monster perched block. HVS for climbers who can use their feet.
FA. Joe Brown 1950

❶ August Arete . . . . HVS 5b
14m. Climb the crack on the right of the holly then move out right to reach the the arete which is climbed on slopers.
FA. Al Parker 1959

❷ Telli E3 6a
10m. Climb the centre of the bald slab to the break. A crucial mantelshelf leads to a standing position and a final difficult move up the pebbly slab. The right-hand variation is an inferior but easier E2 5c/6a depending on reach.
FA. Steve Bancroft 1978

Opposite is the side wall of the Calvary Buttress.

❸ Traversty . . . . . . HVS 6a
12m. From an embedded block make bouldery moves to flakes and a horizontal crack. Pull up and right to the ledge then climb the final wall trending left.
FA. Al Parker 1959

❹ Rib Chimney . . . . HVD
14m. The dark cleft is climbed by classical back and foot techniques (the nail-scratched holds prove it's a classic) to ledges and the eponymous dividing fin. Finish more easily up its left-hand side.

❺ Calvary E4 6a
18m. A classic gritstone gripper on which the protection is just about adequate. Start up a crack then swing out left and make a fierce mantelshelf move to reach a creaking flake. Up this (good large Friend out left) then move left up a shallow scoop to a ledge (crucial small Friend). Layback up and teeter right, or harder, move right and climb the bulging headwall direct.
FA. Gabe Regan 1976

CALVARY BUTTRESS
A fine buttress with one of grit's classic frighteners in the form of *Calvary*. With modern gear the route should be safe enough though it requires a circumspect approach. If the route is too bland perhaps *Defying Destiny* might be more to your liking.

❻ Defying Destiny . . . E6 6b
18m. A superb taxing line up the centre of the wall. Climb the initial crack then move right and gain the next break with difficulty. Dubious Friends out left protect a pull on some tiny flakes and a sprint for the thin finishing crack. A **Direct Start** is **6b**.
FA. Bill Turner 1982

❼ Dark Reign . . . E5 6b
18m. The right-hand arete of the Calvary Buttress is climbed on its left-hand side throughout. Protection is from especially poor Friend placements and the crucial reach has a potential ground fall. From good gear finish up the rounded final moves.
FA. Mark Turnbull 1999

Descent

Dover's Wall 150m →

Wharncliffe
Dovestone Tor
Rivelin
Bamford
Stanage
Burbage North
Higgar Tor
Burbage South
Millstone
Lawrencefield
Yarncliffe
Froggatt
Curbar
Gardoms
Birchen
Chatsworth
Cratcliffe

8 Chockstone Chimney . . . . . . HVD 4a
18m. The rift that cleaves the centre of the buttress, passing the chock (crux) early on. Safe but distinctly graunchy.

9 Cleft Wall Route 1 . . . . . . HS 4b
14m. Start in the middle of the wall and take the obvious zigzag crack to the wide and awkward final section.

10 Cleft Wall Route 2 . . . . VS 5a
12m. Just right is a continuous crack running the full height of the buttress. It is safe but awkward, especially towards the top.

THE UNCONQUERABLES

11 The Little Unconquerable . . HVS 5a
10m. The left-hand crack is a mild test of fist-jamming proficiency. From the rock platform sprint up the leaning crack, a large Friend protects. Thought by some to be the hardest of the three; it isn't.
FA. Joe Brown 1953

12 The Left Unconquerable . . E1 5b
16m. The leaning crack succumbs to jamming leading to an indifferent rest at the horizontal break. Lace it then make the crucial precarious layback moves up and left to reach a ladder of jugs. A great contender for your first grit E1.
FA. Tom Probert 1949

13 Vanquished E5 6b
14m. The upper wall between the two cracks has a stopper move using a piss-poor pocket.
FA. Tony Ryan 1988

THE UNCONQUERABLES
Home to a trio of classic cracks including T*he Right Unconquerable*, perhaps the most vaunted of all grit-stone outings. Doing all three *Unconquerable* cracks in under an hour is a way of spicing up ascents when you have done them all a few times.

14 The Right Unconquerable . . HVS 5a
16m. One of gritstone's greatest classics, now getting a bit battered. Start up the polished central crack then stride right to the flake. Layback the nose to reach easier climbing and a rest below the final roof. The belly flop direct finish is best, though a traverse left to a short crack is an easier option. A high stepping **Direct Start** is 6a and out of keeping with the rest of the climb.
FA. Joe Brown 1949

15 Monday Blue E2 5b
16m. The right arete of the wall has runners just below the crux, but that is a fair way off the ground. Finish as for *Right Unconquerable*.
FA. Ernie Marshall 1981

16 Curving Chimney . . . . VDiff
16m. A good example of its type. Making upward progress is awkward, slipping back down is easy. The upper section is less of a struggle.

17 Curving Buttress . . E2 5b
14m. From the left-hand end of a ledge climb the blunt rib (micro wires to the left) and make hard moves up and right to a ledge in the middle of the wall. Continue over a bulge. The **Direct Start** is a reachy E1 6a.
FA. Eric Byne 1930s

Afternoon | 20 min

Descent

10

11

Descent

1

2

3 4 5 6 7 8 9 12 13

Unconquearables Area 150m

B.A.W.'s Crawl 30m

DOVER'S WALL and CLEFT WING AREA

The well-fissured Dover's Wall is a popular spot; the last gasp of the superb right-hand side of the cliff. There are a bunch of good cracks here and some more open routes as well as the strange goings on around the *Cleft Wing*.
APPROACH - The buttresses from Dover's Wall rightwards are usually approached from the Hook's Car parking below the Popular End.

1 Newhaven . . . . **Diff**
6m. The pleasant corner at the left-hand side of the wall.

2 Dover's Wall, Route 3 . . . . **VS 4c**
10m. Follow the ramp at the left-hand end of the wall and then the bulging crack to an awkward finish.
FA. Les Gillot, early 1960s

3 Nothing to do with Dover . . . **HVS 5a**
12m. Climb the straightforward crack and then the bulges above. Pleasantly strenuous.
FA. Clive Jones 1978

4 Dover's Wall, Route 2 . . . **HVS 5a**
12m. Climb the thin crack (third from the right) to reach a thrilling finish up the overhanging flakes.

5 Dover's Wall, Route 1 . . . . **HS 4b**
12m. The thin crack (second from the right) leads to a rock spike which is passed awkwardly on the left.
FA. Harry Dover early 1930s

6 Dover's Wall, Route 4 . . . . **VS 4b**
10m. Climb the tricky crack immediately left of the right-hand arete of the wall to an awkward bulge.
FA. Dave Gregory 1970s

7 Wing Buttress Gully . . . . **Diff**
12m. The obvious cleft is kind of compelling.

Just to the right is a buttress with a deep dingy recess formed by a huge leaning flake.

8 On a Wing and Prayer . . **E1 5c**
12m. Start on the left and gain a small ledge 3m up the arete. Continue awkwardly over a nose then climb the side wall immediately left of the roof to finish at a rocking stone.
FA. Graham Parkes 1996

9 Wing Buttress . . . . . . **VS 5b**
14m. Start on the left wall at some polished footholds and make delicate moves to better holds. Swing left along a horizontal break to pass the arete and climb the steep wall and a crack.

10 5.9 Finish **5.10a**
12m. Follow the previous climb but continue to the roof then cross this rightwards via a thin flake to an ungainly exit.
FA. Clive Jones 1977

11 Cleft Wing . . . . **VS 5b**
12m. Start as for the previous route to reach the flake crack that runs up to the overhang. About face, flop across the gap, and swing rapidly round the arete to easy ground.
FA. Joe Brown 1953

12 Cleft Wing Superdirect . . . . **VS 4c**
12m. Climb up into the back of the gloomy recess then hand-traverse the overhanging right-hand wall. Swing round the arete and finish more easily.
FA. Joe Brown 1958

13 Taking a Winger **E2 5c**
12m. The centre of the front face of the Wing on sloping holds.
FA. Graham Parkes 1996

Side tabs: Wharncliffe, Dovestone Tor, Rivelin, Bamford, Stanage, Burbage North, Higgar Tor, Burbage South, Millstone, Lawrencefield, Yarncliffe, Froggatt, Curbar, Gardoms, Birchen, Chatsworth, Cratcliffe

Unconquerables Area 150m

Dover's Wall | Cleft Wing Area | BAW's Crawl Area | Verandah Buttress | Roundabout Buttress | Martello Buttress | Heaven Crack Area | Mississippi Buttress | Balcony Buttress

N — About 50m

BAW'S CRAWL AREA

Although only short the classic routes on *Pedlar's Slab* and the *BAW'S Crawl* buttress make the area worth a visit. The contrast between the two pieces of rock is extreme, one a near holdless slab and the other a huge jutting overhang, select your poison.

⑭ The Punk .... VS 4b
10m. The hanging crack in the north face of the buttress is accessed by a short hand-traverse from the gully. Care with rope-work required.
FA. Steve Bancroft 1973

⑮ Cemetery Waits ... E7 6c
8m. The hanging left arete of the buttress is taxing in the extreme. Only the tall need bother and a substantial spotting team might be a good idea.
FA. Joe Brown (the younger) 1996

⑯ Shine On E7 6c
10m. Direct over the main overhang to the crack of *The Punk*. Cross the roof via a thin flake (small wires) then make difficult moves up using the obvious poor pockets.
FA. Robin Barker 1992

⑰ BAW's Crawl .... HVS 5a
10m. From the boulder below the overhang swing your feet in to the break high on the right then shuffle onto the front face. A couple of moves of proper climbing to get you to the top.
FA. Joe Brown, Nat Allen, Wilf White 1953

⑱ Punklet E1 5c
8m. The centre of the front face of the buttress requires a fierce pull on small holds to reach the break (crux). The finish uses rounded holds, though soloists often sneak off right.
FA. Steve Bancroft 1976

⑲ Pedlar's Rib E1 5c
12m. The smart rib is climbed via a series of small layaways to a horizontal break and good jams. Swing rapidly right to easier ground. Unprotected until after the crux.
FA. Jim Perrin 1967

⑳ Pedlar's Arete .... HVS 5b
10m. Climb the blunt arete using flakes (small wires) to a ledge then traverse right to finish up *Pedlar's Slab*.
FA. Don Morrison et al early 1960s

㉑ Keep Pedalling E2 5c
10m. Climb the blunt rib left of *Pedlar's Slab* directly to the ledge on the arete then finish direct on sloping holds.
FA. Chris Craggs 1991

㉒ Pedlar's Slab .... HVS 5c
10m. A solo problem up the centre of the smooth slab with a technical start (unless you jump). Continue more easily though with care.
FA. Barry Pedlar early 1960s

VERANDAH BUTTRESS

These impressively steep and multiple-stacked overhangs are home to a variety of hard climbs. The original classic of *Guillotine* has now been eclipsed by more modern, more direct, and inevitably harder, offerings. The shorter walls to the right have a nice set of pitches at a markedly lower grade than the front face.

Descent

Descent

BAW's Crawl Area

---

❶ Plastic Dream   E3 6a
14m. The undercut left arete of the buttress is hard to start. The obvious, but risky, technique of an ankle-lock in the first break (ouch) does work but don't fall off. Once established things get easier.
FA. Ed Wood 1977

❷ Headless Chicken   E5 6b
14m. Climb the wall leftwards via a line of small flakes then stretch left to holds below the obvious loose flake. Keep right of this to reach the overhang then step left and pull over with difficulty to the final easy wall.
FA. Neil Foster 1994

❸ Off With His Head   E4 6a
14m. Climb the centre of the face to a tiny ledge. Step left and go up to the lip of the first overhang then trend left past the scarred runner-slot to hard moves over the nose. Another hard move using a prominent pocket, leads through the final roof to a break and an easy finish.
FA. Andy Barker 1982

❹ Guillotine Direct   E4 6b
14m. Start as for *Off With His Head* but at the roof step right and pull through just right of the scar to join the original.
FA. John Allen 1987

❺ The Guillotine   E3 5c
16m. Start up the centre of the lower wall but swing right (poor wires) below the overhangs to a rest on the right. Traverse the narrow hanging wall leftwards (gripping and hard for the long legged) until past the arete. Cross the final overhang using the flake or the horizontal breaks on the left.
FA. Ed Drummond (one big peg 1971). FFA. John Allen 1973

❻ The Old Dragon   E2 5b
14m. Climb the steep shallow groove on the right-hand side of the overhanging face to a good ledge. The holds are better than you might expect. Escape off right or finish up the short overhanging crack just to the left.
FA. Bill Birch (one nut) 1968. FFA. John Allen 1973

❼ Verandah Buttress   S 5b
14m. The sloping shelf of *The Verandah* is gained at its bottom right-hand corner, which usually requires a torrid struggle. The loss of a useful block many years ago may explain the current difficulties. From the scoop traverse left to finish up the exposed arete of the buttress. About 4a after the start.

❽ Butcher Crack   HVS 5b
10m. Start as for *Verandah Buttress* to the shelf then continue direct via a short crack and a final long stretch from an upside-down jam.
FA. Peter Biven 1954

❾ Greengrocer Wall   HVS 5c
10m. The wall the left of the corner cracks has a hard start using a thin diagonal crack. Continue up the wall passing a useful lump to a reachy finish.
FA. Ray Burgess early 1950s

❿ Verandah Cracks   Diff
8m. The twin cracks in the angle are pleasant if short.
FA. Don Morrison et al early 1960s

⓫ Verandah Wall   VS 4c
10m. The centre of the wall to the right of the corner has some rounded holds and is steep.
FA. Don Morrison early 1960s

⓬ Cocktails   VS 4c
8m. From the small overhang trend left though the bulge then finish directly up the rib.
FA. Dave Gregory 1993

Wharncliffe
Dovestone Tor
Rivelin
Bamford
Stanage
Burbage North
Higgar Tor
Burbage South
Millstone
Lawrencefield
Yarncliffe
Froggatt
Curbar
Gardoms
Birchen
Chatsworth
Cratcliffe

⑬ Verandah Pillar . . . . ☼▢ **HS 4b**
8m. Just right, climb the left-facing flakes to an tricky finish.
FA. Dick Brown 1951

⑭ The Confectioner . . . . ▢ **VS 5a**
6m. The rib on the right is approached from the right.

ROUNDABOUT BUTTRESS
This square, jutting buttress has a closely-packed set of routes. Although only short they are all steep enough to be quite memorable and they tend to be less busy than some of the adjacent areas.

⑮ Intermediate Buttress . . . . ☼▢ **VDiff**
10m. Climb up the left-hand edge of the north-facing wall via a series of good breaks.

⑯ The Nose . . . . ②▢ **VS 4b**
12m. Start as for the previous route but hand-traverse out to the right along the lower pair of breaks to reach and climb the mildly-exposed arete.
FA. Joe Brown 1954

⑰ Jaygo's Pipe . . . . ☼◣▢ **VS 4c**
10m. Start under the centre of the north face of the buttress and pull straight through the bulges then climb the face to a rounded exit.
FA. Bruce Goodwin 1994

⑱ Second Wind . . . . . . ☼◣▢ **HVS 5c**
12m. From the centre of the west-facing wall of the buttress hand-traverse left and pull into a short crack with difficulty. Continue up the right-hand side of the arete via a tricky bulge.
FA. Tony Ryan 1986

⑲ Swings . . . . ①▩▢ **E1 5c**
10m. Climb the centre of the buttress on small holds to jugs and runners. Continue up the steep groove and overhang.
FA. Tony Walker 1983

⑳ Turf Crack . . . . ☼▢ **VDiff**
8m. The groove gives a short piece of well-protected bridging and contains not a vestige of grass.
FA. Dick Brown 1951

㉑ Little Tower . . . . ▢ **HS 4b**
8m. Climb the short arete, on its left-hand side, avoiding *Turf Crack*, so that you don't earn two ticks in one go.
FA. Dick Brown 1951

㉒ 49 Bikinis . . . . ☼◪▢ **HVS 5a**
8m. Climb steeply up the centre of the buttress and then pull through the overhangs that cap the wall.
FA. Bill Briggs 1993

Descent

Change in viewing angle

Descent

Verandah Buttress 60m

MARTELLO BUTTRESS

Originally named because of its resemblance to the Martello Towers set up on the south coast back in 1804 as protection against a possible invasion by Napoleon and his army. Unlike those towers, this buttress contains some fine routes with steep starts and rounded finishes.

1 Narrowing Chimney . . . . `S 4a`
8m. The steep chimney on the far left of the buttress that narrows as it rises.

2 Byne's Route . . . . `HS 4b`
14m. Climb into a recess then hand traverse right to a short jamming-crack which is followed as it zigzags to a finish up the wall just left of the arete.
FA. Eric Byne early 1930s

3 Zel . . . . `VS 4c`
12m. Climb *Byne's Route* to the top of the crack then climb the wall leftwards to the arete and follow this on its right-hand side.
FA. Gary Gibson 1979

4 Choux Fleur . . . . `E1 5c`
14m. Struggle around the right-hand edge of the overhang then reach left to a block. Use this to get established on the wall then finish direct by easier climbing.
FA. Brian Rossiter 1992

**5 Another Game
of Bowls Sir Walter?** . . . . `E1 5b`
14m. Climb a short flake just right of the arete to its end then make awkward moves to better holds. Continue steeply keeping right of the arete throughout.
FA. Chris Craggs 1992. The name is a historical blooper confusing the Armada with Napoleon's mob, I was only 200 years out!

6 Martello Buttress . . . . . `VS 4c`
16m. The original route of the buttress has optional starts, both hard. Climb either side of the large jammed block to gain its tip then continue directly for 6m until the small platform on the left can be reached. Move left then finish up the arete.
FA. Fergus Graham 1922

7 The Scoop . . . . `HVS 5b`
16m. Start to the right of *Martello Buttress* where a second jammed block offers a way through the bulges. Move up and left into an open shallow scoop where long reaches and rounded breaks give excellent sustained climbing.
FA. Rodney Wilson 1959

8 Bloodshot . . . . . . `E3 5c`
16m. Start up a leaning groove on the right and move up and left to a small ledge. Step left and climb the overhang on sloping holds linked by long reaches.
FA. Gabriel Regan 1979

9 The Scoop . . . . `VS 4c`
16m. Two routes with the same name, on the same page, strange (but also check out page 113). Climb the steep slanting crack awkwardly almost as far as *Martello Cracks* and then trend back left to climb the left-hand edge of the open scoop.

10 Martello Cracks . . . . `Mod`
10m. The parallel cracks in the slabby angle form a pleasant introduction to grit.

11 Mistella . . . . `VDiff`
12m. Ascend *Martello Cracks* for 3m then traverse right to finish up the middle of the slabby face.

Wharncliffe
Dovestone Tor
Rivelin
Bamford
Stanage
Burbage North
Higgar Tor
Burbage South
Millstone
Lawrencefield
Yarncliffe
Froggatt
Curbar
Gardoms
Birchen
Chatsworth
Cratcliffe

Descent

Mississippi Buttress

Wharncliffe | Dovestone Tor | Rivelin | Bamford | Stanage | Burbage North | Higgar Tor | Burbage South | Millstone | Lawrencefield | Yarncliffe | Froggatt | Curbar | Gardoms | Birchen | Chatsworth | Cratcliffe

HEAVEN CRACK AREA

The big cracks of *Heaven* and *Hell* are the showpiece of this sector although there is plenty of other stuff to keep people busy including the frequently-frustrating *Fading Star*. *Heaven Crack* was once described as having the roughest rock on the cliff, well I am not sure about that, though it is certainly pretty abrasive.

⑫ Phlegethoa **E1 5c**
12m. From below the nose swing right onto the arete and make a tricky move to get established, then continue to the horizontal break and the easy upper arete. A **Direct Start** is a fingery **6a**.
FA. Jim Perrin 1967

⑬ Fading Star **E3 6b**
12m. Start up the centre of the wall to the roof. Move right through this and make a fierce move to reach the next break. The tall will be able to mantelshelf it but shorties may have to resort to pulling on the non-existent pebbles. The tricky and unprotected lower section can be avoided by either of the starts of *Phlegethoa*.
FA. Gary Gibson 1979

⑭ Saliva **E1 5b**
16m. Climb the thin crack on the right then make a committing traverse leftwards until it is possible to climb up and left to finish steeply up the right-hand side of the arete. For those tedious types who insist "it used to be VS" - yes it did and it was two notches under-graded!
FA. Peter Biven 1955

⑮ Ashes **E3 5c**
12m. From the thin crack of *Saliva* continue boldly to a large horizontal break and the first useful runners. Finish up the steep wall above on jams and rounded holds.
FA. John Fleming 1981

⑯ Devil's Chimney .... **Diff**
12m. The dark rift that separate the walls is tackled in traditional style to an awkward narrowing exit.

⑰ Step-ladder Crack ...... **VS 5a**
14m. From a short distance up *Devil's Chimney* pull awkwardly right to gain the crack. Climb this then work up rightwards to finish at the top of *Hell Crack*.
FA. Ted Howard early 1950s

⑱ Step-ladder Crack Direct . **HVS 5c**
12m. Climb directly into the base of the crack with difficulty then finish up the short wall where the regular route scoots off right.

⑲ Hell Crack .... **VS 4b**
14m. The black and bulging jamming crack is taken direct and is superb. The initial overhang is taxing though well protected and will seek out any weakness in your jamming technique. Once established, the rest of the crack is straightforward.

⑳ Still in Limbo **E1 5b**
10m. The groove, overhang and wall somewhere between *Heaven* and *Hell* - hence the name. A rocking block in the first big break is of material assistance, then finish up the wall.
FA. Chris Craggs 1993

㉑ Heaven Crack .... **VDiff**
10m. The flake crack in the left-hand wall of the descent gully is a juggy dream which, like all good dreams, is over far too soon. Layback the flakes to a juggy exit where they end.

Wharncliffe
Dovestone Tor
Rivelin
Bamford
Stanage
Burbage North
Higgar Tor
Burbage South
Millstone
Lawrencefield
Yarncliffe
Froggatt
Curbar
Gardoms
Birchen
Chatsworth
Cratcliffe

Descent down chimney

Heaven Crack Area

MISSISSIPPI BUTTRESS

Possibly the finest buttress on the whole cliff, a great bulwark of gritstone with a superb set of climbs. *Mississippi Buttress Direct* is one of the very best VS routes anywhere on grit and the nearby offerings of *Congo Corner* at HVS and *The Link* at E1 means that these ever-popular grades are well covered. Towards the lower end of the grade spectrum, *Mississippi Chimney* is a good beginner's route and *Amazon Crack* is an excellent Severe.

❶ Acheron **E1 5b**
16m. An exhilarating route taking the left-hand side of *The Louisiana Rib*. A reachy and fierce pull from the horizontal break form the bold crux and makes you realise you are dealing with an E1 that thinks it's an E2.
FA. Jim Perrin 1967

❷ The Louisiana Rib . . . . . . **VS 4c**
18m. A devious and excellent way up the buttress. Climb the crack on the left then traverse to the right arete. Up this awkwardly, just left of the arete for a couple of moves, then move left on to the front face to finish.
FA. Dick Brown 1950

❸ Mississippi Chimney . . . . . **VDiff**
18m. Enter the chimney by a blocky crack. Above this the main fissure is followed more easily. A good beginner's climb.
FA. J.W. Puttrell late 1800s

❹ Dark Continent **E1 5c**
20m. The lowest overhang has a flake crack. Climb through the roof using the crack then follow *Congo Corner* to the end of its initial traverse. The wall above is climbed by a hard semi-mantelshelf (large Friends in the deep horizontal) then move slightly left to finish through the final bulges.
FA. Phil Burke 1978

❺ Congo Corner . . . . **HVS 5b**
24m. Tackle the thin crack to below the overhangs then traverse up and left until a good horizontal break is reached. Move back right and make a tricky move to gain a good ledge. From here a precarious layaway move leads to the beckoning horn and a more delicate finish. A breathtaking pitch of peerless quality.
FA. Peter Biven 1954

❻ The Link **E1 5b**
22m. A very sustained way up the face. Climb *Congo Corner* to where it heads off left then push on through the bulges, on creaky flakes, to where a swing left allows you to join *Congo Corner* again just below its upper crux. Finish up this.
FA. Chris Craggs 1974

❼ Mississippi Buttress Direct . **VS 4c**
22m. The flake line that splits the centre of buttress is one of Stanage's pre-eminent VS routes. Start in a leaning groove and climb this steeply to a bridged rest below bulges. Pass this awkwardly and then follow the fabulous crack above which eases gradually. *2nd 1/11/03*
FA. Roy Horseman 1927

Balcony Buttress

⑧ Mississippi Variant ... HVS 5a
24m. A historical route which has been superseded by the Direct but still gets done since the climbing is so good. Follow *Mississippi Buttress Direct* to below its crux then move right to a right-trending flake. Climb this steeply to an overhang and make difficult moves out right to gain a small ledge and an easier finish diagonally to the right.
FA. Bernard Simonds 1930s

⑨ Mississippi Variant Direct E1 5b
20m. Climb through the overhangs on the right to a ledge then from the left-hand end of this (low runners) step awkwardly up and left (much harder for the short - give yourself an E2 5c) to reach a sloping ledge on the previous route. Finish up this.
FA. Bill Birch 1968

⑩ Stanleyville E4 5c
20m. A harrowing lead up the centre of the smooth wall. Climb the rib to the ledge on the previous climb then make worrying moves to a horizontal break (a very poor Friend 3.5 is the best you can get here). Make a crucial mantelshelf and finish up the final section of *Mississippi Variant*.
FA. John Allen 1973

⑪ Puzzlelock E5 6a
18m. The blunt rib in the centre of the face gives another bold pitch on small holds and with little in the way of useful protection until above the crux. A bit of an eliminate.
FA. Gary Gibson 1981

⑫ Morrison's Redoubt E1 5b
18m. A good route with a bold start. From a block (low Friend) climb the wall using tiny layaways to a good horizontal slot. Continue up a short vertical crack then a wider one, trending right to the top.
FA. Don Morrison early 1960s

⑬ Melancholy Witness E3 5c
18m. An eliminate making the best of the rock on the right-hand side of the wall. Start just right of *Morrison's Redoubt* at a short arete. Climb the left wall of the arete to runners in the slot on *Morrison's Redoubt*. Then move up right on flakes before rejoining *Morrison's Redoubt* to finish.
FA. Gary Gibson 1981   LEAD 11/10/03

⑭ Amazon Crack ...... S 4a
12m. The undercut flaky crack near the right edge of the wide wall is awkward to access because of the overhanging start. Once reached the main crack soon eases to a juggy but steep gambol.

⑮ Fallen Pillar Chimney .... Diff
12m. The narrowing rift in the gully to the right leads to an awkward exit where the slumped tower blocks the way. Bridge past this then exit to the right.

⑯ Fairy Castle Crack ...... VDiff
12m. The angular groove on the right leads past a small overhang and into the continuation groove.

Change in viewing angle

Descent

Descent

Mississippi Buttress

Afternoon | 15 min

BALCONY BUTTRESS

A tall buttress with a heathery ledge at half-height on its front face and a series of cracks in the north-facing side wall. The classic of *Balcony Buttress* always appears to have a team in-situ though there are other routes here worth doing such as *Centre Stage*.

① Fairy Chimney . . . . Diff
12m. The parallel cracks in the groove on the left-hand side of the buttress lead past a block and into a shallow chimney.
FA. Fred Pigott early 1920s

② Balcony Climb . . . . HS 4b
12m. The pleasantly-sustained leaning crack left of the niches in the north-facing wall is followed by sustained and steep jamming.
FA. Fred Pigott early 1920s

③ Balcony Cracks . . . . S 4a
14m. Climb to the upper niche, passing a huge jammed block, then take the left arete until it is possible to pull rightwards over the bulge and finish up exposed flakes in the final wall.

④ Exit Stage Left E1 5b
18m. Start under the left arete of the front face of the buttress and climb the bulges (a leg-lock may help) to ledges. The next set of bulges are quite reachy. Move left finish up the wall around the arete.
FA. Chris Craggs 1993

⑤ Centre Stage . . . . HVS 5a
18m. Start at ledges below the centre of the face and trend left then right through the initial overhangs. Keep left of the wide crack on *Balcony Buttress* then, from the heather ledge, pull strenuously through the centre of the roof to finish at a notch.
FA. Chris Craggs 1993

⑥ Balcony Buttress . . . . S 4a
20m. A great classic with the gloss to prove it. From the flat ledge below the right arete of the face trend left to a wide crack. Climb this to a heathery ledge then move to the left to an awkward flake on the exposed arete. 2nd 1|11|03
FA. Lewis Coxon 1922

⑦ The Flue . . . . HVD
14m. Climb the left-hand of a pair of parallel cracks then the wide left trending rift to a narrow and exposed exit.

⑧ Scoop Crack . . . . HS 4b
14m. Climb the right-hand parallel crack in a shallow groove and then its continuation passing the inverted V-shaped niche with difficulty. Finish more easily.

⑨ Balcony Corner . . . . Diff
14m. Climb the short wall into a left-facing corner with a prominent block overhang. Pass the left-hand side of this to reach easy ground.

TWIN CHIMNEYS BUTTRESS

⑩ Needle Crack . . . . HS 4a
10m. Start from a boulder and trend right to enter a shallow groove which leads to an exit under the Needle.
Nat Allen 1958

⑪ Agony Crack . . . . HVS 4c
12m. Climb the awkward thin crack in the blunt arete to an uncomfortable ledge then attack the continuation crack that splits the overhang by jamming and laybacking. Oh the ecstasy!
FA. Len Chapman 1940

⑫ Thrombosis . . . . VS 4c
12m. Climb the groove on the right to a ledge then the left-hand narrow crack that rises from the ledge.
FA. Don Morrison early 1960s

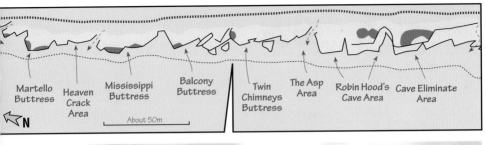

Martello Buttress · Heaven Crack Area · Mississippi Buttress · Balcony Buttress · Twin Chimneys Buttress · The Asp Area · Robin Hood's Cave Area · Cave Eliminate Area

About 50m

N

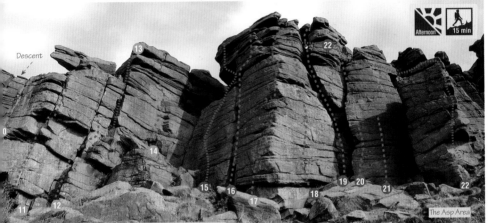

Descent

Afternoon · 15 min

The Asp Area

TWIN CHIMNEYS BUTTRESS

From the thuggery of *Agony Crack* to the delicacy of *Twin Chimneys Buttress*, here is a small section of contrasting routes including some quality low grade routes.

⑬ Rigor Mortis .... VS 4c
14m. Climb *Thrombosis* to the ledge then continue up the right-hand crack with a finish up the arete if required. Not the stiff proposition the name suggests
FA. Don Morrison early 1960s

⑭ Thrombosis .... HS 4b
10m. From the gully climb the shallow groove to a steep but juggy exit via the horizontal breaks.
FA. Don Morrison early 1960s

⑮ Bark Don't Bite E1 5c
14m. Climb the slab to the cave and then the cracks in the roof trending left to a finish up the hanging arete.
FA. Gary Gibson 1980

⑯ Crack and Cave .... VDiff
18m. Climb the boot-width crack to the right-hand edge of the prominent circular cave then move out right to finish up the face in a fine position.
FA. Eric Byne 1950

⑰ Twin Chimneys Buttress .... VS 4c
18m. The rounded arete has a bold start. Make slippery moves to the arete then climb to a detached block. A difficult move gains the upper section which is better protected and easier.
FA. Lewis Coxon 1922

⑱ Lucy's Joy E1 5b
18m. The steep narrowing slab has tricky and poorly protected moves to pass the bulge. Unfortunately it is relatively easy to avoid the crux on its left.

⑲ Left Twin Chimney ...... Mod
14m. The left-hand fork of the prominent Y-shaped chimney system is pleasantly mild. Another good introductory route to this strange game of ours.
FA. J.W.Puttrell late 1800s

⑳ Right Twin Chimney ...... VDiff
14m. Climb the stepped rib just right of the chimney for 5m then the chimney itself. Starting direct is rather easier but a bit of a green grovel.
FA. J.W.Puttrell late 1800s

㉑ Bobsnob E1 5a
10m. The unprotected slab behind the block is climbed delicalty, trending rightwards.
FA. Chris Craggs 1983

㉒ Little John's Step ...... S 4b
25m. A tortuous expedition but with some good climbing. Pull through the initial overhang and climb the outer edge of the block (many finish at this point). Stride across on to the main face and move left and climb just right of *Right Twin Chimney* for a couple of moves then traverse left to finish up the final easy section of *Twin Chimneys Buttress*.

Wharncliffe · Dovestone Tor · Rivelin · Bamford · Stanage · Burbage North · Higgar Tor · Burbage South · Millstone · Lawrencefield · Yarncliffe · Froggatt · Curbar · Gardoms · Birchen · Chatsworth · Cratcliffe

Wharncliffe
Dovestone Tor
Rivelin
Bamford
Stanage
Burbage North
Higgar Tor
Burbage South
Millstone
Lawrencefield
Yarncliffe
Froggatt
Curbar
Gardoms
Birchen
Chatsworth
Cratcliffe

THE ASP AREA

This small area has two major routes: the fierce but well-protected crack of *The Asp* and the bold and airy *Boc No Buttress*. There are several short routes in the bay to the left of *The Asp* which have not been described before. However they follow obvious lines and are all well marked. They were checked in 1993 and are described here in detail for the first time hence the rather modern sounding names.

❶ Awl . . . . S 4a
12m. Climb the delicate left arete of the buttress and then the face on the left of the final nose.

❷ Bean . . . . VS 5a
14m. The narrow slab gives delicate moves just below the ledge that cuts across the buttress. Finish through the overhang at a thin crack.
FA. Bruce Goodwin 1992

❸ Dun . . . . HS 4b
14m. The blunt left arete of the central groove gives good moves. Finish through the overhang as for the last route.
FA. John Street 1992

❹ Bee . . . . VDiff
12m. A mild crack which leads to an even easier groove. A worthwhile beginner's route.

❺ Four . . . . VS 4c
12m. Climb the right-hand face to a ledge. The upper arete is climbed via a couple of small overlaps.
FA. Bruce Goodwin 1992

❻ The Asp E3 6a
12m. A classic finger crack. Gain the base of the crack from the left using a big pocket or (harder) from directly below. Perfect wired runners protect a crucial layback move at two-thirds height. The finishing crack is bold.
FA. Ed Drummond 1975

❼ Boc No Buttress E4 6a
14m. A well-positioned climb that has just about enough protection. Climb *The Asp* to the good runners then hand-traverse (hard for the short) to the arete along a poor set of pockets. Continue up the arete past a solitary good runner (medium wire) slot.
FA. Steve Bancroft 1979

ROBIN HOOD'S CAVE AREA

❽ Wuthering E2 5b
20m. A devious classic with some unique moves. Climb the chimney (a high sling runner is naughty but normal) until it is possible to bridge out along a low line of pockets and bounce onto the left-hand arete. Step onto the front face then traverse left and up to a slot in the centre of the face which takes a selection of small gear. When suitably sorted trend left to a shallow groove just short of the arete. *Photo page 139.*
FA. Ed Drummond 1973

**❾ Robin Hood's
Chockstone Chimney** . . . . . . S 4a
16m. The deep chimney is slick and awkward until the chock-stone is passed. Protection is good throughout and the upper section is much easier.
FA. Fred Pigott et al early 1920s

❿ Withered Thing E2 6a
16m. Climb the centre of the face passing the overlap with considerable difficulty. Side runners protect, pity really, time it was soloed and given a proper grade!
FA. Chris Hamper 1978

Whamcliffe
Dovestone Tor
Rivelin
Bamford
Stanage
Burbage North
Higgar Tor
Burbage South
Millstone
Lawrencefield
Yarncliffe
Froggatt
Curbar
Gardoms
Birchen
Chatsworth
Cratcliffe

ROBIN HOOD'S CAVE AREA

The fabled Robin Hood's Cave is located along a short shelf half way up Robin Hood's Gully. This superb bivvy site has been used by generations of climbers; please respect it if you stop here. Recent complaints from the residents of Hathersage about revellers in the cave keeping them awake at night appear unlikely!

There are many great routes within this arena across the grade spectrum with the combination of *Robin Hood's Cave Innominate and Harding's Super Direct Finish* being the pick of the bunch.

⑪ Paucity .... 🔲🔲🔲 **HVS 5b**
18m. A good varied route. Climb an open groove to the left-hand side of a narrow roof, step left and follow the delicate groove to ledges. Finish up the wall above.
FA. Don Morrison et al early 1960s

⑫ Robin Hood's Crack ..... 🔲🔲 **VDiff**
18m. Climb the crack in the open groove to the overhang then hand-traverse out the right to reach the arete. Climb to a large ledge then ascend the wall left of the cave entrance.
FA. Eric Byne early 1930s

⑬ Tea-leaf Crack .... 🔲🔲 **HVD**
16m. In the left wall of the big gully is a crack with a slot in its left wall. Climb the flake to the ledges by the cave then step left to join and finish as for *Robin Hood's Crack*.
FA. Alpha Club members 1959

The next two routes start near the top of the gully on the right-hand side where a large hole provides a thread runner.

⑭ Last Ice Cream .... 🔲 **E2 5c**
8m. Thread the hole then head out left to climb the short but steep arete that hangs over the gully.
FA. Paul Mitchell 1982

⑮ Just One Cornetto ...... 🔲🔲 **E2 5c**
8m. Thread the hole then pull rightwards onto the wall. Climb it steeply on spaced flat holds.
FA. Chris Craggs 1993

⑯ Cave Gully Wall ..... 🔲🔲🔲 **HVS 5a**
14m. From the boulders climb the tricky slab (small wire to the right) to the left-hand twin cave. Move right and climb the narrow rib between the caves and the steep shallow groove above on good flat holds. The initial slab is often avoided by traversing in from the left above it, passing 'the Bad Step' to reach the right-hand cave.
FA. Alf Bridge 1932

**⑰ Robin Hood's
Cave Innominate** .... 🔲🔲 **VS 4c**
14m. The beckoning crack is reached by a precarious traverse from the left or direct (**5a/b**) by a hard mantelshelf. It provides perfect, though shiny, finger jams and runners, and leads to the *Right Twin Cave*. Move up and right to a good stance on a higher ledge. Escape easily out right across the balcony.
FA. Alf Bridge 1932

⑱ Harding's Super Direct Finish 🔲🔲 **HVS 5a**
6m. From the balcony step left and make a long reach round the roof from undercuts to locate jugs then sprint up the short but highly-exposed final wall.
FA. Peter Harding 1946

**⑲ RH Cave Innominate/
Harding's Finish** .... 🔲🔲 **HVS 5a**
20m. A combo of the previous two routes is one of the best HVS routes on the edge and earns three ticks in one go. Miss out the stance to get the full thrilling effect.

133

Descent (awkward)

Robin Hood's Cave Area

CAVE ELIMINATE AREA

A fine 'blank' wall with a couple of fingery outings on the Desperation wall. The larger buttress to the left has the classic of *Cave Arete* and the excellent *Cave Eliminate*. The short walls to the right have some easier climbs. Further right is the ever-popular *Ellis's Eliminate*, a true test of jamming ability, and the technical *Good Friday* plus the excellent but neglected *Right Twin Crack*.

❶ Carpe Diem **E6 6c**
16m. Climb the middle of the wall to an odd block and continue leftwards to holds under the roof. Reach back right for a pocket on the lip and make desperate moves past the bulge. Finish more easily.
FA. Neil Foster 1994

❷ Cave Eliminate . . . **E2 6a**
16m. A boulder problem start (V3) up a leaning rib leads to a good ledge at 5m (this start can be avoided by a much easier traverse from the left reducing the grade of the route to 5c). Pull through the notch in the overhang with difficulty (useful micro-Friend in a thin pocket) and finish leftwards up the wall on green, sloping holds.
FA. John Allen 1973

❸ Cave Arete . . . . **HVS 5a**
16m. A much-photographed route. The first ledge on the arete is accessed from the right awkwardly then make long reaches (5b for the short) to gain better holds higher up the arete. The upper section is more delicate. Escape off right across the top of the chimney or through the cave system. *Harding's Super Direct Finish* is just to the left and is also worth considering.
FA> Don Morrison early 1960s

❹ Robin Hood's Balcony Cave Direct . . . . **VDiff**
16m. The imposing chimney is climbed on polished holds to reach the balcony (stance). Escape right or, better, finish through the overhang by a couple of weird moves on jugs; Sev 4b.
FA. Fred Pigott et al early 1920s

❺ Broken Arrow **E1 5b**
6m. The wide crack that hangs over the chimney is awkward to access through it eases once past the first overhang.
FA. Graham Parkes 2000

❻ Constipation **E4 6a**
14m. A problem requiring some exertion. Climb the face just right of the arete (poor Friend 1.5) using tiny holds away on the right and a worrying slap for the break. The upper part is easier.
FA. John Allen 1973

❼ Pacific Ocean Wall . . . **E5 6b**
14m. Start as for *Constipation* then move out right and climb the wall by sustained hard moves on tiny holds. Pre-placed side runners in *Desperation* protect all but the final moves.
FA. John Allen 1983

❽ Desperation **E1 5c**
12m. The lower section of the smooth wall is climbed via a problem start on the right (6a for short climbers). Swing left then attain a standing position in the break. The upper section then follows the thin crack and gradually eases.
FA. Bob Brayshaw 1959

❾ Rubber Band . . . . **VS 4b**
20m. Follow *Robin Hood's Staircase* until just below the cliff top then traverse left along the prominent horizontal break on jams to finish up the left-hand arete.
FA. John Allen 1972

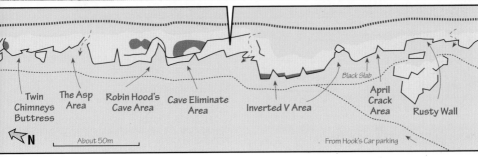

Twin Chimneys Buttress · The Asp Area · Robin Hood's Cave Area · Cave Eliminate Area · Inverted V Area · April Crack Area · Rusty Wall

Black Slab

N · About 50m · From Hook's Car parking

10 Robin Hood's Staircase .... **VDiff**
10m. The weakness running diagonally leftwards up the wall is relatively straightforward but unprotected.

11 Titbit .... **VS 4c**
8m. The crack in the side-wall has solid jams and a gritty exit.
FA. Don Morrison late 1950s

12 Muesli .... **HS 4c**
8m. The blunt arete has an awkward start and then eases.
FA. Bruce Goodwin 1992

13 Cornflakes .... **S 4b**
8m. The face right of the arete starting from the block.

14 Boot Crack .... **VDiff**
8m. A boot-wide crack that splits the centre of the short wall.

15 Soft Shoe .... **HS 4c**
8m. Climb the centre of the wall using a shallow flake crack.
FA. Bruce Goodwin 1992

16 Twin Cracks .... **VDiff**
12m. Climb the right-hand of a pair of crack for 5m then stride left and follow the left twin to a leftwards escape under the great capping slab.

17 Right Twin Crack .... **VS 4c**
12m. Follow the right-hand crack. It gives good finger jamming and all the difficulties are well protected.
FA. Rodney Wilson late 1950s

18 Good Friday .... **HVS 5b**
16m. Start along *Ellis's Eliminate* but make a difficult pull on poor holds and a precarious high step to access the centre of the fine wall.
FA. Pete Green 1977

19 Ellis's Eliminate .... **VS 4c**
20m. A good test of how your jamming is coming on! Traverse the obvious horizontal break on solid lockers out to the nose. Finish up the juggy arete in a dramatic setting.
FA. Gilbert Ellis 1950

Descent
(awkward)

Cave Eliminate Area

INVERTED V AREA

Bishop's Route, *Inverted V* and *Robin Hood's Right-hand Buttress Direct* are a trio of superb outings from the 1920s. The latter two are as popular as any routes on the cliff, whilst the first is a bit of an unsung gem. All the other routes hereabouts are well worth doing, get them checked out.

① Inverted V .... VS 4b
22m. The superb V-shaped cleft. Follow the initial polished crack and deepening groove to a roofed-in recess. Continue up to the overhang (it used to be traditional to take a stance here, in the Birdcage) and traverse right (threads) to finish up the exposed crack that splits the right edge of the roof.
FA. Cyril Ward 1922

② Retroversion ..... HVS 4c
22m. Climb *Inverted V* for 5m then traverse the right wall along the lowest break to the hanging arete. Once back in balance finish up the rounded rib in a fine position.
FA. Don Morrison 1960s

③ Robin Hood's
Right-hand Buttress Direct . HS 4a
22m. A great route tackling the soaring wide crack splitting the centre of the magnificent face. Climb to the large overhang and shuffle out right to reach a small ledge below the main crack. From here route finding is not a problem, although protection can be unless you have a healthy supply of 'big guns'.
FA. Cyril Ward 1922. Also known as 'Button Hook'.

④ Cold Turkey .... HVS 5a
22m. Start up the flake in the left rib of *Straight Crack* then step left on to the fine face and climb it direct. If you fancy a change from *Christmas Crack* on 25th December, how about this one?
FA. John Allen, Christmas Day 1973

⑤ Straight Crack .... VS 4c
20m. The central line of the buttress is excellent. Climb into the wide chimney and, either climb to the roof and shuffle left, or take the flake-crack on the left arete as for *Cold Turkey*. From ledges easier climbing leads past the overhang to the finishing chimney. A few slings for a whole set of threads might be found of use.

⑥ Robin Hood Zigzag ..... S 4a
24m. A wandering outing with a lot of good climbing. Start up the wide chimney then traverse out right to a good stance, and a possible stance. Continue up the crack left of the holly to a ledge and then the wall above this to a niche. Step right for a nicely exposed finish.
FA. Cyril Ward 1922

⑦ Spring into Action .... HVS 5b
22m. Bridge the wide chimney until it is possible to swing out onto the right arete. Continue to the ledge (stance) then climb the centre of the steep wall behind the ledge with a long reach or two.
FA. Graham Parkes 1996

⑧ Bishop's Route .... S 4a
26m. An excellent expedition, unstarred in every previous guidebook! Start at the base of *Zigzag Flake Crack* and climb the leftwards-leaning crack to a good ledge. Continue up the corner crack right of the holly to a higher ledge then make tricky moves to gain the flakes above. Climb these to a horizontal break just below the cliff top and finish direct.
FA. Henry Bishop 1920s

⑨ Zagrete .... VS 4b
20m. Follow the previous climb to the ledge but step out right and climb the well-positioned thin crack near the arete to a fine finish on flutings.
FA. John Loy early 1960s

Descent

Whamcliffe
Dovestone Tor
Rivelin
Bamford
Stanage
Burbage North
Higgar Tor
Burbage South
Millstone
Lawrencefield
Yarncliffe
Froggatt
Curbar
Gardoms
Birchen
Chatsworth
Cratcliffe

10 Zigzag Flake Crack . . . . 🏿🏿 [____] **VS 4b**
20m. The tall (and strangely straight) flake is awkward and not too well protected. Improvise up this to a good ledge on top of the flake and finish up the short wall behind, or step left for more exposure.
FA. Herbert Hartley 1929

11 Coconut Ice . . . . 🏿🏿 [____] **E2 5b**
16m. A route with a good lower section. Climb the wall via couple of long reaches (big Friend to the left) to reach easier terrain. As the wall gets ever narrower escape becomes the best option.
FA. Gary Gibson 1981

12 Ice Boat . . . . 🏿🏿 [____] **E1 5c**
14m. A popular little eliminate. From a short crack climb the fingery wall to the traverse of *The Little Flake Crack*. Continue up the wall above trending slighty right past a couple of long reaches.
FA. John Allen 1983

13 The Little Flake Crack . . 🏿🏿 [____] **VS 5a**
14m. The front face of the huge flake has a smaller hanging flake set in its right-hand side. Reach this from the chimney by a tricky traverse using polished footholds then layback up it rapidly to easy ground. A short wall leads to the cliff top or escape up the groove on the right.
FA. Frank Elliott 1930

14 Flake Chimney . . . . [____] **S 4a**
16m. The chimney in the left-hand side of the bay can be climbed inside or outside of the chockstones. The subterranean route is more secure, but is also very claustrophobic, the outer one is more precarious and probably worth **VS**.

15 Hybrid . . . . 🏿 [____] **E1 5b**
16m. Climb the rounded pillar between the two chimneys at the back of the bay to its top. Then tackle the capping overhang with difficulty using the flake on the right-hand tip of the nose.

16 Pedestal Chimney . . . . 🏿 [____] **Diff**
14m. Climb the slippery groove to the left of the pedestal then follow the deepening gully above to an exit under the huge chockstone.

17 Wright's Route . . . . 🏿 [____] **VS 4c**
16m. The steep groove to the right of the pedestal is bridged and jammed to its top. Step up and make a short exposed hand traverse out right to enter, and finish up, the hanging corner.

18 Wall of Sound . . . 🏿🏿🏿🏿 [____] **E6 6b**
16m. A desperate route up the scooped wall. Climb the thin crack then move right via an enormous reach to a break. Continue slightly rightwards using a pocket to gain the right arete and an easy finish. Poor wires may protect.
FA. John Allen 1983

**19 Whillans' Pendulum
and Black Magic . . . .** 🏿🏿 [____] **HVS 5b**
16m. Start beneath overhangs and monkey rightwards until it is possible to gain a ledge on the front face. Move up awkwardly then step left on to the narrow side face of the slab and ascend this delicately. Large Friends protect the precarious crux moves.
FA. Don Whillans 1958. FA. (BM) Giles Barker 1976

137

Descent --→

Whillan's Pendulum

Rusty Wall

Inverted V Area

APRIL CRACK AREA

About as classic as classic grit gets, with the superb offerings of *April Crack* and the *Trinities*, as well as the excellent *Hargreaves' Original* on the Black Slab. The latter route is the site of the famous leaping exploits of Alf Bridge.

❶ Hargreaves' Original Route .... VS 4c

18m. One of Stanage's finest VS routes. From a boulder pull up and left to the base of the slab then move up and right to a ledge. Continuing up the centre of the slab trending slightly rightwards. Well protected nowadays with a big enough rack of Friends.
FA. Albert Hargreaves 1928

❷ The Flange ..... HVS 5b

16m. Steep pulls gain the prominent niche at 4m (overhead gear but hard work). Continue up the flake of 'the flange' then the steep slab on rounded holds to a final short crack.
FA. Peter Biven 1956

❸ April Crack .... HS 4b

16m. The steep crack in the open corner is awkward to start (easiest on the right) then gives fine sustained bridging and laybacking. Protection is perfect throughout.
FA. Herbert Hartley 1928

❹ Easter Rib E1 5b

16m. Delicate. Climb the shallow groove just to the left of the nose (technical crux) then swing right and up to a deep horizontal break. From good runners teeter up the bold rib to the final juggy arete.
FA. Peter Biven 1956

❺ Christmas Crack .... HS 4a

16m. This long straight crack is a must. Climb a V-shaped groove to the crack and follow it with pleasure. The final leaning corner is awkward and there is also an exposed alternative to the left. This and *Christmas Curry* at Tremadog are the only routes where you will be queuing on December 25th every year.
FA. George Bower 1926

❻ Central Trinity .... VS 4c

16m. To the right is a vertical crack that ends at 6m. Climb this then traverse left to the base of the continuation crack which is entered by a hard move on thin jams. Follow it more easily into a right-facing corner and finish up this. The **Direct Start** is an unprotected **5a** problem.
FA. Herbert Hartley 1929

❼ Meiosis .... HVS 5b

14m. The wall to the right is climbed direct and features some long reaches between rounded breaks. Protection is good if you are carrying a stack of Friends.
FA. Gary Gibson 1978

❽ Right-hand Trinity .... S 4a

14m. Climb the last continuous crack in the wall direct, initially up a shallow right-facing corner. The crack is a good introduction to the art of hand jamming being mild and protectable.
FA. Herbert Hartley 1928

❾ Fergus Graham's Direct HVS 4c

12m. The wall immediately to the right of the crack is climbed direct. The route is effectively unprotected, although it is possible to lean left to place runners, reducing the grade to VS.
FA. Fergus Graham 1920s

Graham Parkes not wobbling on *Wuthering*, E2 5b, Stanage Popular. *Page 132*

RUSTY WALL

The short wall decorated with a selection of blobs is always popular with the bouldering brigade. The cracks here are all well protected and make good introductions to the grade, well apart from *Green Crack* which is plain awkward when dry and unpleasant when wet.

❶ Topaz **E4 6a**
10m. The arete is climbed on its right-hand side by technical laybacking and long reaches, until a grasping exit to the other-side of the arete becomes essential. Swinging around a couple of moves earlier reduces the grade to a more sane **E1 5b**.
FA. Gary Gibson 1979

❷ Green Crack .... **VS 4b**
10m. The square-cut corner is fine when dry though the final narrow chimney is always an awkward grovel.
FA. Herbert Hartley 1928

❸ Rugosity Wall ...... **HVS 5c**
10m. The wall 2m to the right of *Green Crack* has a fingery start leading to easier-angled climbing which has one more tricky pull.
FA. Chuck Cook - in nailed boots! 1949

❹ Rusty Wall .... **HVS 6a**
10m. The wall immediately left of the crack has hard starting moves. Once the first good hold (a 4c hop away for the tall) is reached things ease. The iron holds keep on popping.
FA. Herbert Hartley 1928

❺ Rusty Crack .... **HVS 5c**
10m. The left-hand crack has a hard start using polished footholds and painful finger-jams. Although hard it is also very protectable with small wires.

❻ Via Media .... **VS 4c**
10m. The protectable right-hand crack finishing up the short chimney above.
FA. Ron Townsend 1949

❼ Via Dexter Direct **E2 5c**
10m. The centre of the wall just right is technical and poorly protected. Variations to the right are easier and inferior.
FA. Tony Moulam 1951

❽ Oblique Crack .... **S 4a**
10m. The crack that bounds the right-hand side of the main section of Rusty Wall. The lower section gives good jamming and leads to a loose chockstone. Finish up easier ground.
FA. Herbert Hartley 1928

❾ Straight Chimney .... **VDiff**
10m. The crack widens as it rises and has awkward moves to pass the small overhang.

HOLLYBUSH CRACK AREA

❿ Narrow Buttress .... **VS 4c**
14m. Climb the right arete then move over on to the left-hand edge briefly before traversing back to the right again and climbing directly to a wild juggy finish. It is often started direct via a tricky 5a move.
FA. Ron Townsend 1949

⓫ Hollybush Crack .... **VDiff**
14m. The clean cut corner-crack is steep and excellent. The lower section has some polished footholds but the more imposing upper part is juggy and proves to be impressive at the grade.
FA. George Bower 1926

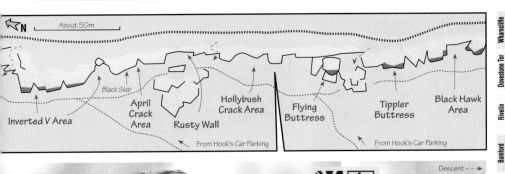

HOLLYBUSH CRACK AREA

Another very popular area with a fine set of climbs including classics at VDiff and HVS and a selection of routes of only a slightly lesser stature.

⑫ Queersville . . . . **HVS 5a**
16m. Start up a projecting flange on the right side of the bay then stretch out left to flat ledges. Climb to a broken flake under the roof and make a long reach to the ledge above. Swing right and climb the easy wall to finish.
FA. Alan Clarke 1965

⑬ The Nose **E3 5c**
14m. A worthwhile but neglected outing. Climb the strenuous bulging arete on small holds to a ledge. Step left and tackle the more precarious upper section via some bold laybacking.
FA. Andy Bailey 1985

⑭ Yosemite Wall **E2 5b**
16m. A varied route. Climb into a small recess then make difficult moves (easier on the left) to the ledge above. Poor runners in the thin crack protect moves on sloping holds up the steep slab just right.
FA. Alan Clarke 1965

⑮ Leaning Buttress Gully . . . . . **VS 4c**
16m. The left-hand crack in the square recess with hard moves to pass the overhang. Above this move right into the next climb to avoid the hanging gardens.
FA. Jim Lomas early 1930s

⑯ Hangover . . . . **VS 4c**
16m. Take the right-hand crack in the recess. Pass the overhang with difficulty then follow easier ground up the continuation groove above.
FA. Bob Brayshaw 1957

⑰ Leaning Buttress Direct . . . **HVS 5b**
16m. The long main face of the buttress is climbed direct with a hard move to leave the ledge at 6m.
FA. Fergus Graham 1922

⑱ Leaning Buttress Indirect . . **VDiff**
16m. A wandering route with an exposed finish. Climb the corner crack to ledges then traverse out on to the front of the buttress and climb its left-hand edge.

⑲ Leaning Buttress Crack . . . **VDiff**
14m. The long groove is followed throughout. It is well protected and very pleasant.

Tippler Buttress

Descent

Hollybush Crack Area

Change in viewing angle

Afternoon | 12 min

FLYING BUTTRESS

One of the most recognisable profiles on gritstone is the steep slab and series of stacked overhangs of *Flying Buttress*; join the queue. *Flying Buttress Direct* launches through the centre of the overhangs and is a real adrenaline trip. Across the descent gully The Grey Wall offers milder though much more serious sport.

① Wedge Rib . . . . VS 5a
14m. The axe-edge rib in the gully has a delightful start (just about worth a star) leading to easier climbing up the broader buttress above.

② Flying Buttress Gully . . . . Diff
14m. The long blocky gully gives a pleasant but neglected low-grade route, also used as away down by the proficient.

③ Flying Buttress . . . . HVD
24m. A classic. Wander up the unprotected 'question-mark' slab to its top left-hand corner. The undercut groove here is tricky to enter and leads to an exposed slab climbed rightwards to a ledge and a finish on jugs. Walk off to the right or finish up the short wall behind.
FA. Fergus Graham 1922

④ Goodbye Toulouse E1 5b
16m. An exciting route across the left-hand side of the big roof. Climb the slab to the curving flake in the overhang then start using fist jams (large Friend protection) before trending to the right to finish just right of the nose on good holds.
FA. Gary Gibson 1978

⑤ Flying Buttress Direct . . E1 5b
16m. Exhilarating climbing on large holds, low in the grade but a real thriller the first time you launch across the roofs. Climb the slab then the centre of the roof, first right then back left with a variety of heel-hooks and a touch of brute force.
FA. Paul Grey 1966

⑥ Kirkus's Corner . . . E1 5b
14m. A good route with a bold finale. Climb the edge of the slab to the right end of the overhangs and pull through these at a short vertical crack (perfect wires). Step left into an open groove and bridge up this to a rounded exit. Perhaps only HVS for those who don't mind exposed padding. *Photo on cover.*
FA. Colin Kirkus 1934

⑦ Jitterbug Buttress . . . . S 4b
12m. In the back of the gully is a narrow buttress. Climb the wall to the capping overhang and then sneak off rightwards below the final overhangs. The direct finish is VS 4c.
FA. Eric Byne 1950

To the right is Avalanche Gully, an easy descent. The right-hand side of this is Grey Wall. All the routes here are poorly protected and as such require a circumspect approach.

⑧ The Kirkus Original . . . VS 4b
12m. Start from a block to the right of the base of the gully. Go up the face to harder moves at half height (holds to the right) which lead to a scary mantelshelf and then easier ground. Unprotected.
FA. Colin Kirkus 1930s

⑨ Jitter Face . . . . HS 4a
14m. Start below the centre of the face and climb until sloping holds lead diagonally right towards the arete. After a couple of moves up traverse back left to join *The Kirkus Original*. Unprotected and above a poor landing; care required.

⑩ Townsend's Variation . . HVS 4c
14m. Take the lowest possible line up the edge of the face on shelving footholds and then move around on to the exposed face where bold moves up the rib reach superb finishing jugs. Easy enough but don't consider falling as it is completely unprotected.
FA. Ron Townsend 1949

Wharncliffe | Dovestone Tor | Rivelin | Bamford | Stanage | Burbage North | Higgar Tor | Burbage South | Millstone | Lawrencefield | Yarncliffe | Froggatt | Curbar | Gardoms | Birchen | Chatsworth | Cratcliffe

TIPPLER BUTTRESS

An impressive buttress which is home to a fine a set of strenuous routes. From the boldness of *Censor*, through the brutality of *The Unprintable* to the daunting roof of *The Dangler* and the surprising technicality of *The Tippler*. The strong and proficient will love the place, the weak and timid will probably walk on by.

At the other extremity of the climbing experience *Castle Chimney* is a great beginner's route.

TIPPLER THREAD - There has sometimes been a thread fixed in the roof of the Tippler. With modern protection this thread is no longer necessary; please don't replace it.

① Censor   **E3 5c**
16m. An intimidating route with fine climbing. From boulders gain the shallow corner (dubious small wires). Climb to the roof, swing right and commit yourself to the bulge making strenuous then delicate moves to stand on the nose. Easier but still-bold climbing remains.
FA. Jim Perrin 1967

② The Unprintable **E1 5b**
14m. Follow the deceptively awkward left-hand crack into a confined recess. The exit from here is difficult and swearing usually helps. Swing into a right-facing layback (knees useful) before sprinting to safety.
FA. Don Whillans 1952

③ The Dangler **E2 5c**
16m. The archetypal roof-crack. Climb the right-hand thin crack into a cave (thread) then head out into space. A long reach gains the break above the lip from where a good flat hold in the first horizontal break above and left of the lip is of assistance.
FA. Joe Brown 1954

④ Tippler Direct **E3 6a**
16m. A excellent piece of roof climbing. Climb through the stacked overhangs to a hanging position where a massive lock-off move or a short leap is needed to reach the break under the final roof. Finish up the crux of the normal route.
FA. Jim Reading 1976

⑤ The Tippler **E1 5b**
18m. A classic route and a tough challenge at the grade! Climb the right-hand edge past a tricky overlap to the big overhang. Traverse left then grope up and left for better-than-expected jams. Make the crux moves (try facing right) to get established on the final wall.
FA. Barry Webb 1964

⑥ Paranoid **E5 6b**
14m. Technical climbing over the right-hand side of the roof. Follow *Tippler Direct* to the roof then move right and make a desperate reach to poor holds. Use these to pull over. Shorties will need to approach the reach from the left.
FA. Johnny Woodward 1981

⑦ The 9 o'clock Watershed   **E6 6c**
14m. Taxing. Climb the side-wall of the Tippler Buttress until it is possible to step onto the arete. An undercut in the roof allows a good hold to be reached, leaving a precarious finale.
FA. Neil Foster 1994

BLACK HAWK AREA

⑧ Castle Chimney . . . . **Mod**
20m. The profound chimney splitting the buttresses is worthwhile but neglected. Enter over blocks and head into the cliff until it is possible to bridge up to daylight at a large platform. Choose a way to the cliff top.
FA. J.W.Puttrell 1904

⑨ Master of Disguise **E6 6c**
14m. A short and thrilling problem. Start left of *Chameleon* and climb the mottled wall until it is possible to traverse out right to below the roof on the regular route. Pull left (RP above) gain the arete with difficulty and finish with a flourish.
FA. Neil Foster 1994

Manchester
Buttress
Area

BLACK HAWK AREA

Possibly the most popular section of the most popular cliff in the country and with good reason. There are classics galore here especially in the lower grades. It is a place you will enjoy and keep returning to. If it is busy consider walking a bit further down the edge to the delights of the Robin Hood and Mississippi areas.

⑩ Chameleon . . . . . . ▨▨▨ [____] **E4 6a**
16m. An intimidating route up the hanging tower. Climb the lower wall to jams below the overhang. Climb this with difficulty (good RP up and left) to reach a right-slanting ramp. Hand-traverse up this to gain the arete and a juggy finale.
FA. Ed Drummond 1975

⑪ Black Hawk Bastion . . . ▨▨ [____] **E2 5c**
16m. The stepped groove is okay up to the big square overhang where committing moves lead left to a wild finish up the hanging left arete of the final groove.
FA. John Allen 1975

⑫ Eliminator . . . . ▨▨ [____] **HVS 5b**
14m. A fine climb up the arete and wall left of the angular corner. The arete is technical in its lower reaches to a short vertical crack. More strenuous climbing leads up the short wall, on spaced holds, to the final shallow groove.
FA. Alan Clarke 1965

L 5/03

⑬ Castle Crack . . . . ▨ [____] **HS 4b**
18m. The slippery right-angled corner is climbed to ledges by laybacking or awkward jamming. Finish direct, or more in keeping, out to the right.
FA. Henry Bishop et al early 1910s

⑭ Black Hawk . . . . ▨▨ [____] **HS 4c**
14m. Climb the crack right of the corner and the overhang to a ledge then step right and follow a shallow crack that leads to a better ledge. Finish up the right-hand crack above.
FA. Eric Byne early 1930s

⑮ Prudence . . . . ▨ [____] **HVS 5b**
16m. A worthwhile direct line. Start in the V-shaped groove and climb this to ledges. Step right and follow the thin crack until just below its top then pull straight up to reach ledges and a finish up the wall.
FA. Chris Craggs 1997

⑯ Black Hawk Traverse Left . . ▨ [____] **VDiff**
18m. An ever-popular outing. Go up the polished groove in the centre of the wall and make the 'Bishop's Stride' move around the bulge to the left. Continue up and then leftwards to a good ledge and possible belay on the Parapet and then choose a suitable finish. *Photo page 87.*
FA. Henry Bishop early 1910s

⑰ Tribute to Joy . . . . . . ▨▨ [____] **E6 6c**
14m. Climb the shallow groove to the break and then access the slab with the greatest of difficulty. Reclimbed after the loss of crucial pebbles; others may since have gone west.
FA. Mike Lea 1985. Reclimbed by Don Honneyman 2000. L 5/03

⑱ Black Hawk Hell Crack . . . . ▨ [____] **S 4a**
14m. The long crack in the right side of the wall is climbed direct. It is steep, juggy and well protected using slings.
FA. Eric Byne early 1930s

⑲ Black Hawk Traverse Right . ▨ [____] **Diff**
16m. Start to the left of the prominent chimney and follow scratched footholds rightwards to a crack and climb this to bulges. Step right and climb the main fissure to the capping overhang and escape out the left.
FA. Henry Bishop early 1910s. Also known for a time as Blizzard Chimney.

⑲ Gargoyle Variant . . . . ▨ [____] **HS 4b**
14m. Start under the hanging left arete of the buttress and climb the awkward wide crack to the overhangs. Traverse out to the right to below the large loose block, gain this carefully and finish more easily trending rightwards up the face.

Wharncliffe · Dovestone Tor · Rivelin · Bamford · Stanage · Burbage North · Higgar Tor · Burbage South · Millstone · Lawrencefield · Yarncliffe · Froggatt · Curbar · Gardoms · Birchen · Chatsworth · Cratcliffe

Descent behind chockstone

Black Hawk Area

Afternoon 10 min

MANCHESTER BUTTRESS AREA

The eponymous Mancunian classic is well worth doing, as is *Gargoyle Buttress*. Despite their popularity the trio of routes in the back of the bay are less worthwhile, although they are definitely better led than top-roped.

① Gargoyle Buttress . . . . VS 4b
14m. Start at the right toe of the buttress and after a couple of moves follow a horizontal traverse crack out to the left. Pull up on the suspect perched 'boulder' with care then finish up the centre of the wall above trending slightly rightwards. *Photo page 143.*
FA. Ron Townsend 1949

② Physiology . . . . VDiff
12m. The left-hand crack is arguably the best of the trio leading steeply to an easy finishing groove.

③ Sociology . . . . S 4a
The centre of the narrow face is best climbed direct to a finish up an easy groove. Rather escapable.

④ Anatomy . . . . VDiff
12m. The right-hand corner is climbed to a move left at the awkward overhang and a finish up the continuation corner. The obvious **Direct Finish** is *Anotherology* - **S 4a**.
FA. (Anotherology) Dave Gregory 2000

⑤ Tinker's Crack . . . . VS 4c
12m. The narrow wall to the right is split vertically in its upper part by a thin crack. Pull over a bulge to gain the crack and follow it to tricky moves where it disappears.
FA. Don Morrison et al early 1960s

⑥ Beggar's Crack . . . . VS 4c
12m. The wider crack to the right starts off easily but has awkward moves to pass the small overlap before easing again.

⑦ Manchester Buttress . . . . HS 4b
16m. Start up the crack in the arete then move left to bypass the first overhang. Move up to a deep break then make an awkward traverse back to the right (fist jams) to get established on a ledge round the corner. Finish direct. A good route to practise your double rope technique on.
FA. Maurice Linnel early 1930s

GROTTO SLAB AREA

⑧ Cakestand . . . . S 4b
8m. The narrow pillar on the right-hand side of the bay is followed throughout with a couple of long reaches. The final tricky nose is easily avoidable.

⑨ Cool Groove . . . . S 4a
10m. The open groove steepens as it rises giving steady bridging to a tricky exit.

⑩ Lancashire Wall . . . . HVS 5a
12m. The centre of the wall has a delicate start from a block and a fine finish up the leaning front face of the final block.
FA. Dave Kenyon late 1970s. A Lancashire raider.

⑪ Crack and Corner . . . . HVD 4b
16m. Set in the arete in an attractive groove. Enter this using an unhelpful set of polished holds; frequently frustrating! Continue up the excellent groove to a good ledge below an overhanging block. Overcome this at its left-hand corner by a short struggle.

Along right margin (top to bottom): Wharncliffe · Dovestone Tor · Rivelin · Bamford · Stanage · Burbage North · Higgar Tor · Burbage South · Millstone · Lawrencefield · Yarncliffe · Froggatt · Curbar · Gardoms · Birchen · Chatsworth · Cratcliffe

⑫ Heather Wall . . . . 🔢🔣 ▭ **VS 4c**

14m. The excellent steep face is climbed using cracks to reach a deeper vertical crack. Difficult moves gain a ledge then a right-trending scoop. From the large ledge above finish up the easy corner on the right. The right-hand start is a worthwhile 5a.

⑬ Chimp's Corner . . . . 🔣 ▭ **VS 5a**

12m. An odd route with some entertaining moves. Monkey up the steep blocky corner to its top then trend left up the wall to below the final large roof. Cross this using a superb curly jug to a belly-flop landing.

⑭ Grotto Slab . . . . 🔣 ▭ **Diff**

12m. Much used as a descent route but also a pleasant beginners' route. Start at the toe of the slab and ascend to its tip. A couple of awkward short corners complete the route. A longer and easier version can be made by taking the lower slab on its right.
FA. Henry Bishop et al early 1910s

⑮ Grotto Wall . . . . . 🔣🔣🔣 ▭ **HVS 4c**

12m. Start right of the slumped flake in an unsavoury pit and gain the shallow left-facing groove which is climbed to an awkward exit. Continue up the final wall trending rightwards on better holds.

GROTTO SLAB AREA

Crack and Corner and *Heather Wall* are the big ticks here. They are so popular that usually you will have to join the queue. *Grotto Slab* is an excellent beginner's climb.

⑯ Green Wall . . . . ▭ **VS 4b**

10m. The crack in the wall just left of the narrow chimney is okay when not the colour the name suggests.

⑰ Capstone Chimney . . . . . 🔣 ▭ **Diff**

8m. The shallow open chimney is most easily climbed up its left-hand corner to a steep exit.

⑱ Little Ernie . . . . ▭ **S 4a**

8m. Start on the left and trend right across the buttress via ledges to reach easy ground.

⑲ Big Chris . . . . ▭ **HVS 5a**

8m. The centre of the face starting down and right is followed via a thin crack to a tricky finale using the bottom-like fissure.
FA. Chris Craggs 1993

147

Afternoon | 10 min

Descent - - - →

Grotto Slab Area

RUGOSITY CRACK AREA

With the exception of the excellent *Rugosity Crack*, this section has less to offer than its near neighbours. However its location at this end of the crag will ensure its popularity.

❶ In Earnest . . . . 　　HVS 5a
10m. The pleasant arete of the bay by laybacking.
FA. Chris Craggs 1993

❷ Recess Wall . . . . 　　HVD
10m. The left slanting groove in the recess using some well polished holds and side-stepping a bevy of bulges.

❸ Right Wall Route . . . . 　　HVD
10m. Start as for the previous climb but follow the right-trending flakes to a crack that splits the right-hand edge of the capping overhang.

❹ Randolf Cheerleader . . . 　　E3 6a
10m. Climb a blunt rib then make thin fingery moves up and left to a short crack which is much easier.
FA. Mark Stokes 1983

❺ Gullible's Travels . . 　　E1 5b
10m. From the centre of the wall trend right delicately with hard moves to reach the incipient crack and then easier ground. Good climbing protected by small Friends.
FA. Brian Pallet 1963

❻ The 3-D Wall . . . . 　　E2 6a
8m. The wall to the left of the black chimney has good moves (long reaches) though the option of rightward escape rather spoils the overall impression.
FA. Gary Gibson 1979

❼ Black Chimney . . . . 　　Mod
8m. The dark rift behind the tower is a good introduction to that kind of thing as long as you aren't claustrophobic.

❽ South Sea Charmer . . . . 　　HVS 5b
10m. Start up *Rugosity Crack* but step out on to the hanging left arete at the earliest opportunity and finish up this.
FA. Paul Williams 1978

❾ Rugosity Crack . . . . . 　　HVS 5b
10m. The prominent thin crack which splits the narrow tower to the left is a little gem. It would get three stars were it on a lesser crag! Climb to a ledge then finger-jam the central section to a steep finish on flat holds.
FA. Pat Fearnehough early 1960s

❿ Niche Wall Direct . . . . . . 　　HS 4b
10m. Pleasant and well-protected. Climb the awkward chimney crack to the niche then take the steep continuation finger crack above.

⓫ Nicheless Climb . . . . 　　S 4a
10m. Mantelshelf onto a flat ledge then climb the awkward wide crack above.

MANTELPIECE BUTTRESS AREA

⓬ Hoaxer's Crack . . . . 　　HS 4b
8m. The thin and fingery crack just right of the chimney.

⓭ Trivial Pursuit . . . . 　　VS 5a
8m. Climb the wall passing a suspect flake to a steep finish.

Descent (awkward)

Wharncliffe Dov

Rivelin

Bamford

Stanage

Burbage North

Higgar Tor

Burbage South

Millstone

Lawrencefield

Yarncliffe

Froggatt

Curbar

Gardoms

Birchen

Chatsworth

Cratcliffe

MANTELPIECE BUTTRESS AREA
This area is almost always busy with top-ropers and groups because of the fine set of low grade routes. In amongst the easy fare are several fine little roof problems which are often soloed.

Afternoon 10 min

14 Small Crack .... **VDiff**
8m. The thin crack has some solid jams and some slippery footholds but isn't smaller than its neighbours. *Photo page 29.*

15 Ground Glass .... **VS 4c**
8m. A shallow groove is climbed to the tricky wall above.

16 Plate Glass .... **VS 4b**
8m. The polished footholds in the centre of the slab lead to easier climbing. Harder for the short.

17 Carborundum .... **VS 5a**
8m. The right-hand side of the slab has a couple of long reaches and is much less polished than the other routes here.
FA. Chris Craggs 1993

18 Mantelpiece Crack .... **Diff 4a**
8m. The right-slanting crack is very nice.

19 Mantelpiece Buttress ..... **Diff**
8m. The left-slanting groove is reached from the right though a more **Direct Start** is possible (**4b**) if you are feeling technical.

20 Mantelpiece Buttress Direct **HVS 5b**
8m. The crack in the overhang gives a short tussle.

21 Fragile Mantel .... **VS 5a**
8m. Climb past the right-hand edge of the narrow overhang by a long reach for the ledge. Finish easily.
FA. Chris Craggs 1993

22 Mantelpiece Right .... **HVD**
8m. The shallow groove in the right edge of the wall.

23 Zip Crack .... **Mod**
6m. The short V-groove.

24 Monkey Crack .... **VD 4a**
6m. The steep crack on the left-hand side of *Square Buttress.*

Descent - - - →

25 Square Buttress Direct ...... **VS 5a**
6m. The steep front face.

26 Square Buttress Arete ...... **VS 4c**
6m. The right-hand arete on its right-hand side.

27 Square Buttress Wall ...... **VS 4b**
6m. The right wall of the buttress.

28 Gashed Crack .... **VS 5a**
6m. The awkward undercut crack in the last buttress.

29 Suzanne **E1 6a**
8m. A classic problem up the centre of the last buttress. Reaching the large break above the overhang often involves a lurch. Continue up sloping rock.
FA. Reg Addey 1965

30 Finale .... **HVS 6a**
8m. The right-hand arete is gained with difficulty.

APPARENT NORTH BUTTRESS

A steep buttress seamed by diagonal cracks and home to the biggest concentration of hard routes on the cliff. Fortunately the recent new routers didn't follow on from Len Millsom's idea and create finishing holds, so several of the climbs have desperate final sequences. Exquisite!
APPROACH - Park on the road leading down to Hook's Car parking. A track leads across to the prominent buttress.

① Apparent North . . . . **HVS 5b**
10m. On the far left a short steep crack can be reached from a boulder. Follow this to jams below the roof before moving round onto the front face. The expected desperate finish is made much easier using a couple of ancient well-chipped holds.
FA. Len Millsom early 1960s

② Skinless Wonder **E6 6c**
10m. An extended boulder problem which is V8 above a pile of mats. Start up a small hanging arete at the left-hand edge of the face and make a hard move on undercuts to reach the break of _Apparent North_. Finish rightwards.
FA. Richie Patterson 1993

③ Stanage Without Oxygen **E5 6c**
10m. The easiest 'hard' route on this buttress, predating the other desperates by 10 years; it will still leave you winded. Climb the left-hand side of the front face of the buttress aiming for the right edge of the capping roof, to a finish up the chipped holds of _Apparent North_. Significantly easier in cool conditions.
FA. John Allen 1983

④ Little Women **E7 7a**
10m. A high-quality modern desperate. Gain the obvious shelf, place Friend runners in the highest horizontal break, then head up and rightwards using a series of poor holds linked by hard moves to reach a typically sloping finish.
FA. John Welford 1997

⑤ Groove is in the Heart **E7 7a**
8m. A series of technical and fingery moves through the stacked overlaps in the scoop to yet another rounded finish. Only led with pre-placed RPs to-date.
FA. Neil Bentley 1998

⑥ Black Car Burning **E7 6c**
8m. Another arduous climb up the vertical face on the right. Start under the shallow feature that is _Groove is in the Heart_ and trend right to poor holds under the roof. Make a hard move to a good hold on the lip and finish rapidly with a series of long reaches. _Photo page 89_.
FA. Robin Barker 1993

⑦ True North . . . . **VS 4c**
8m. From the large boulder jammed in the gully, climb the right-hand side of the blunt arete on the left, finishing up a short wall by a long reach.
FA. Len Millsom early 1960s

⑧ Mating Toads . . . . **5c (V2)**
The rib is a delightful little problem. Try it with and without the right-hand arete for maximum enjoyment.

⑨ Hamper's Hang . . . . **6b (V6)**
A superb traverse starting at the back of the cut-away on the left and following the break and sloping ledge rightwards. Curiously it is only V5 in reverse.
FA. Chris Hamper 1980s

BOULDERING - This is one of the more popular bouldering locations on Stanage. There are plenty of problems on to the left (looking in) of Apparent North Buttress, and all the way around to, and including, the Cowper Stone. However the main reason people come here to boulder is to do _Hamper's Hang_.

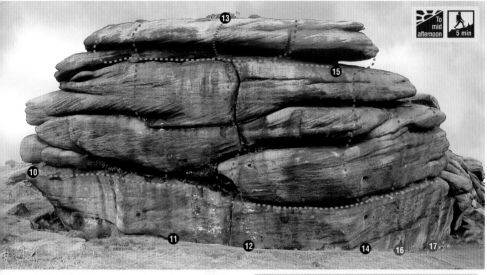

To mid afternoon — 5 min

Wherncliffe
Dovestone Tor
Rivelin
Bamford
Stanage
Burbage North
Higgar Tor
Burbage South
Millstone
Lawrencefield
Yarncliffe
Froggatt
Curbar
Gardoms
Birchen
Chatsworth
Cratcliffe

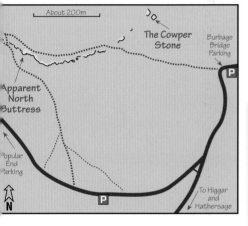

About 200m

The Cowper Stone

Burbage Bridge Parking

Apparent North Buttress

Popular End Parking

To Higgar and Hathersage

N

THE COWPER STONE

This isolated block of rock presents Stanage's last gasp, and what a tough task master it is. There is only a small collection of routes on this glorified boulder, but they include the worst set of holds, and biggest collection of rounded breaks anywhere in the Peak. Climbers unused to gritstone might wonder at the grades of some of the routes.
APPROACH - The best direct approach is from the parking at Burbage Bridge along a well-travelled path.

13 Warmlove **E6 7a**
8m. The direct finish to *Snug as a Thug on a Jug* involves an extraordinary reach for a useful pebble (no long reach symbol; look at the first ascensionist). Once you have got the pebble make a desperate grovelling exit. As hard as they come!
FA. Johnny Dawes 1995

14 Breakdance **E4 6b**
8m. The bulging right-hand arete of the leaning front face of the buttress. Wild and weird contortions can be used but they aren't strictly necessary. The finish is rounded in the extreme.
FA. Johnny Dawes 1985

15 Traverse of the Gritstone Gods **E4 6b**
14m. A superb and arduous right-to-left traverse of the buttress starting up *Breakdance* and finishing on the left arete. Follow the highest horizontal break throughout by using a series of sloping holds, flared jams and backbreaking contortions.
FA. Johnny Dawes, John Allen, Mark Stokes 1986

16 Leyroy Slips a Disc . . . **6c (V9)**
Poor holds up the right-hand wall.
FA. John Allen 1986

17 Head Spin . . . . **6a (V3)**
The right-hand side of the wall on rounded holds to a finish using a crusty flake.
FA. Mark Stokes 1986

10 Zippy's Traverse . . . **6c (V9)**
The lowest break gives an arduous outing. Sustained, technical and horribly rounded. Fortunately the ground is never very far away. Just the right-hand side wall is **V6**.
FA. Zippy (Mark Pretty) 1985

11 Sad Amongst Friends **E7 6c**
8m. Climb the impossible-looking central section of the face to a finish using a red 'wart' on the lip of the final overhang. The lower section is bold and easier for the short. The finish is well protected and quite bizarre.
FA. Johnny Dawes (solo!) 1984

12 Snug as a Thug on a Jug **E4 6b**
8m. Start up the flared crack in the right-hand side of the face and follow this to flutings on its left. Move right to a short flared corner and an elephant's arse finish.
FA. Paul Mitchell 1983

BURBAGE NORTH

Burbage North is one of the favourite locations of many climbers. Unlike its dark counterpart to the south, or the intimidating bulk of Higgar to the west, its reputation is one of friendly routes in a picturesque setting. Fine summer evenings will see the place swarming with enthusiastic locals grabbing a quick route or two, or doing a spot of bouldering before the sun goes down. Its proximity to the road, and plentiful short and amenably-graded routes, means that it is also popular with outdoor centres although they tend to focus their activity on the initial sections and a short 3 minute extension to your approach walk will significantly reduce the crowds.

As a crag it has less to offer in the mega-classic category, compared to it near-neighbours, however there is hardly a bad route on the edge and certainly all of the ones described here are worth doing. The rock is much the same quality as on the other edges but overall the crag is on a smaller scale. Often you will only have time to place a couple of runners before the top is reached, which is why the place is so popular with boulderers and soloists.

BOULDERING - The main edge is extremely popular with boulderers and these areas are briefly described in the following pages. Two other areas of interest are the Burbage Bridge boulders (directly below the man-made tower by the parking spot) and Burbage West which is the area of edge opposite the parking.

APPROACH (SK264826)

Burbage Bridge, at the north end of Burbage Valley, has two parking areas which usually have enough spaces for all visitors. However on busy weekends you may struggle to find a spot. Either wait for someone to leave or park up at Higgar Tor and walk back across (10 mins). From the parking by the Bridge, there are three paths. The main path (the Green Drive) goes down the side of the valley, a small path breaks left from this and heads along the base of the edge. There is also a crag-top path which is useful for reaching the far areas.

CONDITIONS

The edge faces south west and catches the sun from the mid-morning onwards. This means it can get very hot in summer. It is exposed to any bad weather but dries very quickly after rain although a few routes can be a bit sandy.

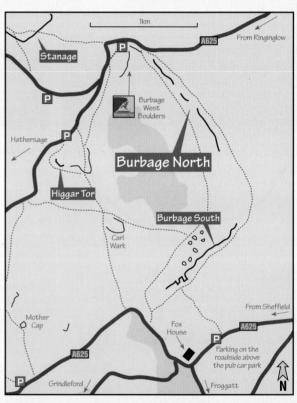

OTHER GUIDEBOOKS - A more complete list of routes at Burbage North is published in the 1991 BMC *Froggatt* guide. The bouldering is in the 1998 Peak Bouldering ROCKFAX.

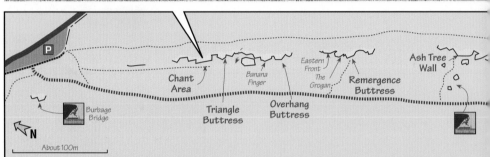

Whamcliffe · Dovestone Tor · Rivelin · Bamford · Stanage · Burbage North · Higgar Tor · Burbage South · Millstone · Lawrencefield · Yarncliffe · Froggatt · Curbar · Gardoms · Birchen · Chatsworth · Cratcliffe

THE CHANT

The first section of Burbage offers plenty of bouldering and short routes which are always immensely popular This is partly because of their accessibility and partly because of their quality. *The Chant* is a great first HVS and the whole area is ideal for getting the feel of the rock.

❶ Route 1 . . . . **S 4b**
6m. The left arete of the wall is a good 'starter for ten'.

❷ Route 1.5 . . . . **VS 5b**
6m. The wall just right of the arete has hard initial moves.

❸ Route 2 . . . . **S 4a**
6m. Climb the steep wall and crack, 3m right of the arete, using ancient chipped holds to start.

❹ Route 1.5 . . . . **VS 5a**
6m. A fingery little number between the cracks.
FA. Jim Rubery 1991

❺ Route 3 . . . . **VD 4a**
6m. The zig-zag crack in the centre of the wall has a slippery start and is juggy above.

❻ Route 4 . . . . **VS 5b**
6m. Just left of the arete is a thin wall which eases with height.

Past a gap of 5m of easy rock is another fine but short wall.

❼ Cranberry Crack . . . . **VDiff**
6m. The gradually-widening and left-slanting crack.
FA. Albert Shutt 1951

❽ The Chant . . . . **HVS 5a**
6m. The centre of the wall leads to tricky right-facing mantelshelf. Once wired it is a candidate for your first HVS solo.
FA. Alan Clarke late 1950s

❾ 20 Foot Crack . . . . . . **S 4b**
6.15m. Thin jams and slippery footholds always make this one feel harder than it should.

❿ The Curse . . . . . . **VS 5b**
8m. A fine boulder-problem start requiring some crimping for success. It can be particularly aptly named for the short.
Photo page 153.

⓫ Lost in France . . . . **VS 5c**
8m. Another technical start on tiny holds but it eases rapidly after the first couple of pulls.

Wharncliffe
Dovestone Tor
Rivelin
Bamford
Stanage
Burbage North
Higgar Tor
Burbage South
Millstone
Lawrencefield
Yarncliffe
Froggatt
Curbar
Gardoms
Birchen
Chatsworth
Cratcliffe

TRIANGLE BUTTRESS

The second section of the edge has a fair selection of lower-grade climbs and more good bouldering including a fine low-level traverse. The lower section of the wall of *Little White Jug* often seeps after rain.

⑫ Little Plumb . . . . **Diff**
8m. A straightforward blocky crack on the left offers a worthy introductory climb.

⑬ Base Over Apex . . . . **VS 4c**
8m. The wall right of the crack has one long reach. Finish up the short, hanging groove.
FA. Chris Craggs 1991

⑭ Baseless . . . . **VDiff**
8m. The straight crack immediately to the left of the nose of the buttress steepens towards the top.

⑮ Triangle Buttress Arete . . **VDiff**
8m. Climb the arete with tricky moves onto a sloping shelf early on and then easier but still-pleasant climbing above.
FA. Eric Byne 1932

BOULDERING - Most of the routes on this section make good entertainment for confident boulderers. For those after more technical fayre try some of the many eliminates around the start of *The Curse*, or the small roof 5m left of *Route 1*.

⑯ Triangle Buttress Direct . . . **S 4a**
8m. The wall just right of the arete is steep and juggy and has a couple of long reaches early on. A problem start just right is 5a/b with tricky moves to reach and pass the small overhang.

⑰ Triangle Crack . . . . **HVD**
8m. The awkward, narrowing corner crack can be a struggle although at least the protection is good. A good place to learn to bridge.

⑱ Leaning Wall Direct . . . **VS 5a**
8m. Fingery (and often wet) moves on small sharp holds lead up the wall just right into the base of the much easier upper crack. Many variations exist.
FA. Ron Townsend 1957

⑲ Little White Jug . . . . . . **VS 4c**
8m. The leaning and juggy wall to the right of the crack leads steeply to a grovelling mantelshelf exit on jams under a conveniently-placed block or a crumbling little edge.
FA. Andy Hall 1977

⑳ Big Black 'un . . . . **HVS 5a**
10m. Climb the juggy wall just right via series of bulges to another mantelshelf exit.

㉑ Leaning Wall . . . . **S 4a**
10m. The hanging crack in the centre of the wall is most easily approached by an awkward traverse from the easy ground on the the right.

㉒ Steptoe . . . . **Mod**
8m. Easy cracks and blocks on the right-hand side of the wall give another pleasant beginner's outing.

From mid morning | 3 min

Overhang Buttress

Descent

BANANA FINGER

This legendary buttress of tiered overhangs is home to the classic *Banana Finger* boulder problem and all its derivatives. Ropes are rarely used here.

Once you have climbed all the *Banana Finger* variations, sit yourself down in the cave to the left and climb out. Turning the lip is interesting!

① Monkey Corner . . . . **VDiff**
8m. Climb the steep and juggy groove on the left of the buttress. Swing right at the bulge to easier ground.

② Banana Finger . . . . **6a (V3)**
8m. A classic boulder problem. From the centre of the buttress finger-traverse left and cross the overlaps (knees help) to easy ground. The **Direct Start** is 6b (V5). A knee-bar is of some help so avoid wearing shorts. Also remember to squeaky clean your right boot otherwise you may end up shinning yourself.
FA. Ed Drummond 1971

③ Monkey Wall . . . . **Mod**
8m. The centre of the face trending left is about as mild as they come. If you find this one scary, you are in the wrong game.

④ Monk On . . . . **HVS 5b**
8m. Sadly the overhang on the right can be outflanked by keeping left, although that is cheating.
FA. Steve Bancroft 1981

To the right is a big roof split by a fierce-looking crack.

⑤ Ad Infinitum . . . . **S 4a**
14m. A well-positioned left-to-right girdle following the obvious line above the roofs and finishing up the far arete.

⑥ Wednesday Climb . . . . **HVS 5b**
8m. The roof crack is a struggle any day of the week and is easiest if you stay away from the crack as much as possible.
FA. Pat Fearneough early 1960s

⑦ Overhanging Buttress Direct **S 4a**
10m. Use shiny holds to climb to the roof, step right to pass this and finish more easily up the fine slab.

⑧ Overhanging Buttress Arete . **Mod**
8m. The juggy arete often has top ropers in situ.

⑨ Burgess Buttress . . . . **Mod**
6m. Across the gully is another popular beginner's climb.

OVERHANGING BUTTRESS

A popular buttress with the top-rope brigade, although *Wednesday Climb* doesn't appear to interest them as much as the other routes here. *Ad Infinitum* is a nicely exposed traverse that sees little traffic.

Descent

Eastern Front 50m

Descent

From mid morning | 3 min

Whamcliffe | Dovestone Tor | Rivelin | Bamford | Stanage | Burbage North | Higgar Tor | Burbage South | Millstone | Lawrencefield | Yarncliffe | Froggatt | Curbar | Gardoms | Birchen | Chatsworth | Cratcliffe

Wharncliffe
Dovestone Tor
Rivelin
Bamford
Stanage
Burbage North
Higgar Tor
Burbage South
Millstone
Lawrencefield
Yarncliffe
Froggatt
Curbar
Gardoms
Birchen
Chatsworth
Cratcliffe

Grogan 20m

EASTERN FRONT
Up and left from *Remergence* is a short wall split centrally by a crack and home to four worthwhile micro-routes.

**1 All Quiet on the
Eastern Front** E1 6a
6m. Gain the left arete by a cross-hands traverse from the left and then climb it rapidly. The **Direct Start** is a desperate V8 (6c) problem that sees many attempts and few successes.
FA. Ed Drummond 1978

2 The Busker .... VS 4c
6m. The steep slab on the right gets a bit close to the crack for real purity of line though it has some good moves.
FA. Steve Bancroft 1982

3 Bracken Crack .... S 4a
6m. The central crack is more awkward than it looks and is a bit wide to protect easily.

4 Green Slab .... VS 4c
6m. A juggy wall with one awkward move up a leaning groove and is easier above.

In the left-hand side of the next buttress is a compelling crack.

5 The Grogan .... HVS 5b
8m. The thin slanting crack is protectable but a struggle; fat fingers do not help at all.
FA. Gerry Rogan 1964

6 Wollock .... HVS 4c
8m. Trend right up the wall then finish direct. Quite reachy in its central section and the rightward exit is only really worth VS.
FA. Dave Gregory 1964

7 Pulcherrime .... VS 4b
8m. The left-slanting crack is stormed on solid jams.
FA. King Edward VII School party early 1950s

8 Slanting Crack .... VDiff
8m. A bit of a grovel up the wide crack.

9 Small is Beautiful .. E4 6c
8m. The tiny wall to the right. The grade is for climbing it direct. An easier **6b** version is available for those who slink off right.
FA. John Allen 1985

THE GROGAN
The wall set back left from *Remergence* is split by three obvious cracks. On the far left the thinnest crack of *The Grogan* is a classic finger shredder whereas the wide fissure of *Pulcherrime* gives good jamming. Not too much of interest to boulderers but okay for soloists.

Remergence 5m

Descent

11

16

15

9

10

11

11

12

13

14

Ash Tree Wall 100m
(Use top or
bottom paths)

REMERGENCE BUTTRESS
The most impressive buttress at this end of Burbage is the tiered overhangs of *Remergence*. The classics of *Mutiny Crack* and *Remergence* are test-pieces from two generations apart: how times change! The lower section of the buttress is very popular with boulderers and with the exception of *Mutiny Crack*, ropes are rarely used here.

The lower roof has countless eliminates around the main lines described here.
20m right of this buttress is a tiny slab which has a remarkable 6 problems on its 3m width. They get gradually harder from left to right.

⑩ Stomach Traverse . . . . . . 🔲 **VS 4c**
14m. Swarm onto the arete of the buttress then move up to the roof. Either grovel along the ledge (historically accurate but very precarious) or, more sensibly, hand-traverse the ledge all the way to *Mutiny Crack*. Not well protected.
FA. Eric Byne 1932

⑪ Tiptoe . . . . 🔲 **VS 4c**
16m. Start as for the previous climb but from the arete step down and tiptoe right to *Mutiny Crack*. Continue around the arete and back to the base of the cliff. Make sure you have clean boots otherwise you may annoy a few boulderers by mucking up their handholds.
FA. Chris Craggs 1972

⑫ Remergence . . . . . 🔲 **E4 6b**
12m. The centre of the lower roof is passed with difficulty using the well-chalked slots in the roof to gain a flatty above - a great V5 problem, though the very tall can just jump past it. The final roof is crossed via a strenuous long reach, fortunately with good Friend protection.
FA. Steve Bancroft 1977

⑬ Blind Date . . . . 🔲 **E4 7a**
12m. Often this is only climbed as a boulder problem start over the first roof (a classic V9). However there is a full route here and the E4 bit is over the top roof but it is 'only' 6b.
FA. Al Rouse 1984

⑭ Mutiny Crack . . . . 🔲 **HS 4b**
10m. The crack that splits a whole bevy of bulges is a glorious 'jug-fest' once the initial large overhang is passed.
FA. Eric Byrom 1934

⑮ Meddle . . . . 🔲 **HVS 5a**
10m. The arete of the buttress is climbed on its right-hand side then take the short wall above. Move left to finish up the centre of the delicate perched slab.
FA. Dennis Carr 1976

⑯ Detour . . . . 🔲 **HVD**
8m. Climb the groove on the far right to a rapid escape out left below the big capping overhang.
FA. Ron Townsend 1957

Whamcliffe · Dovestone Tor · Rivelin · Bamford · Stanage · Burbage North · Higgar Tor · Burbage South · Millstone · Lawrencefield · Yarncliffe · Froggatt · Curbar · Gardoms · Birchen · Chatsworth · Cratcliffe

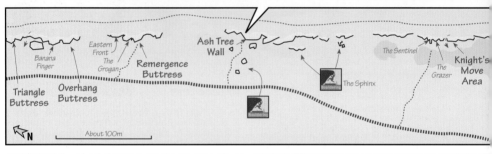

① Ivy Tree . . . . 🔳 HVS 5b
8m. A problem up the wall and arete, with gear in the break.
FA. Dave Gregory 1977

② All Star's Goal . . . . . . 🔳 E1 6a
8m. Climb the centre of the wall trending left to a deep horizontal break and finish direct with difficulty.
FA. Colin Banton 1977

③ Evening Wall . . . . 🔳 E1 5b
8m. As for *A.S.G.* but trend right to finish just left of the arete.
FA. Dave Gregory 1964

④ Wall Chimney . . . . 🔳 S 4a
8m. The narrow rift in the north-facing wall is a struggle.

⑤ Happily Ever After . . . . 🔳 E6 6c
8m. The centre of the wall is climbed direct passing the nose and finishing on pockets. Preplaced runners protect.
FA. Richie Patterson 1995. Supersedes Nefertiti (John Allen 1989) which stepped in from the left.

⑥ Wall Corner . . . . 🔳 HVD 4a
10m. Climb left of the arete steeply to reach a crack, which is then followed throughout.

⑦ Ash Tree Variations . . . 🔳 VS 5b
12m. Climb the fingery wall to the break then step right to finish up the more-delicate slab.

⑧ Ash Tree Wall . . . . . . 🔳 HVD
14m. Climb the fist-width crack to its end then traverse left to the pleasant open groove.

⑨ Ash Tree Crack . . . . 🔳 VDiff
12m. The first continuous crack on the wall gives good, easy jamming and as expected can be well protected.

⑩ Bilberry Crack . . . . 🔳 VDiff
12m. The sweet little number right again.

⑪ Bilberry Face . . . . 🔳 VDiff
12m. The unremarkable parallel cracks on the far right.

Wharncliffe
Dovestone Tor
Rivelin
Bamford
Stanage
Burbage North
Higgar Tor
Burbage South
Millstone
Lawrencefield
Yarncliffe
Froggatt
Curbar
Gardoms
Birchen
Chatsworth
Cratcliffe

ASH TREE WALL

This wall contains a good selection of lower grade routes that are often quieter that you might expect on such a popular cliff. Some pleasant cracks make the routes here worth a visit for those early leads or if you want to brush up on your jamming techniques.

To the left the walls are shorter and provide a few blanker routes and the odd extended boulder problem whilst to the right are three desperate offerings on the *Living in Oxford* block.

⑫ Nirvana E6 6b
8m. The side wall of the block is climbed from left to right and has a dynamic finish.
FA. Darren Thomas 1994

⑬ Living in Oxford . . . E7 6c
10m. The arete of the protruding block to the right sees few (one so far) repeats. Follow the right-hand side of the arete with extreme difficulty and mediocre protection.
FA. Johnny Dawes 1989

⑭ Superstition . . . E8 7a
8m. The astounding blank wall on the right is state of the art.
FA. Miles Gibson 1999

⑮ Green Chimney . . . . VDiff
8m. The wide crack to the right of the block is tricky to get established in. No queues for this one.

BOULDERING - Below Ash Tree Wall is a small set of reasonable boulders. The shorter routes on the edge also provide some sport. This includes the classic start to *Ash Tree Variations*. For some excellent harder stuff locate the block about 30m right (looking in) of *Living in Oxford*.
The Sphinx - See the map. Another area where the edge is short enough to offer some good extended problems. Search out the fine arete of *Cleo's Nose*.

Wharncliffe
Dovestone Tor
Rivelin
Bamford
Stanage
Burbage North
Higgar Tor
Burbage South
Millstone
Lawrencefield
Yarncliffe
Froggatt
Curbar
Gardoms
Birchen
Chatsworth
Cratcliffe

← Ash Tree Wall 200m
‹-- - - Descent

THE SENTINEL

As you progress down the edge things start to become more impressive with a series of jutting buttresses with routes across a spread of grades. The timid will enjoy the *Black Slab* routes whilst the strong should head straight for *Now or Never* and *The Sentinel*.

From mid morning — 15 min

❶ Stepped Crack .... Mod
8m. The easy groove on the left.

❷ Black Slab Arete .... S 4a
10m. From half way up *Stepped Crack* swing right around the arete awkwardly and finish up a shallow groove.

❸ Black Slab .... VS 4b
8m. Climb the pleasant slab and more delicate arete above.

❹ Black Slab Variation .... Diff
8m. The shallow scoop and groove just before the angle.

❺ Now or Never E1 5b
12m. Layback the curving black flake and monkey around the corner to a ledge. The delicate upper arete is a real contrast.
FA. John Allen 1971

❻ Sentinel Chimney ...... VDiff
10m. The rift left of the imposing, hanging arete.

❼ The Sentinel E2 5c
10m. The narrow projecting buttress has a couple of powerful moves just below the top.
FA. Dennis Carr 1977

❽ Sentinel Crack .... Diff
10m. The slanting crack on the right-hand side of the prow is (much) easier than its Chatsworth namesake.

❾ High Flyer E3 5b
8m. Climb the bold bulge from right to left.
FA. Gary Gibson 1978

❿ The Grazer .... VS 4c
8m. The leaning, jamming-crack is not misnamed for most.

⓫ Lieback .... VS 4c
8m. A shallow groove leads to a layback flake just to the left.

⓬ Ringo .... S 4a
8m. A straight crack with an awkward bulge.

THE GRAZER

Another selection of cracks and chimneys. If your jamming is not up to scratch then this area might be worth a visit. The classics of the *Knight's Move* area are located just to the right but there is plenty here to extend your day, or to tick if the routes to the right are crowded.

Descent

From mid morning — 15 min

⑬ Ring Climb . . . . ☐ S 4a
8m. Climb the central flaky-crack to its top then the short wall.

⑭ Ring Chimney . . . . ☐ Diff
8m. The deep chimney is fairly straightforward.

⑮ Agnostic's Arete . . . . . 🔲🔲 ☐ VS 5a
8m. Believe it or not this is the pleasantly technical arete.
FA. Clive Jones 1977

KNIGHT'S MOVE AREA

⑯ Still Orange . . . . 🔲 ☐ S 4a
12m. Climb the easy slanting ramp-line then step right into the steeper right-hand branch.
FA. Dave Gregory (his first new route) 1956

⑰ Green Crack . . . . 🔲 ☐ VDiff
12m. The long wide crack that leans to the right is a rather awkward customer to climb and also to protect.

⑱ Dover's Progress . . . . ☐ HVS 5a
14m. Climb the narrow wall past the cannonball slots. Delicate and not well protected though a micro-Friend helps.
FA. Harry Dover 1932

⑲ Hollyash Crack . . . . 🔲 ☐ VS 4b
14m. The long crack that bends right at the top is tricky in its central section and is a good intro to off-width techniques.
FA. Harry Dover 1932

⑳ Knight's Move . . . . 🔲 ☐ HVS 5a
16m. One of the best routes on Burbage North. Climb past some holes then take the thin cracks that pass the left-hand side of the long roof. Continue up the wall above, following the flakes out to the right to finish.
FA. Gilbert Ellis 1933

KNIGHT'S MOVE AREA
To the right is the tallest buttress on the edge recognised by a large overhang on the right with a healthy holly under it. There are several worthwhile routes hereabouts with the superb *Knight's Move* being especially memorable. The little extra walking involved with getting here tends to keep some of the crowds away.

㉑ Peter's Progress . . . . . 🔲🔲 ☐ VS 4c
20m. Climb *Knight's Move* until you reach the break above the level of the big roof. Follow this all the way to *Great Crack* and an easy finish.
FA. Peter Biven 1953

㉒ Arme Blanche . . . . . . 🔲🔲 ☐ E5 6a
14m. Claw a way past the left-hand edge of the overlap to reach easier ground. A side-runner is usual though it has been done without.
FA. Gary Gibson 1981

㉓ Great Crack . . . . 🔲🔲 ☐ VS 5a
14m. Squirm up the deep corner behind the holly to the overhang then shuffle right and battle awkwardly past the lip to enter the easier upper crack.
FA. Harry Dover 1932

㉔ The Big Chimney . . . . ☐ HVD
12m. The deep cleft leads to a capping-stone which is most easily passed on the right.

㉕ The Rainmaker . . . . 🔲 ☐ HVS 5a
10m. Pull over the flat roof then climb the face above.
FA. Keith Sharples 1977

㉖ Big Chimney Arete . . . . . . 🔲 ☐ HS 4b
10m. The arete on its right side by pleasantly mild laybacking.

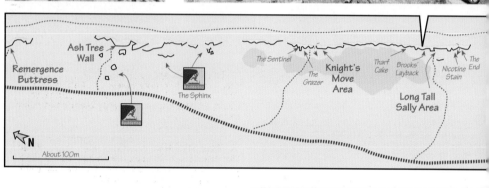

THARF CAKE and BROOKS' LAYBACK

This isolated area has a good collection of lower-grade routes that are quite short and usually quieter than the area just to the right. *Brooks' Layback* is a gem.

APPROACH - Direct approach from Knight's Move Area is awkward. Better is to use the upper or lower paths paths. *Tharf Cake* is on an isolated buttress split by parallel cracks which is situated about 30m left of the more continuous section leading to the Long Tall Sally Area.

① **First Crack** . . . . **S 4a**

8m. An awkward left-leaning crack that bounds the buttress

② **Tharf Cake** . . . . **HVS 5a**

8m. The left-hand side of the face on small holds and pockets.
FA. John Parkin 1977

③ **Left Twin Crack** . . . . **HVD**

8m. It's all in the name.

④ **Right Twin Crack** . . . . **S 4a**

8m. ...and again. Tricky in its middle section.

⑤ **Farcical Arete** . . . . **S 4a**

8m. The pleasant arete is climbed on its right-hand side throughout and is unprotected.

30m right of Tharf Cake is a fine series of square-cut buttresses, just to the right of the Long Tall Sally Area.

⑥ **The Irrepressible Urge** **E1 5b**

8m. The front face of the first square buttress trending right.
FA. Colin Banton 1978

⑦ **Small Arctic Mammal** **E1 6a**

8m. A boulder problem up the arete on its right-hand. A little artificial. No touching *Left Recess Crack*!
FA. Mark Millar late 1970s

⑧ **Left Recess Crack** . . . . **S 3c**

8m. The crack in the left-hand angle.

⑨ **Right Recess Crack** . . . . **HS 4a**

8m. The mirror image in the opposite angle.

⑩ **Ace** . . . . **HVS 4b**

8m. A narrow protruding arete which can be climbed first on the left and then up its crest. Delicate, sustained and gearless.

⑪ **Thrall's Thrutch** . . . . **S 4a**

8m. A well-named wide crack - be warned.

⑫ **Brooks' Layback** . . . . **VS 4b**

8m. The short right-angled corner crack starts from a ledge and is just too thin for good jams, hence the name.
FA. Rupert Brooks 1932

⑬ **Wobblestone Crack** . . . . . . **VDiff**

8m. The crack with wobbling stones eases with height.

Wharncliffe
Dovestone Tor
Rivelin
Bamford
Stanage
Burbage North
Higgar Tor
Burbage South
Millstone
Lawrencefield
Yarncliffe
Froggatt
Curbar
Gardoms
Birchen
Chatsworth
Cratcliffe

LONG TALL SALLY

This is possibly the best selection of routes on the cliff and well worth the walk. *Amazon Crack* is a brilliant jamming crack, the blank corner of *Long Tall Sally* is compelling, and there are other gems to delight.
DIRECT APPROACH - Walk along the cliff top path for about 15 minutes, until you are past the small wooded area below the crag, before descending to the crag base.

14 Hollybush Gully . . . . VDiff
8m. A square-cut slot which is really more of a chimney.

15 The Screamer E1 5c
8m. The thin crack in the right wall of the gully/chimney has good enough gear to ensure no screamers need be taken.
FA. Colin Banton 1978

16 Gazebo Watusi E6 6b
10m. An impressive soaring arete with runners at almost exactly half height.
FA. Jonny Needham early 1990s

17 Obscenity . . . . VS 4c
12m. The steep wide crack is a bugger of a battle, especially at the bulge where the recent loss of a good hold has compounded the difficulties. Other expletives might be found more appropriate by some.
FA. Nip Craven 1948

18 Amazon Crack . . . . VS 4b
12m. A glorious fissure in the shallow corner which is quite superb and far too short. One of grits best short cracks.
FA. Jack Macleod 1932

19 Amazon Gully . . . . Mod
10m. The deep rift just right with a tall flake in its back gives a pleasant beginners route. It is often used as a way down by the technically proficient.

20 Boney Moroney E1 5c
10m. The fierce-looking thin crack is easier than it appears thanks to hidden holds. Keep left for the best of them.
FA. Jack Street 1969

21 Long Tall Sally E1 5b
10m. A superb climb up the blank groove. Many people's first Extreme lead which is surprising since it isn't a push-over. Passing the bulge is the crux, requiring faith in friction; protection is good. *Photo page 157.*
FA. Alan Clarke early 1960s

22 Three Blind Mice . . E7 6c
10m. Fine technical climbing up the blank arching wall. Use a couple of pockets on the right to climb the lower leaning wall leftwards, pass the bulge and finish direct.
FA. Dave Pegg (solo) 1994

23 Greeny Crack . . . . VS 4b
10m. The steep right-hand corner is juggy, well protected and only occasionally green.

24 Rhapsody in Green . . . . . VS 5a
8m. A delicate lower arete leads to a grassy ledge. Continue up the leaning arete above
FA. Colin Banton 1978

25 Left Studio Climb . . . . VDiff
8m. The left-hand crack system in the recess.

26 Right Studio Climb . . . . VDiff
8m. ....and the right-hand one, leading to a ledge and finishing up a groove.

27 Rose Flake . . . . VS 4b
8m. Steep and enjoyable crack climbing on jugs and jams, and with plenty of runners.

28 The Fin E1 5b
8m. The hanging groove is a struggle to enter though at least it has overhead gear. It is much easier above.
FA. Neil Stokes 1971

29 Ai No Corrida E5 6b
8m. Layback boldy up the flying arete. A runner in the next route is only of limited help but it is all you are going to get!
FA. John Allen 1984

Wharncliffe
Dovestone Tor
Rivelin
Bamford
Stanage
Burbage North
Higgar Tor
Burbage South
Millstone
Lawrencefield
Yarncliffe
Froggatt
Curbar
Gardoms
Birchen
Chatsworth
Cratcliffe

Descent - - - - →

From mid morning | 20 min

NICOTINE STAIN and THE END

Burbage North's last gasp has some good micro-routes on quality rock, and a couple of pleasant slabs that might interest those in search of an easy time.

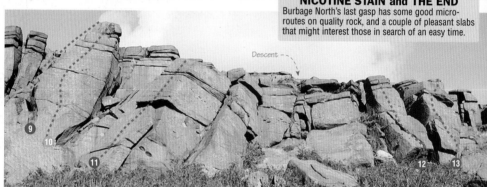

Descent - -

① Right Fin . . . . HVS 5a
8m. An elegant curving flake with a crucial layback move and long stretch before things ease.

② The Enthusiast . . . . HVS 6a
6m. The tricky left arete. For the person who has done everything else on the cliff perhaps?

③ Nicotine Stain E1 6b
6m. The thin seam is easiest if you keep right. A very frustrating problem that sees many floundering attempts.
FA. Al Rouse 1983

④ April Fool . . . . VDiff
6m. Straightforward climbing up the prominent crack

⑤ Approach . . . . HVS 5c
6m. The pocketed wall just right.
FA. Colin Banton 1978

There is some good bouldering here including the superb roof crack in the cave directly below the edge, and some nice problems on the square block 50m right of the last routes above.

⑥ Spider Crack . . . . VS 5b
6m. A pleasantly-technical crack which even has runners.

⑦ The Be All . . . . S 4a
6m. The wide crack.

⑧ The End All . . . . S 4a
6m. Climb the last crack on the wall.

⑨ End Buttress . . . . Mod
8m. A wide crack and slab on the left-hand side of the arete.

⑩ The Penultimate . . . . HVS 5b
8m. The pleasant narrow face. Trend slightly rightwards.
FA. Keith Sharples 1977

⑪ End Slab . . . . Mod
8m. A nice easy slab

⑫ Ender . . . . Diff
8m. The crack in the left-hand side of the face; tricky to start.

⑬ Endste . . . . Diff
8m. The wall and flake above.

HIGGAR TOR

Higgar is a small outcrop with a big impact and steep stuff is the order of the day. Most of the routes will only succumb to a forceful and determined approach and any wavering will be punished with utmost brutality. The abrasive-tool names are a not-very-subtle indication of the nature of the rock on the whole cliff, with the striking line of *The Rasp* being the showpiece. It is typical of many of the other routes: a steep overhanging crack that sometimes affords good jams but is often less accommodating; protection is plentiful but placing it is tiring and the finishes may leave you a breathless and battered soul by the time you reach the top. There is a theory that the routes feel under-graded because the block is slowly tipping forward as time passes. I don't think Joe Brown would agree, he was just good at climbing steep and uncompromising cracks.

Although the Leaning Block is the main event, the shorter walls to either side also have some worthwhile offerings but even here don't expect any soft touches.

APPROACH (SK255819)

Higgar is on the west side of the Burbage Valley and it overlooks the road leading down to Hathersage. Roadside parking is available on the right-hand side of as it starts its descent towards the valley. From the parking walk down the road for about 100m to a stile on the left (there is also parking for 2 or 3 cars opposite this stile). Cross the stile and contour the hillside to the right. The cliff appears as you round the ridge and is less than 5 minutes from the car.

CONDITIONS

Higgar is high and exposed and will catch all the sun, wind and rain that is going. The steepness might make you think that there is something here in wet weather but the sloping finishes are hard enough without the addition of water. Having said that you will find some dry bouldering along the base. The ever-present wind means this is one usable venue through the midge season.

BOULDERING - Higgar has become very popular amongst boulderers over the last few years. The area of interest is around to the east side of the Tor, facing Burbage North. Here are many problems including some classics around the low roof nearest the parking spot on the more-usual approach to the summit of the Tor.

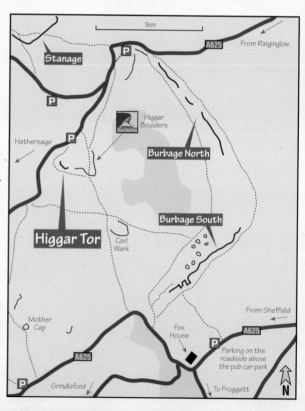

OTHER GUIDEBOOKS - A more complete list of routes at Higgar Tor is published in the 1991 BMC *Froggatt* guide. The bouldering is in the 1998 Peak Bouldering ROCKFAX.

Descent (behind block)

Rock Around the Block

Approach from parking

Leaning Block

Wharncliffe
Dovestone Tor
Rivelin
Bamford
Stanage
Burbage North
Higgar Tor
Burbage South
Millstone
Lawrencefield
Yarncliffe
Froggatt
Curbar
Gardoms
Birchen
Chatsworth
Cratcliffe

HIGGAR TOR - LEFT

The low wall left of the Leaning Block has a series of steep routes which have a similar reputation to those on its big brother to the right. Most of the routes follow steep cracks and proficiency in jamming is near-essential.

❶ The Warding . . . . **VDiff**
6m. The shallow groove near the left-hand edge of the wall is almost to easy to a 'proper' Higgar Tor route.

❷ Aceldama **E4 6a**
8m. The wall is short on length, big on impact, unprotected and with a harrowing exit.
FA. Gary Gibson (solo) 1980

❸ Mighty Atom **E3 5c**
8m. Thin cracks lead to good runners in the second break and a gripping exit too far above them for comfort.
FA. Steve Bancroft 1975

❹ Brillo **E1 5c**
8m. Follow the left arete of the central recess and the thin cracks directly above it. It can be gritty after rain.
FA. Chris Craggs 1987

❺ The Riffler . . . . **HVS 5a**
8m. Strenuously climb the roof of the cave/recess (loose blocks?) and the crack and groove above.

❻ The Cotter . . . . **HVS 5a**
8m. Take the right arete of the central blocky recess and the thin crack directly above it.

❼ The Rat's Tail . . . . . . **VS 4c**
8m. The hand-crack in a shallow groove gives good jamming throughout and is possibly the least brutal pitch on this part of the cliff.

❽ The Reamer . . . . **VS 4c**
8m. Climb the left edge of the deep gully via ledges to a thin crack which gives a couple of good moves
FA. Dave Gregory 1964

❾ Leaning Block Gully . . . . **Mod**
10m. Straightforward and often used in descent though 'back and foot' practice can be had by staying near the front and passing to the outside of the jammed block.

❿ The Sander **E4 6a**
10m. The north-facing side-wall of the Leaning Block is most easily reached from the opposite side of the gully; a direct start is possible but a bit artificial. The upper section of the face has one off-balance stopper move to reach the hanging crack and then easier ground.
FA. Jerry Peel 1972

Wharncliffe
Dovestone Tor
Rivelin
Bamford
Stanage
Burbage North
Higgar Tor
Burbage South
Millstone
Lawrencefield
Yarncliffe
Froggatt
Curbar
Gardoms
Birchen
Chatsworth
Cratcliffe

THE LEANING BLOCK

The main feature of the cliff is the impressive chunk of rock that is the Leaning Block. *The Rasp* is one of the best E2s in the Peak and the side wall has the classic jamming crack of *The File* which gets the morning sun. The top of the block can be reached by a short steep scramble up the back.

❶ Block and Tackle ... E6 6c
12m. The arete on its right-hand side is a taxing and gymnastic effort. Start as for *The Sander* but swing around to the front of the arete at a jug. Move up to a good break and tackle the central section to reach a still difficult finish up the final arete.
FA. Neil Foster 1994

❷ Surform ... E1 5b
14m. Start up the leaning flake and follow it by steep laybacking until a tricky traverse leads left to gain a small ledge. Bridge the corner then escape out left onto slabby rock, climbed right-wards to the summit.
FA. Joe Brown 1958

❸ The Rasp ... E2 5b
14m. Monumental, a contender for the best grit route in the Peak! Sprint up the layback flakes trending right to a rest on jams at deep horizontal break. More laybacking up and right leads to unobvious jug-hauling to gain an uncomfortable half-rest in a niche. Escape out right awkwardly (rounded hand traverse or ungainly grovel using undercuts in the roof) to finish up a wide crack. A brilliant belay is located just above. *Photo page 40.*
FA. Joe Brown 1956

❹ Rasp Direct ... E4 6a
12m. A gnarly finger-crack and tough layback lead rapidly to the crux of the regular route and then its poor rest in the niche. Once suitably recovered pull straight over the roof to a bellyflop landing of the highest calibre.
FA. Steve Bancroft 1975

❺ Flute of Hope ... E3 5c
14m. The butch diagonal. Climb the blunt rib on the right-hand side of the face to a flake. Follow this to its end and make a sapping hand-traverse left to reach the crux of *The Rasp*. Up this to the niche then traverse left under the roofs and finish through a notch.
FA. 1971 (two pts) Ed Drummond. FFA. Ron Fawcett 1977

❻ Bat Out of Hell ... E5 6a
12m. An exciting direct line above the initial rib of *Flute of Hope*. From the top of *Flute's* flake climb the wall via a long reach or a double-shuffle from the snapped flake. Finish with a flourish. A Friend 2.5 above the crux is hard-to-place but essential, especially if you intend to fly. *Photo page 167.*
FA. Paul Bolger 1979

❼ Linkline ... E5 6b
12m. Follow *Bat Out of Hell* to the first break then step right to gain a prominent rugosity. Stand on this to reach the next break then continue direct via powerful moves to the niche at the end of *The Rasp's* traverse.
FA. Neil Foster 1993

8 Rowley Birkin QC . . . E6 6c
12m. Follow the arete left of *The File*. Steady climbing leads to good Friends. Precarious moves on tiny undercuts and pebbles, followed by a slap for a sloping break leads to easy ground or back into space.
FA. Ben Moon 1990s. Climbed on its right-hand side and claimed as Rowley Birkin QC by Percy Bishton 1998

9 The File . . . . VS 4c
10m. The compelling crack in the south-facing wall eats Friends and also the flesh of the uninitiated. The initial roof is the crux, although interest is well maintained to a superb, juggy finish.
Photo page 36.
FA. Don Whillans 1956

10 Paddock . . . . VDiff
6m. From a block climb the zig-zag cracks.
FA. Dave Gregory 1964

11 Greymalkin . . . . S 4a
6m. From the block, trend right up the face following a thin crack to a final long reach.
FA. Dave Gregory 1964

12 Hecate . . . . VDiff
6m. The juggy groove and arete just to the right.
FA. Dave Gregory 1964

13 Rock Around the Block . . . E5 6a
The girdle of the left wall and the Leaning Block is an epic. (See previous page for line of first pitch.)
1) 5a, 10m. Start up *The Warding* and follow the break to a belay on the arete of the gully.
2) 6a, 10m. Step up and fall across the gully to a crack on the side of the block. Follow this rightwards round the arete and continue (crux) to a belay in the niche of *Surform*.
3) 5c, 10m. Make a wild hand-traverse across *Bat out of Hell* to the arete. Either finish up *The File*, or (if persistent) belay and...
4) 4c, 8m. ...continue on the lower of 2 breaks, until you can step off at the back of the Block.
FA. Chris Craggs, Colin Binks 1982

FAR RIGHT
To the right the crag continues as a collection of short buttresses to a tower capped by an overhang. This is a good place to escape the crowds.

14 Achilles' Heel E2 5c
10m. Climb flakes awkwardly to below the roof then escape right to the arete and an easy finish.
The direct finish is *Laze* **E2 5c**.
FA. Gerry Rogan early 1960s. FA. (Laze) John Allen 1975

15 Root Decay E4 6b
10m. Boulder up the wall to runners (poor landing) then trend right to finish.
FA. Mike Lea 1988

16 Stretcher Case E2 5c
8m. The centre of the wall behind the holly is reachy and all the holds slope horribly.
FA. Chris Craggs 1979

17 Splint . . . . HVS 5a
8m. The right arete of the wall on its left-hand side.
FA. Colin Binks 1979

The final section of rock has a small collection of short routes on good rock, and is always quiet.

18 Loki's Way . . . . S 4a
6m. Climb the crack just around the arete to a finish on the left.
FA. Dave Gregory 1964

19 Fricka's Crack . . . . VS 4a
6m. The thinner crack right again leads to an awkward exit.
FA. Dave Gregory 1964

20 Freya's Climb . . . . VDiff
6m. The final crack in the face.
FA. Dave Gregory 1964

Wharncliffe · Dovestone Tor · Rivelin · Bamford · Stanage · Burbage North · Higgar Tor · Burbage South · Millstone · Lawrencefield · Yarncliffe · Froggatt · Curbar · Gardoms · Birchen · Chatsworth · Cratcliffe

BURBAGE SOUTH

Wharncliffe
Dovestone Tor
Rivelin
Bamford
Stanage
Burbage North
Higgar Tor
Burbage South
Millstone
Lawrencefield
Yarncliffe
Froggatt
Curbar
Gardoms
Birchen
Chatsworth
Cratcliffe

The South Edge of the Burbage Valley has never acquired the popularity of its northern brother. Its grim and shady aspect doesn't help but it is probably more to do with the uncompromising appearance of the various buttresses which has limited the popularity of the place to true aficionados. The surprising fact is that Burbage South is home of several of the hardest routes on gritstone which makes them amongst the hardest traditional challenges anywhere in the world. A successful ascent of the likes of *Captain Invincible*, *Parthian Shot* and *Equilibrium* will more than likely make the news section on the various web sites and magazines of the climbing world. Don't be put off though, in amongst all these big names are plenty of other fine routes across the grade range.

BOULDERING - The boulders below Brooks' Crack area are amongst the most popular bouldering locations in the Peak with countless problems in a delightful setting. The bouldering on the actual edge is covered in the following pages.

APPROACH (SK266810)

The best approach is from the Fox House end of the valley from one of the several limited parking spots.
Fox House - Park on the grass verge on the roadside above the pub. Walk up the hill and pick up a path which crosses the wall and leads across the moor to the Quarries.
Green Drive - There is a very limited parking spot (4 cars) at the end of the main valley path. Walk up the Green Drive and head right up the hill to reach the quarries.
Toad's Mouth Bridge - Beyond the bridge there is one short section on which you are allowed to park and that is the section with dotted centre lines on the Padley Gorge side of the road which is about 250m from the bridge. On all other sections, where the centre line is unbroken, you will be ticketed. To reach the edge, walk back over the bridge and either cross a stile and then a bog to gain the main path, or walk up the road and gain the Green Drive approach.

CONDITIONS

Burbage South faces northwest, only gets the sun late in the day from April to September but can be a welcome retreat in hot weather. It tends to be green and lichenous after rain.

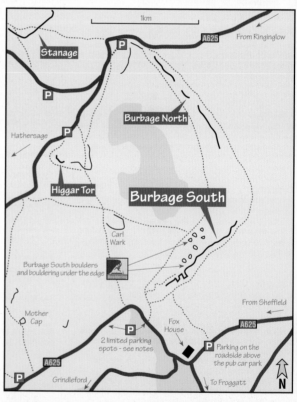

OTHER GUIDEBOOKS - A more complete list of routes at Burbage South is published in the 1991 BMC *Froggatt* guide. The bouldering is in the 1998 Peak Bouldering ROCKFAX.

grunt grimace grin...

Great days out on the Peak District edges are what it's all about... We've been living here and testing our equipment in this environment for over 40 years now, that's some grunt too. We know this has helped us make some really great gear. So if it's too wet to climb or this picture of Neil Bentley pushing the envelope on Equilibrium scares you - why not take some time out and go and decide if all our effort was worthwhile. It may make you grimace like this copy or it may just make you grin!

GORE-TEX

The ultralight multifunctional Lhotse Jacket. 3 layer Ascent XCR Goretex

Local Stockists
- Outside-Calver 01433 631111 • Outside-Hathersage 01433 651 936 • Outside-Sheffield 0114 279 7427 • Peak Store-Bakewell 01629 815 681 • Hitch n Hike-Bamford 01433 651 013 • CCC-Sheffield 0114 272 9733 • Magic Mountain-Glossop 01457 854424

For a complete list of stockists...
phone 01457 854424
or visit www.mountain-equipment.co.uk

MOUNTAIN
EQUIPMENT

eil Bentley on the first ascent of Equilibrium E10 7a Photo: Richard Heap

BURBAGE SOUTH *Far Left*

Wharncliffe
Dovestone Tor
Rivelin
Bamford
Stanage
Burbage North
Higgar Tor
Burbage South
Millstone
Lawrencefield
Yarncliffe
Froggatt
Curbar
Gardoms
Birchen
Chatsworth
Cratcliffe

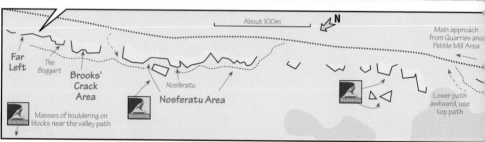

FAR LEFT

At the far left-hand end of Burbage South is a series of tiny buttresses with about twenty routes up to 7m high mostly in the lower grades, though with a few harder outings. The first routes listed are 20m left of the tall tower of *The Boggart* where a pair of thin cracks can be found in a shady recess.

1 Split Nose . . . . VS 5a
6m. A split nose on the left gained from a nearby boulder.

2 The Gnat . . . . HVS 5b
6m. The left-hand crack gives a short and safe struggle.
FA. Neil Stokes 1972

3 Midge . . . . HVS 5c
6m. The right-hand crack is just a (s)midge harder.
FA. Neil Stokes 1972

4 Every Man's Misery . . . . . . VS 5a
6m. The wide right-leaning crack is a thrash and is well named.

5 Triglyph . . . . VS 4b
6m. More graunchy climbing up the right-hand crack.
FA. Dave Gregory 1964

6 The Thistle Funnel . . . . VDiff
8m. The crack splitting an arete and the side wall above.
FA. Dave Gregory 1964

7 Stampede E8 6c
8m. The fearsome left arete of the tower on its left-hand side.
FA. Simon Jones 1995

8 Roof Route . . . . VS 4c
8m. A curiously-named route up the crack in the slabby angle. Surprisingly awkward but large gear and big feet both help.
FA. Jack Macleod 1934

9 Gable Route . . . . VS 4c
8m. Climb the flake in the arete then the pleasantly-balancy edge of the slab above.
FA. Mark Vallance 1977

10 The Gutter . . . . HVS 5a
8m. The steep crack leads on gruesome jams to a ledge. The corner behind is easier.
FA. Dave Gregory 1977

THE BOGGART and BROOKS' CRACK

Past an easy descent gully the edge increases in height with two dramatic buttresses.

11 Lethargic Arete . . . . S 4a
8m. If you can be bothered, climb the crack just left of the arete to reach the slabby upper section.
FA. Joe Brown 1951

12 Charlie's Crack . . . . HVS 5b
10m. Leap into the curving crack from the left and make a tricky pull to easier ground. Step left to finish up slabby rock.
FA. Charlie Curtis 1961

13 Life Assurance E6 6b
8m. Thin smearing up the slab above the curving crack of *Charlie's*. Runners in the crack become less and less useful as the crux approaches. Get that policy checked.
FA. John Dunne 1988

THE BOGGART and BROOKS' CRACK

A couple of imposing towers, the finest on all Burbage, are home to a great set of routes from VS to E10 - so there is something for almost everyone. They receive late evening sun in the summer and can be a useful retreat on those rare hot days. *Brooks'* and *Byne's Cracks* are sterling efforts from the 1930s.

14 Tower Climb . . . . HS 4b
12m. Climb awkward twin cracks (the left-hand pair of three) to a chimney and a finish up a flake.
FA. Byron Connelly 1934

15 Tower Crack . . . . HVS 5a
12m. The right-hand crack leads to a ledge. From here a short layback flake on the right gives the protectable crux.
FA. Geoff Sutton 1957

16 Balance It Is E7 6c
14m. The stunning left arete of the buttress is approached via *Boggart L.H.* and gives superb committing laybacking that is a matter of maintaining a sense of equilibrium, or is that the other arete. An RP4 might be found useful.
FA. Neil Foster 1995

17 Boggart Left-hand . . E4 6a
14m. Gain the thin hanging crack from the left by an extended reach (a side runner brings it down to E2) then sprint to the easier ground of the central crack system.
FA. Steve Bancroft 1976

18 Boggart E2 6b
14m. The thin (and anciently chipped) incipient crack is technical to the first decent hold, things ease above. Usually soloed by the proficient as placing runners is hard work and blocks a semi-crucial finger jam. *Photo page 7.*
FA. John Allen 1975

19 Equilibrium . . . E10 7a
14m. The right-hand arete is current state of the art. From runners below mid-height climb the arete to a grasping exit. May require a helmet and massive fliers. Simply stunning. *Photo page 173.*
FA. Neil Bentley 2000

20 Tower Chimney . . . . Diff
14m. The long chimney groove to a caving-type exit is fun!

21 The Braille Trail E7 6c
10m. A superbly-named line of pebbles and brush marks on the impressive north face are traversed to the exposed arete (poor hand-placed blade peg and six-inch-nail runners). Climb desperately into the thin crack and finish easily.
FA. Johnny Dawes 1984

22 Parthian Shot E9 6c
16m. An awesome route up the prow which is still almost as hard as they come. Lurch left out of *Brook's Crack* and stack wires behind the creaky flake. These protect a harrowing set of moves up and left to the final gripping rock-over.
FA. John Dunne 1989

23 Brooks' Crack . . . . HVS 5a
14m. The left-hand crack is approached up a clean-cut groove to reach a recess. Steep and insecure moves gain the upper cave then good jamming leads to an awkward exit.
FA. Rupert Brooks 1934

24 Byne's Crack . . . . VS 4b
14m. The right-hand crack is juggy and excellent giving great jamming and bridging. Don't fall over the edge at the top.
FA. Eric Byne 1934

25 Ron, Ring Home! . . E5 6c
8m. Fingery and unprotected climbing up the blank wall left of the arete of *The Knock*. Fierce and seldom climbed.
FA. Ron Fawcett 1986

26 The Knock E5 6a
8m. A superb and committing arete with the crux, and some rather battered protection, right at the top. Arguments about the grade (E4 vs E5) continue; its easy for E5 and hard for E4.
FA. John Allen 1975

27 Keep Crack . . . . VS 5a
10m. The groove leads to a ledge and a steeper continuation corner which is bridged with difficulty.
FA. Alan Clark early 1960s

Wharncliffe
Dovestone Tor
Rivelin
Bamford
Stanage
Burbage North
Higgar Tor
Burbage South
Millstone
Lawrencefield
Yarncliffe
Froggatt
Curbar
Gardoms
Birchen
Chatsworth
Cratcliffe

Descent (awkward)

Descent

1 10m (on north-facing wall)

Brooks' Crack Area 30m

Evening | 18 min

1 Captain Sensible E1 5b
8m. Thin cracks in the north-facing slab are often a bit green.
FA. Steve Webster 1977

2 Ladder Gully .... Mod
8m. The gully is most frequently used as a descent route.

3 Recurring Nightmare .. E5 6b
8m. The rib to the right of the gully is hard exactly where you don't want it to be.
FA. Andy Barker (solo) 1982

4 Macleod's Crack .... VDiff
8m. The crack has an awkward start but eases rapidly.

5 Fade Away E1 6a
8m. A decent little micro-route up the steep prow. From the crack on the right reach left and climb the rib direct to a good hold. Pull onto the wall on the left and finish direct.
FA. Paul Mitchell 1982

6 Dowel Crack .... VS 4c
8m. The crack to the right of the prow. The piece of dowel originally used for protection is still in place though its use is not recommended.
FA. Dave Gregory 1964

7 The Iron Hand .... S 4a
8m. Starting from a block climb the short corner crack.

NOSFERATU AREA

The central section of the cliff is a series of small buttress and some meaty cracks. Although first appearances may leave you rather underwhelmed there are some good routes across a spread of grades, that are well worth a visit when a cool venue is required. The whole area is green once the autumnal rains start and stays that way into the spring. *Nosferatu* is the big classic and being on a projecting buttress stays cleaner.
DIRECT APPROACH - Stay on the cliff-top path, past the quarries and lower walls until the next continuous section of edge appears.

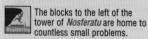

Bouldering The blocks to the left of the tower of *Nosferatu* are home to countless small problems.

Evening | 18 min

Descent

Descent

Route 7 above boulders

8 Sorb E2 5c
10m. Balancy climbing up the left arete of the buttress (poor landing) leads to a good horizontal break and runners. An immense reach is all that remains.
FA. Dennis Carr 1976

9 Nosferatu E5 6b
12m. From the fallen block that used to form the start of *Sorb* climb the right-hand arete with cunning (for that read toe and heel hooking) and using crimpy holds to a reach for a ledge. Finish up the arete or, more directly, via an extended but safe dyno.
FA. Andy Barker 1980

10 Reginald .... VS 4b
10m. Climb the narrow blocky chimney to a rightwards exit.
FA. Nat Allen 1951

11 The Attitude Inspector E3 6c
10m. Climb the leaning wall with difficulty to ledges. A runner on the left protects the upper section. The start is a classic boulder problem (V8) involving a huge leap.
FA. Mark Wilford 1979

12 Nathaniel .... HVS 5b
10m. The right-hand chimney crack gets harder with height. Big fists and big cams are both a considerable help.
FA. Nat Allen 1951

13 The Knack E1 5c
6m. The beckoning, hanging groove is difficult to get established in but is much easier once the first decent hold has been grasped.
FA. John Allen 1971

14 Nick Knack Paddywack . E2 6b
8m. Start below a flake in the left-hand wall of the gully. Pull up to a break then traverse left and climb the wall to the top. The route can also be started direct from *The Knack*.
FA. Andy Barker 1982

15 Less Bent .... S 4a
6m. Climb the arete to the big horizontal break then move left around the arete to find a finish.

16 Zig-zag .... VS 4c
10m. Climb the crescent-shaped crack to the break then scuttle left around the arete to finish as for the previous route.

17 No Zag .... HVS 5b
8m. Climb the flake of *Zig-zag* to the break then step right to gain the widening hanging crack awkwardly and climb it with considerable difficulty.

18 Unfinished Symphony ...... HVS 5b
8m. Tackle the short hanging crack by leaping into it from the blocks on the right. Short but action packed!
FA. John Allen 1974

19 Ribbed Corner .... Mod
8m. The crack on the right or the blocks on the left lead to a groove which is also mild.
FA. Joe Brown (no kidding) 1951

20 The Staircase .... HS 4a
8m. The steep stepped cracks just left of the arete are juggy but quite powerful for the grade.

21 The Drainpipe .... S 4a
8m. A steep groove around to the right is furnished with good holds and runners.

Wharncliffe · Dovestone Tor · Rivelin · Bamford · Stanage · Burbage North · Higgar Tor · Burbage South · Millstone · Lawrencefield · Yarncliffe · Froggatt · Curbar · Gardoms · Birchen · Chatsworth · Cratcliffe

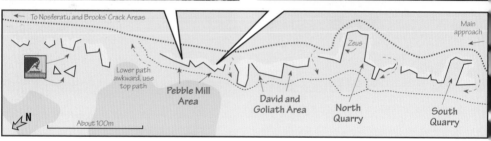

PEBBLE MILL

A fine buttress home to one of John Allen's classic pebble-pulling routes of the 1970s, *Pebble Mill*. Up and left is a smaller slab with some easier offerings.

❶ Broddle . . . . **VS 5a**
8m. The left arete has a tricky mantelshelf start and soon eases.
FA. Dave Gregory 1964

❷ Limmock . . . . **HVS 5b**
10m. The centre of the slab has a slippery and reachy start. The upper section is much easier and has runners.
FA. Dave Gregory 1964

❸ Lino . . . . **HVS 5a**
10m. Precarious moves up the right arete on flaky holds.
FA. Dave Gregory 1964

BOULDERING - There is plenty of good bouldering to be had around the base of the edge. Also worth a look is the collection of boulders about 100m further along the edge, passed on the way to the *Nosferatu* and *Brooks' Crack* areas.

❹ The Birth of Liquid Desires . . . . **HVS 5a**
6m. A minor line up the scooped slab left of the crack. There is no gear until the easy ground at the top.
FA. Clive Jones (solo) 1977

❺ Wazzock . . . . **S 4a**
8m. A pleasant crack to the left of the smooth slab.
FA. Dave Gregory 1964

❻ Pebble Mill **E5 6b**
12m. Layback the lower arete sketchily on its left-hand side to a ledge on the right. Teeter up to better holds (the crux for shorties) and a romp. The tall might think the route 'only E4'.
FA. John Allen 1976

❼ We Ain't Gonna Pay No Toll . . **E5 6b**
12m. An inferior right-hand start to *Pebble Mill*. Boulder out the wall to gain a break. Finger-traverse this onto the slab.
FA. John Allen (solo) 1987

❽ Dork Child **E1 5c**
8m. Between *Pebble Mill* and *Above and Beyond* is a long slabby buttress. Start at the base of this and make a boulder problem start (V2) to a ledge then continue up the wall above finishing just left of the arete.
FA. John Allen 1976

Graham Parkes laid back on *David*, HVS 4c, Burbage South. *Page 180*

Descent

Descent – –

Pebble Mill 20m

DAVID and GOLIATH AREA
A fine buttress of magnificent rock spilt by two of grit's better known cracks and bounded by two excellent though arduous arete climbs. The slab of *Saul* is there for those who prefer their sport to be of a more delicate nature.

**❶ Above and Beyond
the Kinaesthetic Barrier** ☐☐☐☐ **E4 6b**
6m. A highly technical route up the arete. Use the war-time bullet-marks to reach the first jugs, runners and the final balancy moves. The crux is the lower moves but the top is scary and a mat of only limited use.
FA. John Allen 1976

❷ Samson . . . . ☐☐☐ **E6 7a**
12m. From large cams in the top of *Goliath* swing out left to a big pocket then make one desperate move upwards to an easier finish. A big swing if you fall but only one hard move
FA. Jerry Moffatt 1997

❸ Goliath . . . . ☐☐☐☐ **E4 5c**
10m. An unrelenting struggle up the wide crack. At least it is protectable nowadays by the biggest cams and an in-situ thread in the depths of the crack. It is also possible to layback the outer edge of the crack - at least on a top rope, but it is hardly cricket. *Photo page 39.*
FA. Don Whillans 1958

❹ David . . . . ☐☐ **HVS 4c**
10m. The parallel-sided crack is best sprinted, passing a big chockstone en route. A short and sweet route that is unfortunately over far too soon. *Photo page 179.*

❺ Sling Shot . . . . ☐☐ **HVS 5b**
14m. Make a rising traverse up the ramp to reach *David* then climb the wide crack until a swinging hand-traverse leads around the arete to reach the final moves of *Goliath*.
FA. Chris Craggs 1984

❻ Messiah . . . . ☐☐☐ **E6 6c**
10m. A stunning arete which still sees few suitors. It is climbed by technical laybacking to reach holds and runners in the break (Friend 0.5) and a hard finish.
FA. Jerry Moffatt 1984

❼ Rollerwall . . . . ☐☐ **E5 6c**
10m. A thin left-hand start to *Saul* which utilises some old chipped holds. They were filled in some years ago but the cement has gradually eroded, grow your nails for this one.
FA. Ron Fawcett 1987

❽ Saul . . . . ☐☐ **VS 5b**
10m. The steep quarried slab has a pleasing technical start trending right to a ledge and a mantelshelf. Step back left to an easier finish.
FA. Dave Gregory 1964

Whamcliffe
Dovestone Tor
Rivelin
Bamford
Stanage
Burbage North
Higgar Tor
Burbage South
Millstone
Lawrencefield
Yarncliffe
Froggatt
Curbar
Gardoms
Birchen
Chatsworth
Cratcliffe

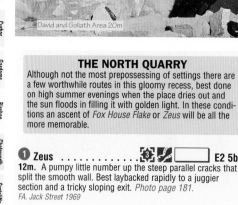

David and Goliath Area 20m

THE NORTH QUARRY

Although not the most prepossessing of settings there are a few worthwhile routes in this gloomy recess, best done on high summer evenings when the place dries out and the sun floods in filling it with golden light. In these conditions an ascent of *Fox House Flake* or *Zeus* will be all the more memorable.

❶ Zeus **E2 5b**
12m. A pumpy little number up the steep parallel cracks that split the smooth wall. Best laybacked rapidly to a juggier section and a tricky sloping exit. *Photo page 181.*
FA. Jack Street 1969

❷ Hades . . . . **HVS 5b**
12m. The slanting V-shaped groove gives a well-protected struggle that is a complete nightmare if at all greasy, and it usually is.
FA. Gerry Rogan early 1960s

❸ Fox House Flake . . . . **VS 4b**
14m. A pleasant diagonal crack leads rightwards usually by a hand-traverse to a steeper finale up the ledgy wall.
FA. Frank Burgess 1934

❹ The Cock . . . . **VS 4c**
12m. The cheeky groove on the right is steep to where it joins *Fox House Flake*.
FA. Gerry Rogan early 1960s

❺ Coldest Crack **E2 5c**
14m. In the back wall of the quarry is this thin crack, unclimbable for 50 weeks of most years. If you find it in condition, get it done.
FA. Mick Fowler 1976

❻ Millwheel Wall **E1 5b**
12m. The blunt arete has a slippery start to the big ledge. Climb the centre of the steep slab trending slightly rightwards, a good test of footwork, to better holds, and even the odd runner (wires and micro-friends) and a brisk mantelshelf finish.
FA. Len Millsom solo 1958

❼ Dunkley's Eliminate . . . . . . **VS 4c**
12m. Mantelshelf onto the ledge from the 'Flintstone's spare-wheel' then climb the well-positioned left arete which has good runners and holds. Swing around left for an exposed finish.

❽ Pretzel Logic **E3 6a**
12m. A counter-diagonal to *MWW* is fingery and unprotected.
FA. Dave Jones 1979

❾ Burssola . . . . **HVS 5b**
8m. The thin crack in the wall to the right is more stubborn than it looks. Fortunately the gear is good.
FA. John Allen (solo) 1975

Descent

Adjoining

North Quarry 60m

Whamcliffe
Dovestone Tor
Rivelin
Bamford
Stanage
Burbage North
Higgar Tor
Burbage South
Millstone
Lawrencefield
Yarncliffe
Froggatt
Curbar
Gardoms
Birchen
Chatsworth
Cratcliffe

THE SOUTH QUARRY

The Southern Burbage Quarry is about as grim as its neighbour although it is worth a visit to view the amazing Cioch Block with its 'dotted line' of drill holes; it looks like they were preparing to blow the whole thing up! Here is a small collection of hard routes and a few lesser offerings. Most of the routes are only climbable after a dry spell.

⑩ The Verdict . . . . ▢ **E2 6a**
10m. A deep V-shaped groove on the far left is brutal struggle. Thankfully the gear is good.
FA. Ken Jones 1972

⑪ The Old Bailey . . . . ▢ **HVS 5b**
14m. The deep blocky groove leads to a large chockstone and tough exit. Ferns can be a nuisance!

⑫ Wizard Ridge . . 🔲🔲🔲🔲 ▢ **E? 7?**
16m. The truly fantastic arete that cuts the air like a knife.
FA. TBA

⑬ The Simpering Savage . 🔲🔲 ▢ **E5 6b**
20m. The diagonal crack is finger traversed (peg) with great difficulty to turf lumps, *The Old Bailey* and a possible stance. Continue across the wall (5a) to the top of *The Verdict*.
FA. Paul Mitchell 1981

⑭ Poisoned Dwarf . . . . . . 🔲🔲 ▢ **HVS 5c**
8m. Thin cracks which used to give good pegging practice. Try finger jamming instead. A good V2 problem.

⑮ The Dover and Ellis Chimney 🔲 ▢ **E1 5b**
16m. The historical (hysterical?) cleft in the back corner of the quarry. Passing the wide upper section is the crux. Often sandy.
FA. Harry Dover, Gilbert Ellis 1932

⑯ Silent Spring . . . . . 🔲🔲🔲 ▢ **E4 5c**
An exposed girdle of the Cioch (Gaelic for tit) Block.
1) 5c, 12m. Start in the dirty gully on the left and cross a thin slab to a stance on the front (easiest with preplaced rope).
2) 5c, 12m. Continue right and then down before traversing out to the arete and a fine finish. Some of the many ancient bolts passed on route can be clipped although none should be trusted.
FA. Steve Bancroft, John Allen 1975

⑰ Off Spring . . . . . . 🔲🔲🔲 ▢ **E5 6b**
10m. Exciting climbing in a dramatic position and much easier for the tall. From a position on the arete (abseil approach) traverse the parallel cracks on the north-west wall then move up and right to finish phlegmatically up the short ramp.
FA. Johnny Dawes 1985

⑱ Captain Invincible . 🔲🔲🔲 ▢ **E8 6c**
16m. Free climbs the old aid route up the awesome north-west face of the Cioch. Climb the technical arete then follow the thin parallel cracks out left to an 'easy' finish up *Off Spring*. A bunch of ten-year-old pegs protect. Astounding!
FA. Sean Myles 1991

MILLSTONE

The greatest of all the gritstone quarries with sheer walls, stunning smooth corners and crack lines that are pure inspiration. Although cracks have become untrendy over recent years the ones you find here are not the dreaded off-widths. Many of the routes were originally aid climbs up hair-line cracks and the repeated inserting and removing of pegs widened the crack enough to allow access to (thin!) fingers, pointed toes and plentiful medium-wire protection. It is worth putting a bit of extra thought into your rack before setting off up one of these of finger-sized cracks since often you will need to make repeated use of the same size wire. But it is not just about cracks since there are also many fine corners and aretes formed by the thoughtful quarrying of the various bays. The section from *Green Death* to the Keyhole Cave could not have been designed better even if a climber had been in charge of the dynamite. Well maybe they might have done something about the unstable finishes since some of the exits are a little dangerous where sub-aerial weathering had started to erode the rock before it was exposed by the quarrymen. These 'crisp-bread' finishes require care and it is always a good idea to place an extra bomber-wire or two before trying to top out.

> **BOULDERING -** The bouldering on the crag is mentioned on page 192. Also of interest is the block of Mother Cap, the smaller Over Owler Tor and the excellent Secret Garden.

APPROACH (SK248804)

It used to be possible to drive up to the quarry via a whole network of old tracks (belaying from the van with the radio on while bashing pegs into grit, days of such decadence). The modern alternative is the extensive (or is that expensive?) Pay and Display car park just to the east of the Surprise View (a bend on the A625 with a sudden and shocking vista of the Hope Valley). Tracks lead out of the northwest corner of this over a ridge into the quarry, 5 minutes away. See close up map on page 199.

CONDITIONS

Although the quarry is a series of bays it offers less shelter than you might expect. Some of the far bays, and the Keyhole Cave, may be slightly less windy. The sun arrives on most of the crag in the afternoon but the North Bay is shady until late afternoon in the Summer and can be useful in hot weather. The walls dry quickly but become green in winter.

> **OTHER GUIDEBOOKS -** A more complete list of routes at Millstone is published in the 1991 BMC *Froggatt* guidebook. The bouldering, including Mother Cap, Over Owler Tor and the Secret Garden is in the 1998 Peak Bouldering ROCKFAX.

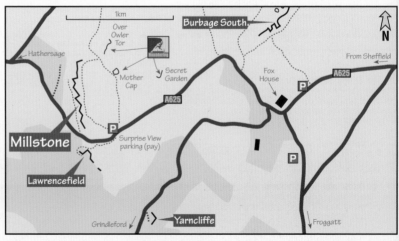

The crux moves on *Erb*, E2 5c, Millstone. *Page 190*

Wharncliffe
Dovestone Tor
Rivelin
Bamford
Stanage
Burbage North
Higgar Tor
Burbage South
Millstone
Lawrencefield
Yarncliffe
Froggatt
Curbar
Gardoms
Birchen
Chatsworth
Cratcliffe

←--- Descent

Evening | 15 min

NORTH BAY

A rather gloomy spot at the left-hand extremity of the cliff that only sees the sun late on in the summer, although that makes it a good venue to escape from the heat. The routes included some excellent steep cracks in the E1 to E3 range and some more recent horrors.

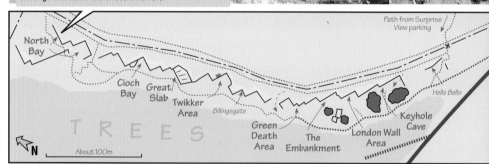

Path from Surprise View parking

North Bay

Cioch Bay Great Slab Twikker Area *Billingsgate*

Green Death Area The Embankment London Wall Area Keyhole Cave

Hells Bells

T R E E S

N About 100m

---

❶ Scrimsel . . . . ☐ **VS 4c**
12m. A long crack which is rather too blocky to be very good.

❷ Brimstone . . . . ☐ **E2 5b**
12m. From blocks, climb the steep crack to a crux just below the top. Sharp holds keep coming, but can you keep pulling?
FFA. Henry Barber 1973

❸ Satan's Slit . . . . ☐ **HVS 5b**
14m. The wider leaning crack, with a kink early on, is entered from the left and climbed rapidly on jams and jugs, passing an uncomfortable niche. Steep and pumpy sport.
FAA. John Loy 1964

❹ Gates of Mordor . . . . . . ☐ **E3 5c**
16m. The pod and leaning hand-crack is a strenuous number. It swallows medium Friends by the shed load. The initial groove feels a grovel but the crux is right at the very top.
FA. Hank Pasquill 1969

❺ Hacklespur . . . . ☐ **HVS 5b**
16m. Millstone's attempt at an answer to *Peapod*. Unfortunately it doesn't quite carry it off.
FAA. Alan Clarke 1960. FFA. John Loy (2nd man on the aided ascent) 1962

❻ Estremo . . . . ☐ **HVS 5a**
16m. The wide twisting crack is easier than it looks if you enjoy fist jamming. Pull over the roof and sprint up the short layback.
FAA. Ted Howard early 1960s

Descent

Wharncliffe
Dovestone Tor
Rivelin
Bamford
Stanage
Burbage North
Higgar Tor
Burbage South
Millstone
Lawrencefield
Yarncliffe
Froggatt
Curbar
Gardoms
Birchen
Chatsworth
Cratcliffe

Evening   15 min

Cloch Bay 100m

7 Gimbals . . . . HVS 5b
18m. A long groove is climbed to the overhang. Pull through this and climb the wall on the right via shallow groove.
FA. Mick Fowler 1976

8 Mother's Pride E6 6c
18m. A fierce thin finger crack leads to a band of overhangs. Pull into the steep leaning groove and finish up this.
FA. (London Pride) Mick Fowler 1976, (Which Way Up Robitho) Paul Evans 1988. Reclimbed as a single pitch up the bottom of LP and the top of WWUR by Mike Lea, 2001, and renamed Mother's Pride.

9 Perplexity E6 6b
18m. The steep arete is technical as far as a band of crusty rock. Step right and climb the difficult slanting groove and the headwall. Holds were chipped off after the first ascent but it is still climbable at pretty much the same grade.
FA. Johnny Dawes 1984

10 Plexity . . . . HVS 5a
12m. The fine steep crack in the centre of the wall leads through a series of bulges to a ledge out on the right. Traverse back left (crux) above the roof and sprint for the top.
FA. Joe Brown 1957

11 Remembrance Day . . . . . . VS 4c
12m. Climb the deep main groove at the back of the bay on its right-hand side to ledges and a finish up the continuation groove above the grass ledge.
FA. Ted Howard 1960

12 Day Dream . . . . VS 4b
20m. Climb the rib to the right of the main corner. Above thin cracks and a shallow groove lead to a ledge. Follow the continuation crack in the steep wall to a loose finish.
FA. John Loy early 1960s

13 Rainy Day . . . . VS 4b
20m. At the right-hand side of the ledge is a crack in a groove. Climb this to a ledge then take the continuation past a couple of tiny grassy ledges to the final steep crack of *Day Dream*.
FA. Alan Clarke early 1960s

14 Top Loader . . . E7 6c
28m. The groove and hair-line cracks to the left of *Saville Street* are climbed until it is possible to trend right to reach the arete. Step back left and make more hard moves to the grass cornice and an interesting finish. A pair of new pegs protect.
FA. Mike Lea 2001

15 Saville Street E3 6a
28m. The superb finger-crack in the right wall of the bay. Gain the top of the pedestal awkwardly and climb the leaning crack to crucial moves into a niche. Exit steeply to easy ground.
FAA. Reg Pillinger early 1960s. FFA. John Allen 1975

16 Soho Sally . . . . HVS 5b
18m. Climb the flake on the right to ledges. From here follow the shallow groove above until it becomes necessary to swing onto the exposed left arete. Care required with the finish.
FA. Geoff Birtles 1975

CIOCH BAY

The main feature of this bay is the narrow tower of the Cioch leaning against its left-hand side and, just left again, the steep jamming crack of *Dexterity*. The right wall has some pleasant offerings although the exits need a careful approach; this is classic 'chest of drawers' territory.

1 March Hare . . . . 🔲🔲 **E2 5b**
14m. The square-cut arete is climbed on its left-hand side and becomes a mite harrowing towards the top. Staying with the arete is best and trending left is the easier option. From the ledge escape right or finish up:
FA. Gabe Regan 1975

2 April Arete . . . . 🔲 **HVS 4c**
14m. The upper arete is gained most easily from the right. Pleasant though poorly protected, and featuring a huge chipped hold. The **Direct Start** to the left of *March Hare* is a poor **6b**.
FA. Alan Clarke early 1960s

3 Dextrous Hare . . . . . . 🔲🔲 **E3 5c**
14m. A tenuous crack and tiny groove are approached on small flat edges and entered by a wild layback. The crack right of the arete offers a top pitch at an easier grade.
FA. Martin Taylor 1976

4 Dexterity . . . . . . 🔲🔲🔲 **E1 5b**
20m. Pumpy climbing up the crack that cleaves the wall. Where it thins, either pull out left, or better and even pumpier, finish direct. Traverse off or finish up the grotty wall at the back.
FAA. Harold Drasdo 1957

5 Cioch Corner . . . . 🔲 **S 4a**
26m. Climb the deep groove to the tip of the Cioch and a possible belay. Finish up the nicely exposed arete above.
FA. Alan Clarke 1956

6 Mayday . . . . 🔲 **HVS 5a**
22m. Climb the balancy arete of the Cioch to its tip and a finish up the continuation arete of *Cioch Corner*.
FA. Alan Clarke early 1960s

7 Supra Direct . . . . 🔲🔲 **E1 5b**
22m. The once-pegged crack up the front of the Cioch proves tricky at the bulge. From its tip easy ground leads to the top or escape down and right via stepped ledges.
FAA. Mike James 1959. FFA. (nearly) Pete Brayshaw 1975

The well-cracked wall to the right has a couple of half-reasonable low grade offerings. GREAT CARE is needed with the exits.

8 Close Shave . . . . 🔲 **S 4a**
24m. Climb cracks to the right of the Cioch, trending right then left back to reach the ledge and a belay. Finish up the deep groove at the back of the ledge.
FA. Alan Clarke 1956

9 Boomerang . . . . 🔲 **S 4a**
24m. Left of the main groove follow the line of cracks and corners left then right to a ledge. Escape rightwards with care.
FA. John Loy (solo) early 1960s

The right wall of the bay has a couple of agreeable slabby routes although protection is a bit sparse.

10 Only Just . . . . 🔲🔲 **E2 5b**
18m. Start just right of a wide crack and climb the groove to a ledge. Continue up the delicate and poorly-protected shallow groove directly above. Side runners reduce the grade.
FA. Ernie Marshall 1959

11 Eartha . . . . 🔲 **HS 4a**
20m. Follow *Only Just* to the ledge then step right and climb the pleasant flake-crack up the slabby face.

Wharncliffe
Dovestone Tor
Rivelin
Bamford
Stanage
Burbage North
Higgar Tor
Burbage South
Millstone
Lawrencefield
Yarncliffe
Froggatt
Curbar
Gardoms
Birchen
Chatsworth
Cratcliffe

GREAT SLAB

A fine sheet of quarried gritstone with a collection of routes across the grades. *Great Slab* is one of the best lower grade routes in the quarry and there is a selection of harder climbs that demand precise footwork. The bay tends to be particularly green after rain.

12 Svelt . . . . **HVS 5a**
20m. The slabby groove up the left-hand edge of the slab gives good climbing to a ledge at its top (possible stance on the right). Then step back left to climb either of the steep grooves above the lower pitch, the left-hand one is easiest and most pleasant. Care with the exit needed.
FA. Al Parker, Martin Boysen 1962

13 The Snivelling Shit . . **E5 6a**
14m. The razor-edged iron coruscations (above an ankle-snapping flake) lead left then back right to the top of the slab. Escape up or down *Great Slab*. The only gear is a Friend 4 located above all difficulties, it is not much use! Perhaps it is worth trying this one in ski boots.
FA. Bob Millward 1978

14 The Moronic Chippings . . **VS 4a**
14m. A line of small and spaced chipped holds (shades of Yorkshire) lead all the way up the slab, or do they run out?? Finish up or down *Great Slab*.
FA. Unknown (no surprise there then)

15 Great Slab . . . . **HS 4b**
28m. Climb the slippery crack which splits the right-hand side of the slab as it runs leftwards, poorly protected. Move back slightly right and then make a short traverse to a good ledge above the centre of the slab (possible belay). Climb the corner-crack to a ledge then move right and round the arete to an excavated chimney with a rather unstable exit.
FA. Alan Maskery 1952. FFA. Al Parker 1957

16 Sex Dwarves **E3 6b**
10m. The right-hand edge of the slab has a series of tiny holds that are becoming ever more polished. Keep left to claim the full 'E-grade' or escape off right. A mat reduces it to an extended V4 problem.
FA. Mark Millar 1982

17 Lorica . . . . **VS 4c**
20m. Climb the crack up the right-hand edge of the slab and the short but gripping curving flake above and left (who says it is detached) to a finish up *Great Slab*.

18 Bun Run . . . . **HVS 5a**
20m. Follow *Lorica* to the steepening in the continue up the awkward groove directly above to a finish up *Great Slab*.
FA. Al Evans 1969

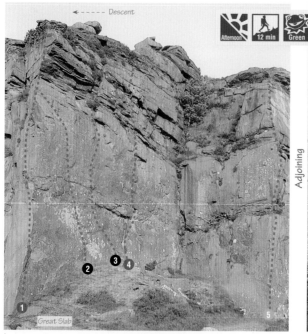

Whamcliffe

Dovestone Tor

Rivelin

Bamford

Stanage

Burbage North

Higgar Tor

Burbage South

Millstone

Lawrencefield

Yarncliffe

Froggatt

Curbar

Gardoms

Birchen

Chatsworth

Cratcliffe

TWIKKER AREA

A fine tall bay with the shallow cave of *Lyon's Corner House* and *Twikker* in its left wall. Several quality routes are located here and the area can be a bit more sheltered than other sections of Millstone although it is occasionally green.

Restrictions may apply in the spring if the ravens are nesting. These will be marked by signs at the crag.

1 Windrete **E2 5b**
14m. The impressive windy arete has low gear (small wires) and mostly good holds. Bold and airy with some suspect rock.
FA. Al Evans 1969

2 Breeze Mugger **E5 6b**
14m. Climb to a break (gear) then make hard moves up before moving left to a finish on the arete of *Windrete*.
FA. Paul Dearden 1990

3 Meeze Brugger **E5 6b**
14m. Climb the wall first left then right. The hard bit is standing on the only good hold on the lower wall. Finish up suspect rock.
FA. Ron Fawcett 1984

4 Eros **E1 5b**
14m. The steep crack in the left wall of the bay has good holds and runners though some of the rock has a temporary feel about it. Finish with care.
FFA. Paul Grayson 1969

5 Lyons Corner House Direct . . . **HVS 5a**
28m. An excellent and well-protected pitch up the long arete. Manages to avoid all the crucial sections on the regular route.

6 Lyons Corner House . . . . . **HVS 5a**
30m. An expedition up the left edge of the bay that can be split at a belay in the cave but is usually done in one mega run-out. A short awkward groove (4b) leads into the cave. Up the corner to the roof then traverse to the left arete and make difficult moves to the security of a narrow ledge. The leaning wall right of the arete leads to ledges and a finish up the spectacularly positioned arete.
FAA. Kit Twyford, George Leaver 1957

7 Erb **E2 5c**
28m. From the cave climb left then right to pass the central overlap awkwardly by finger jamming and a tough mantelshelf. Finish up the wide gritty crack above. *Photo page 185.*
FA. Alan Clarke early 1960s. FFA. Tom Proctor 1975

8 Twikker **E3 5c**
28m. The right-hand side of the cave leads to the lip of the roof which is passed with difficulty (stepping in from the ledge on the right is taboo at the grade) to gain the upper slab. Pass the cave (seasonal Raven's nest) to the final crack which gives tenuous finger-jamming to a sandy exit.
FA. Dave Johnson 1956. FFA. Tom Proctor 1975

9 Lubric . . . . **HVS 5b**
28m. From the big cave trend right to the foot of the smooth corner. This gives good climbing when it isn't full of grass!
FA. Alan Clarke early 1960s

10 Pinstone Street **E2 5c**
28m. The crack right of the corner turns mean (and a bit loose) at the overhang. Once past the bulges continue more easily stepping right at the ledge system to the final crack.
FA. Dave Johnson 1956. FFA. (well almost) Al Evans 1969

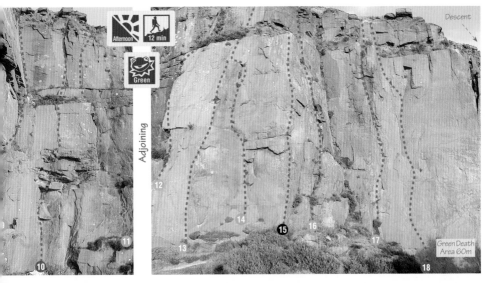

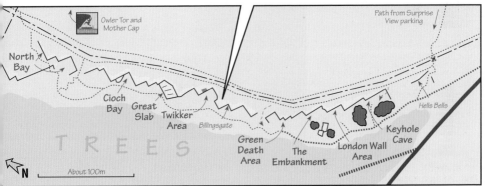

Wharncliffe
Dovestone Tor
Rivelin
Bamford
Stanage
Burbage North
Higgar Tor
Burbage South
Millstone
Lawrencefield
Yarncliffe
Froggatt
Curbar
Gardoms
Birchen
Chatsworth
Cratcliffe

① Diamond Groove .... 🔷⬜ **HVS 5b**
8m. Start at a grass ledge under the centre of the wall and climb to higher ledge. Move left to a groove which leads to a third ledge. Finish up the thin crack in the wall behind.
A. John Loy early 1960s

② Flapjack .... 🔷⬜ **VS 4b**
4m. The shallow groove in the left-hand side of the protruding buttress is pleasant. Finish up the prominent crack above.
A. Jack Soper 1956

③ Neatfeet .... 🔷⬜ **VS 5a**
4m. Climb the square-cut arete to join the upper section of the previous climb.

④ SSS .... 🔷⬜ **VS 4b**
4m. The stepped groove on the right-hand side of the projecting buttress leads to an exit by the finish of *Flapjack*.
A. Jack Soper early 1960s

⑮ Winter's Grip ...... 🔷🤍⬜ **E6 6b**
22m. The steep square-cut arete is an unrelenting gripper. The only runner is too low to be any use!
FA. Neil Foster (solo) 1983

⑯ Keelhaul .... 🔷⬜ **VS 4c**
16m. The hanging flake on the left wall of the grassy groove is approached up a short corner. Care with the finish required.
FA. John Loy (solo) early 1960s

⑰ Quiddity .... 🔷⬜ **HVS 5a**
16m. An impressive arete pitch. There more holds and runners than appearances suggest fortunately!
FA. John Loy early 1960s

⑱ Billingsgate .... 🔷⬜ **E1 5b**
18m. The open scoop gives fine technical climbing (past lots of rather tired small-wire slots) to an exit on the left. Once described as 'like a well protected *Green Death*', well it ain't.
FFA. Steve Chadwick 1969

GREEN DEATH AREA

This is the most impressive part of the quarry with a series of truly stunning lines. From the old classics of *Great North Road* and *Crewcut*, through to the classic scary 70s outings of *Green Death* and *Edge Lane*, and onto to the fantastic line of *The Master's Edge*, there are routes here to dream of through the long winter nights. The rock dries quickly although it can be green in the winter. Fence-post belays at the top of the wall are a long way back, which may require the use of a spare rope.

BOULDERING - There is some good bouldering at Millstone which is surprising for a 25m high quarry. However concentrating on the blank walls and aretes at the base of the crag there are several classic problems. The best are at the start of *Green Death* and around the Embankment slab.

GEAR FOR THE BORE HOLES - The bore holes are essential for protection on this section. There are various methods of fiddling devices into them including certain specialist caming devices and Friends 2.5s on two cams only! One of the most surprising and solid solutions is to use a large Rock (about size 7 or 8) or small Hex (size 5) on cord. Shove it into the hole thin end first with the cord doubled back over the top. Bombproof! Try it in the low holes on *Jealous Pensioner* before heading onto those big airy aretes.

The top of Billingsgate

Descent

---

❶ Stone Dri . . . . 🗝️🖼️🎽 ☐ E2 6a
20m. The blank corner delicately past a perched flake to a taxing bridging sequence which is much easier for the tall.
FA. (1 pt) John Regan 1976. FFA. Dave Humphries 1977

❷ Crewcut . . . . 🗝️🖼️🎽 VS 4c
22m. Layback the imposing straight past a good resting ledge. Chockstones or large Friend runners protect. Those heading to the States might want to 'off-width' it just for the practice.
FA. Alan Clarke 1963

❸ Xanadu . . . . 🗝️🖼️ ☐ E1 5b
1) **4c, 20m.** From part way up *Crewcut* follow the ledge out right to reach the large corner and climb to the ledge above.
2) **5b, 25m.** The main angle gives an excellent pitch when clean. Finish by a wild hand-traverse out to the right arete.
FA. Keith Myhill, Al Evans 1969

❹ Jealous Pensioner . 🗝️🖼️🎽 ☐ E4 5c
22m. The centre of the drilled wall gives an odd pitch with worrying stretches to and from the midway ledge. Ingenious use of both the horizontal and vertical bore holes for protection can make it feel much safer.
FA. Jim Burton 1978

❺ Xanadu Direct . . . . 🗝️🖼️🎽 ☐ E3 5c
22m. A wild and weird piece of bridging up the blank corner. The tall can bridge but shorties will have to shuffle, feet on one wall, hands on the other, honest!
FA. Hank Pasquill 1974

❻ Adios Amigo . . . . . 🗝️🖼️🎽 ☐ E5 6b
16m. Climb the right wall of the corner on bore holes and small edges. Protection for what it is worth is in the holes.
FA. Mark Leach 1985

❼ Great West Road . . 🗝️🖼️🎽 ☐ E2 5b
Fine climbing with two impressive and contrasting pitches.
1) **5b, 18m.** Layback up the huge flake to a tiny ledge. The upper part is steeper and technical, leading to a massive terrace.
2) **E2, 16m.** The upper arete is delicate and effectively unprotected. The forty-year-old golo should not be trusted!
FAA. Dave Johnson 1957. FFA. Al Evans 1965

❽ Edge Lane . . . . 🗝️🖼️ ☐ E5 5c
18m. The magnificent scalloped arete is unprotected where it matters although gear can be fiddled in the half-height bore holes. Not for the faint of heart, because from the crux you will hit the ground, gear or not!
FA. Alan McHardy 1974

← – Descent

Whamcliffe
Dovestone Tor
Rivelin
Bamford
Stanage
Burbage North
Higgar Tor
Burbage South
Millstone
Lawrencefield
Yarncliffe
Froggatt
Curbar
Gardoms
Birchen
Chatsworth
Cratcliffe

⑨ Green Death . . . . 🔲🔲 **E5 5c**

18m. The superb blank groove can be approached from a short way up *Edge Lane* by a tricky traverse, the alternative being a pile of stones or a choice of 6b to 7a problems. The crucial upper section has a solitary (old) peg runner in the right wall, just above the first crux and just below the second. Finish using a tiny chipped hold. Continue up the easy corner or abseil carefully from the chipped spike on the left.
FA. Tom Proctor 1969. F Winter A. Tom Proctor early 1970s

⑩ The Master's Edge . . 🔲🔲🔲 **E7 6c**

18m. One of the major routes of the 80s up the clean-cut arete. A hard starting section enables the sanctuary of the bore holes to be reached (gear). Continue with rising anxiety to a final wild leap which is about twice as far off the ground as your last runner. There is a fixed belay on a bunch of pegs at the top.
FA. Ron Fawcett late 29December 1983

⑪ Great Arete . . . . 🔲🔲 **E5 5c**

16m. The upper arete is delicate and mighty serious. Start on the ledge and climb the arete, first on the right and then on the left. A low bunch of peg runners might just save your life!
FA. Tom Proctor 1975

⑫ Knightsbridge . . . . 🔲🔲🔲 **E2 5c**

34m. A fine thin crack which is one of Millstone's classic E2s. Most people start by scrambling up *Scoop Crack* to the mid-height ledge. The steep lower corner crack is best done early in the year before the ferns take over (5b).
FFA. Tom Proctor

⑬ Scoop Crack . . . . 🔲🔲 **VS 4b**

32m. Climb the cracks in the broken arete to the big ledge and a stance. Take the blocky continuation in the left wall which eases with height.

⑭ The Scoop . . . . 🔲🔲 **Diff**

35m. A worthwhile mild offering in this crucible of daring deeds. The ramp leads left then steep rock is climbed leftwards, all very pleasant, to the huge ledge. The juggy corner behind is followed all the way to the moor.

⑮ Clock People . . . . 🔲🔲🔲 **E6 6c**

14m. One the aid climbers missed up a hairline crack in the steep slab. Technical in the extreme.
FA. Ron Fawcett 1984

⑯ Watling Street . . . . 🔲🔲 **E3 5b**

16m. Start from the big ledge and climb the arete left of the cental section of *Great North Road*. Delicate and unprotected.
FAA. Len Millsom early 1960s

⑰ Great North Road . . . . 🔲🔲 **HVS 5a**

32m. One of the great classics of the quarry up the magnificent long corner. It has a crucial central layback/bridging groove and tricky final roof. It can be split into three short pitches if require, though is best done as one huge run-out.
FAA. Peter Biven, Trevor Peck 1956. FFA. Joe Brown 1957

Descent

Green
Death
Area

Escape Route
from the ledges

Afternoon | 8 min

THE EMBANKMENT
A superb sheet of rock named after a similar but inferior feature in London. Once the place to learn to aid climb, this is now the home of the finest set of finger cracks in the Peak.

❶ Technical Master . . . . . 🔲 6b (V4)
6m. The arete is a classic boulder problem. The left-hand side is also 6b but worth V5. The shortest three star route in the Peak perhaps? It has also been done one-handed, dream on!
FA. Keith Myhill late 1960s

❷ Blind Bat . . . . 🔲 E4 5c
14m. Bold climbing up the wall right of the upper part of *GNR*. A runner in *Embankment 1* is a good idea then climb the wall leftwards on flat holds passing an ancient peg runner.
FAA. Les Bonnington late 1960s. FFA. Mick Fowler 1976

❸ Embankment 1 . . . . . 🔲 E1 5b
1) **VS 4c, 12m.** The first crack and flake lead past an angle iron to the ledge. Often done as a route in its own right.
2) **5b, 12m.** Climb the thin crack to a steep exit. *Photo opposite.*
FFA. John Allen 1975

❹ Embankment 2 . . . . 🔲 VS 4c
1) **4c, 12m.** Climb the twin cracks. A big boot on your left foot may be useful. The right-hand crack on its own is provides fine E2 5c finger-jamming practice.
2) **4b, 12m.** From the ledge finish up the groove to a loose exit.

❺ Scritto's Republic . . 🔲 E7 6b
16m. The wall between the cracks with both runners and holds in short supply.
FA. Ron Fawcett 1982

❻ Embankment 3 . . . . . 🔲 E1 5b
1) **5b, 14m.** An excellent and popular finger jamming exercise. Passing the in-situ tat at 12m is the tricky bit. *Photo page 3.*
2) **5b, 12m.** The thin crack in the upper wall, left of the groove, has hard moves low down.
FFA. Ed Drummond 1975

❼ Time For Tea . . . . 🔲 E3 5c
20m. Low in the grade but spooky. Follow the crack to a poor rest below the blank upper section. Fill the cracks with runners then traverse left boldly to better holds. Either finish straight up or continue traversing to finish close to *Embankment 3*; both options are about the same grade and are equally scary.
FA. Ed Drummond 1975

❽ Tea for Two . . . . . 🔲 E4 6a
20m. The direct finish to *Time for Tea* is bold, technical and not well protected. Is it your cup of tea?
FA. Ian Riddington 1982

❾ Time For Tea Original . . 🔲 E1 5b
22m. From the poor rest below the blank upper section on *Time for Tea* traverse right to join and finish up *Embankment 4*. Only one independent move but still very worthwhile.
FA. Ken Wilkinson 1974

❿ Embankment 4 . . . . . . 🔲 E1 5b
22m. The right-hand crack started from blocks has thin moves up the crack and superb groove above to a shelving exit.
FFA. Chris Addy 1975

Katherine Schirmacher on pitch 2 of *Embankment 1*, E1 5b, Millstone.
Photo: Ian Parnell. *Opposite*

←--- Descent

Descent
beyond Keyhole Caves
----►

Afternoon | 8 min

Whamcliffe | Dovestone Tor | Rivelin | Bamford | Stanage | Burbage North | Higgar Tor | Burbage South | Millstone | Lawrencefield | Yarncliffe | Froggatt | Curbar | Gardoms | Birchen | Chatsworth | Cratcliffe

Embankment Slab

Keyhole Cave
100m

LONDON WALL AREA
A superb set of cracks and grooves including the magnificent *London Wall*, the superb *Bond Street* and the pretty reasonable *Great Portland Street*.

❶ Whitehall .... HVS 5b
26m. The deep angle is straightforward (4b) to below the upper smooth section which gives good technical climbing.
FFA. Keith Myhill 1969

❷ Lotto E1 5c
24m. Disjointed climbing though with some good moves. Easy ledges lead to an stance below a shallow groove (4b). Climb the groove until forced around the arete. Step up then follow the wide break back left and finish over the centre of the roof.
FAA. John Loy early 1960s. FFA. Tom Proctor 1975

❸ Covent Garden .... VS 4b
1) 4b, 15m. A pleasant groove leads via a couple of moves on its left arete to a stance in the corner on the right.
2) 4b, 12m. Shuffle out left to the airy arete (a bit thin on gear) and finish through the bulges in a spectacular position.
FAA. Peter Biven, Trevor Peck 1956

❹ Bond Street .... HVS 5a
20m. A near-perfect jamming crack has hard moves to enter and leave the prominent niche. It will swallow all the protection you can 'afford' to carry.

❺ Monopoly E7 6b
20m. A blank wall with the not unusual combination of technical climbing and little in the way of protection.
FA. Johnny Dawes 1983

❻ Great Portland Street ..... HVS 5b
20m. A tough mantelshelf is required to reach the elegant hanging groove. This then gives excellent steep bridging.
FFA. Alan Clarke 1963

❼ White Wall E5 6b
22m. The smooth wall left of the deep corner could have done with a bit more pegging before it was free climbed. The crux is reaching the overlap although the interest is well maintained.
Photo opposite.
FFA. Steve Bancroft 1976

❽ The Mall .... VS 4c
22m. The sustained right-angled groove is a bit hard at the grade, though protection is excellent. Beware the shelving top.
FAA. Pete Biven, Trevor Peck early 1950s (at A3!) FFA. Joe Brown 1957

❾ London Wall E5 6a
22m. One of the finest crack-climbs in the country sees many suitors and almost as many failures. The initial leaning fissure is as hard as anything on the route, although the leftwards traverse is also taxing and the final breathtaking shallow groove sees many a flier. An essential tick.
FAA. Trevor Peck 1956. FFA. John Allen 1975

❿ Lambeth Chimney .... VS 4b
22m. The shallow chimney on the right-hand side of the wall leads to a ledge. Step around the exposed arete on the left to enter and finish up a shallow groove.

John Arran climbing *White Wall*, E5 6b, at Millstone. Photo: Ian Parnell

KEYHOLE CAVE

A steep wall riven by vertical cracks and featuring two wide red slots known for obvious reasons as the Keyhole Caves. The rock on the faces is good but that in the caves is soft and sandy and many visits into either recess end with a 'never again' vow. *Regent Street* is one of the very best E2s in the Peak. The surrounding walls and trees make this area a touch more sheltered from the wind than other sections of the crag and it is first to get the sun.

Left of the main Keyhole wall is a long wall of poorer rock with a wide jagged crack in its right-hand side.

❶ Brixton Road . . . . 🎿 VDiff
24m. The deep crack is the best low-grade route in the quarry although considerable care is required with the finish. Climb the crack to ledges, move left to a groove and left again onto the arete before scaling the tottering slope to safety.

❷ Sky Walk . . . . 🎿 VS 4b
24m. A well-named route that traverses above the lip of the roof of the Keyhole Cave. It is most easily reached via *Brixton Road* and it is not well protected. Watch for friable holds.
FA. John Loy early 1960s

❸ Adam Smith's
Invisible Hand . . . . 🎿 E6 6b
20m. The superb left arete of the wall. Tat on the mouldy old bolts and a peg round the arete are the only gear.
FA. Johnny Dawes 1984

❹ The Rack . . . . 🎿 E5 6a
20m. Follow the old bolt ladder on a series of sharp and rather snappy holds to the left edge of the cave. Side runners protect.
FFA. Loz Francombe 1982

❺ Oxford Street . . . . . 🎿 E3 6b
22m. The wide left-hand crack (a good HVS 5a pitch) leads to the cave. Then very hard moves through the notch in the overhang (good gear but awkward to place) may allow you onto the easier upper wall.
FAA. Peter Biven 1956. FFA. Phil Burke 1969

❻ Piccadilly Circus . . . . 🎿 E2 5c
24m. The middle finger crack leads to the cave (worthwhile at HVS 5b) and indifferent belays. A tricky traverse left and thin wall gains a ledge on the arete. Trend easily right to finish.
FFA. Steve Bancroft 1976

❼ Coventry Street . . . 🎿 E4 6b
22m. A popular test-piece which means that this is usually the most chalked of the cracks. It gets gradually harder as the cave approaches with a frustrating final move that is easy once you have sat on the gear. The sandy roof above the cave gives a gripping struggle passing a fat old peg (6a). The bottom section is often done on its own at a hard but safe E3. Abseil off a spike.
FAA. Peter Biven 1956. FFA. Steve Bancroft, John Allen 1976

❽ Jermyn Street . . . . 🎿 E5 6a
24m. The thin crack and shallow groove lead to the cave. Climb the right arete (small wires) then traverse the handrail out left (small Friend) feet pedalling in the sand, to get established on the head wall with difficulty. Finish more easily.
FAA. Peter Biven, Trevor Peck 1956. FFA. Tom Proctor 1971

❾ Regent Street . . . . 🎿 E2 5c
22m. The finest finger crack in the Peak (and the country?). Climb steeply to pass the jammed block (possibly the technical crux?) then trend right to a shallow groove and ledges below the soaring final crack. This is best climbed quickly after placing high runners. A final short steep wall completes this gem.
FAA. Peter Biven, Trevor Peck 1956. FFA. Terry King 1968

Cioch Bay

Great Slab

Twikker Area

Billingsgate

Over Owler Tor and Mother Cap

Surprise View parking (pay)

TREES

Green Death Area

The Embankment

London Wall Area

Keyhole Cave

Hells Bells

Lawrencefield

N

About 100m

Whamcliffe · Dovestone Tor · Rivelin · Bamford · Stanage · Burbage North · Higgar Tor · Burbage South · Millstone · Lawrencefield · Yarncliffe · Froggatt · Curbar · Gardoms · Birchen · Chatsworth · Cratcliffe

⑩ Wall Street Crash . . . E5 6b
20m. A good technical route with fingery moves on iron carbonate coruscations. Now a touch bolder due to the removal of the old aid bolts and their replacement with lower pegs. Finish up the steep ramp above.
FFA. Johnny Dawes 1983

⑪ Shaftesbury Avenue . . . HVS 5a
20m. The fist-width crack at the right-hand side of the wall leads to a small overhang, (big cams and big fists help). The wall above the overhang is much easier The exit is loose.
FAA. Peter Biven, Trevor Peck 1956. FFA. Jim Campbell 1967

⑫ The Whore . . . . HVS 5b
20m. Climb the wall to the overhang and layback through this using a finger crack to reach easier ground. Not quite the bitch the name suggests. Another one with a grotty exit
FA. Jim Reading 1975

⑬ Gimcrack . . . . VS 4c
22m. A good jamming crack lead up the wall left of the right-hand cave to enter a shallow right-facing groove. The exit from this requires care as an unstable slope lurks above.
FA. Barry Ingle 1962

Descent

Afternoon · 6 min

14 15   16   17   18 19

HELLS BELLS
A pleasant buttress with some mild offerings which are suitable for those who find the scale of the main quarry a bit intimidating. This is the first piece of decent rock that you arrive at on the normal approach. Descend to the right.

⑭ Chiming Crack . . . . HS 4b
8m. On the left a pair of converging cracks and their continuation give pleasant and well-protected jamming.
FA. Alan Clarke c1960

⑮ Hells Bells . . . . HS 4a
8m. The left-hand of the three grooves is the best route here and is a sample of what the rest of the quarry has to offer. Bridge and jam the well-protected groove to rocky ledges

⑯ Midrift . . . . VDiff
8m. The central groove is pleasantly mild. Another good introduction to the rock and the style of climbing at Millstone.

⑰ Giant's Steps . . . . VDiff
8m. Yet another good starter up the right-hand groove using a series of giant steps.

⑱ Street Legal E2 5c
8m. Climb the smooth face on the right passing an Africa-shaped flake with difficulty.
FA. Paul Cropper 1978

⑲ Blood and Guts
on Botty Street E5 6b
8m. An extended boulder problem up the right-hand arete of the buttress is unprotected and precarious
FA. Allen Williams 1987

LAWRENCEFIELD

The deeply recessed quarry (named after the extensive moor behind the old workings and called Laurencefield on the Harvey Dark Peak map) has been a haunt of climbers since the 1950s. Initially a selection of easy free routes were developed around the pool before the place was transformed into an aid playground with climbers hammering a way up the many thin cracks that split the vertical back wall that rises above the green and greasy pool. By the early 1970s standards of technical ability and the quality of protection, allied to the fact that the majority of the cracks were now wide enough to admit fingertips, meant that many of the aid routes became excellent free climbs in a new route gold rush not see before or since.

Although playing second fiddle to nearby Millstone Quarry, Lawrencefield quarry remains a well-liked venue, with a good set of climbs, a selection of easier and immensely popular routes around Gingerbread Slab and the hard classics on the steep smooth walls around the pool, there is something here for most tastes.

OTHER GUIDEBOOKS - A more complete list of routes at Lawrencefield is published in the 1991 BMC *Froggatt* guidebook.

APPROACH (SK249798)

The quarry is situated near the Surprise View, on the other side of the road to the larger Millstone Quarry. Park at the large Surprise View car park, cross the road and follow a narrow track towards the bend. Just before the bend follow a path down leftwards and through a gate. The quarry lies hidden from view but sandy paths leads down the slope past the end of the rocks into the main bay which is now gradually filling with a sea of silver birch.

CONDITIONS

The quarry is very well sheltered and is ideal on cold or wild days. This fact is well known hence it does get crowded in such conditions. It can be midgy when humid and is a real furnace on clear summer afternoons.

Much of the rock gets very sandy in the summer. It doesn't dry very quickly after rain.

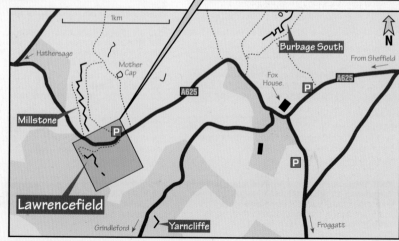

Alan James and Tudor Griffiths on *Pool Wall*, E5 6b, Lawrencefield. Photo: Brian Harley. *Page 202*

LAWRENCEFIELD *Great Harry Area*

← - - - - Descent

GREAT HARRY AREA

The series of walls and grooves to the left of
the pool have a fine collection of middle
grade routes that follow strong natural lines.
Three Tree Climb, Pulpit Route and *Great
Harry* are especially thrilling outings. For
something a little more taxing *Suspense*
takes a trip above the water and getting
involved with *Pool Wall* increases the likeli-
hood of a ducking several-fold.

① Three Tree Climb . . HS 4b
22m. A good route up the left arete of the main
quarry. A steep, juggy start and awkward grooves
lead to a small ledge. A blind grope around the right
arete locates a good flake. Layback on this to reach a
pine tree on a ledge (popular belay spot) then finish
more easily out leftwards.
FA. Albert Shutt 1952

② Great Peter . . . E1 5b
20m. The discontinuous thin crack in the wall to the
right is approached via a steep finger crack and is
pleasantly delicate and well protected with small
wires. Originally aided by Biven hence the name.
FA. Peter Biven 1956. FFA. Clive Jones 1976

③ Pulpit Groove . . . . VDiff
28m. An unsung low grade gem which can be split
into three pitches if required. Climb a short crack to
gain the base of the ramp and follow this to a sitting
stance atop the pulpit (thread belay). Stride across
the gap and follow the exposed ramp to a large ledge
and tree belay. Finish out to the right for the best effect.
FA. Albert Shutt 1952

④ Great Harry . . . . VS 4c
22m. The large corner is jammed and bridged to a stance on
the pulpit. Continue up the wide and awkward corner crack
above to a tricky but well protected exit up a blank groove.
FAA. Harry Hartley 1953

⑤ Scoop Connection E3 5b
22m. Climb the slabby wall rightwards to an indifferent set of
small runners on the arete then teeter left along the scary shelf
to join and finish up *Pulpit Groove*.

⑥ Suspense E2 5c
20m. A route to keep you on your toes. Climb the right wall of
the open corner on finger edges to a rest on the arete then step
around right to a small ledge. Climb the thin cracks in the face
with difficulty (occasional peg runner) to a final long reach.
FAA. Peter Biven 1956. FFA. John Allen 1975

⑦ Pool Wall E5 6b
20m. At low water the direct start to *Suspense* is technical and
bold. Small wires and cams protect sparingly. Above the crux a
bold sprint leads to the crux of the regular route. If the tide is in
the water might just break your fall. *Photo page 201.*
FAA. Alan Clarke 1958. FFA. Roger Greatrick early 1980s.

BELAYS - For most of the routes belays stakes are in place
at the top of the crag, and there is the occasional useful
boulder. Climbers are requested to avoid belaying on the
fence posts that form the boundary of the quarry.

THE POOL WALL

⑧ Lawrencefield Ordinary . . . VDiff
24m. A wandering trip, worth it for the views alone. Gain the
ledge behind the pool from the right and follow it to its left
edge, and belay. Climb a groove then trend left up ledges and
grooves to eventually reach the tree on *Pulpit Groove* and a
stance. Finish out right to maximise the exposure.
FA. Albert Shutt. 1952

⑨ Austin's Variation . . . . VS 4c
10m. The flake and corner above the start of the *Ordinary*
(possible belay below it) give a short and strenuous pitch
though the effort required to get there is not really fully repaid.
FA. Allan Austin 1956

⑩ High Plains Drifter . . E4 6a
20m. A grandly-named outing that wanders its way up the left-
hand side of the wall. Climb a shallow groove to where the wall
steepens then pull right and back left (a wire hooked over an ol
upside-down peg is difficult to place) making long reaches to
gain a narrow resting ledge out on the left. Finish out right,
steeply but on better holds.
FA. Jim Reading 1977

202

Side navigation tabs (right margin): Wharncliffe, Dovestone Tor, Rivelin, Bamford, Stanage, Burbage North, Higgar Tor, Burbage South, Millstone, Lawrencefield, Yarncliffe, Froggatt, Curbar, Gardoms, Birchen, Chatsworth, Cratcliffe

THE POOL WALL
The most imposing bit of rock in the quarry is the fine steep wall behind the pool. Once a practice ground for pegging it now has a fine collection of hard free routes. Over the years a number of climbers have ended up in the pool along with dead sheep, not a pleasant thought For this reason a belay on the starting ledge is a sound idea.
APPROACH - The ledge behind the pool is most easily reached from the right over blocks though at times of high water this can be problematic.

❶ Boulevard **E3 5c**
8m. The left-hand continuous crack system. Start as for *High 'lains Drifter* but move right and attack the crack. Protection is ood and the holds keep appearing but the whole thing is hard ork.
AA. Peter Biven 1956. FFA. Ed Drummond 1975

❷ Von Ryan's Express   **E5 6b**
m. A serious and seldom-attempted gap-filler but with some uality climbing. Start up *Boulevard* and step right below the all. Arrange side-runners then gain a small ledge above. Leave nis with some trepidation and climb the wall just left of *Billy Vhiz* to finish.
A. Tony Ryan1985

❸ Billy Whizz **E2 5c**
8m. The central line on the wall is often well chalked and is igh in the grade. Climb the slab to the base of the steeper rock vires to the right) and sprint up a flake to a deep slot. Step left nd climb the thin crack (desperate for fat fingers) to a trian-ular hole and a final couple of long reaches for the top.
A. Geoff Birtles 1975

❹ High Street **E4 6a**
0m. The right-hand crack system has a taxing start to the eather on *Billy Whizz*. Step right and follow the thin continua-on on good finger locks.
A. Peter Biven 1956. FFA. Jim Reading 1975

⑮ Holy Grail **E4 5c**
8m. The least attractive of the routes on the back wall. Start up *Excalibur* and step left at the steepening. Climb the blocky cracks above to the crest of the wall, however you may first need to remove the grass that manages to obscure the most useful of the finger jams.
FA. Jim Reading 1977

⑯ Excalibur **VS.4c**
20m. The long groove at the right-hand side of the pool (rising challengingly from the lake!) steepens towards the top. It can be greasy after damp weather. The start is probably the tech-nical crux though a couple of layback moves on the upper section feel tough; beware the final blocky moves as the corner keeps getting shorter and shorter.
FA. Peter Biven 1955

Afternoon | 5 min | Sheltered

Scramble off then descend to left

in corner

Red Wall
70m through trees

GINGERBREAD SLAB
Beyond the pool is the attractive and immensely popular sheet of rock know as Gingerbread Slab. This is always a attractive spot for top-roping or tackling your first lead so it can be a bit crowded.
DESCENT - From the top of the slab an awkward scramble leads to the cliff top from where you can walk around left-wards to join the approach path. It is possible to abseil from the trees on the ledge but they are becoming a bit battered so best give them a rest.

❶ Once Pegged Wall . . . . 🔩🧗 ☐ VS 4c
10m. The well-hammered thin cracks in the left wall of the groove have good finger locks and good gear, move onto the left arete to reach for the top.
FAA. Don Morrison. 1955

❷ Morning Glory . . . . 🧗 ☐ E2 5c
10m. Follow the line of old peg holes up the centre of the wall. The route features some good moves but it manages to feel a bit artificial (or at least it used to do!).
FA. Dominic Stainforth

❸ Limpopo Groove . . . . 🔩 ☐ VS 4b
10m. The angular corner above the "grey green greasy waters" has great gear, a tricky central section and a steep finale.
FA. Dave Gregory (solo) 1955

❹ Gingerbread . . . . 🔩 ☐ VS 4b
10m. The left arete of the slab has decent wire runners at half height; so don't fall off the last moves!
FA. Albert Shutt 1952

❺ Meringue . . . . 🔩🕸 ☐ HVS 5a
10m. The thin crack just to the right is delicate above half-height, micro-Friends just about protect the final crucial moves.
FA. Albert Shutt 1953. FFA. John Fearon 1955

❻ Éclair . . . . 🕸 ☐ E1 5b
10m. The thin slab just right has polished holds and no gear and is best top-roped.

❼ Vanilla Slice . . . . 🕸 ☐ E2 5c
10m. The slab just right again is even harder, just as polished, and with the same number of runners.

To the right are a couple of cracks that make good first leads.

❽ Snail Crack . . . . 🔩 ☐ VDiff
18m. The first continuous crack leads up steps to steeper moves and ledges on the left. Meander up easier rock to finish
FA. Albert Shutt 1953

❾ Nailsbane . . . . 🔩 ☐ HVD
18m. The next crack system leans to the left and is followed until it is possible to exit left as for the previous climb.
FA. Albert Shutt 1952

Descend by walking left around the quarry

RED WALL

The quarry continues rightwards from Gingerbread Slab but the quality of rock deteriorates rapidly and the trees have claimed most of the exposed walls as their own. One section which does give some worthwhile routes is a wall rising above a band of sandy red rock and with an arrow-straight corner-crack to its right.
The rock on this wall is often very sandy, especially after rain.
APPROACH - Continue walking through the trees from below the Gingerbread Slab past a pit that holds a seasonal pool. Red Wall is at the point where the path heads up the slope away from the cliff.

⑩ Tyrone . . . . **HVS 5a**
18m. Climb the straightforward crack to its end then the steep wall on good but rather spaced holds. Finish direct up the curving crack for the full effect, or cop out rightwards. The easiest way off from the ledge is to abseil from the tree, alternatively scramble left then right to reach the cliff top and descend well to the left past the pool.

⑪ Nova . . . . **VS 4b**
18m. Climb either of the cracks in the right-hand side of the slab (the right-hand one is easier) to a short jamming crack; up this to a tricky move onto a ledge and an awkward finish on flat holds.
FA. Don Morrison 1956

RED WALL
The next routes are 80m to the right.

⑫ Delectable Direct **E1 5c**
15m. The thin crack in the centre of the wall can be dirty after rain. At other times it is followed direct and is excellent and well protected.
FAA. Peter Biven 1956. FFA. Don Morrison 1964

⑬ Red Wall **E1 5b**
18m. A worthwhile climb though with a fearsome finish. Climb the lower wall rightwards (tricky to start) and a short corner to a sandy ledge and belay. Make a desperate mantelshelf up the wall on the left at the back of the ledge to finish.
FA. Don Morrison 1956

⑭ The Delectable Variation **VS 4c**
24m. Altogether a better way up the wall. Climb *Red Wall* to the sandy ledge stance. Traverse the wall to the left all the way to the arete on a continuously surprising set of holds for an exposed finale.
FA. Don Morrison 1956

⑮ Cordite Crack . . . . **VS 4b**
18m. The wide and intimidating layback crack is best attacked with your bold head on, just blast up it. A couple of big cams is a good idea, but do you really think you will be able to stop to place them?
FA. Peter Biven 1955

Afternoon | 7 min | Sheltered

Whamcliffe
Dovestone Tor
Rivelin
Bamford
Stanage
Burbage North
Higgar Tor
Burbage South
Millstone
Yarncliffe
Lawrencefield
Froggatt
Curbar
Gardoms
Birchen
Chatsworth
Cratcliffe

Wharncliffe
Dovestone Tor
Rivelin
Bamford
Stanage
Burbage North
Higgar Tor
Burbage South
Millstone
Lawrencefield
Yarncliffe
Froggatt
Curbar
Gardoms
Birchen
Chatsworth
Cratcliffe

YARNCLIFFE

A small sheltered quarry that is unfeasibly popular because of its great accessibility. If you arrive and there are more than a couple of outdoor centre/school minibuses parked in the gateway it is probably worth looking elsewhere for your sport. The quarry and nearby edge (not described here but worth a look if you like unexplored jungle) are named after the mill-stones that used to be quarried here; an old name for them was querns and the corruption 'yarn'-cliffe (and also 'Wharn'-cliffe) indicates a location of this ancient industry.

When the quarry was first developed the initial bays had a good collection of face and crack climbs that largely relied upon the recently exposed sharp edged flakes to make progress, unfortunately the battering (especially through abseiling) has led to the premature aging of most of these climbs, perhaps an indication of the future that awaits all our favourite climbing destinations. An added problem is that cliff top erosion means that after rain the routes can be very sandy; polished holds and ball-bearings are not a good combination – care is required especially on the poorly protected faces.

To the right of the initial bays the cliff extends away in a semicircular fashion, and although much of the rock is a bit grotty there are some admirable climbs, including the fine cracks of *Fall Pipe* and *Zapple*, and the magnificent arete of *Crème de la Crème*.

APPROACH (SK255794)

On the southern (uphill) side of the road that runs between Fox House and Grindleford is a large gated entrance, with parking for up to half a dozen carefully placed vehicles.

The nearest rock is only seconds away, on the left through the gate, whilst the other good sector is up the old tarmaced (correct spelling) track, straight on once through the gate. Avoid turning in the vicinity of the gate, the road is travelled by fast traffic. It is much safer to go down the hill and turn in the entrance of the road that runs down to Grindleford station, only two minutes away.

OTHER GUIDEBOOKS - A more complete list of routes at Yarncliffe is published in the 1991 BMC *Froggatt* guidebook.

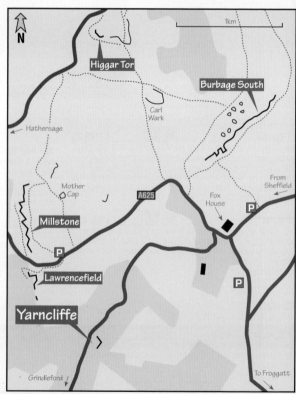

CONDITIONS

The quarry is very sheltered, partly because of its recessed position and partly because of the tree cover. It makes a good venue on cold windy days but can be unpleasantly midgy when the weather is at all humid. In high summer the large number of ants, which do bite when provoked, can be a bit off-putting. It is almost always extremely sandy.

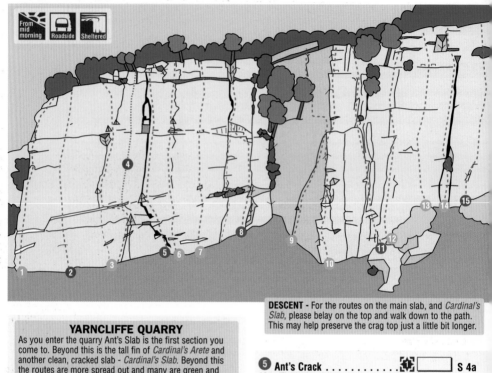

DESCENT - For the routes on the main slab, and *Cardinal's Slab*, please belay on the top and walk down to the path. This may help preserve the crag top just a little bit longer.

YARNCLIFFE QUARRY

As you enter the quarry Ant's Slab is the first section you come to. Beyond this is the tall fin of *Cardinal's Arete* and another clean, cracked slab - *Cardinal's Slab*. Beyond this the routes are more spread out and many are green and overgrown although there is an occasional gem hidden in amongst the trees. Of particular interest to the seasoned Peak connoisseur is the fine crack of *Zapple* and the magnificent, but bold, arete of *Creme de la Creme*. Both of these routes are best approached by walking straight up the track, past the clearing and through the trees to the far bay of the quarry.

① Ant's Arete . . . . 🔦🧗‍♂️ [____] **VS 4b**
16m. The stepped left-hand arete of the quarry is very pleasant, although there is no protection until above the crux.
FA. Nat Allen 1950

② Aphid's Wall . . . . 🔦🧗‍♂️🧗 [____] **E1 5a**
16m. The slabby wall to the right of the arete is poorly protected and the small holds are very rounded.
FA. Dave Gregory 1972

③ Latecomer . . . . 🔦 [____] **VS 4b**
16m. The long thin crack is reached from the right and climbed passing a couple of angular niches. Finish out to the left. It can be started direct by a worthwhile **5a** problem.
FA. Don Morrison 1964

④ Soldier Ant . . . . 🧗 [____] **E3 5c**
16m. The narrow wall between the two cracks is sketchy, slippery and unprotected without recourse to side runners. With side runners it is only E1.
FA. Malcolm Salter 1978

⑤ Ant's Crack . . . . 🔦 [____] **S 4a**
16m. The wide crack in the centre of the slab is a good, if somewhat sandy, introduction to jamming.
FA. Nat Allen 1950

⑥ Ant's Wall . . . . 🔦 [____] **HS 4a**
18m. The steep slab and thin crack just right have good holds and runners. Possibly the best route on the slab.
FA. Dave Gregory 1972

⑦ Formica Slab . . . . 🧗 [____] **HVS 4c**
18m. The steep slab to the left of the parallel cracks is unprotected, just for a change.
FA. Dave Gregory 1972

⑧ Angular Climb . . . . [____] **HVD**
18m. The parallel cracks, set in the right-hand side of the slab, starting up the right-hand one then stepping left. The original line started up the thin left-hand crack at **Severe**. The right-hand crack in its entirety is *Centipede*, it is now overgrown in its upper section.

⑨ Hidden Crack . . . . [____] **VS 5a**
24m. The thin diagonal crack in the left-hand side wall runs out to the arete. Step back left along a ledge to find the hidden crack and a steeper juggy finish. Alternatively, finish up *Cardinal's Arete* at **VS 4b**.
FA. Dave Gregory 1971

⑩ Cardinal's Arete . . . . . . 🔦🧗 [____] **VS 4c**
20m. The undercut arete has a steep start and is pleasant above leading to a delicate finale which can be avoided on the right.
Photo page 207.
FA. Don Chapman 1951

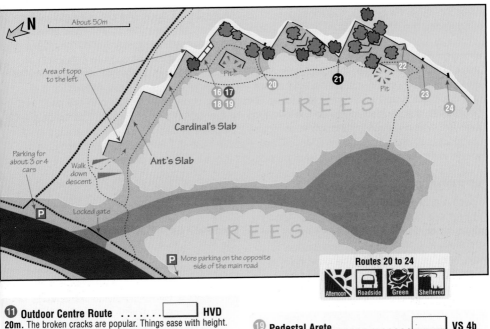

Routes 20 to 24
Afternoon · Roadside · Green · Sheltered

⑪ Outdoor Centre Route ...... HVD
20m. The broken cracks are popular. Things ease with height.

⑫ Cardinal's Slab .... VS 4c
20m. The long thin crack up the left-hand edge of the slab.
FA. Dave Gregory 1972

⑬ Threatened .... HVS 4c
20m. The rather sketchy slab right again can be green and has the odd creaky hold.
FA. Gary Gibson 1978

⑭ Cardinal's Crack ..... VS 4b
20m. The wide crack in the slab leads to a massive tree and blocky finish. It is pleasant enough if you enjoy fist jamming.
FA. Don Chapman 1950

⑮ Chalked Up E1 5a
20m. A shallow groove and hairline crack in the centre of the next slab are easiest, as might be expected, when chalked up.
FA. Giles Barker 1978

The next routes are marked on the map. The first four are on the wall and arete just beyond Cardinal's Slab.

⑯ Sulu .... HVS 5a
20m. This thin crack just left of the arete is steep as far as a good ledge. Continue on the left until forced right to finish.
FA. J.R.Barker 1971

⑰ Rhythm of Cruelty E3 5b
20m. The right-hand side of the steep arete is pushy as far as the ledge. Finish more easily.
FA. Phil Wilson 1979

⑱ Capital Cracks .... VS 4c
20m. A crack two metres right of the arete leads to a ledge. Step right and follow the continuation crack to the top.
FA. Dave Gregory 1971

⑲ Pedestal Arete .... VS 4b
22m. Start on the right and follow a series of giant steps out left to the arete. Finish as for *Sulu.*
FA. Nat Allen 1951

The next routes are located in amongst the trees and bushes as you work rightwards around the quarry.

⑳ S.T.P. .... VS 4c
14m. Follow the crack just left of the arete to a tree belay. Pleasant when clean.
FA. W.Phillips 1971

㉑ Creme de la Creme E6 6b
16m. The magnificent central arete of the quarry still sees few ascents. One peg runner at half-height may be in place. The boulder problem start needs a lot of padding to be made safe.
FA. Ron Fawcett 1977

㉒ Fall Pipe .... VS 4c
16m. Across the bay is the finest wall in the quarry, split on the left by a long crack which gives good jamming and bridging when it is dry. Sadly it is often a bit overgrown.
FA. Ted Howard 1964

㉓ Zapple .... HVS 5b
20m. The superb finger and hand crack that splits the centre of the wall is an essential Peak crack-climb!
FA. Pete Brown 1971

㉔ Trised Crack .... VS 4c
15m. The flaky crack to the right gives slippery laybacking and can be somewhat overgrown once the season is under way.
FA. Don Cowan 1951

FROGGATT

After Stanage, Froggatt is the most popular of the eastern Edges; the cliff is relatively low lying, faces the afternoon sun, and has many routes of an angle that is less than is usual for gritstone. There is as high a concentration of quality routes here as on any of the edges and although Froggatt is renowned for its superb open slabs, it also has a great collection of crack climbs. Sections of the cliff, especially the right-hand end, were quarried in antiquity; the abandoned millstones still lie where they were left when the industry collapsed. It is strange to think that such great routes as *Green Gut*, *Brown's Eliminate* and the peerless *Great Slab* are as man-made as the offerings on the nation's indoor walls! The crack climbs here are well protected, although in complete contrast the slab routes are invariably bold; the grades of *Sunset Slab* (HVS 4b), *Three Pebble Slab* (E1 5a) and *Great Slab* (E3 5b) speak volumes, as they are are serious outings requiring a wary approach.

APPROACH (SK249764)

There are two usual approaches to the cliff:
1) From parking by the bend on the B6045 a short distance below the Grouse Inn. If this is full there is a National Trust car park a little way back up the road on the downhill side. Follow the hillcrest footpath to a stream and white gate then onto the cliff, 15 to 20 minutes from the car. The first section of the main edge is 100m before the prominent bulk of Froggatt Pinnacle.
2) From a small lay-by (up to 6 vehicles) on the bend below the Chequers Inn. Walk back up the road past an old horse trough, then turn right and follow a steepening track straight up the hill to arrive at the Downhill racer area.

CONDITIONS

Froggatt is low lying enough to escape the worst of the weather but high enough not to be bothered by the clinging greenery that affected the more sheltered gritstone cliffs. The cliff is climbable all year if the weather is kind. The westerly aspect and low angle of much of the cliff means that the after-noon winter sun warms the rock and makes it well worth a visit on clear winter days. On the odd occasion when an inversion exists, and the Derwent Valley fills with cloud, climbing here is truly magical.

BOULDERING - There is plenty of good bouldering at Froggatt. The Hairpin Boulder is one area not shown on the crag maps and is situated just up the track from the main road on the approach walk.

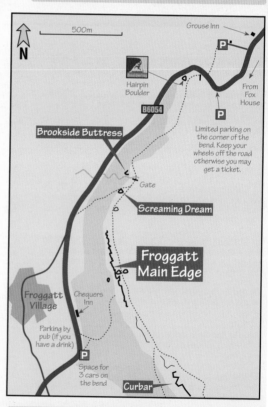

OTHER GUIDEBOOKS - A more complete list of routes at Froggatt is published in the 1991 BMC *Froggatt* guidebook. The bouldering is in the 1998 Peak Bouldering ROCKFAX.

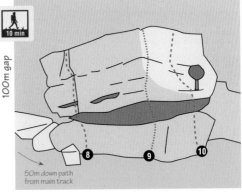

50m down path
from main track

BROOKSIDE BUTTRESS and SCREAMING DREAM

Before you get to the main edge of Froggatt there are two worthy buttresses hidden away from view. One has a fine arete and the other is home to some news-worthy desperates. Both are relatively easy to find, if you know where to look. See map opposite.
BROOKSIDE APPROACH - At the gate on the main approach turn right and follow a small stream downhill. Keep close to the right bank and after about 70m the buttress appears on your right.

---

❶ Neb Crack . . . . **VS 4b**
10m. The crack on the left-hand side of the north-facing wall.
FA. Nat Allen 1956

❷ Dick Van Dyke
Goes Ballistic **E7 6b**
10m. Gain the hanging shallow groove in the wall from the base of *Neb Crack*. Sustained with a high crux and a bad landing.
FA. Dave Pegg (solo) 1994

❸ Indoor Fisherman . . **E4 6a**
10m. The superb arete is a mini *Beau Geste* in appearance and one of the unsung gems of Froggatt. Climb direct up flakes then a hard move leads to a horizontal break, a rest and gear. Make use of all of these then pull up the rounded finish.
FA. Steve Bancroft 1977

❹ Crooked Start . . . . **VS 4c**
10m. Climb the wide cracks on the front face of the buttress. Head right at the top to the finish of the next route.
FA. Wilf White 1956

❺ Tinsel's Triangle . . . . **S 4a**
8m. The arete on the right and the flake-crack above.
FA. Wilf White, Tinsel Allen 1956

There are two routes on the green side-wall of the buttress, above the stream.

❻ Piledriver . . . . **HVS 5b**
6m. On the side wall of the buttress, climb the thin crack and move left onto the slab. Can be started direct at 6a but it is usually much too green.
FA. Al Evans 1977. Direct by Steve Bancroft 1977

❼ Brookside Crack . . . . **Diff**
6m. The grass and fern-filled crack by the side of the brook.
FA. Wilf White 1956

SCREAMING DREAM APPROACH - 100m after the gate, locate a small track leading diagonally down off the main track. 50m down here a steep block overhangs the path.

❽ The Screaming Dream . . **E7 7a**
6m. The desperate crack on the left-hand side.
FA. Mark Leach 1987

❾ Renegade Master . . **E8 6c**
7m. The hanging arete starting from the left. The micro-wires are usually pre-placed which reduces the grade to E7.
FA. Jerry Moffatt 1995. Soloed by Tom Briggs 2001.

❿ The Famous Chris Ellis . **E4 6a**
8m. Climb the right-hand side of the block and make a scary move onto the ledge.
FA. Paul Mitchell, Chris Ellis 1984

Whamcliffe · Dovestone Tor · Rivelin · Bamford · Stanage · Burbage North · Higgar Tor · Burbage South · Millstone · Lawrencefield · Yarncliffe · Froggatt · Curbar · Gardoms · Birchen · Chatsworth · Cratcliffe

Benign Lives 20m

Change in viewing angle

Evening

Afternoon | 15 min

STRAPIOMBO BUTTRESS

A splendid buttress with two great grit-ticks both of which have hotly-debated grades. There are also a few modern desperates but there is little here in the lower grades. Although the front face gets the afternoon sun, *Strapiombante* faces north and can be cooler in hot weather.
APPROACH - See map on page 216.

① Strapiombante E1 5b
8m. A fine route to break into the grade, strenuous and quite bold though with good gear to catch you in the event of muffing the final long reach. Trend right up the wall to a break (small Friends) then back left to a strenuous final move. *Photo opposite.*
FA. Dave Brearly 1962

② Strapadictomy E5 6b
9m. Hard work but well protected and low in the grade. Climb the short arete to runners, then lean out (large wire in the flake) and layback (crux) onto the flake; about face and finish briskly.
FA. John Allen 1976

③ Cock Robin E6 7a
10m. With preplaced (and preclipped?) gear in *Strapadictomy*, climb the wall to the right to the protruding boss. Now try and stand up (easier for the short) then finish up the slab.
FA. Robin Barker 1994. Without preplaced gear.

④ Strappotente E7 7a
10m. The eliminate line right of *Cock Robin*. Head straight through the centre of the roof, place gear in the lip, then grovel and press to reach the top.
FA. Seb Grieve 1999

⑤ Strapiombo E1 5b
9m. The roof crack to the right is a battle. The use of knees and loss of copious skin are pretty much par for the course.
FA. Don Whillans 1956

BOULDERING - The hard traverse of *The Ape Drape* is on the block down and right (looking out) of *Strapiombante*. See map on next page.

⑥ English Overhang ...... VS 4c
9m. The wide crack right of the roof is an awkward struggle.
FA. Dave Gregory 1978

⑦ Scarper's Triangle ...... VS 5a
9m. Climb leftwards out of the capped corner then pull back onto the slab. This leads to a finishing crack.
FA. John Fearon 1957

⑧ Parallel Piped E3 5c
6m. The reachy left arete, with gear in the half-height break. Harder for the short. A good introduction to harder gritstone arete climbing.
FA. Graham Hoey 1986

⑨ Benign Lives E7 6c
8m. The blank slab just right is almost pebbleless, completely protectionless and rarely attempted except on a top-rope or above a huge pile of mats. Graded for ascents without the mats!
FA. Johnny Dawes (solo) 1984

⑩ Mild E4 6b
7m. Step off the mid-height ledge as for *Benign Lives*. Move up rightwards to the arete past a thin flake and a pocket.
FA. Julian Lines (solo)1992

Sunset Slab 100m

Wharncliffe · Dovestone Tor · Rivelin · Bamford · Stanage · Burbage North · Higgar Tor · Burbage South · Millstone · Lawrencefield · Yarncliffe · Froggatt · Curbar · Gardoms · Birchen · Chatsworth · Cratcliffe

Scramble descent

Beau Geste

SUNSET SLAB

This is the first of many fine slabs at Froggatt. The routes up the cracks are very friendly but the others need a steady and confident approach as protection is minimal.
APPROACH - See map on page 216.

❶ Science Friction . . . E6 6a
12m. Very bold friction climbing up the arete left of *North Climb* with gear at just below half-height. Pretty much a solo where it matters. Can be dirty.
FA. Mark Miller 1980

❷ North Climb . . . . S 4a
12m. The wide crack on the left was a good effort for its day. It is certainly better suited to tweeds than lycra!
FA. J.W.Puttrell 1906

❸ What's Up Doc? E2 5b
12m. A filler-in. Attempt to climb the slab about 1m to the right of *North Climb*. Very serious and precarious.
FA. Graham Hulley 1990

❹ Sundowner E2 5a
12m. The centre of the slab crossing *Sunset Slab*. Friction climbing on poor pockets with the crux near the top. A naughty side-runner on the right lowers the grade a couple of notches. The line shown here incorporates the relatively easy direct start to *Sunset Slab* which makes a logical and independent route.
FA. John Allen 1972

❺ Sunset Slab . . . . HVS 4b
14m. The main route of the slab is protectionless except for a poor large Friend which may be of psychological help. From the initial crack trend left via shelving ledges to a flake and teeter up this. The crux is one move higher than you might expect.
Photo opposite.
FA. Joe Brown 1948

❻ Sunset Crack . . . . HS 4c
12m. The awkward undercut crack has enough runners to make up for the previous two offerings! The initial bulge is the crux and the route has its fair share of sloping holds but on the whole it is pretty friendly even at HS.
FA. Len Chapman 1948

❼ Turret Crack . . . . HS 4b
12m. The next crack just right is awkward and blocky at the start, awkward and steep just below the top.
FA. Don Chapman 1948

The block-choked gully just right offers an easy way down after the tricky initial slither under the chockstone.

❽ Slab and Crack . . . . Diff
10m. The ramp in the right wall of the gully.
FA. Nat Allen 1948

The unprotected crux of *Sunset Slab*, HVS 4b, Froggatt. *Opposite*

Wharncliffe
Dovestone Tor
Rivelin
Bamford
Stanage
Burbage North
Higgar Tor
Burbage South
Millstone
Lawrencefield
Yarncliffe
Froggatt
Curbar
Gardoms
Birchen
Chatsworth
Cratcliffe

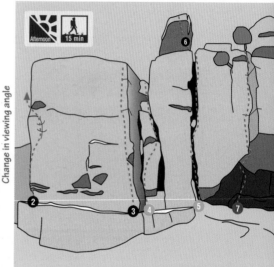

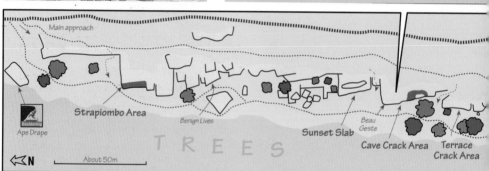

BEAU GESTE

The impressive and grim north-facing wall and arete just right of *Sunset Slab* is home to two major routes.

❶ Soul Doubt **E8 6c**

12m. Low and poor gear almost protects this hard and scary climb up the blank wall. Use the thin crack to reach the ramp and make some very hard moves on pebbles and a pocket to reach salvation.

FA. Adrian Berry 2000. Ramp-art (Martin Veale (solo) 1986) gained the ramp and then escaped left into the gully.

❷ Beau Geste **E7 6c**

14m. The soaring arete is the classic hard route of the crag. Relatively easy climbing up the groove in the lower arete (RPs) and a worrying move right along the break gains some much needed gear (Friends). Back at the arete, make a desperate move to reach a thin crack on the left (crucial Rock 1 or RP3, very hard to place) and finish off the rest of the arete. Please don't stand on the pebble as there is only half of it left now! Three ropes are normal to protect the line.

FA. Johnny Woodward 1982

CAVE CRACK AREA

❸ Epiphany Left-hand . . . **E6 6b**

12m. Climb the fine soaring arete on its left-hand side throughout, with a slight detour at half-height to place gear. A sustained and gripping pitch

FA. Nick Dixon 1990s, starting up the crack on the left. Direct start added by Ben Heason 1999. It was originally climbed on its right-hand side at E4 6a (Phil Burke 1970s).

❹ Holly Groove . . . . **VS 4c**

12m. The slippery twin cracks in the long hollyless groove. Start up the left one step into the right, then finish up a wide easy chimney.

FA. Slim Sorrell 1948

❺ Hawk's Nest Crack . . . . **VS 4c**

12m. The classic jamming crack is a bit of a battle, with useful chockstone (knees almost obligatory). From the ledge finish over the exposed jutting flake on the left for an extra thrill.

FA. Joe Brown 1948

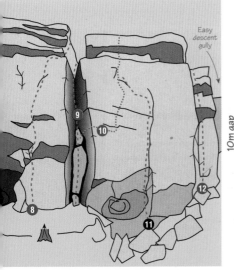

TERRACE CRACK AREA

10m gap

Afternoon 15 min

Tody's Wall Area 10m

CAVE CRACK AREA

Past the arete of *Beau Geste* is a tree-filled area shading a section with some good vertical cracks and a slightly dingy cave. The area may be cooler in the Summer (at least for the belayer) and the cave provides shelter in the rain.

6 Horizontal Pleasure **E5 6b**
..m. The big roof above *Hawk Nest Crack*. Start up the crack ..hen move left under the roof (Friend 4). Span out to the lip ..sing foot jams and a slot on the right of the roof. Slap (crux) ..or a horizontal break, traverse right to a good hold and a Friend ... Finish direct, delicately.
A. Andy Healy 1999

7 Cave Crack **E2 5c**
.2m. A bruising battle for most. From a thread hand-traverse ..he greasy flange and fist-jam the roof crack; hint: it helps to ..ead with the right at the lip. Once established on the front face ..hings ease instantly. A HVS from when men were men.
A. Joe Brown 1950

8 Cave Wall **E3 5c**
.2m. Bold and precarious. From the right rib of the cave ..oulder up and right to a small ledge, a Friend in the undercut ..p and left may encourage you to the ledge but won't help on ..he crux! Scary balance moves lead to better holds and a rapid ..xit to the right. If you haven't had enough, finish over the roofs ..hat cap the wall.
A. Don Whillans 1958

9 Swimmer's Chimney . . . . . **S 4a**
.2m. The deep and ever-narrowing chimney around to the ..ight. Breast stroke appears to work best and don't flounder!
A. J.W.Puttrell 1890s

10 Brightside **E2 5c**
.2m. From half way up the chimney squirm around the arete on ..he right and climb the wall by a hard move, things soon ease.
A. Phil Burke 1980

11 Greedy Pig **E5 6b**
12m. The searing thin crack that forms a direct start to the last climb is fiercely technical and has gear which is hard to place.
FA. Paul Mitchell 1981

12 Avalanche **E2 6a**
11m. The groove on the right-hand side of the wall has a particularly hard pull over the roof.
FA. Daniel Lee 1981. The old version fell down.

TERRACE CRACK AREA

An ancient quarried wall undercut by a section of soft red rock. The upper wall provides a couple of thin, hard wall climbs with sparse gear. Thankfully the crack on the right is a much more pleasant affair.

13 Mean Streak **E6 6b**
12m. The wall right of the arete has low runners and gradually improving holds but is bold in the extreme. Sadly chipped.
FA. Dominic Lee 1981

14 The Gully Joke **E3 5c**
15m. Climb the flake left of the steep crack, place runners on the right then teeter out left and climb the wall on small hidden holds. Bold and historically undergraded - but not any more.
FA. John Allen 1975

15 Terrace Crack . . . . **VS 4b**
12m. The long blocky crack was once quarried and is unusual for the age. It is juggy, well protected and worthwhile.
FA. Freda Rylett early 1940s

16 Bud **E7 6c**
10m. The leaning left arete of the slender buttress to the right of the gully, right of *Terrace Crack*. Technical and bold up to a nasty slap for a jug (RPs in crack on the right). A strange move enables you to stand on the jug and romp to the top.
FA. Andy Popp 1990s

Wharncliffe
Dovestone Tor
Rivelin
Bamford
Stanage
Burbage North
Higgar Tor
Burbage South
Millstone
Lawrencefield
Yarncliffe
Froggatt
Curbar
Gardoms
Birchen
Chatsworth
Cratcliffe

217

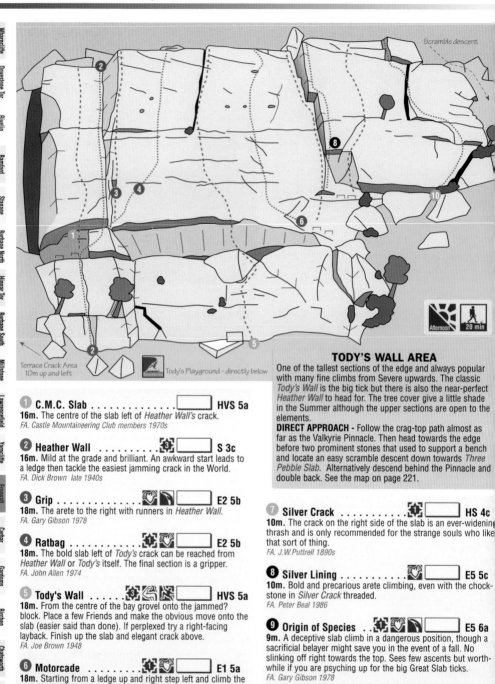

Scramble descent

Terrace Crack Area
10m up and left

Tody's Playground - directly below

Wharncliffe | Dovestone Tor | Rivelin | Bamford | Stanage | Burbage North | Higgar Tor | Burbage South | Millstone | Lawrencefield | Yarncliffe | Froggatt | Curbar | Gardoms | Birchen | Chatsworth | Cratcliffe

TODY'S WALL AREA

One of the tallest sections of the edge and always popular with many fine climbs from Severe upwards. The classic *Tody's Wall* is the big tick but there is also the near-perfect *Heather Wall* to head for. The tree cover give a little shade in the Summer although the upper sections are open to the elements.

DIRECT APPROACH - Follow the crag-top path almost as far as the Valkyrie Pinnacle. Then head towards the edge before two prominent stones that used to support a bench and locate an easy scramble descent down towards *Three Pebble Slab*. Alternatively descend behind the Pinnacle and double back. See the map on page 221.

❶ C.M.C. Slab .... ☐ **HVS 5a**
16m. The centre of the slab left of *Heather Wall's* crack.
FA. Castle Mountaineering Club members 1970s

❷ Heather Wall .... ☐ **S 3c**
16m. Mild at the grade and brilliant. An awkward start leads to a ledge then tackle the easiest jamming crack in the World.
FA. Dick Brown late 1940s

❸ Grip .... ☐ **E2 5b**
18m. The arete to the right with runners in *Heather Wall*.
FA. Gary Gibson 1978

❹ Ratbag .... ☐ **E2 5b**
18m. The bold slab left of *Tody's* crack can be reached from *Heather Wall* or *Tody's* itself. The final section is a gripper.
FA. John Allen 1974

❺ Tody's Wall ..... ☐ **HVS 5a**
18m. From the centre of the bay grovel onto the jammed? block. Place a few Friends and make the obvious move onto the slab (easier said than done). If perplexed try a right-facing layback. Finish up the slab and elegant crack above.
FA. Joe Brown 1948

❻ Motorcade .... ☐ **E1 5a**
18m. Starting from a ledge up and right step left and climb the centre of the pocketed slab right of *Tody's* crack. Large low Friends protect, but not very adequately.
FA. D.Warriner 1969

❼ Silver Crack .... ☐ **HS 4c**
10m. The crack on the right side of the slab is an ever-widening thrash and is only recommended for the strange souls who like that sort of thing.
FA. J.W.Puttrell 1890s

❽ Silver Lining .... ☐ **E5 5c**
10m. Bold and precarious arete climbing, even with the chockstone in *Silver Crack* threaded.
FA. Peter Beal 1986

❾ Origin of Species .. ☐ **E5 6a**
9m. A deceptive slab climb in a dangerous position, though a sacrificial belayer might save you in the event of a fall. No slinking off right towards the top. Sees few ascents but worthwhile if you are psyching up for the big Great Slab ticks.
FA. Gary Gibson 1978

❿ Bollard Crack .... ☐ **VS 4c**
8m. The kinked crack to the right is a bit of a bollard! The star is for people who enjoy ruining perfectly good clothing.
FA. Slim Sorrell 1948

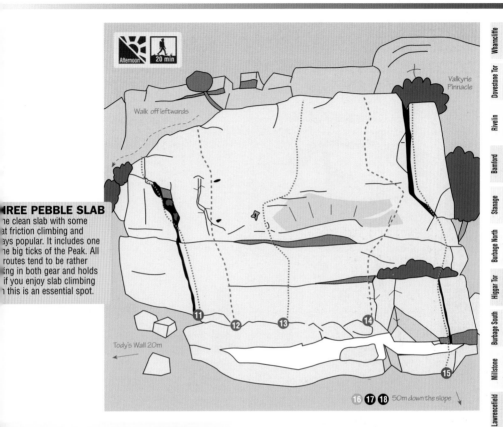

Afternoon | 20 min

Valkyrie Pinnacle

Walk off leftwards

REE PEBBLE SLAB
ne clean slab with some
at friction climbing and
ays popular. It includes one
he big ticks of the Peak. All
routes tend to be rather
ing in both gear and holds
if you enjoy slab climbing
this is an essential spot.

Tody's Wall 20m

11 12 13 14

15

16 17 18 50m down the slope

Wharncliffe · Dovestone Tor · Rivelin · Bamford · Stanage · Burbage North · Higgar Tor · Burbage South · Millstone · Lawrencefield · Yarncliffe · Froggatt · Curbar · Gardoms · Birchen · Chatsworth · Cratcliffe

① Soft Option . . . . [ ] **VDiff**
m. On the left-hand edge of the slab is a widening crack.
limb this and slink off leftwards at the top.
. Dave Gregory 1960s

② Two-sided Triangle . . . . . [1] [ ] **E1 5b**
0m. A mini Three Pebble which has a harder move but is less
atisfying. The line follows the slab just to the right of the tiny
orner. Once again finish on the mid-height ledge.
. Gary Gibson 1978

③ Three Pebble Slab . . . . [3] [♥] [ ] **E1 5a**
2m. One of the classic Froggatt slabs which is always good
ub-fodder in the great grade debate. Climb to a hole (small
ire) rock up and right and pad to safety. Easy for E1 but the
nal friction slab will test your bottle and boots, especially if
ou tackle it direct. *Photo page 223.*
. Joe Brown 1948

④ Four Pebble Slab . . . . . [1] [♥] [ ] **E3 5c**
2m. More than just a pebble harder than its neighbour. Trend
ght up the steep lower wall via awkward ledges to runners
en step left and 'sketch' up the slab on barely adequate holds.
. John Allen 1972

⑤ Grey Slab . . . . [1] [ ] **S 4b**
2m. The lower wall leads steeply to the wide and oddly named
rack. Get thrashing!
. Rucksack Club members 1903-4

*There are three routes on the huge split block directly below
Three Pebble Slab. This can be reached easily by following a
path below the slab that loops down.*

⑯ Heather in My Face . . . . [ ] **HVS 5b**
6m. The left arete (looking uphill) of the upper block.
Unprotected but only short.
FA. Andy Grill (solo) 1994

⑰ Turd Burglar . . . . . [1] [♥] [ ] [ ] **E6 6c**
8m. The main face of the upper block. Climb the slab which
leads to a sloping roof, skirt around this on the left. The name
is not a reflection of the quality of the climb
FA. Nick Dixon 1987

⑱ Dogs Die in Hot Cars . . [1] [ ] [ ] **E6 7a**
8m. Climb the overlaps on the right-hand side of the upper
boulder. A hand-placed peg is used for protection.
FA. Iain Farrar 2000

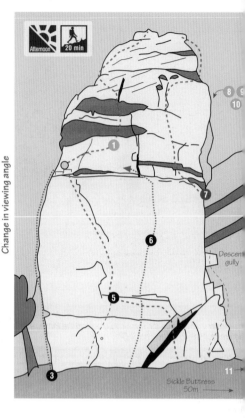

Change in viewing angle

Summit equipped with abseil point

Tody's Wall below and left

Descent gully

Sickle Buttress 50m →

VALKYRIE PINNACLE

The unmistakable square bulk of Froggatt Pinnacle is home to one great classic and a set of only slightly less worthy offerings. Some of the harder routes are of a bouldery nature and don't reach the summit. For the other routes which do go all the way the summit is thoughtfully equipped with a chunky abseil ring.

❶ Valkyrie .... HVS 5a
20m. One of the Peak's classic HVS routes which has two wonderful, contrasting pitches.
1) 5a, 10m. The slanting jamming crack and a short traverse lead to a stance on the arete (awkward belays).
2) 5a, 10m. Step right, climb the wall (bomber Rock 9) and move left and mantelshelf (crux) to the easy upper slab. Enjoy the summit experience then abseil from the ring.
FA. Joe Brown, Wilf White 1949

❷ Neon Dust E6 7a
The wall between the crack and arete has a desperate start followed by easier (6b) climbing above on gradually improving finger holds. It is usually just done as a V10 boulder problem before scuttling off left to the *Valkyrie* crack.
FA. Ron Fawcett 1983

❸ Narcissus E6 6b
18m. The blunt arete of the pinnacle is increasingly taxing, with the crux just where you don't want it! Easier with padding but graded for an ascent without. Finish up or down *Valkyrie*.
FA. Steve Bancroft (solo) 1976

❹ Narcissus II E5 6b
18m. Not pitch 2 to *Narcissus* but a continuation above the *Valkyrie* crack. Pull over and aim for the flared crack which leads to the top. There may be an old stuck wire in place.
FA. Steve Bancroft 1979

❺ Oedipus Ring
Your Mother E4 6b
8m. A taxing traverse from the right along the sloping finger break gains the base of a shallow flake. A committing long stretch and ancient chipped hold (lest we forget) reaches the sanctuary of the *Valkyrie* stance. It can be started direct but this involves another more blatant chipped hold and is only 6a. On top of that it is historically less satisfying.
FA. Tom Proctor (solo) 1968

❻ The Mint 400 .. E6 6b
9m. A boulder problem up the wall gains the break of *Oedipus*. Launch up the seemingly holdless wall above to gain the upper break. Escape left. A serious and technical undertaking.
FA. Ron Fawcett 1983. Direct start added at a later date.

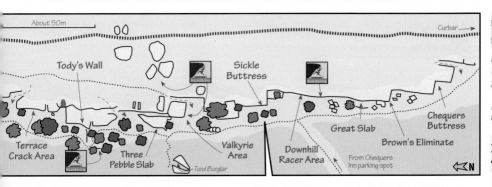

About 50m — Curbar →

Tody's Wall — Sickle Buttress — Chequers Buttress — Great Slab — Brown's Eliminate — Terrace Crack Area — Three Pebble Slab — Turd Burglar — Valkyrie Area — Downhill Racer Area — From Chequers Inn parking spot — N

(Side tabs: Wharncliffe, Dovestone Tor, Rivelin, Bamford, Stanage, Burbage North, Higgar Tor, Burbage South, Millstone, Lawrencefield, Yarncliffe, Froggatt, Curbar, Gardoms, Birchen, Chatsworth, Cratcliffe)

BOULDERING - There are several good bouldering spots at this end of Froggatt.

Tody's Playground - Short wall hidden below *Tody's Wall*.
Pinnacle Boulders - Large boulders on the top of the crag.
The Pinnacle - Several problems around *Oedipus*.
Joe's Slab - Thin slab below *Slab Recess*.

Afternoon — 20 min

Downhill Racer Area 20m

he next routes start up the blocky gully behind the Pinnacle nd are reached by a short scramble.

7 Pinnacle Arete . . . . 🔲🔲🔲 **E2 5b**
6m. Neglected but well worthwhile. From the gully traverse left along the lowest break, pass the arete and pull up to gain a dge. Climb the groove then step up and right to better holds nd a quick sprint finish.
A. Slim Sorrell 1948

8 Chapman's Crack . . . . 🔲 **VS 4c**
m. Start at the top of the gully. Traverse left above the gully in position of some exposure and climb the short crack. The asiest way up the Pinnacle.
A. Len Chapman 1948

9 Route One . . . . 🔲🔲 **VS 5a**
m. The short north-east arete yields to a tough mantelshelf. n impressive route for its day and a viable way down for the chnically proficient or those with rubber legs.
A. Henry Bishop 1912

10 Pinnacle Face . . . . . . 🔲🔲 **VS 5b**
0m. From the top of the gully below the back arete teeter right ong shelving ledges then climb the wall passing a useful and ther unusual hole.
A. Gilbert Ellis 1947

ack down at ground level is a clean-cut crack in the wall right f the gully that runs up behind the Pinnacle.

11 Diamond Crack . . . . . 🔲🔲 **HS 4b**
m. The slanting crack gives a fine exercise in jamming - steep, trenuous and well protected. A popular route for logging your rst flight time! And by the way who said Joe Brown invented and-jamming?
A. Henry Bishop 1913

SICKLE BUTTRESS
This short wall has a clean crack at its left-hand side. It is situated just to the left of the popular Downhill Racer Area.

12 Broken Crack . . . . 🔲🔲 **HVS 5a**
10m. The jamming crack is best approached by a swift layback.
FA. Joe Brown 1948

13 Sickle Buttress . . . . 🔲 **VDiff**
12m. Climb onto the ledges then follow them out to the right-hand arete of the buttress and finish up a shallow groove.
FA. R.Davies 1945

14 Sickle Buttress Direct . . . . 🔲 **VS 4c**
12m. Finish up the centre of the wall instead of moving right.
FA. Joe Brown 1948

15 Performing Flea . . . . . . 🔲🔲 **HVS 5a**
12m. Climb the arete and the wall above.
FA. Matt Boyer 1985. The old route Sickle Buttress Arete fell down.

Afternoon | 20 min

Awkward scramble descent here or walk
to gully behind Valkyrie Pinnacle

Alternative
descent at
end of crag

Great Slab

Sickle Buttress 5m

DOWNHILL RACER AREA

The most popular area at Froggatt has some great climbs in the lower grades and a famous blank slab. However it is showing signs of wear and tear, and the whole area can be very crowded on busy weekends.

DIRECT APPROACH - From the crag-top path descend the gully behind the Valkyrie Pinnacle and follow the lower path. Alternatively continue to the end of the crag and double back. The area is situated at the top of the Chequers Inn approach path for those coming up the hill. See map on previous page.

1 Long John's Slab . . . . . 🔢🏆 ▢ **E3 5c**
14m. From a lurking boulder mantelshelf onto a narrow ledge then use the old peg hole (6a for the short) to gain finger holds and easier climbing. Unprotected but the hard bit can be made safe with some padding.
FA. Al Rouse (solo) 1969

2 Downhill Racer . . . 🔢🏆🏆 ▢ **E4 6a**
16m. Climb the slab left of the shallow groove then step left and make a fierce fingery mantelshelf to better holds and an uphill finger traverse to ledges. One awkward move remains. The route is unprotected unless you faff about with a runner in the boulders below *Long John's* and one in the corner on the right. I did and still hit the ground from the crux!
FA. Pete Livesey 1977

3 Slab Recess Direct . . . . . 🔢 ▢ **HS 4b**
14m. The shallow corner has an unhelpful set of sloping and slippery holds. The upper half is a doddle.
FA. Joe Brown 1948

4 Joe's Direct Start . . . . . 🔢🏁 ▢ **5c (V2)**
4m. A classic boulder problem up the face to the right via a mantelshelf is worthy of description and a minute of your time. Variations are countless, with the technical mantelshelf on the left arete being the best (6a (V3)).
FA. Joe Brown 1950s

5 Slab Recess . . . . 🔢 ▢ **Diff**
16m. The best beginners route on the cliff, do yourself a favou and don't top rope it. Climb the cracks on the right then move along a ledge to the flake in the centre of the face. A mild layback up this leads into the final corner.
FA. Sandy Alton 1948

6 Gamma . . . . 🔢 ▢ **VDiff**
12m. The obvious continuation to start of the previous climb.
FA. Nat Allen 1951

7 Allen's Slab . . . . 🔢 ▢ **S 4a**
16m. Start up *Gamma* but follow the diagonal crack out right t a heathery ledge. Finish up the juggy wall just left to the left of the next crack (*Trapeze Direct*).
FA. Nat Allen 1951

8 Polyp Piece . . . . . 🔢🏁🏆 ▢ **E7 6c**
10m. Climb the blank slab on very poor footholds and under-cuts direct to the traverse of *Allen's Slab*. Graded for a solo ascent, it is E5 with a side runner in the diagonal crack of *Allen's Slab*.
FA. Nick Dixon 1987 (with a side runner). Ben Heason 2000 (solo)

9 Trapeze Direct . . . . 🔢 ▢ **VS 4c**
12m. The easy crack leads to a bulge split by a thin crack. Fill i full of runners and reach for a huge jug above. Heave away to easy ground. A safe first VS lead.
FA. Wilf White 1948

10 Trapeze . . . . 🔢 ▢ **VDiff**
14m. Follow *Trapeze Direct* to the bulge then swing right along a break to gain an open groove. Climb this to the top.
FA. R.Davis 1945

11 Nursery Slab . . . . ▢ **Mod**
10m. The well-named cracks and blocks to the left of The Grea Slab. Often used as a way down by the competent.
FA. J.W.Puttrell 1906

Whamcliffe · Dovestone Tor · Rivelin · Bamford · Stanage · Burbage North · Higgar Tor · Burbage South · Millstone · Lawrencefield · Yarncliffe · Froggatt · Curbar · Gardoms · Birchen · Chatsworth · Cratcliffe

Downhill Racer Area

Descent at end of crag

Brown's Eliminate Area

Afternoon / 20 min

THE GREAT SLAB

This is finest gritstone slab in the Peak District. It has a magnificent set of routes from Joe Brown's original *Great Slab* to the ultra-technical *Toy Boy*. With the exception of the crack of *Synopsis* there isn't a runner on the whole wall. Most of the routes are graded for solo ascents although top roping is pretty much the norm.

❶ Heartless Hare E5 5c
12m. The left-hand side of the slab is a bold undertaking passing a ledge then two tiny left-facing flakes. Often climbed with side-runners (as high as your consciousness allows) at a more friendly E3.
FA. Steve Bancroft 1975

❷ Jugged Hare E6 6a
14m. A right-hand finish to *Heartless Hare* using small holds to gain a thin break and a steep spooky finish. A distant side-runner is of little use. Once chipped, subsequently filled in but now gradually eroded over the years.
FA. Johnny Dawes 1983

❸ Great Slab E3 5b
18m. Not very hard but still unprotected and a touch precarious. Trend right up a delicate ramp to a ledge, 'piano-play' right (crux featuring slippery footholds) then climb the steeper wall on flatties. Harder for the short.
FA. Joe Brown 1951

❹ Art Brut E7 6b
15m. The direct finish above the start of Great Slab following a line midway between *Jugged Hare* and *Hairless Heart*.
FA. Dave Thomas 1990s

❺ Hairless Heart E5 5c
15m. The central line on the slab is superb. Follow *Great Slab* to its rest then friction up the slab to the curving flake and follow this to a rapid exit rightwards.
FA. John Allen (solo) 1975

❻ Hairy Heart E6 6a
15m. A more direct finish to *Great Slab*, after its crux climb the right-hand of the pair of overlaps.
FA. Mick Fowler 1975

❼ Artless E5 6b
15m. The right-trending ramp below the centre of the slab is gained awkwardly (try jumping!) and climbed via a hard dyno/slap or a harder rock-over. Then move up and right to join and finish up *Great Slab*.
FA. John Allen (solo) 1976

❽ Artless/Hairless Heart E5 6b
18m. This combination, which also includes reversing the crux of *Great Slab* is the finest slab route on grit - period!
FA. John Allen (solo) 1975/76

❾ Toy Boy E7 7a
15m. There are no visible holds on this one, however armed with your magnifying glass you might just find something to curl your fingernails over. Progress depends on leaps between the micro edges until you reach the finish of *Great Slab*. Ensure you wear a stiff pair of boots for this one!
FA. Ron Fawcett 1986

❿ Synopsis E2 5c
14m. The old peg crack looks like a refugee from Millstone. The crux is at an awkward height off the ground, with barely comforting wires to protect, just before the flat holds arrive.
FA. Steve Bancroft 1974. Aid climbed by Nat Allen in 1952.

⓫ Beta .... VDiff
15m. The long blocky corner feels out of place.
FA. Nat Allen 1951

⓬ Spine Chiller Start . 6b (V5
15m. The left-hand arete of the block to the right of Great Slab is most notable for the boulder problem start. Sit down at the back of the cave and pull out up the slanting crack. The upper section is a scary E4 5c.
FA. Steve Bancroft 1984. Start added at a later date by persons unknown.

Mo on First Ascent of Slingshot
V13
Froggatt Edge, England

Contact: Big Stone
Tel:0114 263 4261
Email: info@bigstone.co.uk
www.lasportiva.com

LA SPORTIVA

The Great Slab

4m gap

Afternoon 20 min

BROWN'S ELIMINATE AREA

This area is steeper than the rest of Froggatt and the signs of quarrying are more evident. There are some great cracks which offer strenuous but well-protected climbing from Severe to E2. However the first routes are more in keeping with the bold climbs elsewhere on the crag up a magnificent clean wall with a prominent sharp arete.

❶ Flake Gully . . . . **Diff**
15m. Climb the gully behind the detached block then traverse left until the steep but juggy wall can be climbed.

❷ Brown's Eliminate **E2 5b**
16m. An impressive route with an intimidating reputation. Usually soloed or top-roped although there is gear at half-height. From the corner trend left to a ledge (low Friend runners to the left) then climb the wall on small flakes until things ease. The arete all the way is sustained from the bottom and worth a very bold **E3 5c**.
FA. Joe Brown 1948

❸ Armaggedon **E3 5c**
12m. This would be a fine wall climb if it wasn't so escapable. Make a hard move to the ledge then continue direct on positive holds past a couple of longish reaches to the top. Side runners reduce the grade to E2 and can be placed from the route.
FA. Alec Burns 1977

❹ Green Gut . . . . **HS 4a**
14m. The superb and squeaky-clean corner took a couple of days of digging before the first ascent. Nowadays it is just a question of finding the end of the queue.
FA. Nat Allen 1948

❺ Pedestal Crack . . . . **HVS 5a**
14m. The long crack which runs into a flake near the top has an awkward move level with the big roof on the right.
FA. Joe Brown 1948

❻ Sling Shot . . . . . . **7b (V13)**
Ultra-hard bouldering through the bulge right of *Pedestal Crack*. It was well padded for the first solo ascent. *Photo page 225.*
FA. Mo Overfield 2000. Top-roped by Jerry Moffatt in 1988.

❼ Chequers Groove . . **7a (V11)**
A similar but lesser boulder problem to *Sling Shot* up the groove and overlaps just left of the *Big Crack*.
FA. Jerry Moffatt 2000

❽ The Big Crack **E2 5b**
15m. Jugs and jams lead to a spike then bolder moves gain the base of the wide upper crack. This is awkward though occasional good holds out left do help. A big outing!
FFA. John Syrett 1973. In 1955 the mighty Whillans used a machine nut for aid.

❾ Circus/Hard Cheddar . . . **E7 6b**
15m. Excellent bold and technical wall climbing. Originally done with side-runners on the *Circus* upper section (at E6) but has now been done without.
FA. (Hard Cheddar) Tom Proctor 1977, (Circus) Daniel Lee 1982

❿ Stiff Cheese **E2 5c**
12m. A short and very stiff crack. You will probably get pumped if you try to place gear, better to jump off onto your mat.
FA. Steve Bancroft 1974

⓫ Beech Nut **E1 5c**
12m. Hard to crack! Easier to solo.
FA. Don Whillans, Nat Allen 1951

Whamcliffe · Dovestone Tor · Rivelin · Bamford · Stanage · Burbage North · Higgar Tor · Burbage South · Millstone · Lawrencefield · Yarncliffe · Froggatt · Curbar · Gardoms · Birchen · Chatsworth · Cratcliffe

Change in viewing angle

Descent

From mid morning | 20 min

CHEQUERS BUTTRESS

The final buttress at Froggatt is a tall undercut tower. The two famous *Chequers* routes provide contrasting challenges: the *Crack* is a short and savage affair which sees many valiant struggles, the *Buttress* gives more airy climbing in a splendid position.

⑫ Chequers Crack . . . . . . HVS 5c
14m. The thin finger crack (crux) leads to the break (good hold in the roof) and an easier upper section on solid jams. Much easier to solo than to lead if you are up to it, but don't fall off.
FA. Don Whillans 1951

⑬ Spock's Missing/
Business Lunch . . . E5 6c
14m. Boulder out the roof right of *Chequer's Crack* for your *Business Lunch* then climb the upper wall direct, with runners in both *Chequer's Crack* and *Chequers Buttress* if you can reach them. *Spock*'s *Missing* is E5 6b if climbed on its own.
FA. (SM) Ron Fawcett 1981, (BL) John Allen 1984

⑭ Sole Power 6c (V9)
Extended bouldering up the hanging fin to the right. Rarely climbed. Finish as you wish. Given E5 6c as a route.
FA. Jerry Moffatt 1983

⑮ Bacteria Cafeteria . . . . HVS 5b
14m. A direct line but inferior to its neighbours. Climb the wall left of the flake to the break, continue direct up cracks to finish.
FA. Gary Gibson 1979

⑯ Chequers Climb . . . . . . VS 4c
20m. Devious but worthwhile, double ropes are sensible. Climb the ramp then traverse round the arete to access the upper section of *Chequer's Crack*.
FA. Joe Brown 1949

⑰ Chequers Buttress . . . . HVS 5a
14m. The final Froggatt classic. Climb the slippery ramp then the side-wall diagonally leftwards to a good large wire. Make a barn door move left to the jug on the arete. The finish above is both easy and spectacular.
FA. John Gosling 1962

⑱ Solomon's Crack VDiff
12m. The awkward slanting ramp and wider upper crack are all very historical. The thinner left-hand crack near the top gives an alternative Severe finish.
FA. J.W.Puttrell 1890

⑲ Janker's Crack . . . . HS 4b
10m. The first crack in the wall to the right is approached by a crack and is an awkward battle to enter.
FA. Joe Brown 1948

⑳ Janker's Groove . . . . . . VS 4c
10m. The right-hand of the grooves is approached from the previous climb. The direct start is a classic featuring a heave on a fist-crunching **6b** jam, you can thank Whillans for that.
FA. Joe Brown 1948

㉑ Janker's End . . . . VS 4c
10m. Continue the traverse from *Janker's Groove* under the roof. Climb a short groove and rock back left onto the arete.
FA. Joe Brown 1948

Wharncliffe
Dovestone Tor
Rivelin
Bamford
Stanage
Burbage North
Higgar Tor
Burbage South
Millstone
Lawrencefield
Yarncliffe
Froggatt
Curbar
Gardoms
Birchen
Chatsworth
Cratcliffe

CURBAR

An edge with a fierce and well-deserved reputation as a tough task master. The routes are generally hard, intimidating and strenuous and this not a place for climbers who like their sport to be elegant, dainty and air-conditioned. Many of the routes feature steep crack climbing and the lack of such features in the nation's climbing walls is part of the reason these feel so damn hard. Hauling up a 45-degree overhanging wall, liberally covered in bolt-ons, is not much use when the only available hold is a parallel crack slightly wider than your fist. However it is not just the cracks that are hard here, by some quirk of nature most of the other routes tend to be in the upper reaches of their respective grades and a soft-touch on Curbar is a rare find indeed. So why on earth would anyone want to come and climb here? Well, like many great challenges, the meaner the task appears at first, the greater the sense of satisfaction when you overcome it. The 'challenges' on Curbar are as fine as any on grit and the likes of *Peapod, L'Horla, Elder Crack, Right Eliminate, Moon Walk* and *Profit of Doom* are an essential part of any gritstone climber's aspirations.

BOULDERING - There is some great bouldering on the blocks below the main edge. These are reached by walking down the road and following a path from the bend.

APPROACH (SK257752)

The edge is situated in a majestic position overlooking the villages of Curbar and Calver. The road through Curbar village leads up the hill to a pay and display car park just to the east of Curbar Gap. This car park can also be reached from a turning off the A625, just above Gardoms Edge. From here a short walk over the top leads to the Eliminates Wall on the main edge. There are a few free parking spots on the road below Curbar Gap but these are often full. Roadside parking here is sometimes possible but you may get a ticket, especially if you block the road.
Alternatively the cliff can be reached from Froggatt by heading south, gently uphill to the start of the cliff, a couple of minutes away. The start of the 'business end' is another ten minutes walk.

CONDITIONS

The edge is typical of most of the eastern edges: quick-drying, exposed to the afternoon sun but with the potential to be windy and cold in bad weather.

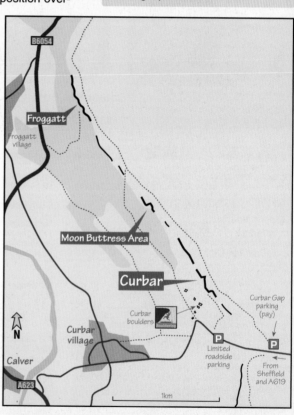

OTHER GUIDEBOOKS - A more complete list of routes at Curbar is published in the 1991 BMC *Froggatt* guidebook. The bouldering is in the 1998 Peak Bouldering ROCKFAX.

Whamcliffe · Dovestone Tor · Rivelin · Bamford · Stanage · Burbage North · Higgar Tor · Burbage South · Millstone · Lawrencefield · Yarncliffe · Froggatt · **Curbar** · Gardoms · Birchen · Chatsworth · Cratcliffe

← - - - - Descent

Afternoon · 15 min

① Black Nix Wall . . . . . . 🔲🔲🔲 **E1 5c**
8m. The technical wall just right of a short open corner trending right via some thin flakes.
FA. Steve Bancroft (after Black Nick failed) 1976

② Mastiff Wall . . . . 🔲🔲 **VS 4c**
8m. Thin cracks in the wall lead to a steep and tricky exit. Fortunately it is well protected.
FA. Nat Allen 1964

③ Camel Ticks . . . . 🔲🔲 **E3 6a**
10m. A bold little problem up the thin groove and the wall to the left of *Rat Scabies*.
FA. Mike Hammill (solo) 1987

④ Rat Scabies . . . . 🔲🔲🔲🔲 **E4 6b**
10m. The delightfully named centre of the wall has a gruesome 'stopper' mantelshelf move to pass the bulge.
FA. Gabe Regan mid 1970s

⑤ Bulldog Crack . . . . 🔲🔲 **S 4b**
10m. The groove that bounds the wall requires a tenacious approach especially in its upper section.
FA. K. Brindley 1950

⑥ John's Arete . . . . 🔲🔲🔲 **E1 5b**
10m. The square, jutting arete and wall above are pleasantly technical but not something you would want to fall off.
FA. Steve Bancroft 1975

⑦ Derwent Groove . . . . 🔲 **S 4a**
10m. The open corner is awkward towards the top.
FA. Nat Allen 1950

⑧ Cool Moon . . . . 🔲🔲🔲🔲🔲 **E7 6c**
12m. A brilliant bold climb up the thin flakes and sinuous cracks. The hard lower section has no gear but a side-runner in *Moon Walk* drops the grade one notch. Higher up small Friends protect.
FA. Daniel Lee (with side-runners) 1981. Thomas de Gay (solo) 1999

MOON BUTTRESS AREA
One of Curbar's finest buttresses with some great classics covering the spectrum from Brown's 1950 test-piece of *Sorrell's Sorrow* through to the Dawes' 1986 heart-stopper of *The End of the Affair*.
APPROACH - From the parking at Curbar Gap follow the cliff top path northward towards Froggatt for 15 minutes passing the high point of the path until a series of 'Hippo's Teeth' like outcrops can be seen down to the left in an open gully. Left (looking out) of these is Apollo Buttress and right of them is Moon Buttress. This point can also be reached in 10 minutes walk from *Chequers Buttress* at Froggatt.

Descent

Apollo Buttress opposite

9 Moon Walk **E4 6a**
12m. One of the most perfect grit experiences. A tricky start gains a flake in the arete. This leads to a pause before the sumptuous finishing moves above Friends in the break. Well worth attempting as a true ground-up, on-sight since commitment on the final move will be rewarded, one way or the other.
FA. John Allen 1976

10 Moon Crack **E5 6b**
14m. A fine companion to *Moon Walk*. The bulging crack is a fierce battle with solid wires to protect. At the top of the crack move right to the much easier slabby groove.
FA. John Allen 1975

11 Crack and Slab . . **E7 7a**
12m. Climb *Moon Crack* to above its crux then gain access to the slab above by a wild mantelshelf. Hard smearing and a rounded finish complete the fun.
FA. John Arran 1999

12 Moon Madness . . **E7 6c**
12m. The bulge right of *Moon Crack* is unprotected, reachy and the landing is particularly grim.
FA. Ron Fawcett 1987

13 Sorrell's Sorrow . . . . . **HVS 5a**
12m. The soaring central crack-line is too wide for comfort and too compelling to ignore. Take your big guns on this one.
FA. Joe Brown 1950

14 Mr Softee **E1 6a**
16m. Climb the bulges via a crack (hard for the short) to the break then scuttle left past *Sorrell's Sorrow* (sigh of relief) to finish up *Moon Crack*.
FA. John Allen 1973

15 The End of the Affair . . **E8 6c**
14m. The archetypal grit arete, technical and ultra committing with good runners at one-third height and the crux at the top. The leader's life might be saved if the second man is prepared to jump off the belay ledge, but timing is *kinda* critical!!!
FA. Johnny Dawes 1986

16 Amphitheatre Crack . . . . . **Diff**
8m. A pleasant right-angled groove in the south-facing wall is obviously on the wrong cliff.

17 Gladiator Buttress . . . . **HS 4b**
8m. Climb an arete to a big ledge then either of the cracks above on the left-hand wall of the tower.

18 Hidden Pleasures . . . **E3 6a**
8m. The thin cracks in the narrow tower, small wires protect.
FA. Andy Bailey 1984

19 Twin Crack . . . . **S 4a**
8m. The wide corner crack immediately right of the tower.

20 Ulysses or Bust **E5 6b**
8m. An attractive and unprotected arete. Layaway to the right until it becomes imperative to swap sides.
FA. Neil Foster 1984

21 The Unreachable Star . . **E3 6a**
8m. The thin crack past an extended reach to a rounded exit.
FA. Mark Stokes 1980

22 Dog Leg Crack . . . . **VDiff**
6m. The jamming crack is classic, pity it is so short.

Change in viewing angle

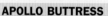

APOLLO BUTTRESS

The central feature of this sector of Curbar is the impressive tall bulk of the Apollo Buttress with its majestic valley face. There is also a collection of (slightly) lesser routes to either side of the main tower.

APPROACH - Follow the cliff top path to the 'Hippo's Teeth' gully and descend this turning left at the bottom to locate the side wall of the buttress.

The first three routes are on the wall to the left of the main bulk of the Apollo Buttress and follow a trio of prominent cracks.

① Buckle's Sister . . . . S 4a
6m. The left-hand crack is (relatively) amenable.
FA. Nat Allen 1950

② Buckle's Brother . . . . HVS 4c
6m. The central crack is an exhausting thrash.
FA. Nat Allen 1950

③ Buckle's Crack . . . . HVS 4c
6m. The right-hand crack is also a battle.
FA. Nat Allen 1950

④ Soyuz E2 5c
10m. The cracks in the north-facing side wall lead to sloping shelf. Before you pump out here stretch awkwardly right and reach for the top. Low in the grade.
FA. John Allen 1972

⑤ Dark Entries E4 6a
10m. Climb the bulges leftwards to a short crack then head right on spaced holds to decent finishing holds.
FA. Ron Fawcett 1980

⑥ Forbidden Planet E4 6b
12m. The flying arete on the right. Climb through the bulges with difficulty to the crucial roof. Undercut past this then sprint for the top. A Friend 3.5 might well prove to be essential.
FA. John Allen 1984

⑦ Apollo E2 5c
16m. Start from a stance on the ledge left of the tower. Climb up and trend right through the imposing bulges via a short crack with one powerful move to reach easier ground. There is an unremarkable lower pitch to the right of *Two Pitch Route*.
FA. John Gosling (with a little tension) 1969

The next two routes start at a lower level.

⑧ Two Pitch Route . . . . VS 4c
1) 4c, 10m. From the base climb a wide crack to ledges then traverse right to pass the arete to a comfortable stance.
2) 4c, 6m. Finish up the fine crack to a superb juggy exit.
FA. Joe Brown 1950

⑨ The League of Gentleman . . . E6 6b
16m. Climb direct up the right edge of the lower wall. Continue over the big roof then climb the big bulges above to join *The Beer Hunter*.
FA. Pete Robins 1999

The following route is usually started from the mid-height ledge. This is reached from the right (looking in).

⑩ The Beer Hunter E3 6a
16m. Climb the right arete of the buttress via a thin crack to a baffling move on a hidden pocket which gives access to the front face. Keep right to finish. Starting up a crack below the upper arete is also an option.
FA. Steve Bancroft 1979

N | About 50m | Overtaker's Buttress 300m

Froggatt 10mins

Moon Buttress Area

Apollo Area

Open gully containing 'Hippo's Teeth'

The End of the Affair

Birthday Groove Area

No easy access along the base of the crag

TREES

THE BRAIN and BIRTHDAY GROOVE AREA
This complex area consists of a series of smaller walls and buttresses scattered up and down the hillside. The lowest buttress with *The Brain* is always popular and the *Diet of Worms* buttress is frequented by the hard-core.

The lower wall (climbed by Two Pitch Route) has 3 other reasonable pitches to the right of a gully

11 Combat les Pellicules .... **HVS 5c**
5m. The short arete to the left of *Big Rocker* is climbed first on the left and then on the right.
FA. Bill McKee 1985

12 For the Good of the Cause **E4 6b**
5m. The right-hand side of the short wall left of *Big Rocker*. A hard start reaches pockets that are followed left to finish as for *Combat les Pellicules*.
FA. Andy Barker 1994

13 The Big Rocker .... **VS 4c**
1) 4c, 10m. Climb a thin crack on the right of the lower wall then a groove in the rib. Move right along a ledge to the arete.
2) 4c, 8m. Climb the arete then move left around the bulge.
FA. John Gosling 1966

The next two routes are on the tower left of pitch 2 of Big Rocker. Reach the start by scrambling up from the right.

14 Rocky Horror Show . **E6 6b**
6m. The short, technical and exposed arete left of pitch 2 of *Big Rocker* is a bit of a ...
FA. Pete Robins 1999

15 Body Torque **E3 5c**
The centre of the west-facing wall with a hard lower section.
FA. Paul Mitchell 1981

Down and right, near the trees, is a slab leading to a tower.

16 Mensa **E6 6b**
14m. Climb the centre of the slab to reach the left-hand arete. Boldly finish up this. A perplexing problem for most.
FA. Neil Foster 1993

17 The Brain .... **VS 4c**
18m. Climb the slabby lower wall trending right to the base of a groove (possible belay). Climb the groove to finish. An interesting alternative finish is to step left onto the arete for more exposure but with no change in grade.
FA. Slim Sorrell late 1940s

Afternoon | 15 min

Descent | Descent

The Brain 25m

Up and right of The Brain is a steep, imposing, axe-edged arete.

18 King of the Swingers **E5 6c**
8m. Climb the wall left of the arete to a pocket (gear) then make a desperate long move left to finish.
FA. Ron Fawcett 1984

19 King Louis **E6 6c**
8m. Start as for the previous route to the runners then make crucial moves up and right to a final mantel which has some ground-fall potential if your second is at all lax.
FA. Chris Wright 1999

20 Diet of Worms **E4 6a**
10m. The arete is approached from the left. A Friend 4 protects the final difficult moves.
FA. Paul Mitchell 1978

21 Slackers **E6 6b**
10m. The direct to the arete is bold, dynamic and elegant.
FA. Robin Barker 1994

22 Birthday Groove **E1 5c**
8m. The groove on the right is a pig to enter but eases above.
FA. Joe Brown 1950

Wharncliffe · Dovestone Tor · Rivelin · Bamford · Stanage · Burbage North · Higgar Tor · Burbage South · Millstone · Lawrencefield · Yarncliffe · Froggatt · Curbar · Gardoms · Birchen · Chatsworth · Cratcliffe

Descent -->

Afternoon 12 min

20m gap

POTTER'S WALL

OVERTAKER'S BUTTRESS and POTTER'S WALL

Long renowned for the route of the same name, the overhang-capped buttress is now best known as home to the Johnny Dawes' desperate of *White Lines* that had to wait over 15 years for a repeat. *Potter's Wall* is the tall buttress to the right of Overtaker's.

APPROACH - Walk along the top of the crag and keep an eye out for the prominent hanging prow which is perched above Overtaker's Buttress. Descend down a steep path about 50m before this which leads under *Potter's Wall*.

❶ Overtaker's Buttress ..... **HVS 5b**
1) 4c, 10m. Reach the groove from the left and at its top traverse right below the overhangs to a ledge and stance.
2) 5b, 8m. Climb the bulging arete to finish.
FA. Don Chapman 1954

❷ Overtaker's Direct **E3 5c**
10m. Climb the groove of the original then the overhang above and left using some rather flexible flakes.
FA. Mike Simpkins 1970s

❸ Snorter **E4 6b**
10m. The centre of the overhangs above *Overtaker's* traverse are tackled with difficulty (crucial Friend 0.5) .
FA. Mike Lea 1999

❹ White Lines **E7 6b**
12m. The centre of the wall by a desperate mantelshelf then the overhangs above via a pocket. Sustained technicalities.
FA. Johnny Dawes 1984

❺ Free Way **E5 6b**
12m. Climb the crack on the right then the left-hand side of the nose by a long stretch for distant pockets. Finish over the bulges that cap the wall.
FA. Pete Robins 1999

There are two routes near the impressive beak above.

❻ Right Triplet Gully .... **VDiff**
8m. Back and foot the deep cleft left of the beak.

❼ Fidget **E1 6a**
6m. Climb the arete below the right edge of the beak then fidget left and stretch for the flake.
FA. John Allen 1973

20m right of Overtaker's Buttress is a narrow wall, with an protruding oblong block on its top, known as Potter's Wall.

❽ Mad Hatter **E2 5c**
8m. Start up a groove on the left-hand side of the wall (or the harder wall to its right). Climb up and then left to the top break finishing with hard moves over the left edge of the capping roof.
FA. John Gosling 1966

❾ Potter's Wall .... **HS 4b**
10m. The discontinuous cracks up the right-hand edge of the buttress have good holds but are light on gear.

❿ Circus of Dinosaurs .... **HVS 4b**
10m. The arete of the wall on its left-hand side has some good moves although avoiding the previous route is not easy.
FA. Roy Bennett 1989

⓫ Grooved Arete .... **VS 4c**
8m. The shallow, stepped grove in the south-facing side wall is good but short-lived. Thought you were on Tryfan for a second?
FA. Mike Simpkins 1966

Wharncliffe
Dovestone Tor
Rivelin
Bamford
Stanage
Burbage North
Higgar Tor
Burbage South
Millstone
Lawrencefield
Yarncliffe
Froggatt
Curbar
Gardoms
Birchen
Chatsworth
Cratcliffe

BARON'S WALL and CALVER WALL

A pair of fine of short steep walls, once quarried but long enough ago for all the damage to have healed. They are home to a good selection of fingery face climbs of a less intimidating nature than is usual for Curbar.

⑫ Smoke ont' Watter **E1 6a**
8m. A boulder problem start (6a) leads to a ledge. An awkward and scary move up left gains a thin hanging crack which leads more easily to the top.
FA. Nicky Stokes 1976

⑬ Baron's Wall . . . . **HVS 5b**
8m. The right-hand crack is gained from the right. Again the start is quite problematical especially for the short.
FA. Joe Brown (the Baron) late 1950s

⑭ Blockhead . . . . **VS 4c**
8m. Climb direct past the triangular niche to a steep finish.
FA. Dave Gregory 1978

⑮ Sweet Gene Vincent . . . . **HVS 5b**
10m. Take the wall right of *Blockhead* to the break. Step left and climb the technical thin crack in the wall.
FA. Gary Gibson (solo) 1978

⑯ Saddy **E2 5b**
10m. The thin crack in the centre of the wall is harder than it looks, doesn't accept wires easily and has a pumpy finish.
FA. Steve Bancroft 1977

⑰ Wall Climb . . . . **VS 5a**
10m. The shallow right-trending groove is tricky to reach.
FA. Joe Brown 1950

⑱ Top Secret **E1 5c**
8m. The right-hand arete of the wall. Bridging is not an option.
FA. Gary Gibson 1981

⑲ Calver Chimney . . . . **Mod**
8m. An easy tick and possible descent route up/down the gully.

⑳ Calver Wall . . . . **VS 4b**
8m. Climb the easy wall left of a tree to a ledge. Finish up the short, but perfect, jamming crack above.

㉑ Brindle Crack . . . . **HS 4b**
10m. As for *Calver Wall* to the ledge but step right to reach and climb the right-hand branch of the crack.

㉒ Polar Crack . . . . **VS 4b**
8m. Start to the right of the tree and climb the wall leftwards to reach the rightmost crack in the upper wall.

25m right is a tall buttress with a short blank groove on the left.

㉓ The Corner . . . . **HVS 5b**
8m. The blank corner is bridged. Low in the grade.
FA. Joe Brown 1955

㉔ Flying Buttress . . . . **S 4a**
12m. The left-hand side of the buttress via a groove and cracks.

㉕ Flying Buttress Right . . . . **S 4a**
10m. The right-hand side of the buttress also gives a worthwhile climb.

KAYAK SLAB

That rarity on Curbar, a brace of slabs. It isn't all good news though, the routes are generally tough and there is hardly a runner between the seven climbs here. If you're feeling bold and technical, step this way, and don't forget your life-jacket.

The first 3 routes described are 50m to the left of the Kayak Slab, in a small, north-facing bay with two clean cracks.

① Inch Crack .... **VS 4b**
6m. The left-hand crack is short and steep.

② Little Innominate .... **HVS 5a**
6m. The right-hand crack is narrower and harder.

③ Lepton **E2 6b**
6m. The bouldery arete to the right of the cracks. Finish to the right or go direct for an E3 tick.
FA. Al Rouse 1978

Back to the more important stuff.

④ Kayak **E2 5b**
8m. The left-hand side of the central slab trending right. Hard for the short. The final break will take runners but by then the difficulties are all over.
FA. Colin Mortlock 1964

⑤ Finger Distance **E3 6b**
10m. The pocketed centre of the slab is tenuous and unprotected. The right-hand start, using the big pocket, is only 6a for the short but true technicians will ignore this and climb direct.
FA. Gary Gibson 1980

⑥ El Vino Collapso **E5 6b**
8m. Stagger up the right-hand side of the slab to a crucial stretch for thank-God jugs.
FA. John Allen 1985

⑦ Canoe **E3 6a**
6m. The pocketed left-hand edge of the right-hand slab.
FA. Ed Drummond early 1970s

⑧ Stopper **E5 6b**
6m. Right again with the final stopper moves forming the crux.
FA. Ron Fawcett 1987

⑨ White Water **E6 6c**
6m. The sustained and unprotected slab just to the right.
FA. Johnny Dawes 1984

⑩ Done Years Ago **E3 6b**
6m. Head right past a pair of overlaps to the juggy arete.
FA. Johnny Dawes 1984

AVALANCHE WALL AREA

⑪ Portrait of a Legend **E4 6b**
8m. Climb the fierce thin cracks in the left-hand side of the wall past a deep break to a steeper finish.
FA. John Allen 1987

⑫ Avalanche Wall ..... **HVS 5a**
12m. One of the few Curbar routes which are 'low in their grade'. Twin cracks lead past blocks to steeper flaky cracks that are best tackled rapidly. Not a loose as the name suggests.
Photo page 239.
FA. Joe Brown 1950

⑬ One Step Beyond .. **E6 6b**
20m. From *Avalanche Wall* traverse the steep slab rightwards passing a runner slot and crucial high step to an easier finish just left of the far arete.
FA. Ron Fawcett 1980

⑭ Slab and Crack **E7 6c**
14m. The centre of the steep slab is a Curbar test-piece, being both technical and bold. Climb directly to the runner slot on *One Step Beyond* then continue up the sustained thin crack above. An RP2 is useful in the crack but it is hard to place.
FA. Johnny Dawes 1986

--- Descent

AVALANCHE WALL

A couple of low grade classics and two truly desperate outings are the main draws of this once-quarried bay. *PMC1* is Curbar's best 'easier' climb, *Avalanche Wall* is as popular as any HVS route hereabouts.

⑮ Doctor Doolittle — **E10 7a**
5m. Stunning hard route starting up *Slab and Crack* and then making a desperate traverse left into *One Step Beyond*. Above he crux of this break left and tackle the head wall by extremely enuous moves. The grade is a guess since John gave it H9 7a eferring to head pointing rather than an on-sight.
A. John Arran 10th November 2001

⑯ Owl's Arete — **VS 4b**
4m. The well-cracked arete is steep for one move in its central section. It disappoints somewhat above.
A. Slim Sorrell 1949

⑰ Predator — **E2 5c**
The thin crack on the right is rather unsatisfying. The bulge is he crux (knee-bar rest) and although the ledges on the right are difficult to avoid, avoid them you must!
A. John Allen 1976

⑱ Argosy Crack — **VS 4b**
14m. The wide crack in the corner is good practice for dirty American off-widths and great at wrecking clothes old or new.
A. Slim Sorrell late 1940s

⑲ P.M.C. 1 — **HS 4a**
16m. The cracks to the right of the corner lead steeply to a edge (possible stance on the left). Trend right up the wall to a spike (tape runner) and an exposed finish on sloping holds.
A. Bob Tomsett 1948

← - - Descent

Elder Crack Area

— Descent beyond Avalanche Wall

Afternoon 6 min

Descent behind L'Horla

Avalanche Wall

L'Horla Area 30m

ELDER CRACK AREA

Not surprisingly the tallest section of Curbar is also home to some of its very best routes. These aren't just three star classics, the main 5 outings here are major landmarks in any climbing career. However the difficulty level is high and most competent climbers may only manage to tick *Elder Crack* in a normal lifetime. Those who progress on to manage *Profit of Doom* can consider themselves to have pretty much tamed most of Curbar. Those lucky few who manage the other routes here have truly joined the elite.

❶ Profit of Doom **E5 6b**
18m. The superb hanging groove in the arete is best approached directly up the steep and awkward crack below it although those impatient individuals who can't wait to get at the main event often climb the wall to the left. Gear in the back of the groove is hard to place, especially for the short. Once suitably protected bridge-a-way to glory making suitable use of the left-hand arete. Many pre-place the wire on abseil which reduces the grade to E4. *Photo page 229.*
FA. John Allen 1975

❷ Rigid Digit **E5 6b**
18m. Climb the direct start to *Profit of Doom* to below the crucial groove and place the *Profit* runner. Use a flake to start a sequence heading up and right to access the other tantalising hanging groove (more runners) and a hard finishing sequence.
FA. Ron Fawcett 1980

❸ Janus **E7 6b**
16m. The long, shallow, leaning groove that cleaves the front of the tower is arduous and superb. One of the very best lines on grit. Small wires protect throughout but it is a good idea to place a solid runner early on to avoid them unzipping in the (inevitable) event of a fall.
FA. Johnny Dawes 1986. Originally given E7 7a "because the grooves looked like 2 sevens".

❹ Elder Crack **E2 5b**
18m. The imposing narrowing fissure is one of gritstone's great ticks. A brambly, blocky crack leads to the sentry-box. Runners can be placed deep in the crack (although not when wearing a helmet) however a large cam is the simpler modern method. Shin up the outside of the crack to a jug on the left arete then get established in the upper crack with difficulty. The wide upper crack is a little easier, just keep laybacking. Brilliant.
FA. Joe Brown 1950. Given VS - must have been more holds on it then.

❺ Knockin' on Heaven's Door **E9 6c**
18m. Well named. Climb the superb, steep wall initially up a shallow groove, then centrally with increasing apprehension to a final desperate sequence on ancient bullet marks. Originally done with a (hand) pre-placed peg runner by starting on the right. The direct start was added before it was finally soloed.
FA. Andy Pollitt 1988. Direct start added by Richie Patterson while repeating the route in 1996 and the whole route was renamed Born Slippy. Ben Tetler soloed the original line in 1999.

❻ Keeper's Crack .... **HS 4b**
14m. The crack on the right is too wide for comfort although the upper section, behind the ledge, is easier. Another grovel from way back when.
FA. Slim Sorrell 1949

❼ Bill and Ben **E4 6b**
16m. Climb the arete to ledges then the easier (E2 5c) exposed continuation over on the left. Not much in the way of gear.
FA. Johnny Dawes 1984

Whamcliffe · Dovestone Tor · Rivelin · Bamford · Stanage · Burbage North · Higgar Tor · Burbage South · Millstone · Lawrencefield · Yarncliffe · Froggatt · Curbar · Gardoms · Birchen · Chadworth · Cratcliffe

Descent down the chimney

Change in viewing angle

Descent down the chimney

Toy Are

Elder Crack 20m

From mid morning · 6 min

L'HORLA AREA

Three classic cracks, *Maupassant*, *L'Horla* and *Insanity*, all short and high in the grade, are the perfect introduction to Curbar. How you perform on these will give you an idea of how you are going to cope with the rest of the cliff. Welcome to the big butch world of Curbar.

❶ Slab Route . . . . **S 4a**
10m. Start below the centre of the slab and take the right-trending line of polished holds that steepen as they rise. Escape off left or finish up the groove left of the *Bel Ami* tower.
FA. Chuck Cook 1948

❷ Bel Ami . . . . **VS 4b**
16m. The flake and narrowing crack leads to the crusty arete of the squat tower and a real summit tick. Escape off the back.
FA. Wilf White late 1940s

❸ Green Crack . . . . **HVS 5b**
10m. Stride across the smelly pit then follow the curving flake out right to a poor rest and tricky moves to grasp the bounteous flutings. Finish easily.
FA. Joe Brown (some tension) 1957

❹ Usurper **E4 6a**
12m. The crack just right of the arete leads to a non-rest at the overhang. Progress from here requires some sustained and painful jamming and usually stops most folks in their tracks.
FA. Nicky Stokes 1977

❺ Moonshine **E5 6b**
12m. The thin bulging cracks on the right-hand side of the wall are gained from the right and are especially taxing where the initial crack fizzles. Friend 1.5 and RPs are useful.
FA. Tim Leach 1980

❻ Eclipse **E6 6b**
12m. Start up *Moonshine*, pull over the roof and then continue up the slappy arete above and right. Well positioned.
FA. Pete Robins 1999

❼ Maupassant . . . . **HVS 5a**
10m. A jamming crack leads to a bridged rest, take a big breath and layback to glory. A big chockstone can be lassoed from below, so exactly how good a cowboy are you?
FA. Don Whillans 1955

❽ L'Horla **E1 5b**
10m. The leaning groove is awkward and insecure. At the bulge (high wire and Friend 3 in the notch) leap onto the left arete and finish or flounder with a flourish. Alternatively, ignore the photogenic jug, and pull straight up into the groove. *Photo opposite.*
FA. Joe Brown (some tension) 1957

❾ Insanity **E2 5c**
8m. Put 2 Friend 1.5s on your rack and scuttle up the thin leaning crack by a tottering layback, especially where the side wall disappears (so where do you put your feet?). Easier for the short but always manages to feels a desperate struggle.
FA. Hugh Banner 1958

❿ Committed **E6 6b**
6m. Well named. From part way up the bank on the right cross the side wall leftwards to a hard finish. Very small holds provide a crux start (6c for the short) and tricky (6b) finish, with the ground sweeping increasingly away helping to focus the mind. Might be only E5 for the very tall.
FA. Johnny Dawes (solo) 1984

Stu Littlefair hanging out on *L'Horla*, E1 5b, Curbar. Photo: Simon Richardson. *Opposite*

THE TOY WALL

A series of short problems on impeccable rock. As you might expect most of the routes feel hard for the grade and many are also bold, despite their diminutive size.

❶ Tin Drum **E5 6b**
6m. The fierce thin crack on the left-hand side of the wall is technical and bold.
FA. Dominic Lee 1981

❷ Be Bop Delux **E5 6b**
6m. From the same start as *Tin Drum* step out right and climb the wall with difficulty.
FA. Ron Fawcett 1984

❸ The Toy **E1 5c**
6m. The thin crack splitting the centre of the wall is protectable and gives elegant, fingery climbing which packs far more in than you expect for a climb of its length. The most popular route here (cos this ones got runners!).

❹ Plaything **E2 5c**
6m. The wall and arete right of *Toy* is another bold one.
FA. Gary Gibson 1983

❺ Pretty Face **E1 5b**
6m. The narrow face right of the chimney on small finger-holds.
FA. Paul Mitchell 1975

❻ October Crack .... **HS 4b**
8m. Steep parallel cracks which give pleasant jamming.
FA. Wilf White 1949

❼ Shallow Chimney .... **VDiff**
8m. The eponymous rift just right is the easiest climb for miles and miles.

❽ Grey Face .... **VS 5a**
8m. An oddly-named thin crack. Awkward though safe enough.
FA. Dennis Gray 1964

❾ Thirst for Glory .... **HVS 5b**
6m. An unremarkable wall climb. Head first left then right to finish at a tiny crack.

❿ Pale Complexion .... **VS 4c**
6m. The right arete of the wall on its left-hand side. Start up a crack then follow the arete throughout.

Descent

Descent

This wall is much bigger than that one

THE ELIMINATE'S WALL

The magnificent Eliminates Wall is one of the most intimidating bits of grit around and home to arduous crack climbs from the 50s and desperate face climbs from the 70s, 80s and 90s. Apart from for *The Peapod*, queues are unheard of!

⑪ The Left Eliminate .... | **E1 5c**
12m. The left-hand crack is short and 'ard. The same grade as *Toy* but this one sees a lot less attention. Gaining the narrower upper section is especially difficult.
FA. Joe Brown 1951

⑫ The Zone .. | **E9 6c**
18m. The smooth wall is climbed right then left by desperately fingery climbing which may (or may not) be protected by two skyhooks and absolutely nothing else.
FA. John Arran 1998

⑬ The Peapod .... | **HVS 5b**
18m. Mega-classic. A short slippery crack leads to the base of the pod. Back and foot up this to a difficult exit. Arguments abound about the best way to face; I always prefer leftwards. The awkward upper crack leads to an easy chimney finish.
Photo page 41.
FA. Joe Brown 1951

⑭ Peas of Mind ...... | **E6 6a**
18m. The blunt right arete of *The Peapod* is sustained, unprotected and, except for by the obvious method, inescapable!
FA. Dave Pegg 1994

⑮ The Shape of Things to Come ...... | **E6 6b**
18m. A well-named and impressive face climb between the two biggest cracks. Passing a runner early on, climb the face on finger holds to the base of a tiny shallow groove. Gibber up this to reach easy ground.
FA. Phil Burke 1980

⑯ The Right Eliminate ... | **E3 5b**
18m. Do this and *Great Slab* (in a pair of Wooly's pumps!) on the same day to get a measure of the man. An exhausting and precarious struggle on which upward progress is always too tenuous. The rotating chockstones both help and hinder.
FA. Joe Brown 1951

⑰ Linden ...... | **E6 6b**
18m. Brilliant face climbing, despite the drilled holds. Make a very hard move to leave the block and gain the dodgy flakes (gear includes a spike, supposedly-lassoable from below, which might protect the moves). Then sustained 6a crimpy wall climbing gains better holds and the top before a flash pump occurs. Finish up and right (5a) or escape off left.
FFA. Mick Fowler 1976. Climbed by Ed Drummond in 1973 with two skyhooks for aid. The tiny holes he drilled are still there.

⑱ Happy Heart ..... | **E7 7a**
18m. Climb the incipient crack left of the shallow groove (low side runners) and then the mighty bold wall above.
FA. John Hart 1987

⑲ Hurricane .... | **E4 6a**
24m. A gripper but less so than when it was graded E2. Climb *Scroach* to below its jamming crack then teeter left to gain a shallow ramp. Follow this into wilder and wilder territory until an 'escape' can be made up *Linden*.
FA. Mick Fowler 1977

⑳ Scroach .... | **E2 5c**
22m. From the tip of the tombstone, step left (small wires, tricky to place) and climb the shallow groove and jamming crack to a ledge. Traverse out left and climb the wall to finish.
FA. Ed Drummond 1975

㉑ Hercules .... | **E1 5a**
12m. The wide crack is a good warm-up for the *Eliminates* and might just make you change your 'sports-plan' for the day.
FA. Chuck Cooke 1949

㉒ Alpha .... | **HVD**
10m. The groove just right with tombstone is quite enjoyable and a bit of a contrast to most things hereabouts.
FA. Alpha 1949

Wharncliffe · Dovestone Tor · Rivelin · Bamford · Stanage · Burbage North · Higgar Tor · Burbage South · Millstone · Lawrencefield · Yarncliffe · Froggatt · Curbar · Gardoms · Birchen · Chatsworth · Cratcliffe

GARDOMS

Wharncliffe
Dovestone Tor
Rivelin
Bamford
Stanage
Burbage North
Higgar Tor
Burbage South
Millstone
Lawrencefield
Yarncliffe
Froggatt
Curbar
Gardoms
Birchen
Chatsworth
Cratcliffe

Gardoms tends to be one of those crags which people visit to do a particular route rather than spend a whole day and more often than not it is *Moyer's Buttress* that is top of the hit list. This is indeed a great classic, however there are plenty more worthwhile offerings spread about amongst the buttresses and those who are prepared to pick and choose their base of operations will be rewarded with some delightful and secluded routes. By a quirk of nature the crag excels at the grade E3 5c with *Sleeping Sickness*, *Stormbringer*, *Crocodile* and *Waterloo Sunset* all being great examples of the grade. The climbing they offer tends to be both delicate and strenuous, often with barely adequate and thought-provoking protection.

With the exception of the climbs around Apple Buttress area it is rare to have company on the edge, though in many ways this adds to the appeal since it makes a nice change from the circus atmosphere at the popular end of Stanage and on Froggatt.

 BOULDERING - The crag itself offers little for the boulderer but the boulders passed on the approach walk (known as Gardoms North) are excellent and popular. This is the home to the fine arete of *Soft on the G* (V8) and its various harder derivatives. The south end of the edge has another small set of problems. Although not of the quality of the northern problems the scooped groove of *G-Thang* (V4) is a hidden gem.

APPROACH (SK272736)

The crag is situated above the main A621 Sheffield to Baslow road. It is possible to park on the roadside by the minor cross roads above the crag. Although there are limited spaces, parking here is seldom a problem. Walk down the road, cross a stile and take the right-hand branch of the path towards some boulders (see below). Cross some fences and enter the trees. When you exit the trees the first buttresses are below you on the right.

CONDITIONS

The heavily-wooded base of the crag can make it an unpleasant venue at the colder and damper times of the year when the rock stays green. However the tree-cover does have the advantage of offering shelter from the wind and the general aspect is slightly more north-facing than the other edges offering some respite in very hot weather, albeit only in the morning.

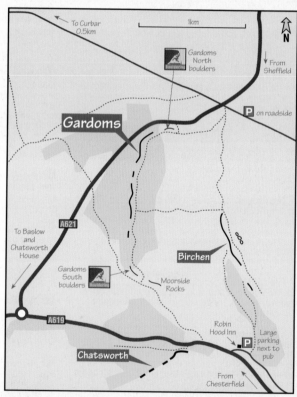

OTHER GUIDEBOOKS - A more complete list of routes at Gardoms is published in the 1996 BMC *Chatsworth* guide. The bouldering is in the 1998 Peak Bouldering ROCKFAX.

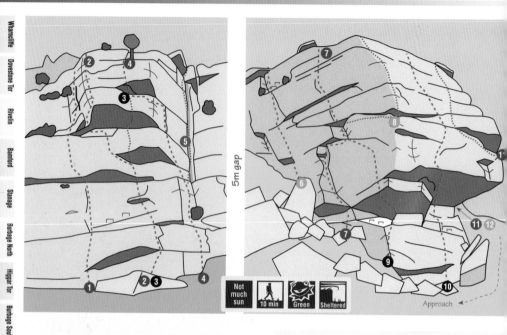

Vertical left margin tabs:
Wharncliffe · Dovestone Tor · Rivelin · Bamford · Stanage · Burbage North · Higgar Tor · Burbage South · Millstone · Lawrencefield · Yarncliffe · Froggatt · Curbar · Gardoms · Birchen · Chatsworth · Cratcliffe

5m gap

Not much sun · 10 min · Green · Sheltered

Approach ←

OVERHANG BUTTRESS AREA

The first section of Gardoms is not the most welcoming bit of rock in the Peak - a dark and dank wall and a large undercut buttress both of which face north-west and are often green and neglected. However there are a few things of interest and the wall will always be a good option in hot weather, providing the midges aren't out. For hard routes *Mickey Finn* and *Spanish Fly* are modern classics. Of the rest, *Sleeping Sickness*, *Four Horsemen* and *Vaya Con Dios* are the pick, the latter appealing to the more perverted gritstone enthusiasts.

APPROACH - (See map on next page). Follow the cliff-top path from the boulders above the road through a small tree-covered section. As you exit the trees head right towards the cliff top and descend an easy blocky slope.

❶ Tsetse Fly E1 5c
14m. Start below the hanging corner that bounds the left edge of the overhang. From a flake gain a ledge where reachy moves give access the corner. Oddly, finish out right up a thin crack.
FA. Mike Browell 1978

❷ Raging Insomnia E3 6a
15m. Climb to the roof using a flake crack. Undercut moves lead left to better holds and a difficult move to gain the hanging arete. Finish more easily.
FA. Keith Sharples 1984

❸ Mickey Finn E6 6b
14m. Start as for the previous route but instead of slinking off tackle the stacked bulges direct. Superb.
FA. Paul Mitchell 1990

❹ Sleeping Sickness E3 5c
14m. Gain the thin crack in the left wall of *Brown Crack* then traverse left below the roof to the front face and a reachy finish.
FA. John Allen 1975

❺ Brown Corner . . . . VDiff
12m. The groove that bounds the right-hand side of the over-hangs was the first route on the edge and remains a struggle.
FA. J.W.Puttrell 1890

Across the gully is a large undercut buttress.

❻ Thunder . . . . VS 4c
8m. The left-hand line on the north wall. Climb leftwards via a couple of cracks and a corner.
FA. Ernie Marshall 1956

❼ Four Horsemen . . . E2 5b
12m. Climb into the niche in the centre of the wall then continue direct to an awkward exit.
FA. Gary Gibson 1981

❽ Lightning Wall . . . . HVS 5a
16m. From *Four Horsemen's* niche follow the descending break until past the arete and then finish delicately up the front.
FA. Don Chapman 1951

❾ The Igloo E5 6b
14m. Pull over the overhang just right of the arete and climb the wall leftwards to finish as for *Four Horsemen*.
FA. John Allen 1986

❿ Spanish Fly E6 6c
14m. The large roofs are tackled centrally (poor wires in the flakes in the roof) to gain the front face and a finish leftwards up the wall. A stiff little problem of considerable quality.
FA. John Allen 1985

Not much sun

10 min Green Sheltered

Change in viewing angle

21
20
18
19 20

Afternoon

Approach

20m to the left

Wharncliffe
Dovestone Tor
Rivelin
Bamford
Stanage
Burbage North
Higgar Tor
Burbage South
Millstone
Lawrencefield
Yarncliffe
Froggatt
Curbar
Gardoms
Birchen
Chatsworth
Cratcliffe

---

⑪ Vaya Con Dios . . . . . [icons] **E2 5c**
20m. Climb the chockstoned crack in the south face to a horizontal break then squirm along this to pass the arete with great delicacy (prayers help more then curses). Stand up awkwardly and then finish more easily.
FA. Allan Austin 1956

⑫ Overhang Buttress Ordinary [icon] **VS 4b**
12m. For those who find passing the arete on the previous route too much, it is possible to writhe into the vertical crack and finish easily. Best book a visit to the chiropractor before tackling this one!
FA. Eric Byne 1934

Immediately on the left as you descend from the cliff-top path is a small tower with two routes.

⑬ Traction . . . . **HS 4b**
10m. The centre of the buttress starting up a crack.
FA. Ernie Marshall 1956

⑭ Gardoms Gate . . . . **VDiff**
10m. The groove in the right arete is climbed to a ledge, where a traverse left leads around to a finish on the north wall.
FA. Keith Axon 1949

⑮ Moyer's Climb . . . . [icon] **S 4a**
14m. From the left edge of the front face climb diagonally right to a finish on the right arete.
FA. Clifford Moyer 1931

⑯ Moyer's Variation . . . . [icon] **S 4a**
12m. The centre of the face climb eases gradually after a rather awkward start.

NOWANDA BUTTRESS
A small buttress with a green north-facing slab and a side wall with two fine cracks which catch the sun.
APPROACH - (See map on next page.) As for Overhang Buttress but continue left along the base of the crag. It can also easily be approached from Garden Face.

⑰ Social Fools **E1 5b**
10m. The right arete of the buttress is started on the right, then swing left and balance up the front face.
FA. Gary Gibson 1981

⑱ Cobweb Arete/Little Wanda **E2 5c**
10m. The arete can be climbed on either side by pleasant but rather artificial moves.
FA. Tim Bevis 1994/Brian Rossiter 1999

⑲ Nowanda . . . . [icon] **HVS 5a**
12m. The first crack in the south-facing wall is worth seeking out by those in search of jamming practice, well protected.
Photo page 245.
FA. Ernie Marshall 1953

⑳ Landsick . . . . [icon] **HVS 5a**
10m. Take the right-hand crack to its end, then swing right and finish with a pull-up to reach a flat hold and heathery ground.
FA. Peter Biven 1953

㉑ Landsick Direct . . . . . [icons] **E3 6a**
8m. Climb direct from the crack by a fierce couple of moves on sloping holds.
FA. Ian Riddington 1981

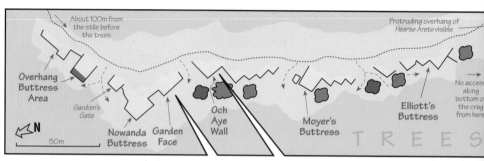

Descent

20m gap

GARDEN FACE and OCH AYE WALL
A buttress which is split by several cracks and round to the right a smooth slab that was quarried long ago.

1 Cave Gully Crack .... S 4a
10m. The steep crack on the far left to ledges and easy ground.

2 Chockstone Crack .... HS 4a
12m. The block-filled rift leads to an exhausting narrow exit.

3 Garden Face Crack ...... HS 4b
14m. The continuous crack just left of the arete is tricky to enter (jig to the left) and is good above.
FA. Clifford Moyer 1931

4 Garden Face Direct .... VS 5a
14m. Start up *Garden Face Crack* then move right onto the wall and climb it direct. Nice positions but sadly a bit artificial.

5 Garden Face Indirect ..... Diff
14m. Just right of the arete climb a short corner and the continuation blocky crack above, it gives steep climbing for the grade.
FA. J.W.Puttrell 1890

Up to the right is a steep, tree-shrouded slab with three worthwhile routes all of which are tricky for the vertically challenged.

6 Och Aye Wall Indirect .... VS 5a
18m. Just right of the arete climb the wall on tiny polished holds to a ledge at 10m. Move to the centre of the wall to finish.

7 Och Aye Wall Direct VS 5b
16m. The centre of the wall has a hard start, which is especially so for the short.
FA. Jack Macleod 1934

8 Tartan Route .... VS 5a
12m. Just out from the corner is another worthwhile line. Once again it has a disproportionately hard start.
FA. Ernie Marshall 1956

Wharncliffe
Dovestone Tor
Rivelin
Bamford
Stanage
Burbage North
Higgar Tor
Burbage South
Millstone
Lawrencefield
Yarncliffe
Froggatt
Curbar
Gardoms
Birchen
Chatsworth
Cratcliffe

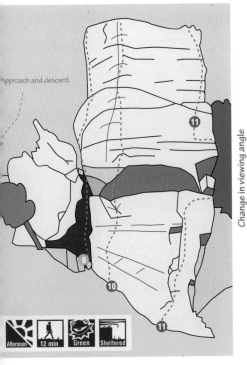

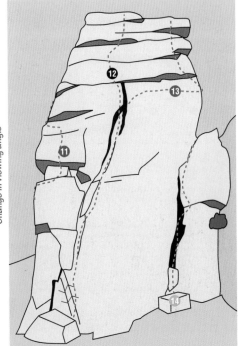

Change in viewing angle

Wharncliffe
Dovestone Tor
Rivelin
Bamford
Stanage
Burbage North
Higgar Tor
Burbage South
Millstone
Lawrencefield
Yarncliffe
Froggatt
Curbar
Gardoms
Birchen
Chatsworth
Cratcliffe

MOYER'S BUTTRESS

The finest buttress at this end of the crag is also home to one of the Peak's best known routes - *Moyer's Buttress*. This brilliant route takes an unlikely line up the tallest arete and gives climbing that is both delicate and strenuous. If you are up to it take a look at *Stormbringer* and *Perfect Day* both of which take equally impressive lines to their easier companion. The wall is well-sheltered but slow to dry when wet and can be green in the spring.

APPROACH - Direct approach can be made from the cliff-top path. The buttress is marked by a pair of large blocks on its rocky crest a few metres below the level of the path.

⑨ Cave Arete . . . . 🔲🔲 **HVS 5a**
8m. Fight up the crack between the giant boulder and the main ace to a good ledge. Then balance up the rib above in a fine osition; a big contrast to the first section.
A. Wilf White 1950

⑩ Stormbringer . . . . 🔲🔲🔲 **E3 5c**
0m. One of a bunch of classic E3 5c routes at Gardom's. Climb the slabby arete to the right of the cave and lean out to each a good jug. A gut-wrenching mantelshelf on this gains the pper wall just right of the rib, which proves to be much more elicate but fortunately has adequate gear.
FA. Dave Morgan 1976. FAA. Pete Biven 1956. Biven reached the mantelshelf using tension, though the moves were done free. The route hen zig-zagged up the final buttress all the way out to Moyer's and back!

⑪ Moyer's Buttress 🔲🔲🔲🔲 **E1 5b**
22m. A major classic, originally led with a single chockstone runner. Climb the cracked slab to the overhang then swing around the arete. Wrestle with the rocking-block before making difficult moves to get back on the front face. The upper slab is very delicate though protection is adequate nowadays.
FA. Peter Biven 1955

⑫ Perfect Day . . . . . 🔲🔲🔲🔲 **E5 6b**
22m. A fine route with a crux which feels more committing than it should do. Climb the wide crack in the steep face to its end. Then the wall above, first left then right (good wires) to a final grasping exit. Reaching the key hold is one thing, using it is another. The direct start is a V7 boulder problem.
FA. Steve Bancroft 1979

⑬ Biven's Crack and the Enigma Variation . . . . 🔲🔲🔲🔲 **E3 5c**
24m. The once-aided jamming crack (on big wooden wedges) is climbed to its end and a swinging escape out right. So far it is *Biven's Crack* - HVS 5b. For the full route move back left onto the wall and climb this to a rounded exit.
*FFA. (Biven's Crack) Jack Street 1966. FAA. Pete Biven 1955
FA. (Enigma Variation) Keith Sharples 1983*

⑭ Keith's Corner Crack . . . . 🔲 **HS 4b**
18m. The short groove which bounds the face to the right is followed to a ledge, finish up easy rock on the left.
FA. Keith Axon 1949

Wharncliffe
Dovestone Tor
Rivelin
Bamford
Stanage
Burbage North
Higgar Tor
Burbage South
Millstone
Lawrencefield
Yarncliffe
Froggatt
Curbar
Gardoms
Birchen
Chatsworth
Cratcliffe

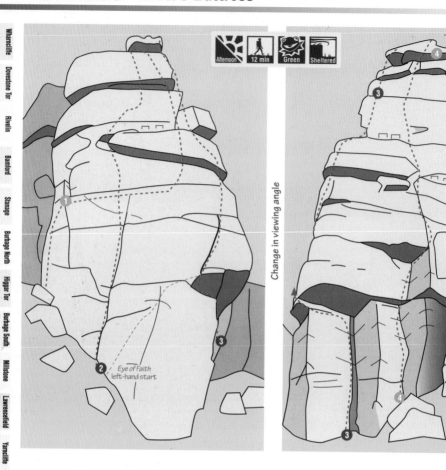

Change in viewing angle

Eye of Faith
left-hand start

ELLIOTT'S BUTTRESS

These days this buttress is more notable for the classic E1, *Eye of Faith* than its historic namesake. This superb climb makes a great 'other route for the day' if you have come to do *Moyer's Buttress*. The trees are getting ever-closer which has resulted in the lower section of the buttress being green when the weather is damp, although usually the main routes stay clean.

APPROACH - See map on previous page. Walk over the top of *Moyer's Buttress* and drop down a gully. Then navigate your way through the undergrowth.
If you wish to continue to any of the routes further right then return to the crag top first.

1 Elliott's Buttress Indirect .. **VS 4b**
16m. Jam along the horizontal break from the gully, out onto the front of the buttress, then climb the steep wall above keeping to the left of the arete.

2 Seventy One White Mice **E2 6a**
16m. Climb the thin crack in the left wall of the buttress to where a perplexing couple of pulls reach a deep break. Continue much more easily up the wall.
FA. Gabe Regan 1981

3 The Eye of Faith **E1 5c**
20m. A fine route which is now more usually climbed by its hard direct start than the cop-out left-hand version from the gully. Climb the groove to the roof then traverse left to the finger crack in the nose. Stuff in the wires while your arms pump out then pull up to reach the crest of the buttress above. Finish up this trending slightly right and in a great position.
FA. Peter Biven 1956

4 Elliott's Buttress Direct . . . **HS 4a**
22m. Climb the groove that bounds the right-hand side of the buttress and the crack on the right to a ledge. Move up and left to the crest of a huge flake and step onto a polished 'lump' before climbing the wall rightwards to the final crack.
FA. Frank Elliott 1934

The way we were, Andy Nicholson, mid 1980s, on *Crocodile*, E3 5c, Gardoms. *Page 253*

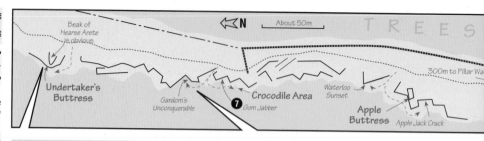

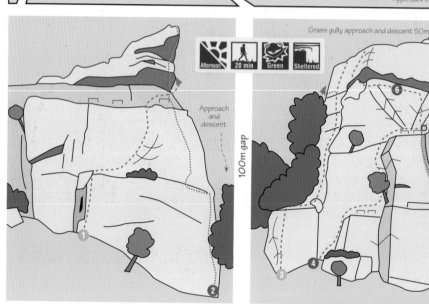

UNDERTAKER'S BUTTRESS

This small, isolated buttress is most notable for the impressive beak of rock hanging over it. Its location hidden in the trees means that it is well sheltered though it can be a bit green and dirty if the weather has been damp.

APPROACH - From the cliff-top above *Moyer's Buttress*, pick out the beak of *Hearse Arete* which interrupts your view towards Chatsworth. The descent is just beyond the arete and involves doubling back under the face.

① Undertaker's Buttress .... 🖼️🔲 **VS 4c**

22m. Start on the left at a short wide crack and climb this to a chockstone then move right and climb the wall (a tad bold) to a possible stance (4c). Climb to the roof then traverse round the arete to the right to a short finishing crack (4b).

FA. Joe Brown 1951

② Hearse Arete .... 🖼️🔲 **E1 5b**

20m. This spectacular-looking route promises more than it delivers. Begin directly below the beak and climb on to a ledge on the left with difficulty. Climb up and right then cross the overhang on good holds. Thrilling but slightly artificial.

FA. Peter Biven (1 peg) 1956

GARDOM'S UNCONQUERABLE

An isolated ancient quarried section which is almost impossible to view from anywhere.

APPROACH - From above *Hearse Arete* continue along the cliff-top path until 30m before the stone wall crossing the path. Double back right down a narrow grassy gully and head rightwards through the trees to the quarried bay.

③ Bilberry Buttress .... 🖼️🔲 **VS 5a**

16m. Climb the rib left of the main bay to a ledge, then follow the exposed arete to the top. The short may need to step left just below the final move into a convenient chimney.

④ Stepped Crack .... 🖼️🔲 **Diff**

16m. The rising ramp-line gives a pleasant low-grade climb to ledges above the *Unconquerable*. Exit right at the top.

⑤ Gardoms Unconquerable .. 🖼️🔲 **VS 4c**

14m. The imposing corner crack can be laybacked, although hidden holds ease the tension. At the top exit right up the wall.

FA. Joe Brown 1950

⑥ Whillans' Blind Variant ... 🖼️🔲 **E1 5b**

10m. From the ledge (belay) above *Gardom's Unconquerable* swing left below the overhangs to pass the arete (loud cries of "Geronimo" are in order) then finish rightwards up the wall.

FA. Don Whillans 1951

Wharncliffe · Dovestone Tor · Rivelin · Bamford · Stanage · Burbage North · Higgar Tor · Burbage South · Millstone · Lawrencefield · Yarncliffe · Froggatt · Curbar · Gardoms · Birchen · Chatsworth · Cratcliffe

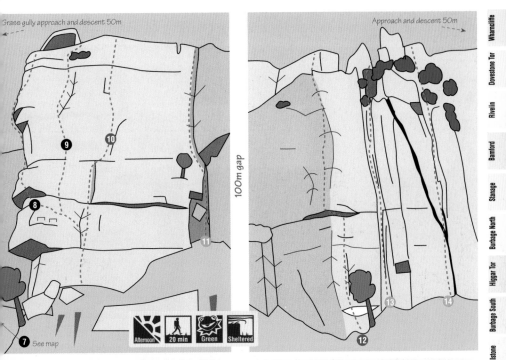

Grass gully approach and descent 50m

Approach and descent 50m

100m gap

⑦ See map

Afternoon · 20 min · Green · Sheltered

CROCODILE AREA

This superb open wall has plenty to offer those after high grade wall climbs though all those here are bold.
APPROACH - At the base of the gully used on the approach to *Gardom's Unconquerable*, turn left and follow the vague path under the crag until you can scramble up to this wall.

The first route is on a wall about 30m left of the steep bulging arete of Make it Snappy.

Gom Jabbar . . . 🔲🔲🔲🔲 **E8 6c**
...m. The hanging arete to the right of a mini *Inverted-V* groove reached from a ledge at 8m. Unprotected, fingery and hard. A de-runner stops a ground fall but not hitting the ledges.
A. Simon Jones 1994

Make it Snappy . . . 🔲🔲🔲🔲 **E6 6b**
...4m. From the centre of the wall move up and left around the arete to a black pocket. Hard moves up and right reach better holds and an airy finish back on the right side of the arete.
A. Neil Foster 1984

Ecky Thump . . . 🔲🔲🔲🔲 **E7 6c**
...2m. The wall just to the right of the arete is bold, fingery and fiercely technical. Oh, and its also light on gear.
A. Andy Popp 1995

Crocodile . . . 🔲🔲 **E3 5c**
...2m. A bold route which is another of Gardom's fine E3 5c cracks. The centre of the wall is pushy in its upper part, the runners and holds are there, though both take some finding.
Photo page 251.
A. Gabe Regan 1975

⑪ Right-hand Crack . . . . . . 🔲🔲 **VS 4c**
10m. The open groove on the right-hand edge of the wall with a useful bonsai tree has its crux right at the top.
FA. Eric Byne 1940

WATERLOO SUNSET

Another isolated buttress with a classic E3 5c.
APPROACH - Continue along the cliff-top path for about 70m beyond the stone wall. When you are almost on top of the tower of *Apple Buttress* ahead, descend back rightwards directly below a cracked wall behind the trees.

⑫ Waterloo Sunset . . . . . 🔲🔲 **E3 5c**
16m. The final, and perhaps the hardest of the Gardom's E3s, is a bold arete climb. Start on the right and climb to a break where runners protect the crucial moves up and left to easier ground. In the event of a flier, head to the right where there is a touch more air-space.
FA. Martin Boysen 1977

⑬ Finale Groove . . . . 🔲 **VS 5a**
16m. The first crack in the fractured face is obviously misnamed. The crux is just above the obvious jamming crack and requires some strenuous pinch-gripping.
FA. David Penlington 1951

⑭ Tree Groove . . . . 🔲 **VS 4b**
12m. Climb the pleasant groove to the right of the centre of the face until level with the eponymous woodwork then move right into a narrow rift to finish. More direct variations are possible.
FA. Clifford Moyer 1934

Wharncliffe · Dovestone Tor · Rivelin · Bamford · Stanage · Burbage North · Higgar Tor · Burbage South · Millstone · Lawrencefield · Yarncliffe · Froggatt · Curbar · Gardoms · Birchen · Chatsworth · Cratcliffe

Wharncliffe · Dovestone Tor · Rivelin · Bamford · Stanage · Burbage North · Higgar Tor · Burbage South · Millstone · Lawrencefield · Yarncliffe · Froggatt · Curbar · Gardoms · Birchen · Chatsworth · Cratcliffe

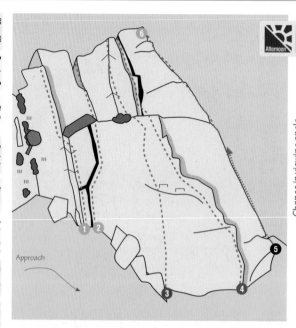

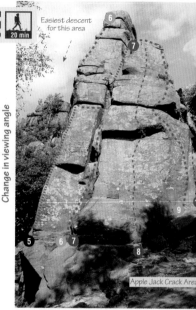

Easiest descent for this area

Change in viewing angle

Apple Jack Crack Area

APPLE BUTTRESS

The best bit of rock at this end of the cliff is the fine jutting rib of Apple Buttress. It is a popular venue mainly because of the pulling-power of the fine *NMC Crack* and the delightful *Apple Arete*. At this point the cliff is just far enough above the approaching foliage to be a good bet for much of the year and the outward views are always great.
APPROACH - Follow the crag-top path for about 150m past the low wall. The tower of Apple Buttress should be visible. Descend a gully before this and work back southwards.

❶ Layback Crack . . . . **VS 4c**
10m. The steep straight-sided crack near the top of the gully is best climbed by .... well you guess!
FA. Wilf White 1950

❷ Flake Crack . . . . **HS 4b**
12m. The central line is tricky at the nose and is climbed on a generous set of holds.
FA. Rupert Brooks 1934

❸ Twilight's Last Gleaming **E2 5b**
14m. Climb the slab to the left of *NMC Crack* to a good ledge and then the rib on the left to the top. A bit of an eliminate but with some good moves.
FA. J.Zonn 1989

❹ N.M.C. Crack . . . . **HVD**
14m. The fine stepped-groove in the north face of the buttress leads to a short crack and mini-summit. Polished and popular but still a very good tick.
FA. Frank Elliott 1930

❺ Apple Arete Direct **E4 5c**
18m. The arete in its entirety is a quality route but very bold requiring difficult laybacking and use of some sloping holds. Worth E2 with side runners.
FA. Gary Gibson 1980

❻ Apple Arete . . . . **VS 4b**
18m. The tall left-hand arete of the buttress is mild at the grade and is a real corker. Climb the central crack to the first break then make a short traverse left to the arete.This is then followed throughout in a photogenic position.
FA. David Penlington 1952

❼ Apple Crack . . . . **VDiff**
16m. The wide crack that splits the front of the buttress leads to a ledge just below the summit. Passing the protruding flake early on is tricky.

❽ Cheeky Monkey **E2 6b**
14m. Climb the overlap and slab up its centre using the obvious pinch on the lip.
FA. Ellison Allcock 1997

❾ Cider Apple . . . . **HS 4a**
16m. Starting around on the right-hand side of the buttress move left to pass the arete then climb the right edge of the slab to a large ledge. The short arete on the final block gives an exposed extension if required.
FA. P. Knapp 1950

❿ Giant's Staircase . . . . **S 4a**
14m. The steep stepped-crack in the side-wall leads to a short slippery layback and then a final steep jamming crack leads to the summit.
FA. Clifford Moyer 1931

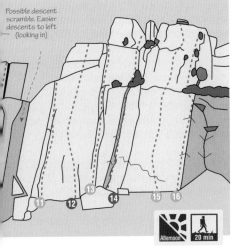

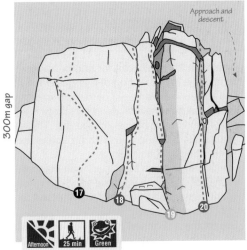

APPLE JACK CRACK

To the right of Apple Buttress is a short slab quarried long ago. This has a pleasant collection of cracks and a couple of harder climbs up the blank slabs between the cracks.

① Bitter . . . . **VS 5a**

n. The thin crack with a useful spike (nut either side or a tape ver it) is technical and slippery but nice and safe. Don't turn tter if you fail.

. Eric Finney 1960s

② Master of Thought . . **E2 5c**

n. Climb the steep slab which is especially sketchy for the ort. Unprotected unless you use side runners, thus dropping e grade a notch. Recent loss of a hold may have made this a uch harder.

. Gary Gibson 1979

③ Velvet Cracks . . . . **VS 4b**

m. The thin crack in the right-hand side of the slab is pleasant, though the closeness of the cracks of the next route is some-ing of a distraction.

. Ernie Marshall 1963

④ Apple Jack Cracks . . . . . . **VDiff**

m. Parallel jamming-cracks splitting the centre of the slab are est gained direct. Short, sweet and well-protected.

⑤ Cydrax . . . . **HVS 5b**

m. A fingery slab leads to a short finishing crack.

. Eric Finney 1957

⑥ Cider . . . . **VS 5a**

m. The delicate right-hand arete of the wall and steeper rock rectly above.

. David Penlington 1950

PILLAR WALL

The main edge gets swamped by trees after Apple Buttress and offers little quality climbing. However about 300m further on is a fine wall which is worth seeking out. It is well-hidden and can be awkward to find. Also the tree cover leaves it green for the early part of the year although this does clean up in the summer.

APPROACH - From the top of *Apple Buttress*, continue along the cliff-top path through some trees. About 80m after the trees finish, and about 100m before a stone wall crosses the path, head right to the cliff top. Skirt south of the most substantial bit of rock and drop down below the wall.

⑰ Charlotte Rampling . **E6 6b**

10m. A fine clean wall with an attractive ramp but the climbing is sustained and bold. Poor gear can be arranged in the break but the lower section is unprotected and the landing is terrible, even with a bouldering mat. Start left of the ramp and make hard moves to get your hands on it. Trend up left to the break then move right and make another hard move to gain the top.

FA. Johnny Dawes 1984

⑱ Left-hand Pillar Crack . . **E1 5b**

10m. An excellent crack climb which is well worth the walk in. Once established on the upper flake a desperate search for footholds proves to be the crux.

FA. Allan Austin 1956

⑲ Right-hand Pillar Crack . . . **HVS 5a**

10m. Harder than it looks and not as good as its neighbour, but while you are in the area you might as well indulge!

FA. Frank Elliott 1930

⑳ Elliott's Crack . . . . **S 4a**

10m. The steep and juggy right-hand crack to an exit on the right is also worth ticking while you are here.

FA. Frank Elliott 1930s

BIRCHEN

Birchen Edge (not as it is so often called Birchens Edge) is one of the more popular edges in the Peak mainly due to the plethora of excellent low-grade routes found here. Because of this it has always been popular with groups of one kind or another and this popularity has led to the polishing of many of the holds. This is at least partly the reason the place has always had a reputation for under-graded routes. Hopefully the wide consultation we have undergone in the writing of this guide will have removed most of these anomalies.

The rock is millstone grit of the expected quality; rough, rounded and well-cracked. Many of the routes are characterised by steep, undercut starts and it is often the case that leaving the ground is the biggest challenge. This explains why there are some routes with odd grades like VDiff 4c and HVS 6a; make the start move and you will most likely find a pleasant slabby wall above.

The popularity with beginners can mean that routes get taken over with top-ropes and that many popular ones become sandy from dirty boots. If you find the main section of the cliff rather busy, a short walk to the right will locate some secluded buttresses and, in all probability, a bit of solitude.

The routes at Birchen tend to have names of a nautical nature linked to the monument on the cliff top that was erected to celebrate Nelson's famous victory at the Battle of Trafalgar.

APPROACH (SK280728)

Birchen Edge runs along the crest of the moor 3km to the east of Baslow village. The usual approach is from the extensive National Trust car park next to to the Robin Hood pub (could be handy later on). From the car park walk up the road to a stile on the left. This gives access to a sandy track that leads to the rocks in 10 to 15 mins. Keeping left at the only fork leads straight to the most popular section of cliff. Heading right at this fork will lead you under Kismet Buttress and to the right-hand end of the main section of the crag. It is also possible to approach the crag from the Gardoms' parking spot (see page 244)

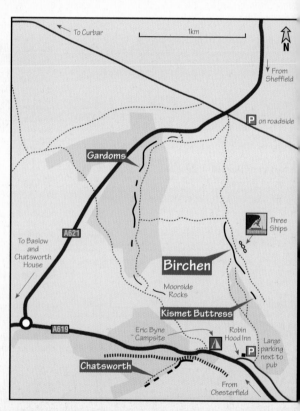

CONDITIONS

The edge is quick-drying, being exposed to the afternoon sun but with the usual potential to be windy and cold in bad weather. It takes virtually no drainage and is probably the fast drying of all the Eastern Edges.

OTHER GUIDEBOOKS - A more complete list of routes at Birchen is published in the 1996 BMC *Chatsworth* guide.

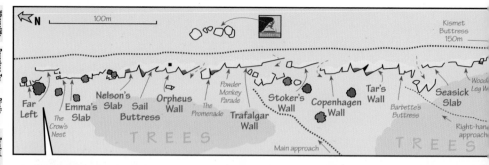

FAR LEFT

The left-hand extremity of the cliff is less popular than the rest of Birchen Edge and as such is a good place for a bit of solitude. *The Gangplank* is a good beginners route - on the blunt end! The wall to the right has a selection of routes that could do with being twice as long.

1 The Gangplank . . . . 🔲 **Mod**
10m. The isolated slab on the far left is followed direct by pleasant balance climbing on footholds that have seen generations of wear, first by 'nails' and more recently by 'rubbers'.

2 Handy Crack . . . . **VDiff**
6m. A chockstoned crack in the left-hand side of the next wall gives a handy introduction to jamming.

3 Visitors Only . . . . 🔲 **HS 4a**
8m. The shallow left-facing groove has a few pleasant moves.

4 All Aboard . . . . 🔲 **Mod**
8m. The central groove in the wall, with a deep crack in its back, is mild.

5 Saltheart Foamfollower . . . 🔲 **HVS 5**
8m. A thin crack in the smooth wall on the right leads to a dee break and tricky finish. Great name for a so-so route.
FA. Bob Higginbotham 1980s

6 Poop Deck Crack . . . . 🔲 **VDiff**
12m. The crack that splits the flat wall to the right leads into a short v-groove.
FA. Reg Schofield early 1930s

THE CROW'S NEST and EMMA'S SLAB

7 The Crow's Nest . . . . . . 🔲 **VS 4c**
14m. Climb the crack on on the right of the block then onto the face on the right. Cross to the base of the slab and balance up this to a delicate final move which is tricky for the short.
FA. Frank Elliott late 1920s

8 Land Ho! . . . . 🔲 **S 4c**
12m. A more direct, but less satisfying version of *The Crow's Nest*. From the ledge at the top of the initial crack climb the left hand arete of the side wall. This bit is only 4b but you have to do the 4c start to get there.

THE CROW'S NEST and EMMA'S SLAB

The first section of the main part of the cliff is home to several worthwhile climbs and is always popular. Many of the routes have become well-polished over the years though despite this the quality of the climbs continues to shine through.

⑨ Scrim Net . . . . 🏃🏻🪨 ⬜ **E1 6a**
2m. The thin crack has a tough move to reach a large hole, runners and easier climbing.
A. Richard Brown (2 pts) 1951. FFA. Len Millsom 1963

⑩ Look-out Arete . . . . 🔧 ⬜ **S 4a**
2m. Climb the chimney of *The Funnel* until it is possible to swing onto the left arete, which is followed in a fine position.
A. Eric Byne 1956

⑪ The Funnel . . . . 🔧 ⬜ **Diff**
2m. The deep chimney is entered awkwardly and is then climbed in 'traditional' fashion. Seasoned gritstoners should smoke up this one.

⑫ Kiss Me Hardy . . . . 🔧 ⬜ **VDiff**
2m. Skip up the right-hand wall of *The Funnel* using a well-glossed hold, then make progress up the awkward crack above using anything that works.
A. Eric Byne early 1930s

3m to the right is a chimney with a huge block of a chockstone.

⑬ Victory Crack . . . . ⬜ **S 4a**
14m. Climb onto the chock then move left to climb the narrow crack that splits the buttress to the left of the gully.
A. Eric Byne, early 1930s

⑭ Victory Gully . . . . ⬜ **S 4a**
12m. Climb onto the chock then continue up the gully (more of a groove really) to a tricky final couple of moves.
FA. Eric Byne, early 1930s

⑮ Emma's Slab . . . . ⬜ **VS 4b**
14m. Climb onto the chock then stride out right and climb to and on through the capping roof.
FA. Ernie Marshall 1952

⑯ Technical Genius . . 🔧📷✋ ⬜ **E1 6c**
4m. The boulder problem start over the low roof just had to be done.
FA Mark Katz 1997

⑰ Emma's Dilemma . . . . 🔧🏃🏻 ⬜ **S 4a**
14m. Worthwhile. Starting just right of a low overhang climb the crack and groove to a steep and well-protected finish up a thin crack.
FA. Eric Byne early 1930s

⑱ Emma's Temptation . . . 🔧🏃🏻 ⬜ **VD 4c**
14m. Climb the slippery slab rightwards to a ledge. Step back left and take the thin crack to the top.
FA. Jack Macleod early 1930s

⑲ Emma's Delight . . . . 🔧 ⬜ **HS 4b**
14m. Start just left of the right-hand edge of the slab and climb straight up the face to gain the final short crack.
FA. Dave Penlington 1952

⑳ Deluded . . . . ⬜ **VS 4c**
12m. Climb easy rock into a grassy niche then the steep and awkward crack and the short bulging wall above and left.

㉑ Emma's Delusion . . . . . . 🔧 ⬜ **S 4a**
12m. From the grassy niche take the bulging right-hand crack which is steep and awkward.

㉒ The Prow . . . . ⬜ **VS 5a**
12m. Pull over a small overhang to gain a ledge then continue up a short wall to a second overhang which is well supplied with jugs.
FA. Chris Craggs 1993

Wharncliffe · Dovestone Tor · Rivelin · Bamford · Stanage · Burbage North · Higgar Tor · Burbage South · Millstone · Lawrencefield · Yarncliffe · Froggatt · Curbar · Gardoms · Birchen · Chatsworth · Cratcliffe

CROW'S NEST AREA 20m

NELSON'S SLAB

An attractive hanging slab that is difficult to access, and a couple of fine buttresses further left, ensure that this particular bit of Birchen Edge is always popular. The well-polished nature of the rock on the *Captain's* routes will keep you on your toes. The oddity of *Telescope Tunnel* is included for cavers who are up here having a rest day.

① Captain's Prerogative . . . . **HS 4c**
12m. The left edge of the slab has a hard start using a vague crack and polished holds. It eases a little above.

② Captain's Bunk . . . . **HS 4b**
12m. The right-hand side of the slab is climbed via a trio of mantelshelves, the last one to reach the ledge of 'the bunk' being the crux. Finish up the groove behind the bunk.
FA. Chuck Cook 1951

③ Telescope Tunnel . . . . **Mod**
14m. One of the most bizarre outings on grit. Climb the easy chimney then move left to enter the claustrophobic slot. Squirm up this, then into the crag to reach easy ground on the other side of the face.

④ Porthole Buttress . . . . **S 4a**
24m. A bit of an expedition. Climb the chimney to a cave and gain the ledge on the right. Follow this to its end then make tricky moves to access the slab further right again. Cross this to its right-hand edge then finish easily.

⑤ Porthole Direct . . . . **VS 4b**
12m. Start 1m right of the chimney and climb up into a shallow corner, passing 'the porthole', to a good ledge. Finish up the leaning, narrowing crack on the left.
FA. Gilbert Ellis 1951

⑥ Captain Birdseye . . . . **VS 4c**
14m. Climb the crack in the left-hand side of the gully to a cave and bridge past this. Step left and climb the overhang on the front of the buttress to finish.
FA. Chris Craggs 1993

⑦ Blind Eye . . . . **S 4b**
14m. A couple of tricky but well-protected moves. Climb up and left into the recess then swing right (runner up and left) on good holds to reach the hanging slab. Climb directly up the slab to finish.
FA. Gilbert Ellis 1952

⑧ Dead Eye . . . . **HVS 6a**
10m. A lower exit pulls through the roof at the obvious notch in the overhang to reach easy ground rapidly.
FA. John Allen 1986

⑨ Nelson's Slab . . . . **VS 5b**
14m. Start under the right-hand edge of the slab and make hard moves up and left via a polished niche (good overhead gear) to reach the slab. Move 2m left then finish direct.
FA. Frank Burgess, early 1930s

⑩ Half Nelson . . . . **HVS 5b**
12m. Start as for the previous route but after the strenuous start trend delicately up to the right to gain a good ledge. Finish direct.
FA. Chris Craggs 1993

The initial steep groove on *Nelson's Nemesis*, VS 4b, Kismet Buttress, Birchen. *Page 271*

SAIL BUTTRESS

A fine piece of rock with a steep left-hand (north-facing) wall and an attractive valley face which is home to some of the best routes on the edge. A three star day is assured if you tick all of these.

❶ Left Ladder Chimney . . . . [   ] **Diff**
12m. The left-hand block filled crevice.

❷ Right Ladder Chimney . . . . . . [   ] **HVD**
12m. The narrow right-hand slot is steeper and harder.

❸ Midshipman/Plain Sailing [icons] **E2 6a**
12m. From a jug climb leftwards to a thin crack then continue up the centre of the wall until under the capping overhang. A long reach from jams and a rounded exit overcome the final roof. Great climbing which is well-protected throughout.
FA. Len Millsom 1963/Gary Gibson 1982

❹ Cold Compass . . . . . . [icons] **E2 6b**
14m. Start from a large sloping block. Pull powerfully over the roof using a flake and pocket high on the right, then follow the direct line to a hard exit. A pre-placed Friend 2 up and left is sensible unless you want to bounce.
FA. Gary Gibson 1980

❺ Sail Buttress . . . . [icon] **HS 4b**
14m. A slippery classic. Start below the steep arete and climb up and right to a good ledge. Use the deep horizontal crack to aid a traverse out to the left to access the final easier slab.
FA. Bert Smith 1934

❻ Ratline . . . . [icons] **E1 5b**
14m. From the ledge on *Sail Buttress* move awkwardly right then step up and right again to reach a good flake. Climb through the bulge by a bold high step to reach the upper slab.
FA. Len Millsom 1963

❼ Amazing Grace . . . [icons] **E2 5c**
14m. The steep and reachy wall right of *Ratline* with a jig right at two thirds height. Avoid the opposite wall.
FA. Wim Verhoeven 1998

❽ Sail Chimney . . . . [icon] **S 4a**
14m. An ancient classic. Climb the initial polished groove then continue directly up the chimney. Back and foot technique is best though squirming up the back also works.
FA. Eric Byne early 1930s

❾ Topsail . . . . [icons] **VS 4c**
12m. To the right is a face with an overhang split by a flake crack. Approach this via a crack (big thread) and power through the bulge. The slab above is easy and a lot less strenuous!
FA. David Penlington 1951

Nelson's Monument
please do not use as an anchor

Afternoon 12 min

Descent

Wharncliffe
Dovestone Tor
Rivelin
Bamford
Stanage
Burbage North
Higgar Tor
Burbage South
Millstone
Lawrencefield
Yarncliffe
Froggatt
Curbar
Gardoms
Birchen
Chatsworth
Cratcliffe

ORPHEUS WALL
To the right is the leaning section of rock that is home to a couple of arduous outings, topped by the monument that celebrates Nelson's victory at Trafalgar. Climbers are asked not to use it as an anchor.

⑩ Monument Chimney Crack . . 🔲 VDiff
14m. Climb into the chimney/groove from the left via a short polished ramp then climb the steep, juggy crack on the left of the main groove.

⑪ Monument Chimney . . . . . . 🔲 VDiff
14m. Start on the left and climb the slab rightwards as for *Monument Chimney Crack* to enter the pleasant open groove. Bridge up this to the monument.
FA. Henry Bishop, early 1910s

ORPHEUS WALL

⑫ Pillar Wall . . . . 🔲 S 4a
14m. Climb an awkward groove directly below the main corner then the centre of the wall on the right direct.
FA. David Penlington 1951

⑬ The Bow . . . . 🔲 S 4a
14m. The arete is gained from the left and is then followed on its right-hand side. The direct start up the steep lower arete is a nice 5c if you don't mind wearing blinkers.

⑭ Orpheus Wall . . . . . . 🔲 HVS 5c
14m. Climb the thin crack just right of the arete to reach the leaning wall and a horizontal slot. Good Friends here protect the bewildering moves to jugs (hint: ignore the standard advice about knees) and exit rapidly to easy ground. Almost worth E1.
FA. Joe Brown 1950

⑮ Peaches . . . . . 🔲 E4 6b
14m. An excellent and arduous route that is obviously on the wrong cliff. Climb the technical slab until the rock begins to lean. Battle on to the prominent hollow where final desperate moves leftwards gain easy ground.
FA. Gary Gibson 1980

⑯ Monument Gully . . . . 🔲 VDiff
14m. Climb the short slab into the chimney. Continue to a roof and exit leftwards to gain a slab and an easy finish.
FA. Henry Bishop, early 1910s

⑰ Monument Gully Buttress . . 🔲 HVS 5b
8m. The arete has tough moves to get standing on the beak at half height, a huge jug on the ledge is helpful. A long-standing Severe from the days when men were men!
FA. Ken Wright 1951

⑱ The Keel . . . . 🔲 HVS 5b
8m. The wall 2m right of the arete has hard moves to get established in the midway break and then eases dramatically. Another route graded Severe for years.

⑲ Naughty Nauticals . . . . . . 🔲 E3 6b
8m. Reach the flake on the lip of the overhang (small wires) then make a baffling couple of moves to gain the slab.
FA. John Allen 1985

THE PROMENADE

One of the most popular beginner's routes around is up the delightful clean slab of *The Promenade* although it is not a good first lead since protection is poor. Further right is the savage undercut bulge of *Gritstone Megamix*, a route that sees few attempts and even fewer successes.

❶ The Promenade .... **Mod**
16m. A good introduction to grit. Climb the left-hand edge of the slab to its crest then traverse right to reach the continuation beyond the cleft. Finish up this.

❷ Promenade Direct ...... **VDiff**
10m. Follow the balancy centre of the slab, on worn holds, to reach easy rock above.

❸ The Chain .... **S 4b**
12m. Climb the right arete of the slab directly (5b) using very polished holds or alternatively traverse in from below the roof on the right (4b). From ledges, climb the middle of the face just to the right.
FA. David Penlington 1951

❹ Gritstone Megamix . **E3 6c**
10m. The roof to the right is nearly impossible! Small pockets in the roof allow a flake to be reached. Once above the bulge the rest is easy. Side-runners protect.
FA. John Allen 1984

❺ Hollybush Gully ..... **VD 4c**
10m. The gully with a jammed boulder at 3m is a frantic fight. The grade of 4c is a guess, how do you grade such a struggle? The upper part is easy romping.

❻ Anchor Traverse .... **S 4c**
12m. From the chock traverse left to the arete. Step around this and ascend the pleasant front face. The section shared with *Hollybush Gully* is 4c, the rest is only 4a.
FA. David Penlington 1952

POWDER MONKEY PARADE

The classic of *Powder Monkey Parade* is worth seeking out though the polished start up *Hollybush Gully* is a thrash. It is a classic route with several harder and more direct variations in the form of a trio of uncharacteristic fiercely technical problems scaling the wall below its traverse. To the right *Admirals' Progress* is an altogether easier option.

Wharncliffe
Dovestone Tor
Rivelin
Bamford
Stanage
Burbage North
Higgar Tor
Burbage South
Millstone
Lawrencefield
Yarncliffe
Froggatt
Curbar
Gardoms
Birchen
Chatsworth
Cratcliffe

Descent

⑦ Powder Monkey Parade   VS 4c
16m. From the chock move right onto the arete, swing round the corner (4b but quite a bit harder for the short who will have to dangle) then teeter out to the right and finish up the well-positioned slab. Excellent.
FA. David Penlington 1951

⑧ Oarsman E1 6b
14m. The thin crack in the slab provides a technical starting move. Once established on the traverse of *Powder Monkey Parade*, finish left over the bulge.
FA. Mark Stokes 1984

⑨ Hornblower E1 6b
12m. The wall just left of the blunt nose is climbed left and right. Pull over the narrow overhang to reach the final slab.
Photo page 257.
FA. 'An unknown youth' 1952

⑩ Obstructive Pensioner . . E4 6c
12m. Use the flakes above the overhanging nose and slopers on the left as well as a 'cheeky gaston' to reach easy ground.
FA. Nick Jennings 2000

⑪ Polaris Exit . . . . Diff
12m. Start up *Admiral's Progress* but move out left past a large protruding block to reach to a short chimney. Rocket up this to the top.

⑫ Admiral's Progress . . . . . Diff
12m. The wide V-chimney is straightforward enough.

TRAFALGAR WALL
This fine slab set above undercut starts, and split centrally by a prominent wide crack, is the most popular section of the crag. Coincidentally it is also the section at the top of the approach path, where climbers first reach the cliff.

⑬ Bulbous Bow E1 5c
12m. The undercut arete is climbed rapidly on its right side and has a couple of technical moves before easing off.
FA. Chris Craggs 1993

⑭ Camperdown Crawl . . . . . VS 4c
14m. Good climbing up the thin crack and wall above. Problem starts are also available at **5b** on the left and **5c** on the right.
FA. Eric Byne 1951

⑮ Barnacle Bulge . . . . VS 4c
14m. The thin crack and/or groove just to its left lead into the base of the wide crack; make like a limpet. From the bottom of the central crack move 2m right and climb directly up the slab.
FA. Stan Moore 1950

⑯ Trafalgar Crack . . . . VD 4a
14m. A once-great route, spoilt by over-use. From a polished block climb shelving and unhelpful rock to gain the centre of the ramp that runs up left into the main crack. Finish up this.
FA. Eric Byne early 1930s

⑰ Trafalgar Wall . . . . S 4b
12m. Start right of the *Trafalgar Crack* and gain the lowest point of the ramp with difficulty, then climb the delicate slab above. Friends provide adequate protection but beware the final rounded moves.

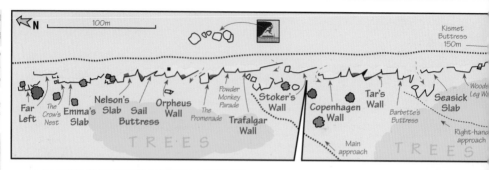

STOKER'S WALL

A short wall with a taller tower above its top left edge, provides a good area for 'quick ticking' or instructions in the basics of gritstone climbing.

① **Bell Bottom Arete** . . . . ☐ S 4a
4m. At the left-hand edge of the wall, gain a hanging groove and then climb the crack in the arete, steep.

② **Sailor's Crack** . . . . ☐ S 4a
4m. Climb the overhanging crack, just right of the arete, on solid jams to a tricky exit. Another steep one.

③ **Sailor's Problem** . . . . ☐ VDiff
6m. The short wall leads into a deep groove, hopefully without too much of a problem.

④ **Reef Knot** . . . . 🔲🔲 ☐ S 4b
6m. The wall to the right has nice moves passing the overlap leading to a rounded finish.
FA. Richard Brown 1951

⑤ **Nautical Crack** . . . . 🔲 ☐ VDiff
6m. The two parallel cracks lead to an inverted-V slot with a block in its base, a tricky couple of moves complete the climb.

⑥ **Yo-Ho Crack** . . . . 🔲 ☐ VDiff
6m. The crack in a shallow corner is approached via a shallow groove and proves to be a hilarious little number.
FA. Reg Schofield early 1930s

⑦ **Rum Wall** . . . . ☐ Diff
6m. Polished holds at the base of the wall lead to thin left-trending cracks above.

⑧ **Stoker's Break** . . . . ☐ VDiff
6m. The short wall leads to ledges at the foot of a slanting ramp, just to the right of a small tree. Continue up the thin crack directly above.
FA. E.J.Clegg 1951

⑨ **Stoker's Hole** . . . . 🔲 ☐ VS 4b
6m. From a block, climb to a ledge then make delicate moves just left of a pale streak, using a rather retiring foothold.
FA. Colin Binks 1993

⑩ **Stoked** . . . . ☐ VDiff
6m. Mantelshelf onto a ledge just right of the streak and follow the thin crack to a tricky couple of moves, just below the top.
FA. CA White 1951

⑪ **Stoker's Wall** . . . . 🔲 ☐ Diff
6m. Climb the face just to the left of an easy crack, close to the right-hand edge of the wall.

Descent
◄ - - - -

Whamcliffe

Dovestone Tor

Rivelin

Bamford

Stanage

Burbage North

Higgar Tor

Burbage South

Millstone

Lawrencefield

Yarncliffe

Froggatt

Curbar

Gardoms

Birchen

Chatsworth

Cratcliffe

COPENHAGEN WALL

The low, undercut face of Copenhagen Wall used to be even lower, the erosion of the ground in front of the cliff has made all the routes a little longer and a good bit harder. To the right the taller tower of the Mast Area has some longer and more amenable offerings.

12 Copenhagen Corner .... **S 4b**
1m. Start on the side-wall to the left of the arete and climb the centre of this using a thin flake.
A. David Penlington 1952

13 Scandiarete .... **VS 5c**
1m. The left-hand arete of the wall is oddly named and technically hard. Start on the right, although a good pocket around to the left may be found to be of passing use.

14 Dane's Delight .... **HS 5b**
1m. The wall 2m right of the arete is hard to start if you are tall and near impossible if you are short. If you can actually do the start one more hard pull remains.

15 Dane's Disgust .... **HS 5b**
1m. Start at a boulder embedded in the ground and climb the face passing the right-hand end of an elongated pocket at half height to a rounded finish.

16 Copenhagen Wall ...... **VS 5a**
10m. Start just left of a pinkish block jammed below the overhang. Using a pocket and flake, reach the first break then trend right more easily on better holds to a finish up the taller buttress above the right-hand edge of the wall.
FA. Norman Kershaw 1951

17 Wonderful Copenhagen . **VS 5a**
10m. Balance up onto the pinkish block from the right then trend right up the wall on sloping holds to join and finish as for the previous route.

18 Mast Gully Ridge ..... **VDiff**
10m. Climb the left arete of the gully on its right-hand side using shelving holds. A start on the left is about 4b.

19 Mast Gully .... **Mod**
10m. The easy rift that splits the buttress is nicely mild.

20 Mast Gully Crack .... **HS 4b**
10m. Climb the crack in the right wall of the gully to a niche, then jam the crack above.

21 Mast Gully Buttress ...... **VS 5a**
12m. Start just right of the gully and climb rightwards to pass the initial bulge then continue more easily.
FA. Gilbert Ellis 1950

To the right is the deep V-cleft known as The Fo'c'sle.

22 Fo'c'sle Wall .... **VS 4c**
12m. Climb the difficult right-trending crack to good pockets and a finish directly up the wall.
FA. David Penlington 1952

23 Fo'c'sle Crack .... **S 4a**
12m. The straight crack and shallow groove just left of the back of the main groove has good holds (apart from at the start).
FA. Reg Schofield early 1930s

24 Fo'c'sle Chimney .... **VDiff**
12m. The main angle of the recess is climbed direct.

25 Fo'c'sle Arete .... **VS 5b**
10m. The right arete of the recess is reached from the left; a pocket up and left is useful. Once established it eases.

26 Broadside **E2 6a**
10m. A long reach right for a hidden pocket and a tricky layback move reach the slanting shallow groove. Finish easily.
FA. G.Warren 1988/Graham Parkes 1993

BOULDERING - The 'Three Ships' above the edge have some limited bouldering possibilities. The hard starts to the 'proper' climbs may also provide some sport for the dedicated boulderer but there is little that could be described as classic.

TAR'S WALL and BARBETTE BUTTRESS

A series of short slabby walls and grooves ending at a prominent flying prow resting on a large block. This another good area for beginners that doesn't have the 'goldfish-bowl' feel of the main sections of the cliff.

❶ The Brigand **E4 7a**
10m. The desperate right-hand side of the face starting from a block and using a poor pocket and bottomless crack.
FA. Mark Katz 1997

❷ Cave Gully .... **VDiff**
10m. The groove above the cave-recess is climbed by some stretchy bridging moves.

❸ Ta Very Much .... **VS 5a**
10m. Climb the right wall of the gully by a good couple of moves via a pocket and small flake.
FA. Chris Craggs 1993

❹ Tar's Arete .... **VDiff**
10m. Approach the arete from the left using well-glossed holds then follow it in splendid isolation,... well nearly.

❺ Ta Ta For Now .... **VS 5a**
8m. Start under the overhang at a pointed spike below the bulges. Pull awkwardly through the overhang and climb the much more delicate slab above.
FA. Chris Craggs 1993

❻ Tar's Crack .... **VDiff**
8m. A steep crack which is awkward to enter. Bridging works best.

❼ Tar's Wall ... . **S 4c**
8m. The centre of the slabby wall has taxing moves to pass the initial bulges.

❽ Tar's Traverse .... **Diff**
10m. A rising traverse across the hanging *Tar's Slab*, from the gully on the far right, to a finish on the arete to the left.

❾ Tar's Corner .... **Diff**
8m. The right-hand arete of the wall on 'slopers'.

❿ Tar's Gully .... **Mod**
10m. Easily up the gully then climb the right wall at the top.

⓫ Pig Head .... **S 4a**
10m. The right-hand arete of the gully is rather impolite.
FA. Ken Holton 1982

⓬ Pigtail .... **HVD 4a**
8m. Climb a leaning groove to easy ground. Quite poky, (or should that be porky) at the grade.
FA. Richard Brown 1951

Wharncliffe

Dovestone Tor

Rivelin

Bamford

Stanage

Burbage North

Higgar Tor

Burbage South

Millstone

Lawrencefield

Yarncliffe

Froggatt

Curbar

Gardoms

Birchen

Chatsworth

Cratcliffe

SEASICK SLAB
ust above the prow of
▸arbette Buttress is a short
lean wall above a level
latform. This has a number
f bouldery little routes
bove a pleasant picnic area.
he obvious but unclimbed
lirect start to Flataback may
epay a visit from a dedi-
ated bouldering team.

⑬ **Wavedance** . . . .  **HS 5b**
ōm. Start at an small jug and climb the wall direct to an over-
grown exit using slopers. Nicely technical.

⑭ **Prow Wall** . . . . **Mod**
3m. Climb the blunt arete to the left of the gully to a steeper
crack at the top.

⑮ **Barbette Crack** . . . . **HS 4b**
ōm. Climb the thin crack to its end then swing left and continue
boldly to a shelving exit. A loose flake has to be used (carefully)
or the final move.

⑯ **Barbette Wall** . . . . **S 4a**
ōm. The left-hand wall of the jutting prow is climbed on an
unusual set of pockets.
FA. David Penlington1951

⑰ **Barbette Buttress** . . . . **S 4b**
ōm. Start from the supporting block and climb the front face of
the prow via the thin crack.

⑱ **Cannonball Crack** . . . . **HVDiff**
3m. The V-shaped groove right of the prow gives good
jamming and is less taxing than appearances might suggest.
FA. Eric Byne early 1930s

⑲ **Cannonball Wall** . . . . **VDiff**
10m. Mantelshelf onto a large block right of the buttress then
step left and climb the centre of the buttress using pockets. A
direct start is about 5a, always assuming you can reach the first
of the holds.

⑳ **Gunner's Gangway** . . . . **Diff**
10m. Start on the right to reach the ledge at the start of the
previous climb and continue up the widening-crack.

SEASICK SLAB

㉑ **Middy's Manoeuvre** . . . . **HS 4c**
6m. The left-hand crack in the short face is a precarious and
exhausting struggle once above the small overhang.

㉒ **Midway** **E1 6a**
6m. This narrow bulging wall is a well-known battle site! Pass
the overhang if you can.

㉓ **Torpedo Tube** . . . . **S 4a**
6m. The central crack is a constricted struggle. Don't burst a
blood vessel on it.

㉔ **Flataback** **E1 6a**
6m. The upper part of the wall to the right could really do with
a direct start. If you muff the crux you may well end up flat on
yer' back.
FA. Quentin Fisher early 1980s

㉕ **Gunner's Groove** . . . . **Diff**
6m. The right-hand crack soon eases although some of the
footholds are well-polished.

㉖ **Seasick Arete** . . . . **HS 5a**
8m. Follow the square arete to a ledge. The final crux move
might make you sick if you blow it. Continue up the short slab
above the ledge.
FA. Ernie Marshall 1951

㉗ **Seasick Slab** . . . . **VD 4b**
8m. A mantelshelf just to the right reaches the same ledge
where it joins and finishes as for *Seasick Slab*.

Kismet Buttress
150m ——

Descent

Seasick Area 10m

Afternoon   10 min

WOODEN LEG WALL

A couple of technically interesting routes in an out-of-the-way setting, you should not have to queue for these. The place gets a bit overgrown with bracken in the height of summer but is fine at all other times.

1 Moby Dick . . . . **S 4a**
12m. Trend left to bypass the edge of the overhangs to where a flake crack gives access to ledges and then the cliff top.
FA. George Sutton 1951

2 Old Codger . . . . **VS 4c**
10m. Climb the bulges in the centre of the face trending left by utilising some small finger flakes just above the overhang. Finish easily.

3 Wooden Leg Wall . . . . . **HVS 5c**
10m. Climb the central bulge trending rightwards by some taxing moves (good small wires protect) to reach easy ground.
FA. Richard Brown (2pts). FFA Len Pearson 1963

KISMET BUTTRESS

8 Implosion . . . . **HVS 5c**
6m. Climb the face left of the thin central crack to a bubbly break from where a long reach should gain the top.
FA. A Russell 1989

9 Explosion . . . . **VS 5a**
6m. The central crack line is strenuous and awkward to protect. Blast up it, boom, boom!
FA. Trevor Baugh 1952

10 Blast Hole Wall . . . . **VS 5b**
6m. Gain the prominent, floral pocket via a long reach from a hole. Stand up with difficulty and finish easily.

4 Owd Gadgee **E1 6b**
10m. Climb the bulges trending right with a desperate mantelshelf onto the sloping ledge on the arete. A pre-placed runner in the previous climb is used at the grade
FA. Colin Binks 1993

5 Stoker's Crack . . . . **S 4b**
8m. Follow the flake-crack that cuts around the right-hand edge of the overhang and then the delicate groove above.

6 Stoker's Saunter . . . . **VDiff**
10m. Climb the crack right of the arete then traverse left around the corner and under the roof to join and finish as for the previous route.

7 Matelot's Meander . . . . **S 4a**
8m. The pleasantly balancy slab to the right of the main angle.

Descent

Wharncliffe

Dovestone Tor

Rivelin

Bamford

Stanage

Burbage North

Higgar Tor

Burbage South

Millstone

Lawrencefield

Yarncliffe

Froggatt

Curbar

Gardoms

Birchen

Chatsworth

Cratcliffe

KISMET BUTTRESS

Birchen's last gasp is not a bad effort. Sheltered and usually quiet, the place is worth a couple of hours if only to tick the stars. *Nelson's Nemesis* is especially worth calling in for if you are passing by, nip up it before that pint in the Robin Hood.

APPROACH - From the main crag go up to the cliff-top path. Turn right (south) and walk above the other areas to the next substantial piece of rock. It can also be reached directly by taking the right-hand approach path and keeping an eye open for the buttress on the right, just above the trees.

⑪ Fuse . . . . **S 4b**
12m. Climb the narrow slab passing a small roof with difficulty. Finish up the side of the prow above for extra interest.

⑫ Gun-Cotton Groove . . . . . . **VDiff**
12m. The grassy crack and shallow groove is a good beginners climb, being well-endowed and well protected.

⑬ Cook's Rib **E1 5c**
12m. Climb the square-fronted buttress direct with the crux passing the low bulge by a fingery stretch. Using either arete lowers the grade to 5b. Not bad for an ancient Severe.

⑭ Horatio's Direct . . . . **VS 4c**
12m. Climb the thin crack in a shallow corner (good wires) then layback up the easier continuation corner. The route can be greasy after rain.

⑮ Horatio's Horror . . . . **S 4a**
14m. The main groove is taken on excellent jams to the overhang and a poor rest. Ape leftwards (the tall can bridge it) to enter and finish up a square-cut groove.
FA. Keith Axon 1949

⑯ Nelson's Nemesis . . . . . . **VS 4b**
16m. Climb the main corner to the roof as for *Horatio's Horror* then traverse right, with a crucial foot change on a shiny nubbin, to reach the base of the continuation crack. Up this to a ledge to an exit on the left on splendid flutings.
Photo page 261.
FA. Keith Axon 1949

⑰ Victory Vice . . . . **VDiff**
12m. The deep, narrowing chimney to the right is hard work but safe. Just get stuck in to it. Despite its name this is not good practice for its Stanage namesake

⑱ For Queen and Country . . **VS 5a**
14m. Climb the face and arete right of the chimney the trend left to cross its upper section and gain a ledge at the foot of a thin crack. Finish up this with long reach for rounded holds.
FA. Izzy Stewart 2001

⑲ Device . . . . **VS 4c**
10m. The buttress is climbed via a mantelshelf, an awkward thin crack and a tricky shelving exit.
Ernie Marshall 1963

⑳ Gunpowder Gully Arete . . . . . . **VDiff**
12m. Climb the left arete of the deep gully and a finish under a large perched flake.

㉑ Gunpowder Gully . . . . . . **Mod**
12m. The gully is another pleasant beginner's climb giving easy bridging.

㉒ Sea Dog Slab . . . . **VDiff**
6m. The front face of the block to right is climbed diagonally from its bottom left corner and is a bit steep to be a real slab.

CHATSWORTH

Wharncliffe
Dovestone Tor
Rivelin
Bamford
Stanage
Burbage North
Higgar Tor
Burbage South
Millstone
Lawrencefield
Yarncliffe
Froggatt
Curbar
Gardoms
Birchen
Chatsworth
Cratcliffe

Retiring and rather neglected, Chatsworth Edge is perhaps the Cinderella of the Easter Edges. The cliff faces north-west and so only receives any real sun on high summer evenings. The slope below the cliff is overgrown with bracken by the start of the summer, making navigation along the foot of the cliff tricky. On top of this a number of large trees growing close to the cliff face have encourage lichen growth in recent years. Despite these rather negative aspects, under the right conditions climbing here is very pleasant, and several of the main buttresses thrust far enough forward to escape the cloying vegetation. The very best of the routes here are the equal of any on grit, and any true gritstoner will one day have to bite the bullet and throw themselves at the likes of *Vibrio*, *Emerald Crack*, *Pearls* and the peerless man-eater that is *Sentinel Crack*. If you like to climb away from the crowds that populate Stanage and Froggatt, it is worth putting Chatsworth on your list of venues.

APPROACH (SK274720)

It used to be traditional to park on the grass verge opposite the old collapsing bridge that leads straight to Sentinel Crack (after which the great route was named). The kerb is high and the traffic flies up and down the road here, it makes MUCH more sense to use the extensive parking by the Robin Hood Inn a little further east from the cliff on the left-hand side of the road. Walk down the footpath for about 150m to a hidden stile on the opposite side of the road. Cross this and follow wooden steps down to a footbridge, on the other side of the river head right over marshy ground to reach a well-made track that runs right-wards towards the rock (and onto that big house just around the corner), less than 10 minutes from the parking. The buttresses further to the right are reached along an indistinct track that weaves up and down across the slope directly below the rocks, it is no fun once the bracken is neck-high!

OTHER GUIDEBOOKS - A more complete list of routes at Chatsworth is published in the 1996 BMC *Chatsworth* guidebook.

CONDITIONS

A rather neglected edge, which can be green and midgy and is perhaps at its best on summer evenings. After rain it is definitely well worth steering clear of, though after any dry spell, especially in spring and autumn, the place becomes well worth a visit. In the heat of summer it can make a morning venue for early risers.

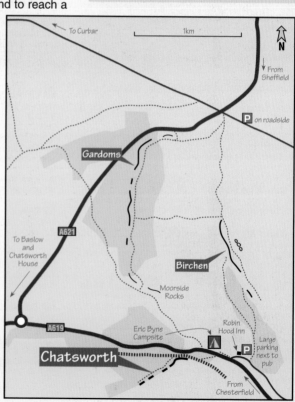

Bruno Marks pulling round the lip of *Sentinel Crack*, E3 5c, Chatsworth. Photo Simon Richardson. *Page 275*

MORT WALL AREA

The first part of the cliff reached has a small collection of pleasant routes generally in the lower grades. *Mort Wall* is a good first HVS being short and safe. If you feel a little 'under-whelmed' by the look of the place just walk another 30 seconds to the right!

① Sidewinder . . . . 🔲 **HVS 5a**
10m. The left arete of the first buttress is pleasant enough.
FA. Paul Harrison 1984

② Mort Wall . . . . 🔲 **HVS 5a**
10m. Climb the centre of the wall, via a niche and finishing through the branches of a collapsing tree. Low in the grade.
FA. Colin Mortlock 1958

③ Slip Arete . . . . 🔲 **E1 5b**
10m. The arete is climbed by an elegant series of balancy moves. Delicate and unprotected.
FA. Gabe Regan 1975

④ Strangler's Groove . . . . . . 🔲 **S 4a**
10m. The angular corner crack is pleasant and well protected.
FA. Don Chapman 1951

⑤ Strangler's Crack . . . . . . 🔲 **VDiff**
10m. A thin finger-crack to the right and then the arete and short wall directly above.
FA. Don Chapman 1951

⑥ Throttled Groove . . . . 🔲 **S 4a**
10m. The deep angular groove gives pleasant climbing.
FA. Don Chapman 1951

⑦ Dumper . . . . 🔲 **E1 5b**
10m. Traverse right from the groove to access the cracks in the centre of the side wall and haul up these to the crowning pine.

⑧ Jumpers . . . . 🔲 **E3 6a**
10m. The leaning prow is juggy, but the jugs are well-spaced and the landing is shocking. Finish up a crack on the right.
FA. Bill Briggs 1976

SENTINEL BUTTRESS

⑨ Leaper . . . . 🔲 **VS 5b**
10m. The undercut arete of the buttress is awkward to access and much easier above.

⑩ Choked Crack . . . . 🔲 **Diff**
10m. Juggy, gritty cracks in the centre of the slab.

⑪ Choked Chimney . . . . 🔲 **VDiff**
10m. The main angle steepens and is very effectively blocked at the top by a big boulder. Exit left.

⑫ Puppet Crack . . . . . 🔲 **HVS 5b**
12m. The leaning crack has a reachy start from the right then gives glorious jamming to a final wide grovel.
FA. Joe Brown (with a little aid from the rope) 1951

Change in viewing angle

SENTINEL BUTTRESS
The imposing buttress that looks out over the old collapsing bridge. *Sentinel Crack* is the one to do, if you feel you are up to it!

Evening · 10 min · Green · Sheltered

⑬ Sentinel Crack E3 5c
16m. An awesome roof crack which is a desperate struggle for most. Climb an awkward groove to a poor rest and then undercut wildly out left. Fist jamming past the lip is especially memorable and will leave its mark for sure.
FA. Don Whillans 1959

⑭ Sentinel Buttress .. E3 5c
14m. Mildly bold but still a cop out! At the roof scuttle right and escape around the arete to a belay (on *Lichen*). There are various ways on from here but *Lichen's* final pitch is the best.
Photo page 273.
FA. Mick Fowler 1977

⑮ Cave Climb .... Diff
14m. The wide crack with chockstones is a bit of a battle to a spider-ridden subterranean exit.
FA. Eric Byne 1928

⑯ Cave Crack .... S 4a
14m. The awkward slanting crack and its easier continuation.
FA. Eric Byne 1920s

⑰ Monk's Park E1 5c
8m. The arete just across the gully is climbed on its right and eases with height. If you blow it head to the right.
FA. Alpha Club members 1963

⑱ Lichen E2 5b
A great right to left girdle which is cleaner than the name suggests. Start up the gully right of *Monk's Park*.
1) 5a, 10m. Climb the gully to a break which leads left to a belay in *Cave Crack*.
2) 5b, 10m. Follow the shelving break left into the corner.
3) 5b, 12m. More sloping, horizontal-break climbing leads to the exposed arete. Finish easily up this.
FA. Keith Myhill 1971

Up the slope behind the trees is a *short, pleasant, slabby wall.*

⑲ Cadenza E3 5c
10m. Climb the rounded arete by unprotected friction moves until it is necessary to escape out right.
FA. Mark Turnbull 1991

⑳ High Step E1 5a
10m. The centre of the slabby wall features the eponymous move, then move left and then back right to finish.
FA. Ernie Marshall 1959

㉑ Price .... HVS 5a
8m. Climb the blunt arete on the right-hand side of the wall to a niche then the wall above on big slopers.
FA. Eric Price 1959

Whamcliffe · Dovestone Tor · Rivelin · Bamford · Stanage · Burbage North · Higgar Tor · Burbage South · Millstone · Lawrencefield · Yarncliffe · Froggatt · Curbar · Gardoms · Birchen · Chatsworth · Cratcliffe

Emperor Buttress
70m

EMERALD BUTTRESS

This tall buttress is home to the classic struggle of *Emerald Crack* and the underrated face climb of *Pearls*.

❶ The Clasp **E3 5b**
12m. The left arete is often green and can leave you grasping.
FA. Martin Boysen 1978

❷ Left Twin Crack . . . . **S 4a**
12m. The wide, straight crack is a battle at the best of times.
FA. Eric Byne early 1930s

❸ Emerald Crack **E3 6a**
14m. The leaning crack is easy enough to two-thirds height, and then it turns mean. Long reaches, thin jams and a tricky exit all add up to an arduous outing.
FA. Joe Brown (1 pt) 1957. FFA. Jim Campbell 1967

❹ Diamond Life **E5 6b**
14m. The right arete on its right-hand side has a bold finale.
FA. Andy Elliott 1987

❺ Pearls **E2 5c**
12m. A route that strings you along! Cracks in the side-wall lead to small runners from where thin moves reach the crest, leaving only a rounded mantelshelf to glory.
FA. Keith Myhill 1971

❻ Double Cave Climb . . . . **VDiff**
12m. The groove on the right-hand side of the face to a chockstoned exit.

VIBRIO BUTTRESS

Across the grassy slope a fine buttress with mid-height overhangs sticks out from the hillside. *Vibro* is the one to do here though the *Direct* is also well worth the effort.

❼ Step Buttress . . . . **VDiff**
14m. Climb the steps up the left-hand side of the front face then move left to the wide crack above the grass ledge.

❽ Good Vibrations **E2 5c**
14m. The left arete of the buttress has a crusty start and a spectacular finale. Climb the upper section on the left then swing around to the right to finish as for *Vibrio*.
FA. Chris Craggs 1990

❾ Vibrio **E1 5b**
16m. The centre of the buttress to a tricky roof and then a short and technical traverse out to the left arete for an easier finish.
FA. Black and Tans Club members 1963

❿ Vibrio Direct **E2 6a**
12m. The 'true' finish is short, sharp and well-protected but still manages to feel scary. Head slightly right from the runner slot.
FA. Keith Myhill (one point of aid) 1971 FFA. John Allen 1976

⓫ Twisted Reach **E4 6b**
10m. The right hand edge of the buttress via a roof crack, a pocket and an extended reach or two.
FA. Bob Berzins 1979

Descent

Descent

Adjoining

21

17

14   16

20

12

19

13   15   17   18

EMPEROR BUTTRESS

The final buttress has some pleasant, if graunchy, low and mid grade climbs and the world class problem of *Desperot*. A good place to escape the crowds though be warned it can be terminally green and slimy.

APPROACH - Follow a small path from below Vibrio Buttress for about 70m through the trees. This path can be completely overgrown in the summer months.

⑫ Emperor Flake Climb   **VDiff**
12m. Climb the left arete of the buttress, then follow flaky cracks on the left-hand wall as they lead out to an exposed finish on the arete.
FA. Eric Byne 1940

⑬ Emperor Crack   **VS 4b**
14m. The long crack in the left-hand side of the face is hard work where it widens; a classic struggle.
FA. Eric Byne 1930s

⑭ The Tyrant   **E2 5c**
14m. From a short distance up *Emperor Crack* move right and climb the left-hand side of the smooth central face.
FA. Geoff Hornby 1993

⑮ Desperot   **E4 7a**
6m. The direct start to *Despot* is truly hard. In the unlikely event of being successful, escape rightwards from the break. The problem was left unnamed, though that used above has become the norm.
FA. Ben Moon 1991

⑯ Despot   **E1 5c**
14m. From a short way up *Empress Crack* follow the lowest break out left onto the wall. Make a difficult reach the next break then climb the centre of the face more easily.
FA. Tim Leach 1977

⑰ Empress Crack   **S 4a**
14m. The long crack on the right side of the wall is enjoyable and amenable. It gives bridging and jamming.
FA. Eric Byne early 1930s

⑱ Prince's Crack   **S 4a**
14m. From a roofed-in alcove move left to access the 'Royal Seat' then finish up the groove behind it.
FA. Eric Byne early 1930s

⑲ Up the Establishment   **HVS 5a**
12m. Bomb up the slanting flake to reach the arete. Climb the left-hand side of it in a pleasantly exposed position.
FA. Chris Craggs 1990

⑳ Anarchist's Arete   **VS 4c**
12m. Climb the groove on the right then traverse left along the break to an exposed finish up the arete.
FA. Don Chapman 1951

㉑ Emperor's Struggle   **S 4a**
12m. The final corner crack is a bit of a thrash. The holly continues to impinge.
FA. Eric Byne early 1930s

Whamcliffe | Dovestone Tor | Rivelin | Bamford | Stanage | Burbage North | Higgar Tor | Burbage South | Millstone | Lawrencefield | Yarncliffe | Froggatt | Curbar | Gardoms | Birchen | Chatsworth | Cratcliffe

CRATCLIFFE

Wharncliffe
Dovestone Tor
Rivelin
Bamford
Stanage
Burbage North
Higgar Tor
Burbage South
Millstone
Lawrencefield
Yarncliffe
Froggatt
Curbar
Gardoms
Birchen
Chatsworth
Cratcliffe

Cratcliffe Tor is one of the most picturesque gritstone crags in the Peak and home to a small, but magnificent set of climbs. Its location away from the main edges, and the lack of any real quality in the lower grades, means that it is seldom busy on the Tor itself, however it is well known as a great bouldering venue. The main area of interest for roped-climbing is the huge open walls that bound Owl Gully. Here the diagonal breaks offer some fine pumpy climbing often traversing out of the gully into impressive positions high on the faces to either side. The breaks offer plenty of protection but being fit enough to hang on and place it is the key. Around the corner from the gully is the dramatic *Suicide Wall*. The routes on this wall are almost impossible to view properly from below so you tend to begin your climb with some trepidation, however once you exit onto the wall above the trees the magnificence of the positions become apparent.

 BOULDERING - The whole area contains some of the best bouldering in the Peak. The main areas of interest are on the beautiful boulders above Cratcliffe Tor, and their close companions in the trees by the Tor. The whole of Robin Hood's Stride offers masses of great bouldering. There is also Eagle Tor, Rowter Rocks and Rheinstor marked on the map below.

APPROACH (SK228625)

The crag is situated in the central Peak, about 5km to the south of Bakewell. There are two approaches.
1) Park by the side of the B5056 Bakewell to Winster road opposite a wide farm entrance. Cross the road and follow the gravel track that leads to the farm but keep left up the hill heading towards the rocky towers of Robin Hood's Stride. Near the top of the of the track is a stile in the wall on the right. Cross this then turn right to locate a horizontal path leading through the trees to the foot of the cliff.
Do not try to reach the Tor via the farm.
2) On the minor road that runs from Alport to Elton there is some limited verge-side parking by a stile in view of Robin Hood's Stride. Follow the collapsed wall towards the Stride then bear left towards the cliff which lies hidden in the trees beyond the corner of the next field.

CONDITIONS

Cratcliffe is low lying and south facing and so is the best-sheltered gritstone cliff in this book. Although the place can be green after rain the cliff is climbable right through the winter and autumn days here can be especially enthralling.

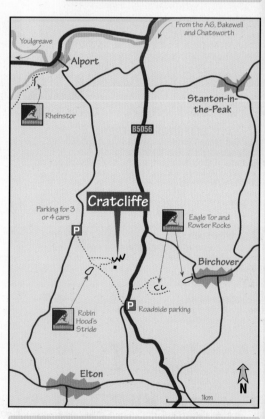

OTHER GUIDEBOOKS - A more complete list of routes at Cratcliffe is published in the 1996 BMC *Chatsworth* guidebook. The bouldering on all the areas mentioned above is covered in the 1998 Peak Bouldering ROCKFAX.

Reaching the invisible jug on *Boot Hill*, E3 5c, Cratcliffe. *Page 281*

HERMIT'S CAVE AREA

The first section of the crag is dominated by a huge yew tree, overshadowing a dark cave. The walls here offer a variety of short steep pitches which are located at several different levels. They can be green and overgrown although the fine prow of *Tom Thumb* will usually be in condition.

THE HERMIT'S CAVE

The cave is partly manmade and is of considerable antiquity. It contains a rough-hewn crucifix and the carved guttering is presumably the inhabitant's attempts to keep his rude abode dry. Please treat the place with the respect it deserves.

① **The Nemesis Exit** .... **HVS 5b**
10m. The crack that splits the overhang above the cave starts off on perfect jams but gradually widens to fist-size and then widens a bit more. Walk off leftwards.
FA. Vin Ridgeway 1951

② **Hermitage Groove** .... **VDiff**
8m. The tree-filled groove is a battle. Walk off left.

③ **Hermitage Crack** .... **VS 4c**
8m. The tricky and polished curving crack was a damn good effort for its day. Sadly it is becoming overgrown. Walk off left.
FA. J.W.Puttrell 1901

The next two routes start from the finishing ledge of the previous routes. This is best reached by walking in from the left under the superb boulder traverse - Jerry's Traverse 6b (V7).

④ **Reticent Mass Murderer** **E4 6b**
8m. Short but exquisite. From the ledge above the cave extemporise a way up the narrow leaning crack. Fat fingers or thin hands make things just a little easier and protection is perfect.
FA. John Allen 1976

⑤ **Genocide** **E6 6c**
8m. The thin flake on the right leads to absurd and extended moves up the short wall above.
FA. Jerry Moffatt 1983

⑥ **Tom Thumb** **E2 5c**
18m. A thin crack in a shallow groove leads rapidly to a ledge on *The Giant's Staircase* (possible belay). From here climb up and left to a ledge then lean back rightwards to enter the spectacular, but short-lived, jamming crack. Once round the roof (try to get your left hand in the highest jam) finish easily.
FA. Tom Proctor 1971

⑦ **The Giant's Staircase** .... **HVS 5a**
18m. An odd route consisting of a series of awkward mantelshelves between stance sized ledges. Trend right up the lower wall then left via polished steps to a final difficult grovel onto the last ledge. Walk off left.
FA. Fred Pigott 1922

⑧ **Bean Stalk** **E2 5c**
18m. The rounded arete used to provide an excellent little route. Sadly the tree at the base is taking control, maybe it has outstayed its welcome? If you do get on it, approach via a wide diagonal crack. Above this there is one fierce pull (small wire) before easing to a superb romp up the rib.
FA. Mike Hardwick 1976

The next two routes start at a higher level; The Amphitheatre, reached by easy scramble from below via a polished groove.

⑨ **Elliott's Unconquerable** .... **HVS 5a**
8m. A short-lived but pleasant piece of jamming with a tricky undercut start.
FA. Frank Elliott 1933

⑩ **Elliott's Right-hand** **E1 5c**
8m. The flake and wall to the right of *Elliott's* main crack has thin moves to reach the wide crack above but soon eases.
FA. Chris Hunter 1977

OWL GULLY - LEFT

To the right are the twin sheer walls that flank either side of the deep rift of *Owl Gully*. These impressive walls contain some of the finest routes around and also one of the most obvious unclimbed problems, the shallow groove nears its left-hand side. The left-hand wall gets more sun and therefore tends to stay cleaner than the other sections of the cliff.

---

① Weston's Chimney . . . . VDiff

6m. Climb the green and slippery chimney to a wide ledge and belay, then climb the narrower continuation in the right wall.
A. Owen Glynne Jones 1897

⑫ Escape/Boot Hill E3 5c

8m. A magnificent arete climb, low in the grade but exciting enough. Climb the greasy chimney then monkey along the break to the arete. Follow this with crucial moves on the left-hand side (the very tall can teeter up the front) to reach a fat juting and the final 'blank' wall with its superb hidden jug. *Photo page 279.*
A. Geoff Sutton 1951. Climbed and claimed again by Tom Proctor 1971

⑬ Nutcracker E2 5c

20m. Start up the gully by the third diagonal zig. Launch out left and hand-traverse out to the arete and a rest. Climb the steep slab (as for the long reach method of *Escape/Boot Hill*) to the roof then exit rightwards as for *Fernhill*. The short will probably find the initial moves desperate and the slab on the front impossible.
FA. Vin Ridgeway, who cracked his nut on the final roof. 1951

⑭ Fern Hill Indirect E3 5c

20m. Devious but superb. It is probably worth placing a runner in the start of the regular route before you start if you don't want to face a massive pendulum when! you muff the crux moves. Follow the diagonal crack as for *Nutcracker* out to a poor rest then climb a shallow groove and the crack that runs back to the right to reach the pumpy crux of *Fern Hill*. Follow this to the top.
FA. Ron Fawcett 1976

⑮ Fern Hill E2 5c

12m. Superb strenuous climbing up the diagonal cracks in the left wall of *Owl Gully*. Start by a thin horizontal crack (the 5th zig) and swing left (small wires can be placed first by bridging out). Make some hard moves to pass the bifurcation then continue along the rising diagonal to the arete and a good rest. Step back right and pull over the finishing with a steep mantelshelf onto a ledge just below the cliff top.
FA. Keith Myhill (one point of aid) 1971

⑯ Owl Gully . . . . VDiff

20m. The deep cleft is a low-grade gem climbed on glossy holds to a substantial chockstone and an exit on the right.

OWL GULLY - RIGHT
The first two routes start from a stance part way up Owl Gully.

① Tiger Traverse . . . . 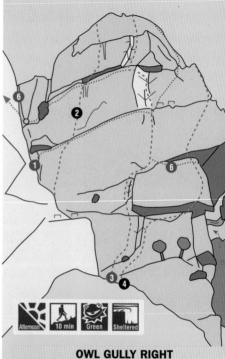 **E2 5b**
16m. A pumpy little number that swings along the rounded break half way up the wall, feet being almost redundant. Escape out right at the end of the traverse.
FA. Peter Harding, Vin Ridgeway 1951

② Nettle Wine **E4 6b**
12m. Technical climbing up the left-hand side of the wall with a spectacular finish. From a little way along *Tiger Traverse* climb the wall to the next break, shimmy right then use the tiny flakes to scale the final blank wall rapidly.
FA. John Hart 1978

③ Five Finger Exercise . . . **E2 5c**
22m. A fine route up the right wall of the gully with a wild finale that catches many out. Pull rightwards over a narrow overlap and climb the wall on small sharp holds (looks harder than it is) and continue to ledges. Fill the horizontal with runners then swing around the arete and power up the hanging flake. Only the weak are spurned, though the timid may have hard time too.
Photo page 5.
FA. Andy Edgar 1976

④ Liquid Assets **E4 6b**
22m. Traverse out onto and then climb the fine square arete to the edge of the huge overhang and then the crimpy wall above. Step out right to reach the upper arete and finish up this.
FA. John Allen 1987

SUICIDE WALL

⑤ Bower Route 1 . . . . **HS 4b**
10m. A short but pleasant pitch that is the easiest way to access the Bower. From a flake make a precarious move right to a polished ledge which leads to a slabby groove debouching in the Bower. Escape is by abseil unless you are proficient at HVS.
FA. Fred Pigott 1922

⑥ Renaissance **E2 6a**
A wandering route with some quality moves.
1) 6a, 10m. Climb the thin hanging crack and its wider continuation until the Bower can be reached by a short traverse right.
2) 5c, 15m. Climb to the giant roof then follow the strenuous hand-traverse out left to the arete. Step left and climb *FFE* to below its crux flake then traverse left to a belay in *Owl Gully*.
3) 5c, 12m. Climb the steep diagonal crack to the right edge of the *Fern Hill* ledge and an awkward exit
FA. Chris Craggs 1985

⑦ Requiem **E3 6a**
A superb outing up the left-hand side of the biggest face on the cliff. The crux moves are fierce but can be avoided by some scary monkey business in the upper branches of the great oak reducing the grade to E2 5c, but not detracting from the quality.
1) 5a, 10m. Climb an overhanging crack straight into the Bower and a belay on the huge tree.
2) 6a, 16m. Climb the desperate crack springing from the right-hand edge of the Bower to a deep horizontal break (or reach the same place from the tip of the tree). Swing left along the break then climb flutings to the final roof, which is passed on the best holds in the world. *Photo page 13.*
FA. Paul Nunn (2 pts) 1970. FFA John Allen 1975

OWL GULLY RIGHT
Although it is slightly overshadowed by its neighbour opposite, the right-hand wall of *Owl Gully* would probably rank as THE wall of the cliff on many other Peak crags. The splendid *Five Finger Exercise* is particularly impressive, giving great climbing, at a reasonable grade, on a line that looks much harder than it is. The wall is often greener than the *Fern Hill* side and receives the sun later in the day.

⑧ The Long Distance Runnel **E5 6c**
16m. The wall between *Requiem* and *Suicide Wall* gives fine climbing. From the Bower climb *Requiem* to the top of the crack. Layback powerfully off the right-hand edge of the long hole to reach a high crimp, then stretch up leftwards to gain the break of *Mordaunt*. Levitate to somehow reach the shallow runnel in the wall above and continue direct to finish.
FA. Neil Foster 1996

⑨ Suicide Wall . . . . **HVS 5a**
30m. A stunning classic following an impressive line of cracks and breaks fairly directly up the steep wall. Climb the abrasive crack, through the chunky tree, and jam onwards to a stance in the Bower. Move right and climb the wall on small finger holds and then a crack to an uncomfortable niche . Layback the crack on the left to the final overhang. Finish with gusto.
FA. Peter Harding, Veronica Lee 1946

⑩ The Child's House **E5 6c**
28m. A big pitch. Start as for *Suicide Wall* but where it trends left follow thinner cracks straight up to rejoin it at the crux wall. Continue to the niche then pull over the bulges and head straight up the final wall and on through the capping bulges.
FA. John Allen 1986

Whamcliffe
Dovestone Tor
Rivelin
Bamford
Stanage
Burbage North
Higgar Tor
Burbage South
Millstone
Lawrencefield
Yarncliffe
Froggatt
Curbar
Gardoms
Birchen
Chatsworth
Cratcliffe

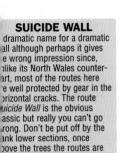

SUICIDE WALL

dramatic name for a dramatic
all although perhaps it gives
e wrong impression since,
like its North Wales counter-
art, most of the routes here
e well protected by gear in the
orizontal cracks. The route
uicide Wall is the obvious
assic but really you can't go
rong. Don't be put off by the
ank lower sections, once
bove the trees the routes are
uperbly exposed and on
onderful clean rock forma-
ons. In the winter the face can
e viewed in all its glory.

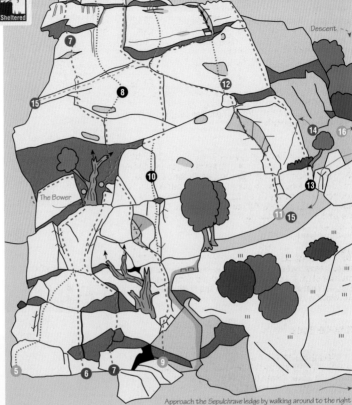

Approach the Sepulchrave ledge by walking around to the right

*tarting from the ledge up and
ight of the foot of Suicide Wall
re several worthwhile routes.
hese are reached by climbing
he steep woodwork filled
himney (Oak Tree Chimney -
'Diff) or more easily by scram-
ling around to the right.

① Sepulchrave .... HVS 5a
8m. Devious climbing up the diagonal cracks in the wall. A
ood jamming crack is climbed to its end. Traverse the continu-
tion leftwards until it is possible to step up and follow another
rack back to the right. The finish lies up the wide crack and is
little easier than it appears from below.
A. Paul Nunn 1970

② Savage Messiah E2 5c
4m. A direct on *Sepulchrave* with only a short independent
ection but what a memorable one! Climb *Sepulchrave's* crack
hen continue directly to enter the large porthole by undercut-
ng and a high step. Finish up the wide chimney above.
A. Rob Burwood 1975

③ Stretch Limo .. E5 6b
4m. The right arete of the *Suicide Wall* face gives good
limbing. Start just right of the crack taken by *Sepulchrave* and
ollow the arete throughout.
A. Andy Cave 2001

④ North Climb .... S 4a
0m. A nail-scratched groove leads to bulges then traverse left
o finish up the airy arete.
A. J.W.Puttrell 1890

⑮ Mordaunt E2 5b
60m. A fine girdle covering impressive territory at a sustained
but amenable grade. Perhaps the best of its genre on grit!
1) 5b, 28m. Follow *Sepulchrave* to the end of its traverse and
continue to *Suicide Wall*. Follow the same line then swing down
to join *Requiem* above its crux and take the wide crack around
the arete to a belay on *Five Finger Exercise*.
2) 5b, 10m. Mantel off the ledge then reverse Tiger Traverse to
a stance in *Owl Gully*.
3) 5b, 10m. From the gully follow the crack of *Renaissance* but
continue out to the arete and a small stance.
4) 5b, 12m. Traverse below the roof to round the arete and
continue into *Weston's Chimney* or, better, finish up *Boot Hill*.
FA. Paul Nunn 1970

*The last route described is on a vertical wall 15m right of North
Climb, above the approach path to the Sepulchrave ledge.*

⑯ Jimmy's Crack .... HVS 5b
12m. The thin cracks zig-zagging up the wall lead to a tree.
Finish up the wall behind.
FA. Chris Hunter (aka Jimmy) 1977

INDEX

INDEX

INDEX